America's Religious Architecture

America's Religious Architecture

Sacred Places for Every Community

Marilyn J. Chiat

Preservation Press

WILEY

John Wiley & Sons, Inc.

NEW YORK   CHICHESTER   WEINHEIM   TORONTO   SINGAPORE   BRISBANE

A cooperative publication with the National Trust for Historic Preservation,
Washington, D.C., chartered by Congress in 1949 to encourage the preservation of sites,
buildings, and communities significant in American history and culture.

This text is printed on acid-free paper.

This publication is designed to provide accurate and
authoritative information in regard to the subject
matter covered. It is sold with the understanding that
the publisher is not engaged in rendering legal, accounting,
or other professional services. If legal advice or other
expert assistance is required, the services of a competent
professional person should be sought.

Designed by Brian Noyes, with production assistance from Dwight McNeill

LIBRARY OF CONGRESS CATALOGING-IN-PUBLICATION DATA
Chiat, Marilyn Joyce Segal.

    America's religious architecture : sacred places for
every community / Marilyn J. Chiat.
        p. cm.
    Includes bibliographical references and index.
    ISBN 0-471-14502-5 (paper : alk. paper)
    1. Church architecture–United States. 2. Synagogue architecture–
United States. 3. Temples–United States. 4. Ethnic architecture–
United States. I. Title.
NA5205.C48 1997   97-7457
726.5' 0973–dc21

 This publication was made possible with funding from the Minnesota Humanities
Commission in cooperation with the National Endowment for the Humanities and
the Minnesota State Legislature.

Printed in the United States of America

10 9 8 7 6 5 4 3 2 1

TO HARVEY

Contents

Preface

THERE ARE OVER A QUARTER MILLION places of worship in the United States, or about one for every 1,000 people. Only a small fraction of that number could be included in this publication, but those selected, I believe, reflect our nation's pluralism, a pluralism that allows each of us the freedom to worship as we please.

The intention of this book is not to focus solely on the most notable or monumental religious buildings in a region. Information on these places of worship is available in other publications, and their futures are quite secure. Rather, I chose buildings that, while often modest in appearance, remain important within the historic, aesthetic, and cultural contexts of their communities. These are the buildings in which many of us worship and are the ones most often threatened with insensitive renovations or demolition.

My journey of discovery of America's historic sacred sites took two forms. In some instances I was able to travel our nation's highways and byways, seeking out places of worship for inclusion in this book, but more often I had to rely on suggestions offered by the staff of a state's historic preservation office, or others who share my love of these buildings.

St. Martin's
Roman Catholic
Church,
Clay County,
Nebraska

While I owe those who responded to my appeal for help an enormous debt of gratitude, the shortcomings of this approach are obvious. Most of the sites are listed on either a local or national register, thus eliminating many important buildings that would warrant inclusion; for this sin of omission, I take full responsibility. However, I do believe the choices made are representative of our nation's vast array of religious architecture–large and small, plain and fancy. Perhaps in future publications I will be able to make amends by focusing in more detail on the buildings in a particular region, including those that are familiar to many of my readers.

What did sadden me throughout my journey was a growing awareness of the loss of far too many of our nation's historic religious buildings. Their spires no longer pierce the sky, their bells have fallen silent, and their vanished walls no longer reverberate with joyous song and prayer. Gone, too, is the vital role these buildings play as sentinels on the increasingly mean streets of our cities. In their places are fast-food restaurants, asphalt parking lots, or worse, nothing–a void where once there was an oasis.

Redundancy is a term commonly used to explain the need to demolish a place of worship. Too many buildings, not enough clergy, solution–destroy one site and merge two congregations. Certainly places of worship can be costly to maintain, but is it not more costly to demolish what is often the finest building in a neighborhood and leave nothing in its place? It is only after the building is gone that people recognize what has been lost–something far more valuable than a place to worship. Often it was the cornerstone of a neighborhood–of a community–that extended far beyond the confines of a particular congregation, ethnic group, or religion.

The further deterioration of a neighborhood can be directly linked to the loss of its religious structures. When these are abandoned or demolished, their members flee the inner city, leaving behind those too impoverished to move, the very people whom all religious faiths claim are most in need of help and support. What now is to be their sentinel, their haven in the midst of the chaos of their surroundings? We are morally obliged to make a greater effort to maintain these often magnificent structures so they may continue to serve not only as neighborhood anchors, but as guardians of our past when all other evidence of that past has disappeared. How else will we remember the vibrant communities of proud new Americans who sacrificed so much to erect these handsome buildings and who were equally proud of their ancient heritages which took visible form in their places of worship?

Buildings are destroyed for reasons other than redundancy–some by forces of nature, others by vandalism, and many are simply abandoned. Their neighborhoods in tatters, their congregants gone, these structures are then transformed into factories or warehouses. At least they still stand, although their former glory, along with their history, too often fades and ultimately disappears. At times, as seen in this book, a few concerned citizens, aware that they are losing an important part of their community's patrimony, rescue these buildings, restore them to their former glory, and once again put them to a use that is not only compatible with their history, but that rejuvenates a neighborhood as well.

This book celebrates our nation's magnificent mosaic that takes visible form in its diverse places of worship. The bulbous silver dome crowning a small Russian Orthodox church rises above the cornfields in Minnesota; a New England meetinghouse is nestled among palm trees on a Hawaiian Island; exotic Moorish synagogues grace neighborhoods in small towns in Mississippi and Texas; and a Presbyterian Church in the guise of an Egyptian Temple can be found in downtown Nashville. This is only a sample of the wonders of religious architecture that await the traveler willing to embark on a journey of discovery–the discovery of the beauty and variety of our nation's sacred sites.

Many people contributed to the realization of this publication, but first and foremost, I must give thanks to Dennis Gimmestad, the Government Programs and Compliance Officer for the Minnesota Historical Society, who supported my interest in historic places of worship and suggested contacting Preservation Press of the National Trust for Historic Preservation about a publication surveying our nation's religious buildings and their preservation. Acknowledgement must also be given to the contributions made by Carol Frenning in the initial phases of this project, but who was unable to see it through to completion.

The Center for the Documentation and Preservation of Places of Worship that I direct is affiliated with the National Conference of Christians and Jews, Inc., Minnesota-Dakotas (NCCJ). The Conference's past and present Executive Directors, Paul O. Sand and Marcy Shapiro, generously provide the Center with office space and services and are enthusiastic supporters of all its projects, including this publication. A special thank you, as well, to my colleague at the NCCJ, Patrick O'Brien, Ph.D., freelance writer, editor, and translator – and computer whiz.

Grants from the Minnesota Humanities Commission (MHC) enabled me to travel to Washington, D.C., to conduct research at the National Register and the Library of Congress and to hire an excellent photography editor, Judith Williams, as well as pay for many of the photographs reproduced in this volume. Cheryl Dickson, the executive director of the MHC, and her staff, Mark Gleason and Jane Cunningham, must also be thanked for the ongoing encouragement they have given me throughout this endeavor.

I AM PARTICULARLY INDEBTED to the staffs of state and local preservation offices as well as other individuals and organizations who responded to my calls for help, generously giving of their time and material. I cannot emphasize enough how valuable their contributions are; this book could not have been written without their assistance. ALABAMA: Robert Gamble; ALASKA: Joan M. Antonson; ARIZONA: Diana Thomas and William Collins; ARKANSAS: Patrick Zollner; CALIFORNIA: E. M. Campbell; COLORADO: Holly Wilson; CONNECTICUT: John Herzan; DELAWARE: Laura Leonard and Gary Sachau; DISTRICT OF COLUMBIA: Stephen J. Raiche; FLORIDA: Barbara E. Mattlick; GEORGIA: Kenneth H. Thomas, Jr.; HAWAII: Dr. Don Hibbard; IDAHO: Belinda Henry Davis; ILLINOIS: Ann V. Swallow; INDIANA: Craig Charron and Suzanne Fischer; IOWA: Bard Todd; KANSAS: Martha Hagedorn-Krass; KENTUCKY: Bob Polsgrove and Julie Risenweber; LOUISIANA: Jonathan Fricker; MAINE: Earle G. Shettleworth, Jr.; MARYLAND: Peter E. Kurtze, Ronald L. Andrews, and Bernard Goldman; MASSACHUSETTS: Betsy Friedberg and Stanley Smith; MICHIGAN: Dr. Kathryn B. Eckert; MINNESOTA: Susan Roth and Charles Nelson; MISSISSIPPI: Richard Cawthon; MISSOURI: Duane Sneddeker and Carolyn Toft; MONTANA: Patricia Bik; NEBRASKA: Joni G. Gilkerson and Bill Callahan; NEVADA: Dr. Julie Nicoletta; NEW HAMPSHIRE: Nancy C. Muller and James L. Garvin; NEW JERSEY: Terry Karschner and Robert W. Craig; NEW MEXICO: Dr. Mary Ann Anders, and Sam Baca, director of Cornerstones, Inc.; NEW YORK: Bernadette Castro; NORTH CAROLINA: Michael T. Southern; NORTH DAKOTA: Louis N. Hafermehl and Rolene Schliesman; OHIO: Amos J. Lovejoy; OKLAHOMA: Cynthia Savage; OREGON: Dr. Leland Gilson and Elisabeth Walton Potter; PENNSYLVANIA: Gregory Ramsey; RHODE ISLAND: Robert Owen Jones; SOUTH CAROLINA: Andrew W. Chandler; SOUTH DAKOTA: Mike Bedau and Michelle Saxman-Rogers; TENNESSEE: Claudette Stager; TEXAS: Jim Steely; UTAH: Max Evans; VERMONT: Elsa Gilbertson; VIRGINIA: Margaret T. Peters; WASHINGTON: Mary Thompson; WEST VIRGINIA: Rodney Collins and Katherine M. Jourdan; WISCONSIN: Jim Draeger; WYOMING: John T. Keck.

A GREAT DEAL OF RESEARCH for this book was conducted at the National Register of Historic Places. Edson Beall and his staff, Jeff Joeckel and Rustin Quaide, provided me with an incredible amount of assistance that made what could have been an impossible task, possible, and for that I am particularly grateful.

A special thank you must be extended to Jan Cigliano, my editor. Besides being an excellent editor whose suggestions certainly improved the quality of this book, I must also commend her for the encouragement she extended to me throughout this entire endeavor. Her unfailing support helped me through some very difficult times.

This book is lovingly dedicated to my husband, Harvey J. Chiat, who has been my traveling companion on many journeys, including the one that has culminated in the writing of this book.

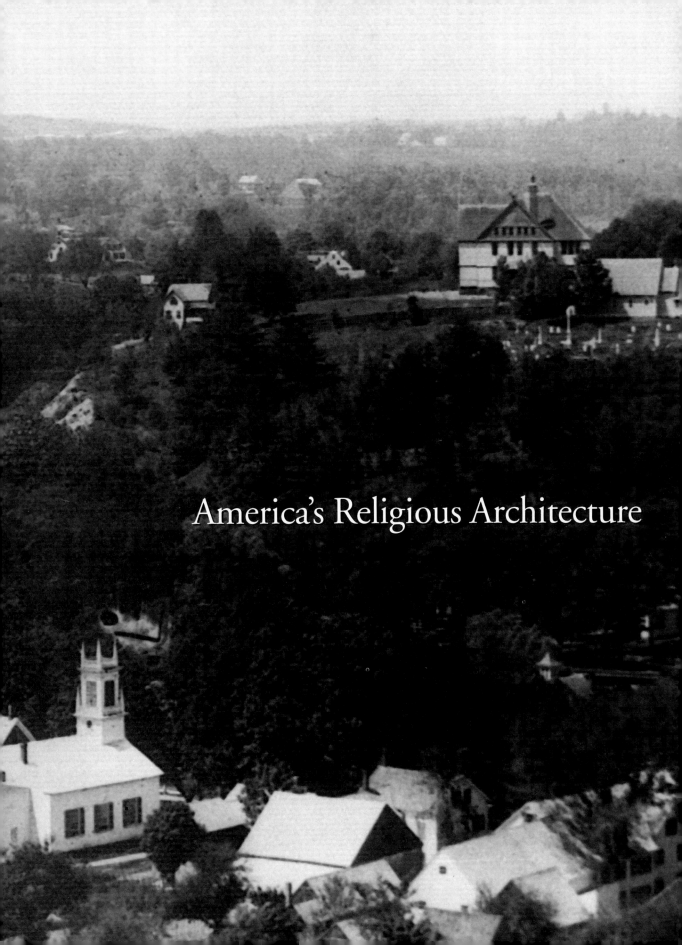

America's Religious Architecture

Introduction

THE STAGE MANAGER in Thornton Wilder's play *Our Town* describes Grover's Corners in New Hampshire as it was on a May day in 1901:

> Up here–is Main Street. Way back there is the railway station; tracks go that way. Polish Town's across the tracks and some Canuck families. Over there is the Congregational Church; across the street's the Presbyterian. Methodist and Unitarian are over there. Baptist is down in the holla' by the river. Catholic Church is over beyond the tracks. [1]

Nearly a century has passed since the stage manager made his observations about Grover's Corners. Many changes have taken place in our nation's towns and cities, but places of worship continue to be among the most visible and defining features of our rural and urban landscapes. From the Lower East Side of New York, where the decaying remains of synagogues still speak of the Jewish immigrants who once filled the tenements and labored in sweatshops, to California's coast, where Spanish missions still serve as reminders of the earliest Europeans to settle here, places of worship bear witness to our nation's diverse heritage.

One geographer describes religious buildings as the "universal element in the American settlement landscape, rural and urban . . . too rich an ore to be overlooked by cultural geo-

San Rafael Roman Catholic Church, La Cueva, New Mexico

graphers or historians."[2] But too often they are overlooked. One can travel throughout the United States and view a stylistic panorama of religious buildings more diverse than anywhere else in the world. All we need to do is pause as we speed along superhighways or hurry through towns and cities on our way to somewhere else and take a moment to look around. We would see places of worship, large and small, elaborate and simple, all with interesting stories to tell about the history of a place and of the people who lived there.

Praising and preserving the past is the theme of this book. Its intent is to pay tribute to historic places of worship located throughout the 50 states and to appraise them for the contributions they make and roles they play within their societies—enhancers of the built environment, cornerstones of many communities, and evidence of this nation's ethnic and religious diversity. Once we have come to appreciate why this diverse heritage deserves our praise, we can then move on to protecting and preserving it for future generations.

The United States is peopled almost entirely by immigrants and their descendants. In fact, only about three people in 100 of the total population are indigenous native Americans—American Indian, Eskimo, Aleutian Islander, and Hawaiian. The rest of us trace our origins back to the ethnic heritages of ancestors scattered throughout the world.

Wherever new immigrants settled, one of their first acts was to establish a congregation and build a place of worship. These historic buildings are among those celebrated in this book. German and Scandinavian pioneers established Lutheran churches in the East and West North Central regions and the Pacific Northwest. Hispanics in the Mountain and Pacific regions, Southern and Eastern Europeans in New England and the Middle Atlantic regions, and French Acadians in southern Louisiana all built Roman Catholic enclaves. Settlers from England and Western Europe seeking religious freedom brought the Baptist faith to the Southern region, where it remains the dominant religion through the end of the twentieth century. Eventually the nation had formed four distinct religious heartlands that are still in place: Baptist in the South, Lutherans in the West North Central farm belt, Roman Catholicism in New England and the Middle Atlantic, and Mormon in Utah and the Mountain states.[3] Minority ethnic groups living in these regions sought to retain their distinctive religious and ethnic identities by erecting their own places of worship, many of which are now lost or endangered. With each loss, the brilliance of the nation's colorful mosaic is further diminished.

Local vernacular architecture also influenced each region's religious architecture. Building materials, climate, topography, available technology, and a congregation's funds all play a part in a building's plan and decoration. America's first-generation immigrants created new building styles that echoed the memories of their pasts while adapting to the realities of a new environment. From the meetinghouses of New England testifying to the persistence of Yankee culture, to the onion domes and towers visible in Chicago's neighborhoods that are reminders of the Eastern Europeans who labored in the city's industries, across the wind-blown prairie dotted with clapboard Gothic churches and synagogues, stretching westward to the adobe churches of New Mexico and the missions of California echoing their Spanish heritage, and finally reaching northward to the Russian Orthodox churches of Alaska and west across the ocean to the Buddhist temples of Hawaii, America's colorful mosaic is clearly visible.

This book's guide to historic religious places is grouped into nine regions:

NEW ENGLAND: Maine, Vermont, New Hampshire, Massachusetts, Connecticut, Rhode Island

MIDDLE ATLANTIC: New York, New Jersey, Pennsylvania

EAST NORTH CENTRAL: Ohio, Indiana, Illinois, Michigan, Wisconsin

WEST NORTH CENTRAL: Minnesota, Iowa, Missouri, Kansas, Nebraska, South Dakota, North Dakota

SOUTH ATLANTIC: Delaware, Maryland, District of Columbia, Virginia, West Virginia, North Carolina, South Carolina, Georgia, Florida

EAST SOUTH CENTRAL: Kentucky, Tennessee, Alabama, Mississippi

WEST SOUTH CENTRAL: Arkansas, Louisiana, Texas, Oklahoma

MOUNTAIN: New Mexico, Colorado, Wyoming, Montana, Idaho, Utah, Arizona, Nevada

PACIFIC: California, Oregon, Washington, Alaska, Hawaii

The selection of the structures profiled herein was based on four criteria: (1) buildings that are listed on the National Register of Historic Places or in local historic registers; (2) buildings representing a particular ethnic culture; (3) buildings whose members have played an important role in a community's history; and (4) buildings of significant architectural merit, including those designed by a major architect, those representative of a major architectural or artistic period, and those having special aesthetic or design features.

The selection is intended to be representative of each region, in order to create a picture and a story for the reader about ethnic and religious diversity and how that diversity is reflected in its historic places of worship.

Perhaps this book will inspire congregations to look at their own buildings as historical artifacts, to document their histories and appearance, and to work toward their preservation. Once begun, documentary material could be stored in a local or regional historical society and be readily available to students and researchers. Then, perhaps, in the future, some ambitious person will carry this effort further, using this valuable collection as a primary resource. Another hope is to inspire additional publications on each of the nation's nine religious and ethnic regions that would include sites that by necessity were omitted here.

NOTES

1. Thornton Wilder, *Our Town: A Play in Three Acts* (New York: Coward McCann, 1938).

2. Wilbur Zelinsky, *The Cultural Geography of the United States* (Englewood Cliffs, NJ: Prentice-Hall, 1973), 101.

3. Barry A. Kosmin and Seymour P. Lachman, *One Nation Under God: Religion in Contemporary American Society* (New York: Harmony Books, 1993), 51.

1

America's Religious Heritage

First Baptist Church,
Providence,
Rhode Island,
drawing by
W. C. Pigeon

ONCE THIS WAS A LAND of tribal religions, whose origins are hidden from history. Then, it became noticeably Protestant, then Protestant and Catholic, then Protestant and Catholic and Jewish and Eastern Orthodox. Then Christianity and Judaism found themselves joined by Buddhism and Hinduism. . . . Then the religion of Muhammed . . . made its way as well to American shores. Pluralism had become the hardy perennial of the American garden.

–Edwin Scott Ganstad, *A Religious History of America*

THE **MOTHER MOSQUE OF AMERICA**, built in 1925, exemplifies America's pluralism. This small rectangular building of white clapboard is topped with an onion-shaped blue dome, and the faithful are called to prayer from its tower-shaped minaret. This mosque stands in the nation's heartland, Cedar Rapids, Iowa.

The existence of a mosque in the Midwest raises important questions. Who were its founders? Where did they come from? When did they arrive? Why did they settle in Iowa? The answers have much to tell about just one group who came to the United States, established a community, and then built a place to carry on its faith. The same questions can be asked about each immigrant group that arrived on the shores of the New World."

The places of worship built by these people–mosque, synagogue, church, or temple–provide important evidence about the history of America's unique religious heritage–a heritage reflected in its religious architecture. To appreciate the panorama of places of worship that unfolds as one travels throughout the nation, it is important first to understand the history of religion in America.

For most Americans, religion has meant a personal affirmation of faith in God and an identification with a religious denomination, but it does not necessarily mean joining or being an active member of that particular group. Religious diversity has been characteristic of the United States since its inception; no other nation approaches it. The country is home to over 1,500 different religious sects, and no doubt even more exist. Many have their roots in Europe. Some, after being transplanted here, splintered into other denominations or synods, making their "family trees" extremely complex, as exemplified by the 75 varieties of Baptists. Enriching the mix are the religious groups that were "made in America": the Church of Jesus Christ of the Latter-day Saints, the Church of Christ, Scientist, and the Seventh-Day Adventist Church, to name the most well known. But this land was not bereft of religious expression prior to the coming of white settlers; the indigenous people had their ancient belief systems and traditions that are only now reemerging after repeated attempts to suppress them.

Not all people with the same ethnic heritage identify with the same religion. As a result, there are fewer ethnic groups in the United States than there are religious sects. This fact does not make the task of defining the term "ethnicity" any less difficult. Here the term is defined as the subjective belief in a common descent based on similarities of cultural patterns, such as customs, language, and shared history; a blood relationship is not necessary. These shared characteristics serve to define a group and distinguish it from others. The term "ethnic" should not be equated with "foreign": ethnic groups as different as Mormon and Yankee have their origins in America. But even with the proliferation of religious sects, the intertwining of religious and ethnic identities in America remained visible. At one time a small market town in Minnesota had five Lutheran churches: Swedish, Norwegian, German, Finnish, and English. The latter was established by the children of immigrants who had intermarried and chose not to affiliate with an ethnic congregation. Completing the town's religious and ethnic composition were two Roman Catholic churches, one German and the other Irish, and a Methodist congregation established by a circuit-riding minister. It was the heartland's version of Wilder's *Our Town*.

This landscape of diversity, however, continues to change through the late twentieth century. As the population of rural areas diminishes, congregations merge, and another religious building becomes redundant. This raises the issue this book addresses: what is to become of the invaluable heritage of America's religious diversity—a diversity that dates back to the nation's founding.

As early as 1686, the English governor of New York, Edmund Andros, in a letter written to the British Board of Trade, described, in some bewilderment, the various religious groups inhabiting his colony: "There are Religions of all sorts, one Church of England, several Presbyterians and Independents, Quakers and Anabaptists of several sects, [and] some Jews. . ."[1] Overwhelmed by multiple demands for the freedom to worship, most of the colonies' English governors attempted to disallow all religions except the Church of England. There were exceptions, however, Roger Williams being one of the more prominent. Expelled from the English colony in Salem, Massachusetts, for advocating religious toleration and liberty, Williams founded a new colony in Providence, Rhode Island, where complete liberty of conscience regarding worship was guaranteed, and established the Baptist Church in America. **The First Baptist Church** in Providence, begun in 1774, is the denomination's oldest church building. Thanks to William Penn's "holy experiment" with religious toleration in the Pennsylvania colony, Quakers fleeing England found a safe haven. **Horsham Friends Meeting House**, constructed in 1804 in Montgomery, Pennsylvania, is the most complete and intact Quaker complex in Pennsylvania.

The struggle for religious freedom ended in 1789, the year that George Washington wrote a letter to the president of **Congregation Yeshuat Israel** (Touro Synagogue) in Newport, Rhode Island, stating his new government's attitude toward religion: ". . . the Government of the United States gives to bigotry no sanction, to persecution no assistance . . . ," that became the law of the land when Congress adopted the First Amendment to the Constitution forbidding the introduction of an established church. The decision to separate church and state was essentially pragmatic. Freedom of worship was viewed by the nation's founders as a necessity if the country was to avoid the religious wars that for centuries had torn Europe apart. The concept of voluntarism—allowing citizens of the land freely to join a faith—fueled a competition among religions for the "unchurched." The Great Awakenings, periods of religious revival that occurred prior to the Revolutionary War and again before the Civil War, stemmed from this competition. The outcome? A proliferation of Protestant denominations that came to dominate the nation's religious character. Another outcome is evident in the appearance of places of worship built across America.

THE FIRST WHITE SETTLERS in sixteenth-century North America were Spanish and French soldiers, explorers, missionaries, and traders, who began arriving soon after Columbus's voyages of discovery. Although their numbers were far fewer than the colonists who followed them, their contributions to the nation's mosaic remains. The beautiful **Mission**

San Xavier del Bac in Tucson, Arizona, is only one of many churches established by Spanish missionaries in the southwest; its architectural style continues to resonate throughout the region.

The story of the utopian Pilgrim Fathers who arrived in the 1620s and the more pragmatic Puritans who soon followed is familiar to us all. Along with families and cultural traditions came new religious practices, many in opposition to their homeland's official religion, representing a vision for a new faith in the New World. Colonists projected that vision of a "congregational way" in the places of worship they constructed. Evidence of these early settlements includes the **Old Ship Meeting House** in Hingham, Massachusetts, dated to 1681 and founded by English dissenters who later became Unitarians, and **Donegal Presbyterian Church** in Lancaster County, Pennsylvania, built in 1732 by Scots-Irish colonists. The "official" Anglican church, rejected by most in the northern colonies, gained a foothold in the South, particularly in Virginia, where **St. Luke's Episcopal Church (Benns Chapel)**, begun in 1632, is the earliest surviving Anglican Gothic style church in America. Other denominations were introduced by Dutch, Swedish, and German settlers, many of whom gravitated to the Middle Atlantic region where they established their own congregations, such as the **Old Dutch**

Reformed Church of Sleepy Hollow in Tarrytown, New York; **Holy Trinity Lutheran Church,** also known as "Old Swedes," in Wilmington, Delaware; and the **Augustus German Lutheran Church** in Trappe, Pennsylvania.

Jewish immigrants fleeing the Inquisition in Brazil arrived in Dutch New Amsterdam in 1647. More than eight decades had to pass before they were able to build a synagogue, Shearith Israel, in 1730; the building has long since been destroyed. Besides being among the first settlers in New York City and Newport, Rhode Island, Jews were also among the first to settle in Charleston, South Carolina. The congregation's first synagogue, **Temple Kahal Kadosh Beth Elohim,** built in 1794, was destroyed by fire in 1838 and replaced with the present Greek Revival building, dedicated in 1841. Also during the colonial period, the increasing need for cheap labor resulted in the importation of thousands of African slaves, who comprised 20 percent of the colonies' total population. Following the Revolutionary War, free blacks in Philadelphia formed an independent congregation that became the first church in the newly formed African Methodist Episcopal denomination. **Mother Bethel A.M.E.** in Philadelphia, erected in 1889-1890, is the congregation's fourth church.

Between 1680 and 1760 the colonial population grew almost tenfold, from approximately 250,000 to over 2 million. The settlers, overwhelmingly British and Protestant, established the enduring character of the dominant American culture and left ample evidence of their presence in their churches, whose architectural style had a lasting impact on the appearance of many of our nation's places of worship. Their preferred model was **St. Martin-in-the-Fields**, a London church designed by Sir James Gibbs and built between 1721

Methodist Tabernacle, Mathews, Virginia

and 1726. Variations of this basilica-plan church with a classical portico at one end and a tower placed back on the roof, began to appear throughout the colonies. **Old North** in Boston, although lacking the portico, is among the best known of this type. But perhaps the finest surviving example that is directly derived from Gibbs's published drawings is the **First Baptist Church** in Providence, Rhode Island, begun in 1775. The style was carried as far west as Hawaii by Congregational missionaries from New England. **Kawaiahao Church** in Honolulu, completed in 1842, is evidence of their efforts. Although St. Martin's was built to celebrate the establishment of a new Protestant dynasty in Great Britain during the reign of Queen Anne, this did not prevent it being used as a model by Roman Catholics. An outstanding example is **St. Joseph Proto-Cathedral** in Bardstown, Kentucky, built by Catholics of English and Irish descent and consecrated in 1819. Even with the predominance of the British people and their customs, widespread European settlement during the colonial era established the religious and ethnic diversity and the regional differences that were to characterize the new nation created in 1776.

DURING AND FOLLOWING the Revolutionary War, immigration to the United States came to a virtual halt. The upheaval in the colonies, coupled with Napoleonic wars throughout Europe, were the contributing factors. At the same time, many colonists began migrating westward, seeking new areas to settle and exploit. Western Virginia (established as the new state of West Virginia in 1863) was one region that attracted Scots-Irish, Welsh, and German settlers. The Methodist Society of America, founded in Baltimore in 1784, sent circuit riders into rural areas where their well-attended outdoor revival meetings successfully enrolled many new settlers into Methodism. Erected in 1922, the **Methodist Tabernacle** near Mathews, Virginia, is one of the state's few surviving Methodist revival shelters. Areas west of the Coastal Plain region of the Carolinas also began to attract settlers, including those who organized **Bethesda Presbyterian Church** in Camden, South Carolina, in 1681. The congregation hired the renowned architect Robert Mills to design its new church in 1832, which is one of the few Mills churches still in existence.

Following the end of hostilities in Europe in 1815, the continent began to experience an unprecedented growth in population and a concomitant decline in its food supply, resulting in the first wave of what was soon to become a deluge of people leaving their homelands to seek a better life in the New World. Numerous Irish peasants fleeing the potato famine and infamous Irish Poor Law of 1838 chose to settle in major urban areas such as New York and Boston, often entering the work force as unskilled laborers. Although impoverished, the immigrants scraped together funds to build churches that were central to their religious and ethnic identity. In South Boston, **Saints Peter and Paul Roman Catholic Church** is visual testimony to their faith and perseverance.

The Corps of Discovery, ordered by Thomas Jefferson in 1804 following the Louisiana Purchase and led by Meriwether Lewis and William Clark, contributed to the opening of vast lands west of the Mississippi River to settlement. It was during this same time that people began to arrive from countries other than those on the European continent, including Canadians heading south and Mexicans moving north. Asians, who were few in number prior to this period, came in search of gold, settling in California's boom towns and in the process introducing an entirely new chapter into the history of America's religious diversity: Buddhism and the architecture of the Far East beautifully preserved in the **Won Lim Temple** in Weaversville, California. However, the enactment by Congress of the Chinese Exclusion Act in 1882 limiting their numbers made these settlers scapegoats for the Panic of 1873 that brought a depression and unemployment to the western states. Meanwhile, Japanese laborers working on American-owned sugar and pineapple plantations on the Hawaiian Islands introduced yet another non-Western faith, Shintoism, that continues to be observed in the **Maui Jinsha Shinto Temple** on the island of Maui.

Increasing numbers of Irish, German, Scandinavian, Dutch, and Swiss immigrants left their homelands in the mid-nineteenth century, propelled by events in Europe and the recruitment efforts by the United States to attract settlers to the vast expanses of land opening as a result of the Louisiana Purchase and the forcible removal of the native peoples. The major attraction was Congress passing the Homestead Act in 1862 promising farmers free land. Land-starved Europeans, notably Scandinavians who constituted the largest northwestern European group after the British and Germans immigrating to America, began settling in the northern states. Protestant churches, particularly Lutheran, dotted the heartland's rural countryside. Most were modest frame structures built in the prevailing Gothic Revival style, preferred by the newly reconstituted and revived Episcopal faith, and introduced into the United States by British architects, Richard Upjohn and James Renwick. Upjohn's monumental **Trinity Episcopal Church** (1847) and Renwick's equally monumental St. Patrick's Cathedral (1853-1880), both in New York City, had an enormous impact on the development of the nation's religious architecture. Many immigrants, including Catholics and Lutherans, came to view the Gothic Revival religious structures, which were so visible in ports of entry, as being appropriately "Christian" while at the same time typically "American." As a result, that style became popular for ethnic groups and faiths other than British and Episcopal. Miniature interpretations of Upjohn's Trinity Church based on designs published in his book *Rural Architecture* (1852) remain a defining image in many small towns and rural areas. Lutheran examples include **St. Jacob's German Lutheran Church** in Montgomery County, Ohio, and **Telemarken Lutheran Church**, built by Norwegians in the

Congregation Beth Israel, Stevens Point, Wisconsin

vicinity of Wallace, South Dakota. Even Jewish immigrants from eastern Europe settling in small market towns began to adapt the Gothic style, minus one important element, the steeple. Congregation Beth Israel in Stevens Point, Wisconsin, recently transformed into a community center, is one surviving example.

Not all German and Scandinavian Lutherans chose to farm; others preferred to live in large cities, taking jobs that opened up in industry, as for example, the flour and lumber mills along the Mississippi River in Minneapolis. The Lutheran churches built in urban areas were often quite different from the modest white clapboard Gothic Revival buildings blanketing the countryside. Central Lutheran Church in Minneapolis is a monumental stone Gothic Revival structure described in its literature as the "Cathedral Church of Lutherans in Minnesota."

The South also attracted new settlers, including many from southern Europe. Roman Catholics moving into ethnic neighborhoods built places of worship, such as the **Cathedral of St. Louis** in New Orleans, that are monumental in size and display, as seen here, aesthetic details reflecting their ethnic identity. Greek Orthodox Christians, whose numbers never came to rival those of the Roman Catholics, were in Florida as early as 1763. Working as laborers under dreadful conditions, their community was on the verge of disap-

Cathedral of
St. Louis,
New Orleans,
Louisiana

pearing when a second influx of Greeks began settling in Tarpon Springs, Florida, to work in the sponge industry. **St. Nicholas Greek Orthodox Cathedral** built in 1943 is testament to their success.

Exotic religious structures were also being built at this time, a reflection of nineteenth-century Romanticism. German Jews in Cincinnati decided to go with the popular Moorish style in synagogue architecture, complete with minarets, for their new building, the **Plum Street Temple** (Isaac Mayer Wise Temple), dedicated in 1866. And in Nashville, Tennessee, the Presbyterians chose the Egyptian Revival style for their new church, the Downtown Presbyterian Church, also known as **Karnak on the Cumberland** built in 1848.

EXTERNAL AND INTERNAL migrations during the post–Civil War era were producing regional shifts in the nation's population: The proportion of people living in the Midwest and West was increasing while the numbers in the Northeast and South began to diminish. African-Americans continued to cluster in southern states, often worshipping in small former slave chapels located on plantations, such as the **Bremo Slave Chapel** in Bremo, Virginia. Over time, African-Americans gained financial strength and were able to build more substantial structures, including the **Orchard**

Street Church in Baltimore, Maryland, dedicated in 1882, and now home to the Baltimore Urban League.

The nation's last major period of immigration, between 1890 and 1920, witnessed the arrival of hundreds of thousands of people from southern and eastern Europe coming to take jobs as unskilled laborers in the nation's rapidly expanding industries. Their large numbers upset the "establishment," resulting in the passage of strict discriminatory immigration legislation in the 1920s. However, by this time over 30 million immigrants had arrived in the United States. Those from eastern and southern Europe followed the pattern of those who came before them, choosing to settle in their own ethnic enclaves, such as the Polish neighborhood in Cambria City in Johnstown, Pennsylvania, that to this day remains clustered around **St. Casimir's Roman Catholic Church.**

Immigration quotas imposed in the 1920s remained in effect (with some modifications) until 1965. Since that time some restrictions have been lifted, resulting in the arrival of immigrants from southeast Asia, Mexico, the Caribbean, and the former Soviet Union. Like those who preceded them, these newcomers, too, have chosen to establish their own distinct places of worship like the **Phat An Buddhist Temple** in a suburb of St. Paul, Minnesota.

BY THE MID-TWENTIETH CENTURY, third-generation Americans were coming of age and, according to scholars studying the sociology of religion in the United States, were transforming the nation from a "land of immigrants" into a "triple melting pot" restructured into three great faiths: Protestant, Catholic, Jew. Unable or unwilling to recover their grandparents' foreign culture, it was argued, they chose instead to identify with their religion, but now in a form that was viewed as American with shared ideals and values. As would be expected, not to identify with one of the three faiths was to be an outsider.[2] As the century progressed, it became increasingly apparent that although most religions have been influenced to some degree by the nation's pervasive Protestant ethos, many religious institutions have quite consciously attempted to maintain their native traditions–architec-tural, liturgical, and cultural. The "triple melting pot" has evolved into a many-hued mosaic. From the Russian Orthodox churches in Alaska, such as **St. Nicholas Russian Orthodox Church** in Eklutna Village, to the small painted German Roman Catholic churches of Schulenburg, Texas, of which the **Nativity of Mary, Blessed Virgin** in High Hill is an excel-lent example, there is clear evidence that the United States population has maintained the nation's religious and ethnic diversity.

Ethnic identity's endurance is central to the stories told about attempts to merge con-gregations. Co-religionists, representing two different ethnic congregations, decided for economic reasons to merge into one congregation. Years following the merger, the two groups continue to sit on opposite sides of the sanctuary's center aisle. Denominations struggling to unite under one banner, as for example the Lutherans under the name Evan-gelical Lutheran Church in America [ELCA], further illustrate how difficult it can be to bring together all the different synods that traditionally have represented different ethnic-ities. Ethnicity and religion in the United States remain intertwined and continue to iden-tify who people are, and even guide where they live. This is not too surprising in a country that takes justifiable pride in its pluralism.

By the end of immigration in the 1920s, the millions who had arrived here included Protestants representing a variety of denominations, Roman Catholics from many nations, Eastern Orthodox of different ethnic origins, Jews of differing cultural perspectives, along with Pietists such as Mennonite and Hutterite, Muslim, Buddhist, and Shinto, plus many others equally important but too numerous to list. Their settlement patterns and places of worship are what give the nation's mosaic its vibrancy and vivid color.

NOTES

1. Edwin Scott Gaustad, *Historical Atlas of Religion in America*, rev. ed. (New York: Harper & Row, 1976), 2.
2. Will Herberg, *Protestant-Catholic-Jew: An Essay in American Religious Sociology* (Garden City, NY: Doubleday & Company, 1956), 272-273.

PRECEDING PAGE:

Old First Presbyterian Church (The Downtown Presbyterian Church, Karnak on Cumberland), Nashville, Tennessee

2

New England

Trinity Church,
Boston,
Massachusetts

THE WELL-KNOWN STORY about the Pilgrims tells of their landing on Plymouth Rock in 1620 and establishing the first permanent white colony in the New World. The Pilgrims were dissenters, Separatists rebelling against the Church of England. Joining them in 1628 were Puritans who went on to establish the Massachusetts Bay Colony in Salem and two years later the city of Boston. The Puritans did not consider themselves dissenters or Separatists, but rather reformers who were trying to "purify" the Church of England of elements of Catholicism. However, when their efforts were rebuffed by the Anglicans they departed for the New World, where they and the Pilgrims went about establishing a "new" England with a new "Church of England," a church governed by a body of believers, not bishops—a church of the "congregational way" as opposed to an episcopal church. Their theocracy gave them the religious freedom they sought, but it was not extended to others. One outcome was Roger Williams fleeing Massachusetts to establish the colony of Rhode Island in 1636, which was to become a haven for all kinds of religious dissenters unwelcome elsewhere in the New World. It was here that Williams established the first Baptist church in America.

Geographers divide New England into two distinct sectors. The east, which was settled first, consisting of Massachusetts, Rhode Island, and Connecticut, is highly urbanized and industrialized. In the years following the Revolutionary War, Boston became the nation's manufacturing and commercial center and set its social and cultural standards. The more rugged north, which was colonized after 1770, including all of Vermont and nearly all of New Hampshire and Maine, continues to retain its independent rural character.

One early observer of the American cultural landscape commented that "the civilization of New England has been like a beacon lit upon a hill, which, after it has diffused its warmth around, tinges the distant horizon with its glow."[1] The beacon's energy came from Great Britain, the nation many colonists fled, but in their baggage came memories of their homeland that were to permeate many areas of their culture, except, at first, their religious architecture. The early colonists refused to even use the term "church" for their places of worship and consciously designed buildings that were in deliberate contradistinction to Anglican churches both in appearance and function. The colonists' simple, unadorned buildings, often surrounded by a palisade, were called meetinghouses, reflecting their Calvinist belief that no distinction should be made between sacred and civil law.

A meetinghouse was a place in which a congregation would gather for secular and religious functions and find shelter at times of attack. It was in these meetinghouses that the increasingly independent colonists would argue issues of religion and democracy. Political independence became as important to them as religious salvation; thus, when the rebellion against British rule began, the Congregational Church, joined by the Presbyterian and most Baptist congregations, were on the side of the Patriots. The Methodist Church chose to side with its Tory leader, John Wesley, and although two-thirds of the signers of the Declaration of Independence were Anglican, most other Anglicans were Loyalists.

The British may have lost the Revolutionary War, but its culture continued to be predominant in the new nation. The war left the Anglican Church in disarray, but recovering quickly under its new banner as the Protestant Episcopal Church, it began to attract prosperous merchants and politicians who, assuming the cultural airs of the British aristocracy, had left the Congregational Church. Thus, as one author has remarked, did "Puritans become Yankees."[2]

Succeeding generations once again began to refer to Christian places of worship as "churches" and didn't hesitate to import architectural styles from England, reinterpreting them by using local technology and materials. In particular, American builders in the eighteenth and early nineteenth centuries were looking at churches designed by two great English architects, Christopher Wren and James Gibbs, adapting them to American needs and ultimately developing a recognizable style that became known as the American church plan: a rectangular red brick or white clapboard porticoed building topped with a multistage tower and steeple. This style, so closely identified with American values, often was the plan of choice for places of worship built by a variety of religious and ethnic groups who immigrated to the New World.

St. Matthew's Episcopal Church, Hallowell, Maine

During the course of the eighteenth century other factors also contributed to the region's changing religious and ethnic landscape. Scots-Irish, Dutch, Flemish, Jewish, French, and Irish immigrants settling in New England began to demand the freedom to worship. Their plea for the separation of church and state received its first clear articulation in a letter that President George Washington sent to the Hebrew congregation in Newport, Rhode Island, in 1790 (see p. 64) that is still read annually at the synagogue. In this letter Washington states clearly that the nation's new government would ". . . give to bigotry no sanction, to persecution no assistance require[ing] only that those who live under its protection shall demean themselves as good citizens."[3]

Successive waves of immigrants arriving throughout the nineteenth and early twentieth centuries brought with them their ethnic traditions and religious beliefs that would need to find expression in a new land. Their stories, as told in the form and decoration of their places of worship, illustrate the Americanization process seen in the merger of stylistic elements from the Old World with those from the New, particularly from meetinghouses and churches built by colonists that were viewed as truly "American."

Maine

MAINE ENCOMPASSES AN AREA that is almost as large as the remainder of New England combined. French and British colonies were established as early as the first decade of the seventeenth century, but by the end of the century the entire district of Maine was under the control of the colony of Massachusetts, where it remained until it was granted statehood in 1820.

Maine's inclement weather, difficult terrain, and territorial battles discouraged all but the most hardy of settlers. These same factors, plus the availability of natural resources, such as white pine, fieldstone, and granite, had an impact on the appearance of the state's places of worship.

The Congregationalists were initially dominant, establishing two congregations by the end of the seventeenth century. The state's oldest extant Congregational church, **The Harpswell Meetinghouse,** was built in Cumberland County in 1757-59. It is typical of the sim-

Old German
Lutheran Church,
Waldoboro, Maine

ple, unadorned meetinghouses that continued to be built in Maine into the nineteenth century, such as the Porter Meetinghouse in Oxford County erected by a Baptist congregation in 1824.

Not all of Maine's earliest settlers were English dissenters. Other hardy souls who braved Maine's demanding climate and terrain to establish a community were a small group of German Lutherans who settled in the vicinity of Waldoboro where, in 1770, they erected their first meetinghouse, the recently restored **Old German Lutheran Church**.

The Anglican Church was not well received by most of the colonists in New England, many of whom were "dissenters." By the end of the eighteenth century Maine had only two Anglican parishes. But the denomination's fate began to change dramatically in the years following the War of Independence, at which time it was reorganized and renamed the Protestant Episcopal Church in America and came to symbolize the success of the former colonists. Dissatisfied with the plain Congregational churches they worshipped in, the newly prosperous former colonists wanted more elaborate buildings that would symbolize what they viewed as American values: entrepreneurship and capitalism. Ironically, in retrospect, they turned to the Episcopal Church and began to erect elaborate buildings in the now favored Gothic style promoted by the English-born architects Richard Upjohn and James Renwick. **St. Matthew's Episcopal Church** in Hallowell, built in 1860, is an almost direct copy of the design for a country church published by Upjohn in his popular and influential book *Rural Architecture*.

Acadian French Roman Catholics migrating south from Nova Scotia began settling in the St. John River Valley in Aroostook County. There they established a parish and built a church, **Our Lady of Mount Carmel (Notre Dame de Mont-Carmel)**. Their descendants continue to comprise most of the region's population, but the church has recently been transformed into a museum and cultural center, L'Association Culturelle et Historique du Mont-Carmel.

Slovak immigrants began arriving in Lisbon Falls in the 1890s to work in the Worumbo textile mill. Unwelcomed by the town's older immigrant community and separated from the mainstream by custom and language, the Slovaks decided to construct their own church. Despite threats of excommunication, they persevered and construction began on Saints Cyril and Methodius Roman Catholic Church in 1923. Although modest in appearance, the one-story brick Gothic Revival building testifies to the determination and achievements of Maine's only Slovak community.

Perhaps one of Maine's most unusual religious complexes is **Shiloh Temple (Rev. Frank W. Sanford's Bible and Missionary Training School)**, built in 1897 for the followers of one man's vision and interpretation of Christianity. It survives as testimony to the rugged individualism of many of the people who came to settle in this state.

Harpswell Meeting House

Harpswell Neck Road (State Route 122), Cumberland County

ARCHITECT / BUILDER:
Elisha Eaton [?]

CONSTRUCTION / DEDICATION DATE:
1757-1759

H ARPSWELL MEETING HOUSE is the oldest extant Congregational meetinghouse in Maine. As was the case with most early places of worship in the United States, the building was designed to function both as a Congregational place of worship and a town meetinghouse. A simple, frame clapboard structure, modest in scale and from the exterior more domestic than public in appearance, its interior reveals its sacred character. Although most of its square box pews have been removed, the paneled high pulpit with sounding board centered on the broad rear wall opposite the entrance remains intact. Since 1843, when a new Congregational church was built across the street from it, the building is used solely as a public meetinghouse—but it remains a historic part of Maine's history that fortunately is essentially intact.

Harpswell
Meeting House,
Cumberland,
Maine (1936 photo)

Old German Lutheran Church

State Route 32 at Kalers Corner, Waldoboro

ARCHITECT / BUILDER:
Re-erected under supervision of Dr. John Christian Walleazer, the pastor
CONSTRUCTION / DEDICATION DATE:
1770-73; re-erected in 1795

T HE BEIGE CLAPBOARD CHURCH that was erected in 1770-73 was rebuilt in 1795 after having been moved across the frozen river because of competing land claims. Erected by German Lutheran immigrants who settled in the area in 1748, its plan reveals influences coming from indigenous meetinghouses they saw in Maine combined with the longitudinal basilica plan brought with them from their homeland. The placement of the pulpit at the long, narrow end of the building opposite a two-story projecting stair hall and entry is typical of churches built throughout Germany, but the openness of its plan, three-sided gallery, paneled box pews, and high pulpit with a sounding board are typical of Maine meetinghouses.

The longitudinal basilica plan leading from the outside secular world to the sacred–the pulpit and altar area–may reflect these congregants' memories of the Gothic basilica-type churches they left behind in the Old World, but it is also a plan that will eventually become the favorite of many Americans, regardless of their ethnicity or religion.

A cemetery which stretches up the hill behind the church dates from the 1700s. Inscriptions on its tombstones provide insights into the hopes, aspirations, and disappointments of the people who built and worshipped here. The church, once abandoned, was recently restored; all its interior fittings remain intact.

Old German Lutheran Church, Waldoboro, Maine

Our Lady of Mount Carmel Roman Catholic Church

(NOTRE DAME DU MONT-CARMEL)
Now: L'ASSOCIATION CULTURELLE ET HISTORIQUE DU MONT-CARMEL

U.S. Route 1, Grand Isle, Aroostook County

ARCHITECT / BUILDER:
Theo Daust, architect
CONSTRUCTION / DEDICATION DATE:
1909

NOTRE DAME DU MONT-CARMEL was built in 1909 to replace the parish's first church, which was transformed into a school and convent. The elaborate clapboard structure is built in a style similar to churches across the St. John River in New Brunswick. Importantly, it remains an intact expression of French Acadian vernacular church architecture, including its twin towers surmounted by octagonal belfries crowned with trumpeting angels. Religious services ceased in the building in 1978, but it has been thoughtfully preserved. In 1984 it was transformed into L'Association Culturelle et Historique du Mont-Carmel, a nonprofit museum and cultural center dedicated to the preservation of the historic, religious, folk, and aesthetic heritages of the whole of the St. John River Valley. The association is governed by a board whose mandate is "preserving the integrity of the former church building through the promotion and presentation of the Acadian culture." Only two of the nineteenth-century French Acadian churches built in the St. John River Valley survive intact. Notre Dame, thanks to the efforts of its new owners, is the better preserved.

Notre Dame de Mont-Carmel (Our Lady of Mount Carmel), Green Isle, Aroostook County, Maine

Shiloh Temple, Bible and Missionary Training School

South of Lisbon Falls on south bank of Androscoggin River

ARCHITECT / BUILDER:
Reverend Frank W. Sanford
CONSTRUCTION / DEDICATION DATE:
1897

S HILOH TEMPLE IS ALL THAT REMAINS of a religious movement similar to Millerism that flourished at the end of the nineteenth century (see p. 73). Its vernacular style combines elements from resort architecture, such as its surrounding porch and mansard roof, and religious architecture, in particular its tall multileveled tower capped by a large gilded metal crown supported on eight columns–a Maine landmark. In a room directly beneath the crown, continuous prayers were said around the clock for nearly 23 years.

Frank W. Sanford, the founder of Shiloh, was an ordained Baptist minister who claimed to be in direct communication with God. Coming at a time when the nation was experiencing a religious revival, Sanford was able to attract followers who did not question his divinity or leadership, and were willing to provide him with large sums of money to build the temple complex, a large quadrangle containing over 500 rooms and capable of housing 1,000 or more people. Sanford's vision was to have Shiloh become the center of an evangelical effort to Christianize the world. Toward that end, he acquired a vessel, the Coronet, and set sail to convert the "heathens." Unfortunately, he knew little about the sea, and with his crew in mutiny, was forced to return to Maine where he was arrested and sentenced to jail. His "Kingdom," however, still exists, with headquarters in New Hampshire, and Shiloh Temple, rarely used, remains an important part of Maine's history.

FACING PAGE:
**Shiloh Temple,
Lisbon Mills,
Maine**

Vermont

VERMONT'S LAKE CHAMPLAIN is named after Samuel de Champlain, the French explorer who visited the region in 1609. The British, following their defeat of the French, gained complete control of the area by 1758. Debates now centered on which colony would control it—New York or New Hampshire. To protect their interests, the colonists organized the Green Mountain Boys under the leadership of Ethan Allen. The war they waged against British domination had its climax in the capture of Ticonderoga on May 10, 1775, considered the first battle in the Revolutionary War. Vermont's petition for statehood, granted in 1791, made it the first state admitted under the nation's new Constitution.

A colonist writing about Vermont in 1790 observed, "As to the character, the manners, the customs, the laws, the policy and the religion of the people in Vermont, it is sufficient to say they are New Englandman." As was often the case in New England, save for Rhode Island, the first church in Vermont's first settlement, Bennington, was Congregational. Erected between 1763 and 1767, it was replaced in 1805 by the present building, **The First Congregational Church**, designed by Lavius Fillmore.

Fillmore was Episcopalian and one of the founders of the first Episcopal Society in Addison County. He was not, however, the designer of the congregation's first church, **St. Stephen's**, a remarkable early example of the Gothic Revival style erected in Middlebury in 1825 after the parish received permission from the town to erect a church on its green.

French Canadian and Irish immigrants brought with them their Roman Catholic faith. The Irish, fleeing the famine in their homeland, began arriving in West Rutland in the 1840s to work in the town's newly opened marble quarry. A frame Catholic church built by the Irish in 1855 was replaced in 1860 by **St. Bridget's Roman Catholic Church**, built at night by Irish quarrymen in the material they knew best–marble; it is the state's first marble church.

Burlington, the largest port on Lake Champlain, provided easy access into the state for French Canadians seeking work in the state's mills, farms, and railroads. Having to share religious services with Irish Catholics made it difficult for the French Canadians to maintain their cultural identity and language. Their request for a separate parish was fulfilled in 1850, and their present church, **St. Joseph Roman Catholic Church**, was built between 1883 and 1887.

Additional quarries began to open at the same time the nation began to experience its last and largest wave of immigration. The Vermont Marble Company and the town of

Proctor were both incorporated in the 1880s. Among those arriving were Swedish immigrants who chose to work in the quarries rather than risk the hardships of homesteading in the Midwest. Most of the buildings in the central village of Proctor are built of marble block masonry, except for St. Paul's Swedish Lutheran Church, a clapboard structure built in 1914 to replace an earlier building that had burned. It could be argued that wood was the building material and technology most familiar to the Swedish carpenters who constructed the church.

The oldest Jewish congregation in Vermont is **Ahavath Garem Synagogue** in Burlington, founded in 1876 as Ohavi Zedek congregation. Most of its founders were immigrant peddlers and merchants catering to the city's expanding population. Their synagogue, acquired in 1885, remains in use by the town's small Jewish community, an important cultural landmark in Vermont where the Jewish population never numbered over 1,500.

First Congregational Church

("OLD FIRST CHURCH")

Monumental Avenue, on Bennington Green at State Route 1, Bennington

ARCHITECT / BUILDER:
Lavius Fillmore

CONSTRUCTION / DEDICATION DATE:
1805

DESIGNED BY LAVIUS FILLMORE, a second cousin of President Millard Fillmore, this church replaced the town's first meetinghouse that was built in 1763-67. The design of the church is similar to plans and designs published by Asher Benjamin in his 1797 book, *The Country Builder's Assistant*. It reflects their common source in now lost early churches of Charles Bulfinch, who in turn drew upon the work of two English architects, James Gibbs and his teacher, Christopher Wren. Gibbs had published plans for his famed London church, St. Martin-in-the-Fields, in his 1728 *Book of Architecture* that was circulated in the United States. It was the design of Gibbs's church, with its classical por-

tico and four-stage tower, that was to have considerable influence on the Federal style as it developed in the United States in the years following the War of Independence.

The church has undergone several remodelings that left little of its original interior intact. However, the high pulpit and box pews have been reconstructed. In addition, the old pews that were originally in the gallery survive, as do the initials and pictures carved into them by bored young worshippers.

First Congregational
Church, Bennington,
Vermont

St. Stephen's Episcopal Church

Main Street, Middlebury

ARCHITECT / BUILDER:
Woodwork by Lavius Fillmore
CONSTRUCTION / DEDICATION DATE:
1826-1827

ALTHOUGH LAVIUS FILLMORE, one of the founders of this congregation, is not specifically documented as the designer of the church, he was on the building committee whose directives were followed by the masons. Records indicate that he was responsible for finishing the interior and exterior woodwork, including wooden tracery in the windows and tower.

The exterior design of the church is a remarkable early interpretation of the Gothic Revival style (and, indeed, the first in Vermont) that did not begin to gain real popularity in the United States until the 1850s following its acceptance as the style of choice by the Episcopal Church in America, as seen in Richard Upjohn's influential Trinity Church built in New York City in 1847. Fillmore's congregation may have elected to build a church in this style to distinguish it from the elaborate Federal Style Congregational Meeting House which he had built just up the street. But it also may reflect Middlebury's perceived competition as a milling center with Lowell, Massachusetts, where a Gothic style Episcopal church, St. Anne's, was completed in 1826. Fillmore did introduce some Federal elements in his design of the interior's woodwork, but little remains, as the result of a later remodeling that included the addition of stained glass windows and a false ceiling. St. Stephens survives, albeit in an altered form, as evidence of the early arrival of the Gothic style in the United States and particularly in Vermont.

**St. Stephen's
Episcopal Church,
Middlebury, Vermont**

St. Bridget's Roman Catholic Church

Corner of Pleasant and Church Streets, West Rutland

ARCHITECT / BUILDER:
Patrick C. Keely, architect
CONSTRUCTION / DEDICATION DATE:
1860-1861

THE FIRST IRISH ROMAN CATHOLICS SETTLING in West Rutland in the 1830s built a small frame church in 1855 that was replaced by the present church in 1861, a time when the town's marble quarry was booming, thanks in part to the Civil War and the need for headstones for the fallen soldiers.

St. Bridget's, an excellent example of Gothic Revival architecture, was designed by Patrick C. Keely, a New York architect who was responsible for designing over 600 cathedrals and churches in the United States, including two others in Vermont.

Built at night by quarrymen who labored all day in the quarries, the marble was donated by the town's own Sheldon and Slason marble company. The first Catholic church in Vermont to be built of stone, St. Bridget's is located on a hill overlooking the town. Its enormous central, two-tier tower and steeple is a landmark that can be seen from miles around. Bishop de Goesbriand, who dedicated the church in 1861, described it as "a substantial structure built of marble of very good proportion and decorated with exquisite taste."

St. Bridget's Roman
Catholic Church,
West Rutland,
Vermont

St. Joseph Roman Catholic Church

29 Allen Street, Burlington

ARCHITECT / BUILDER:
Father Joseph Michaud

CONSTRUCTION / DEDICATION DATE:
1883-1887

S T. JOSEPH, DESIGNED BY FATHER JOSEPH MICHAUD, displays elements borrowed from Renaissance, Baroque, and Classical architecture, anticipating the Beaux Arts style that became popular in the 1890s. Here, however, it reflects the self-taught training of the architect and the attitude of his patron, Monseigneur Ignace Bourget, the Bishop of Montreal. While it was acceptable for the Irish Roman Catholics in Proctor to build their church in the prevailing Gothic Revival style, Monseigneur Bourget considered that style to be alien to French Canada and to Roman Catholicism. Rather, he encouraged Father Michaud to travel to Europe and study Classical, Renaissance, and Baroque churches. The result is the amalgamation of styles seen in this church. For example, the volutes on the exterior of the church are borrowed from the Gesu, an influential Baroque Jesuit church built in Rome in the middle of the sixteenth century, whereas the interior is Neoclassical.

Father Michaud went on to design the new Cathedral of St. James in Montreal, completed in 1894, which is a one-eighth replica of St. Peter's in Rome.

St. Joseph Roman Catholic Church, Burlington, Vermont

Ahavath Garem Synagogue

(ORIGINAL NAME OHAVI ZEDEK)

Archibald and Hyde Streets, Burlington

ARCHITECT / BUILDER:
1902 alterations: Spear Brothers Construction Company
CONSTRUCTION / DEDICATION DATE:
1885-1902

THE SYNAGOGUE'S INAUSPICIOUS BEGINNING was a wooden stone cutter's shed purchased by the newly formed congregation in 1885. A small white frame synagogue was constructed on the shed's foundation. The synagogue remained unchanged until 1902, when it was thoroughly renovated. One member, described in the congregation's history as comprising a committee of one in charge of renovating the synagogue, chose St. Stephen's Church in Winooski, a Gothic Revival building, as a model, minus the steeple. This was an unusual choice for a Jewish house of worship considering the style's close association with Christian ideals, particularly as expressed by architects such as Richard Upjohn and supported by the Episcopal Church. The exterior was also faced with brick at this time and a gallery was added on the interior.

The interior of the building, in contrast to its Gothic style exterior, reveals features traditionally associated with an Eastern European Orthodox Jewish congregation. These include a gallery for women, a *bimah* (platform) and reading table set in the center of the hall, and an Ark or Torah Shrine on a raised platform set against a wall. The beautiful shrine was made by one of the synagogue's members, a tinsmith.

The congregation built a new synagogue in 1952, but a group of members chose to remain in its historic building. The synagogue survives as testimony to the Jewish immigrants who chose to settle outside the mainstream.

Ahavath Garem
Synagogue,
Burlington,
Vermont

Ahavath Garem
Synagogue,
Burlington,
Vermont (interior)

New Hampshire

N EW HAMPSHIRE'S 18 MILES of coastline and harbor were explored by British and French adventurers in the early years of the seventeenth century. The Massachusetts Bay Colony was the first to claim the entire region, but its ownership was not resolved until 1679 when New Hampshire was declared a royal province. Regardless of its "royal" status, the colonists in New Hampshire supported the Patriot cause during the War of Independence and it was the ninth colony to ratify the new nation's Constitution.

The province's first colonists, mainly English, Scot, and Scots-Irish, settled in southern New Hampshire and were followers of the "Congregational way." **Hawke Meeting House,** built in 1755 in Danville, near the border with Massachusetts, is one of the state's oldest Congregational churches. However, soon after its construction, many of its members defected to a Free-Will Baptist church about 2 miles away. The Free-Will Baptist Movement, reacting against the prevailing Calvinism of the traditional Baptists, was attracting many converts in New Hampshire and Maine in the latter part of the eighteenth century. The white clapboard **New Durham Free Will Baptist Church,** built in 1819, considered the Movement's mother church, was founded in 1780 by Benjamin Randall who was born in New Castle, New Hampshire.

The builders of early meetinghouses, such as the one at Danville, very consciously avoided copying Anglican prototypes, particularly the use of the basilica plan progressing along a longitudinal access leading from the entry to the altar that was favored for Anglican churches. For "dissenters" there was no separation between sacred and secular, between priest and parishioner. However, as the memory of English domination faded, so too did the insistence on adhering closely to the democratic principles of the "Congregational way." By the early nineteenth century, numerous Congregational and even Baptist churches, such as the Free Will Baptist in New Durham, were being built that clearly were inspired by Anglican church architecture, particularly drawings of St. Martin-in-the Fields in London designed by James Gibbs. These spired white clapboard or red brick churches often set on a village green still adorn everything from calendars to travel posters and are considered a truly "American" expression of faith. Copied throughout the nation, their ancestry is English, but their accent is American.

The Third Fitzwilliam Meetinghouse, built in 1816–17, is perhaps one of the most photographed of these churches. Designed by Elias Carter and modeled after his church in Templeton, Massachusetts, it reveals his link with his father, an English builder familiar with the work of Christopher Wren and James Gibbs. A close second in popularity is Acworth Congregational Church built in 1821 and known as the Church-on-the-Hill for its picturesque location on an elevated site at the northern end of the town's common. Not all churches in this style are white clapboard. **South Congregational Church** in Newport, built in 1823, is a two-story brick structure considered one of western New Hampshire's finest Federal style churches.

During the Colonial period, other denominations were often forcibly discouraged by government and religious authorities from establishing congregations in New Hampshire, but this did not dissuade three Quaker women who arrived in Dover in 1662. Met by violent opposition, they were "whipped out of town" only to return again the following year when their effort was met with success. Dover's historic Religious Society of Friends Meetinghouse, erected in 1768, is the community's third. At the time of its construction over a third of the population of the town were Quakers.

Washington Church, a modest, white clapboard building, was erected in 1842 for a Christian Connection congregation associated with the Seventh-Day Baptists from England who settled in Newport in 1671. Together they shared a belief that the Sabbath day was Saturday and accepted the prophecy of the second coming of Christ in 1844 advocated by the Millerite Adventist movement, started in Low Hampton, New York, by William Miller (see p. 73). When Miller's prophecy failed, it and the Sabbath day doctrine had to be reexamined. Out of these studies emerged the Seventh-day Adventist Church. Because of the role it played in the formation of doctrine, the Washington Church is considered the "Cradle of the Seventh-day Sabbath in Adventism."

Another denomination established in New Hampshire that has its roots in New York is the Shakers. Canterbury Shaker Village, the fifth Shaker community in the United States, erected its **Meeting House** in 1792. It was the first building in the village and one that has remained virtually unchanged since its completion.

Methodism, thanks to the efforts of circuit-riding preachers, became popular in the state in the early nineteenth century, and by 1850, its churches were outnumbered only by Baptist. Grace United Methodist Church, built in Keene in 1869, is an extravagant Victorian Gothic structure that survives as testimony to the prosperity the state began to experience as its industries expanded in the years following the end of the Civil War.

At that time the state's ethnic and religious composition began to reflect what was happening elsewhere in the nation. Where else but in America would a Russian Orthodox church be built on Petrograd Street in a town named Berlin in a state named after a county in England? This describes the **Holy Resurrection Orthodox Church** built in 1915 by immigrants from Belorussia, the only Orthodox church in northern New Hampshire and northern Maine.

Danville Meeting House

(THE HAWKE MEETING HOUSE)

State highway 111A (North Main Street), Danville

ARCHITECT / BUILDER:
Not available

CONSTRUCTION / DEDICATION DATE:
1755

T HE TWO-AND-ONE-HALF-STORY frame clapboard structure, the oldest in the largest assemblage of early meetinghouses in New England, is a smaller rural replica of earlier prototypes that were built in Portsmouth as early as 1712 and in Kingston, the parent town of Danville, in 1732.

Most of the earlier prototypes are no longer extant, making the almost intact survival of this meetinghouse important to the understanding of the development of this type of religious architecture. Entrances are in the centers of the east, south, and west elevations, but the south elevation and its pair of doors is treated as the main façade. The building still retains many of its early interior features, including on the north wall opposite the main entrance an elevated pulpit reached by a stairway and in front of a deacon's bench.

After 1832 the meetinghouse was used less for religious services and more for town meetings and social affairs. Most of its pews were removed in the 1860s so dances could be held in the building. But in 1911, the Old Meeting House Association was formed to ensure the building's preservation. Funds were raised and the pews on the main floor were replaced. Since then further preservation efforts have been carried out, ensuring the future of this important historic structure.

The Hawke (Danville) Meeting House, Danville, New Hampshire

Free Will Baptist Church

Ridge Road, New Durham

ARCHITECT / BUILDER:
Not available

CONSTRUCTION / DEDICATION DATE:
1819, 1869

LOCATED IN A RURAL AREA a few miles from New Durham, this gable-roofed, clapboard church is significant not only for its architecture, but also for being the mother church of the Free Will Baptist movement that began in New Hampshire and Maine in the latter half of the eighteenth century and spread throughout the United States.

The movement was organized in Durham in 1780 by Benjamin Randall, an itinerant Baptist minister who was invited to town to preach. Doctrinal differences led to Randall and his followers breaking away from the established Baptist church and forming their own congregation. They were ridiculed and known as "Freewillers," a name they then adopted for their denomination, which received official recognition from the State of New Hampshire in 1804.

In 1869, the building was remodeled to its present form. While the frame of 1819 was retained, the structure was given a new two-stage belfry and was embellished with a combination of Greek Revival pilasters and paired Italianate cornice brackets. The church has remained unaltered since this remodeling except for the addition of stamped metal ceiling and wall coverings in the late nineteenth century. It stands alone on high open land, well maintained and preserved by its members.

Free Will
Baptist Church,
New Durham,
New Hampshire

South Congregational Church

(UNITED CHURCH OF CHRIST IN NEWPORT)

58 South Main Street, Newport

ARCHITECT / BUILDER:
John Leach

CONSTRUCTION / DEDICATION DATE:
1823

NEWPORT'S FIRST CONGREGATIONAL CHURCH was erected in 1793. As the town expanded in the early nineteenth century, a rivalry broke out between two factions–Baptists and Congregationalists. The Baptists built a church on the north side of town, and the Congregationalists built theirs on the south side, thus its name.

South Congregational Church (United Church of Christ in Newport), Newport, New Hampshire

The region's abundance of lumber resulted in most New England churches being built of wood by skilled carpenters. This congregation, however, chose brick with popular Federal detailing and a white wooden tower and steeple. The building's exterior retains its original appearance, except for changes to the rear that include the addition of a brick chapel in 1872. The church is most notable for its steeple that is allegedly based on a design by Elias Carter for the First (Federated) Church in Templeton, Massachusetts, designed in 1811. Carter's design is indebted to the work of Asher Benjamin, a well-known American architect whose architectural handbooks, such as *The Country Builder's Assistant*, published in 1797, popularized and Americanized the churches designed and built in England by Christopher Wren and James Gibbs.

In contrast to the exterior, the interior of the church has undergone many changes over time. Restorations undertaken in 1927 removed much of the overlay of Victorian decor, somewhat returning the interior to its original appearance.

Church Family Meeting House

Canterbury Shaker Village, 12 miles northeast of Concord,
and 4 miles south of Belknat-Merrimack county line

ARCHITECT / BUILDER:
Moses Johnson, master builder
CONSTRUCTION / DEDICATION DATE:
1792

T HE MEETING HOUSE is the first building erected by the Shaker community and is among the least changed of the village's 24 surviving historic buildings that are clustered on 13 acres of land. The Meeting House, enclosed by a white picket fence, is on Religious Row, as are the Ministry Shop and the Ministry Barn.

Built by members under the supervision of master builder Moses Johnson, it is modeled after the Meeting House in New Lebanon, also built under Johnson's supervision and completed in 1786. Shaker principles dictated a simple, plain exterior that owes little to then-current architectural styles. The interior reflects Shaker belief that the design of a building was subordinate to their religious beliefs–simple beauty through function.

The frame of the meetinghouse consists of a series of posts and beams that are assembled into H-shaped structural units spaced 4 feet apart along the length of the building. Reflecting Anglo-Dutch carpentry traditions, this frame differs dramatically from the New England frames of later buildings in the village.

Canterbury Shaker Village is considered among the most intact and authentic of the surviving Shaker villages. It is now owned by a nonprofit educational organization, Shaker Village, Inc., and many of its buildings are open to the public.

Church Family
Meeting House,
Shaker Village,
Canterbury,
New Hampshire

Holy Resurrection Orthodox Church

Petrograd Street, Berlin

ARCHITECT / BUILDER:
John Bergesen
CONSTRUCTION / DEDICATION DATE:
1915

COMING FROM ONE OF the most depressed regions of Eastern Europe, Belorussia, the first White Russian immigrants began to settle in Berlin around 1900. Most were single men who came to work in the town's paper mill. Concerned about their bachelor lifestyle and hoping to attract potential mates by improving their "moral and spiritual" life, an official of the mill agreed to contribute to the building of an Orthodox church for the workers. Built by its parishioners, Holy Resurrection reflects their desire to replicate in the New World the style of rural churches in Belorussia dating to the years prior to the Russian Revolution.

The clapboard church, unchanged in appearance since its construction, with its six distinctive golden onion domes, is built on a hillside overlooking Berlin. A two-story building with the church proper upstairs and a large hall at the ground level, its interior houses an important assemblage of Orthodox ritual art and artifacts. As is the case of Orthodox churches in Eastern Europe, the sanctuary does not have any pews; one stands throughout the liturgy. The murals covering the walls depict the trials of Christ and were painted in Boston by Orthodox artists. The iconostasis separating the altar area from the rest of the sanctuary is hung with icons sent from Russia in 1915 by Czar Nicholas II. The church continues to serve its community and remains an important visual reminder of New Hampshire's diverse ethnic and religious heritage.

Holy Resurrection
Orthodox Church,
Berlin,
New Hampshire

Massachusetts

THE PILGRIMS AND PURITANS who settled in Massachusetts in the seventeenth century shared a vision of establishing a "godly" paradise in the wilderness. Their faith, known as the "Congregational way," was more than a religion, it was a way of life. If you did not share their beliefs you were not allowed entry into their land. Even after the British Parliament passed an Act of Toleration in 1689 allowing colonists freedom of worship, the church continued to receive state support until 1834.

Initially the colonists' meetinghouses were simple buildings serving as forts and gathering places—secular and sacred. As the communities prospered, these simple structures were replaced by more substantial multipurpose buildings, such as **Old Ship Meeting House** in Hingham, begun in 1681, which is the only surviving example of a second-generation meetinghouse in New England. It exemplifies Puritan theology rooted in Calvinism that makes no distinction between sacred and civil law. The exterior and interior lack all the pretensions of traditional church architecture, particularly the hierarchical plan of the altar-focused longitudinal basilica favored by the Anglicans.

Despite the Puritans' efforts, the Anglican Church found a receptive audience in Boston—the increasingly prosperous merchant class who retained business ties with England. Their places of worship, and others modeled after them, transformed the city into a veritable repository of Colonial and Federal church architecture. Perhaps two of the best known Colonial churches are King's Chapel designed by Peter Harrison and Christ Church (Old North), by an unknown architect, that were built in 1723. Their appearance owes much to the well-circulated drawings of James Gibbs's famous London church, St. Martin-in-the-Fields, translated into an American idiom by local architects, including Harrison, Charles Bulfinch, Elias Carter, and Asher Benjamin, that became known as the American Church Plan. Other interpretations of this style include **First Church** in Templeton, designed by Elias Carter and built in 1811, which became a prototype for a number of New England churches, and First Church of Christ in Lancaster, built in 1816, considered the finest of the existing New England churches designed by Charles Bulfinch, the nation's first major professional architect.

Boston may have been home to numerous churches, but none allowed African-Americans to be members. In response the city's free black community that dates back to 1796 erected a building on Beacon Hill that was known as the African Meeting House. Built in 1806 and later renamed **The First African Baptist Church**, it is the oldest standing African-

American church building in the nation.

Boston's collage of religious architecture also includes examples of the changes in taste that occurred in the mid- and later nineteenth century as romanticism and its nostalgia for times past became popular. The Gothic Revival style imported from England was favored by the liturgical denominations—Episcopal, Lutheran, and Roman Catholic. The increasing number of Catholic churches being built in the Gothic Revival style in the nineteenth century signaled a shift in the state's Protestant character. Massachusetts had become a destination point for thousands of immigrants seeking jobs in the state's expanding industries. Among the first to arrive were Irish immigrants who began settling in South Boston, a Protestant enclave until the Civil War. There they built one of the city's first Gothic Revival Catholic churches, **Saints Peter and Paul Roman Catholic Church**, constructed from 1848 to 1853.

Nonliturgical denominations, such as the Methodist and Congregationalist, favored the Romanesque Revival style, perhaps because its more expansive interior, lacking the height and length of Gothic churches, had better acoustics and sight lines. Although stone was the preferred building material for Romanesque-style buildings, some were clapboard, including the Wakefield Baptist Church, in Wakefield, designed by William H. Pierson, Jr., and built in 1851.

Our Lady of Good Voyage Roman Catholic Church, Gloucester, Massachusetts

One of the most unique interpretations of the Romanesque style, the famed **Trinity Church** on Copley Square in Boston, was designed by the innovative architect Henry Hobson Richardson. Begun in 1877 and not completed until after Richardson's death in 1886, it combines his unique interpretation of Romanesque architecture, which came to bear his name—Richardsonian Romanesque—with decoration by the artist John La Farge, that together create an integrated truly Romantic late nineteenth-century masterpiece.

Boston is also the headquarters of the Church of Christ, Scientist, founded by Mary Baker Eddy in Lynn in 1865. The First Church of Christ, Scientist, the faith's Mother Church built in 1894, is part of a large center composed of another church added in 1905 and a 1972 office and school addition by I. M. Pei.

Jewish immigrants, initially reluctant to settle in Massachusetts because of its reputation as a "church state," formed a small congregation in Boston in 1843. Over the years their numbers steadily increased, and by the close of immigration in 1924, Boston was home to between 80,000 and 90,000 Jewish people. Several early twentieth-century synagogues survive, including **Congregation Agudath Sholom** (Walnut Street Synagogue) built in Chelsea in 1909, which remains in use, and the Vilna Shul built in 1919, which is being preserved as a cultural center and museum.

Industries developing outside of Boston also attracted immigrant labor, including Greeks working in Lowell's textile mills, who erected **Holy Trinity Greek Orthodox Church** in 1906. Portuguese immigrants in Gloucester found work in the fishing industry and erected **Our Lady of Good Voyage Roman Catholic Church** in 1914, a rare example of Mission style architecture in Massachusetts.

The Old Ship Meeting House

Main Street, Hingham

ARCHITECT / BUILDER:
Not available

CONSTRUCTION / DEDICATION DATE:
1681 (1729, 1755, additions)

I N 1635, 33 COLONISTS from England led by their minister, Peter Hobart, founded the town of Hingham, which was named after their old home. Their first meeting-house was a simple log structure surrounded by a palisade. As the town prospered and grew to 140 families, plans were made to erect a larger and more substantial building, the fifty-eighth meetinghouse built in Massachusetts and one of the largest in New England.

It is unclear how the meetinghouse became known as Old Ship. Originally it was just known as Meeting House and then North Meeting House. Possibly it was a nickname referring to its spire and weathervane acting as a guide for ships along the seacoast. Another theory suggests it is due to the upturned hull-like shape of its interior truss work.

Old Ship has the distinction of being the oldest wooden church in the country. It was enlarged twice–in 1729 and again in 1755 to accommodate a growing congregation. After undergoing "modernization" over the years of its use, the building has been restored to its 1755 appearance.

Old Ship Meeting
House, Hingham,
Massachusetts

The First Church of Templeton

Templeton

ARCHITECT / BUILDER:
Elias Carter

CONSTRUCTION / DEDICATION DATE:
1811

TEMPLETON'S FIRST MEETINGHOUSE was built in 1753 to serve a congregation that was initially Congregational and then mixed Congregational and Unitarian. In 1810, the congregation decided to build a new meetinghouse and hired Elias Carter of Brimfield, Massachusetts, to be the architect. Carter was responsible for the design of a number of New England churches, but this is the earliest of his surviving churches.

Carter's familiarity with the work of Asher Benjamin and Charles Bulfinch, two famed American architects, is visible in the design of this white clapboard building. But he brought to it his own contributions, particularly the tall, shallow pedimented portico in place of a porch and an elaborate tower and steeple that shows his familiarity with the designs of the English architect James Gibbs. Carter's innovations had an influence on churches built elsewhere in Massachusetts and neighboring New Hampshire.

The interior of the church has undergone many changes, including the replacement of its box pews in 1859 with long, curved ones. The high pulpit has also been replaced and the windows behind it covered over. Stained glass windows added in the nineteenth century were removed.

First Church
of Templeton,
Templeton,
Massachusetts

The First African Baptist Church / African Meeting House

8 Smith Court, Boston

ARCHITECT / BUILDER:
Not available

CONSTRUCTION / DEDICATION DATE:
1806

THE FIRST AFRICAN BAPTIST CHURCH was founded in 1805 by one of the largest free black populations in North America, under the leadership of Thomas Paul, an African-American preacher from New Hampshire. Frustrated by being unable to worship in white churches, the blacks formed their own congregation and raised funds to build their own church. One man, a former slave, contributed $1,500. His generosity is commemorated in a marker above the front door that states: "To Cato Gardner, first promoter of this building."

Built by its members with material reclaimed from the neighboring Old West Church then under renovation, the building, lacking a steeple, has been described as simple, but stylistically advanced for its time period. Outstanding features include double quartets of windows on each of three sides and graceful twin staircases leading up to a narrow gallery. The building underwent extensive remodeling in 1855, but in the years that followed it had a tumultuous history reflecting changes occurring in its neighborhood. Some time around the turn of the century, the building was sold to a Jewish congregation who maintained it as a synagogue until 1972, when it was acquired by the Museum of African American History. In 1974, the building was designated a National Historic Landmark and is in the process of undergoing a million-dollar restoration by the National Park Service, which is returning it to its 1855 appearance.

The African Meeting House, Boston, Massachusetts

Saints Peter and Paul Roman Catholic Church

45 West Broadway, South Boston

ARCHITECT / BUILDER:
Gridley J. F. Bryant (int. after fire: Patrick C. Keely)
CONSTRUCTION / DEDICATION DATE:
1848-1853 (rebuilding dates)

A NEW PARISH was formed in the late 1830s to accommodate the increasing number of Irish Catholics who were settling in South Boston. Their church, Saints Peter and Paul, completed in 1843, was destroyed by fire five years later. Not discouraged, they immediately set about building the present church as a replica of the one destroyed. It is an example of the work of Gridley J. F. Bryant, an important Boston architect, and Patrick C. Keely, who was responsible for the design of numerous Catholic churches built in the Northeast.

The building's massive granite base and tower, decorated with blind window recesses, castellated parapets with elaborate finials, and dome, make it a prominent presence on South Boston's main thoroughfare. It has served a wide spectrum of ethnic groups who came to settle in the neighborhood, offering diverse programs ranging from bingo to Headstart. The sanctuary, which has a seating capacity of 750, currently attracts only a handful of people to attend Mass. As a result, the future of this historic church is imperiled.

Saints Peter and
Paul Roman
Catholic Church,
Boston,
Massachusetts

Congregation Agudath Sholom

(WALNUT STREET SYNAGOGUE)

145 Walnut Street, Chelsea

ARCHITECT / BUILDER:
Henry Dustin Joll
CONSTRUCTION / DEDICATION DATE:
1909

I N 1908, THE YEAR CHELSEA was destroyed by fire, nearly one-third of its population was Jewish. Harry Dustin Joll, one of the three architects involved in the rebuilding of the city, designed the synagogue, the largest surviving example of his work. It is also considered to be one of the largest Orthodox synagogues in continuous use in New England.

The synagogue's Romanesque Revival style may have been inspired by the synagogue built in 1886 by Boston's most influential German-Reform congregation, Temple Israel. However, the interior configuration of Agudath Sholom reveals its Orthodox affiliation–it has the Ark (Torah Shrine) against the eastern wall and the *bimah* (platform) in the center of the hall. It also has a balcony reserved for women. Perhaps most remarkable is the synagogue's wall and ceiling frescoes executed by local Jewish artists. At the west end over the women's balcony is a painting of the tomb of Rachel. Over the Ark is a curtained niche filled with Jewish symbols, including the Star of David.

The building has undergone little alteration, but its windows have been damaged by vandals. Most of Chelsea's Jewish residents have departed for the suburbs, but the synagogue continues to serve a small Orthodox congregation that is dedicated to preserving it as a Chelsea and Jewish landmark.

Congregation Agudath Sholom Synagogue, Chelsea, Massachusetts (interior and exterior)

Holy Trinity Greek Orthodox Church

Jefferson and Lewis Street, Lowell

ARCHITECT / BUILDER:
Henry L. Rourke
CONSTRUCTION / DEDICATION DATE:
1906

HOLY TRINITY HAS THE DISTINCTION of being the first church built for a Greek Orthodox congregation in the United States. Greeks began settling in Lowell in the late 1890s; in 1894 they organized "The Washington-Acropolis" society to perpetuate Greek traditions and religion in America, the fourth Greek Orthodox society formed in the United States. The church was incorporated in 1900 and the following year a local architect, Henry L. Rourke, was hired to draw plans for a church. Rourke had visited Hagia Sophia in Constantinople (Istanbul) and thus could fulfill the congregation's request to have a Byzantine style church modeled after that building.

Although the congregation has faced many challenges over the years, religious and economic, the yellow brick domed Greek Cross church, built with the donations of immigrant laborers, remains unchanged and a landmark in its neighborhood, continuing to serve a thriving Greek community.

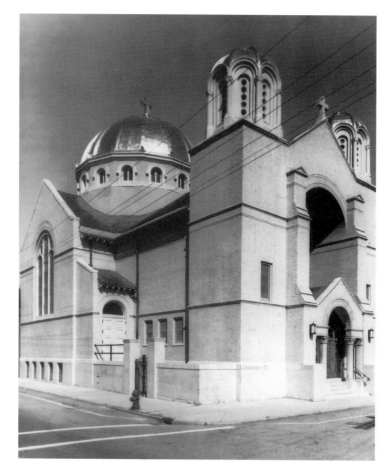

Holy Trinity Greek
Orthodox Church,
Lowell,
Massachusetts

Connecticut

A DUTCH NAVIGATOR CRUISING along the Atlantic Coast in 1614 came across a river known to local Indians as Quonecktacut, or Connecticut, as the name was corrupted by later colonists. When news of his discovery reached New Amsterdam, a group of Dutch colonists set off to establish a trading post near present-day Hartford. A year later, in 1634, colonists from the Massachusetts Bay Company seeking additional land founded several settlements including New Haven, Milford, and Builford. The towns, uniting as New Haven County and following the "Congregational way," restricted citizenship to Puritans. By the end of the century, the Puritans had organized 35 Congregational churches in the colony, and in 1704 made Congregationalism its official religion. Although an Act of Toleration was passed in 1784 allowing for the establishment of other religious institutions, complete disestablishment did not occur until 1843, the year in which the General Assembly first made it legal for Jewish congregations to exist in the state.

Despite the efforts of the Congregationalists, the Anglican Church did make inroads into the colony thanks in part to the efforts of Edmund Andros, the British governor-general of New England. But perhaps more important was the increasing prosperity enjoyed by the Puritans. As they prospered, the austerity of the Congregational Church became less attractive. They were on the way to becoming Yankees and one way to express their financial achievements was in the beauty and glory of their churches. Since the Congregationalists resisted embellishing their places of worship, many "Puritans" turned to the Anglican Church and by 1750 nearly 20 Anglican parishes were established in western Connecticut. Anglicans were allowed to build churches because of a loophole in Connecticut law which stated that all residents were liable to taxation to support the town meetinghouse, which also served as the Congregational place of worship, unless they could demonstrate allegiance to another organized parish. It was this loophole that allowed Godfrey Malbone to build **Old Trinity Church** in Brooklyn, beginning in 1770; this is one of the nation's oldest Episcopal churches.

Connecticut became an independent state in October 1776, and in the decades following the war became a prosperous industrial and commercial center. Although Congregationalism began to wane in these years as the newly revived Episcopal Church grew, Congregational churches continued to be built on village greens. Perhaps the coexistence of faiths in Connecticut at this time is no better illustrated than on the famed New Haven Green platted in 1638. There three churches built between 1812 and 1816 are arranged equidistantly along Temple Street. Two–**Center Church** and **United or Old North Church**–are Congregational and are built in the Federal style promoted by Asher Benjamin; **Trinity Episcopal Church**, completed in 1816, proclaims its Anglican heritage in its Gothic Revival style.

The Federal style church, red brick or white clapboard, set on a village green is the image most people have of New England, but that is a stereotype found on travel posters. Reality is far more interesting and complex as can be seen, for instance, in the African-American churches and Jewish synagogues built in Connecticut.

Unhappy about being forced to sit in the balconies of Hartford's white churches, African-Americans began conducting their own prayer meetings as early as 1816. Ten years later they formed the African Religious Society and acquired a building. **The Metropolitan A.M.E. Zion Church,** built in 1874, grew out of those early years when African-Americans were struggling to establish their own churches in which they could worship as free and equal men and women.

Connecticut's first synagogue was organized in Hartford in 1843, immediately following the General Assembly's legalization of Jewish congregations in the state. The congregation's first building was a church purchased in 1856; it was sold following a fire and the cornerstone for a new structure was laid in 1875. That building, **Temple Beth Israel**, Victorian Romanesque in style, was used by its congregation until 1936 when it was sold to Calvary Temple. It has since been reclaimed by the Jewish community and now functions as the Charter Oak Cultural Center.

The expansion of Connecticut's industries in the years leading up to the Civil War attracted many immigrants, including Irish who settled in Lakeville to work in the town's iron mines. Lacking a Roman Catholic church in which to celebrate Mass, they met in private homes, a school, and even under a tree. Finally, with the help of local Protestants, they were able to purchase land and build the Gothic Revival Catholic Church of St. Mary in 1875.

Following the Civil War, Polish immigrants seeking work in factories began to settle in Hartford, where they built a small Polish Roman Catholic church in 1902. By 1916, the city's Polish community had grown from 400 to 6,000 and a new church, **Saints Cyril and Methodius Roman Catholic Church**, was completed in 1916. Its design and decoration reveal the Polish immigrants' efforts to retain elements from the Old World while accommodating the new.

Further enriching Connecticut's ethnic mix are the descendants of other Eastern and Southern European ethnic groups who began arriving in the early twentieth century. Many settled in New Britain, a town whose name reflects the heritage of its founders. Holy Trinity Russian Orthodox Church, built by Russian immigrants in 1914, is crowned with traditional onion domes. The Assyrians, who came from northwest Iran, established a congregation in 1919 and built a simple brick structure, St. Thomas Assyrian Church (Holy Apostolic and Catholic Church of the East) so they could worship in Aramaic, the original language of their faith.

Old Trinity Episcopal Church

East Side of Church Street, Brooklyn

ARCHITECT / BUILDER:
Godfrey Malbone, designer
CONSTRUCTION / DEDICATION DATE:
1771

GODFREY MALBONE BUILT THIS CHURCH in response to efforts by local Puritans to force him to pay taxes for the building of a new Congregational meetinghouse. Malbone raised the funds for the church, executed its design, and had his black slaves build it. The design pays homage to two well-known American Anglican churches designed by Peter Harrison: King's Chapel in Boston, where Malbone's wife's family worshipped, and Trinity in Newport, Rhode Island, where his father is buried. Harrison's buildings, which precede those of Thomas Jefferson's by almost a generation, reveal a refinement of design and classicism that has been described as a paradigm of good taste in the colonies.

The church is in use on occasion for services, but funds have been provided for the perpetual upkeep of its exterior. Having undergone few changes over the years, it retains many of its original furnishings, including box pews, reading desk, and pulpit; the altar has been replaced. Trinity has the distinction of being the oldest Episcopal church now standing in the oldest diocese in the United States.

Old Trinity
Church, Brooklyn,
Connecticut

Center Church, United (Old North) Church, Trinity Episcopal Church

Temple Street on the Common, New Haven

ARCHITECT / BUILDER:
Center Church plan: Asher Benjamin; Builder: Ithiel Town
CONSTRUCTION / DEDICATION DATE:
1812–1814

Three churches on
New Haven Green:
Center Church,
United or Old
North Church,
Trinity Episcopal
Church

C ENTER CHURCH, BASED ON A PLAN prepared by Asher Benjamin that was purchased for $40, and built by Ithiel Town, is considered an excellent example of a large New England Federal style brick church modeled after James Gibbs's St. Martin-in-the-Fields in London. The exterior of the church remains virtually unchanged; its handsome portico is intact and its elaborate five-stage tower rises to a height of 210 feet. The interior underwent extensive remodeling under the supervision of Henry Austin in 1842–1843. Its original high pulpit was removed at that time and is now located in the Kawaiahao Church (First Church) in Honolulu, Hawaii (see p. 439).

Center Church is one of two churches designed by Ithiel Town that are located on New Haven's green. The second was commissioned by Episcopalians who had apparently requested that Town design a church that would be radically different from its two neighbors, Center Church and Union, both in the Federal style. Town's plan for Trinity Church does represent a radical departure in design and material. Built of local stone, its entrance tower and tall pointed windows are an early interpretation of the Gothic Revival style that was to gain in popularity later in the nineteenth century.

Metropolitan African Methodist Episcopal (A.M.E.) Zion Church

2051 Main Street, Hartford

ARCHITECT / BUILDER:
Not available

CONSTRUCTION / DEDICATION DATE:
1873-1874

THE METROPOLITAN African Methodist Episcopal Zion church building is home to one of Hartford's leading African-American religious organizations, one that is a direct descendant of the city's first African-American church. The congregation had two earlier churches prior to the purchase of the present building in 1926. The large brick High Victorian Gothic style building was constructed in 1873-1874 by a white Methodist congregation. The building proved to be too large and costly for the congregation and it was sold in 1919 to a Jewish congregation who used it as a synagogue for eight years before selling it to Metropolitan A.M.E. Zion.

The church is relatively unchanged from its appearance at the time of its original construction and remains an important landmark in Hartford and a social focal point for its community.

Metropolitan
A.M.E. Zion
Church, Hartford,
Connecticut

Temple Beth Israel

(CALVARY TEMPLE, NOW CHARTER OAK CULTURAL CENTER)

21 Charter Oak Avenue, Hartford

ARCHITECT / BUILDER:
George Keller
CONSTRUCTION / DEDICATION DATE:
1876/1899

THE CONGREGATION'S FIRST SYNAGOGUE was originally a Baptist church purchased in 1854 and remodeled and enlarged in 1865. Sold in 1875 following a fire, the cornerstone for a new temple located in a more fashionable part of town was laid that same year, an event witnessed by over 10,000 people.

The new synagogue, dedicated in 1876, was designed by one of Hartford's leading nineteenth-century architects, George Keller, who was born in Ireland and immigrated to New York City as a child. It is the only religious building Keller designed that included elements largely drawn from Romanesque architecture. He did use similar Romanesque design elements for a jail, residence, and school, but preferred the Gothic style for churches. The choice of Romanesque for the synagogue was probably at the urging of his patrons, who may have been aware of other Romanesque Revival synagogues being built in the United States and in Europe, primarily in Germany. Jews generally were reluctant to build Gothic Revival synagogues because of the style's close association with Christian ideals and church architecture.

The congregation moved to West Hartford in 1935 and the building was then sold to the Calvary Temple; it is now the Charter Oak Cultural Center, home to Jewish and multicultural programs and projects.

Temple Beth Israel Synagogue, now Charter Oak Cultural Center, Hartford, Connecticut

Saints Cyril and Methodius Roman Catholic Church

63 Governor Street, Hartford

ARCHITECT / BUILDER:
Timothy G. O'Connell
CONSTRUCTION / DEDICATION DATE:
1914-1916

ESIGNED FOR A POLISH CONGREGATION by a Boston architect of Irish descent, Saints Cyril and Methodius Church represents a coming together of Polish and American culture. The Romanesque design of the church distinguishes it from other churches in Hartford, but its use of red brick contrasted with white stone and its central tower and spire reflect influences from New England Federal style church architecture.

Whereas the exterior does not reveal the congregants' particular identity, the interior leaves no doubt. Embellished with stenciled Polish folk designs, gilt plaster, and Polish inscriptions and iconography, particularly the distinctive Polish eagle and statues of Polish saints, the interior proclaims the congregants' ethnicity. The design and decoration of this church reflect one congregation's attempt to make accommodations to its new environment while maintaining its traditions and ethnic identity.

Saints Cyril and
Methodius Roman
Catholic Church,
Hartford, Connecticut

Rhode Island

R HODE ISLAND may be the nation's smallest state, but its role in American history is disproportionately large. The first known European to reach its shores was a Florentine explorer sailing under the flag of France who arrived in 1524. A century later came the Dutch, but it was Roger Williams, an English minister banished from Massachusetts for his liberal theological views, who established the colony's first settlement in 1636. Williams's radical belief that people should be allowed to worship as they please embroiled him in bitter controversy with the Massachusetts Puritans, but it foreshadows Thomas Jefferson's "wall of separation" and the First Amendment to the Constitution, which guarantees all citizens religious liberty. Rhode Island's code of laws, adopted in 1647, clearly states that "all men may walk as their consciences persuade them, every one in the name of his God."

Fleeing Salem in 1636, Williams was able to purchase land from friendly Indians where he established a settlement named Providence to commemorate "God's providence to him in his distress." With one of his faithful followers, Ezekiel Holliman, Williams founded the first Baptist church in the colonies, but after just a brief period as a Baptist, he became a Seeker, unsure whether any sort of religious institution was possible. John Clarke picked up the reins of leadership, and the Baptist church began to expand, but at the same time it split into different factions based on theological issues.

A small Baptist meetinghouse built in Providence in 1700 was replaced by a larger building in 1721, and then by a yet grander one, the present **First Baptist Church**, built in 1775 and modeled after drawings of James Gibbs's St. Martin-in-the-Fields. Although it has undergone some alterations, it remains the oldest religious structure of any denomination in Rhode Island and the oldest Baptist church in America.

The colony prospered as large fleets of ships owned by Providence and Newport merchants plied their trade with Africa and the West Indies, trading slaves for molasses to make rum. Blacks, including slaves laboring on the colony's plantations, were denied all rights, but others who sought religious freedom flocked to the colony, many settling in the bustling port of Newport. Quakers, banished from Massachusetts and Connecticut, found a receptive audience in Newport and transformed the town into a center for New England Quakers. Quaker yearly meetings that began in Newport in 1661 continued to be held there with few exceptions until 1905. The town's Quaker Meetinghouse, begun in 1699, has undergone many alterations and additions over the years, but evidence of the original structure can still be seen in the restored building.

The Anglican Church was not welcomed by the colonists, but that began to change following the establishment of the Society for the Propagation of the Gospel in 1701. A mission was established in Newport in 1698, and by 1702, an Anglican church was constructed. It was replaced in 1726 by **Trinity Church**, considered by many to be "the most beautiful Timber Structure in America."

Perhaps the building that most clearly illustrates Rhode Island's acceptance of people of all faiths is the synagogue Peter Harrison designed for Congregation Yeshuat Israel (Salvation of Israel), the **Touro Synagogue**. Dedicated in 1763, it is the nation's oldest surviving synagogue.

Rhode Island may have benefited from the slave trade, but in 1774 it became the first of the colonies to prohibit the importation of slave labor. Another first was the colony's declaration of independence from Britain on May 4, 1776, two months before the other colonies. And yet another first for this small state was the introduction in 1790 of the first water-powered spinning machines that not only led to the growth of its textile industry, but signaled the beginning of the nation's industrial revolution.

Shipyards and whaling contributed to Newport and Providence's continuing prosperity in the years leading up to the Civil War, but with the growth of industry came an influx of immigrant labor. Their arrival not only dramatically changed the state's ethnic and religious composition, it also led to Rhode Island adopting a new state constitution in 1842 which replaced the earlier one that limited the vote to landowners or their oldest sons. Rhode Island now became a study in contrasts—crowded industrial centers like Providence contrasting with Newport where the rich and famous frolicked in their extravagant "cottages" along the beach.

As elsewhere in New England, the first of the "new" immigrant groups to arrive was the Irish. The pattern was always similar: a parish would be established and a modest church built. As the parish prospered, the church would be replaced by one that was more monumental and elaborate. A case in point is St. Michael's Roman Catholic Church, founded in 1857. The congregants initially met in a former Baptist church, a modest frame structure that was used until a new brick building was dedicated in 1868. It, in turn, was replaced by the present church, a monumental building with a distinctive central tower, which was dedicated in 1915.

French-Canadian and Portuguese immigrants formed their own ethnic parishes. French-Canadians settling in Woonsocket's Social district, a congested neighborhood of tenements, mill houses, and textile factories, built an oasis of beauty in 1913, **St. Ann's Roman Catholic Church**. Portuguese who began arriving in Providence in the mid-nineteenth century worshipped in an Irish Catholic church until they organized their own parish in 1885, the third oldest Portuguese parish in the country. In 1905, they built Holy Rosary Church, an ashlar Gothic structure that remains a focal point of community activity.

Perhaps one of the more unusual places of worship in Rhode Island was built by Swedish Lutherans in Providence in 1925, **Gloria Dei Evangelical Lutheran Church**; this is an unusual example of traditional Scandinavian design features combined with elements borrowed from modern styles, including Art Deco.

First Baptist Church

75 North Main Street, Providence

ARCHITECT / BUILDER:
Joseph Brown, architect
CONSTRUCTION / DEDICATION DATE:
1775

JOSEPH BROWN, A PROSPEROUS MERCHANT in Providence and an amateur architect, designed the First Baptist Church's third meetinghouse. After Brown and several members of the building committee traveled to Boston to familiarize themselves with current architectural trends, they came up with this design that stands on the cusp between the old and the new. Brown's plan looks back at earlier foursquare meetinghouses as exemplified by Old Ship in Hingham, Massachusetts. The location of its porch and main entrance at the tower end and the pulpit opposite it replicate the longitudinal church plan introduced by the Anglicans and seen in the design of Trinity Church in Newport. Central entrances on the other two sides reflect the earlier meetinghouse plan, illustrating the building's position as a transition from an old established design to a new one imported from England. English influence is also clearly visible in the church's magnificent tower, copied from one of James Gibbs's designs for his London church, St. Martin-in-the-Fields, and reproduced in his 1728 publication, *Book of Architecture.*

Although the building has undergone changes, a 1950s restoration has essentially returned it to its original appearance.

First Baptist
Church,
Providence,
Rhode Island

Trinity Episcopal Church

141 Spring Street, Newport

ARCHITECT / BUILDER:
Richard Munday, architect
CONSTRUCTION / DEDICATION DATE:
1726

T HE CONSTRUCTION DATE of Trinity Episcopal Church attests to the early success of the Anglican Church to win at least some converts in New England. By 1702 the parish had outgrown its first church, which had been constructed after the establishment of a mission in Newport in 1698, and a decision was made to build a larger, more impressive structure. Richard Munday, a parish member and carpenter, was

selected to design the church. His final design suggests that he was familiar with Christ Church (Old North) in Boston, completed in 1724, except here the building's fabric is rendered in clapboard rather than brick. Its plan is the so-called longitudinal "church plan" with tower favored by Anglicans and based on designs by the English architect James Gibbs. As the congregation grew, it became necessary to enlarge the church. This was accomplished in 1762 by adding two more bays and an apse to the east end of the building.

The three-tiered wineglass pulpit set in the center aisle and the oak altar-table in the chancel are original. The stained glass windows, including several by the studio of Tiffany, were added in the nineteenth century. The entire building underwent restoration in 1988 and appears today much as it did over a century and a half ago.

Trinity Episcopal
Church, Newport,
Rhode Island

Congregation Yeshuat Israel

(TOURO SYNAGOGUE)

72 Touro Street, Newport

ARCHITECT / BUILDER:
Peter Harrison
CONSTRUCTION / DEDICATION DATE:
1763

SEPHARDIC JEWS of Spanish and Portuguese descent began settling in Newport in 1658. Upon receiving a warm welcome, they purchased land for a cemetery, but had to wait over a century for a synagogue. The small congregation met in private homes until the arrival from Amsterdam in 1758 of Isaac de Abraham Touro, a learned Jew who urged the people to organize a congregation and erect a synagogue. The name of the congregation reflects its optimism, "Yeshuat Israel," Salvation of Israel.

The synagogue was designed by Peter Harrison, a well-known amateur architect who had designed King's Chapel, Boston, and Christ Church, Cambridge. Born and educated in England, Harrison was familiar with the work of James Gibbs and, more important in the context of this building, with the work of Joseph Avis. Avis designed Bevis Marks synagogue in London, dedicated in 1701, which in turn was modeled after the great Sephardic synagogue in Amsterdam, completed in 1675 and designed by another Christian architect, Elias Bouman.

Angled so that the Ark (Torah Shrine) faces east toward Jerusalem, the synagogue's plain exterior contrasts with an interior described as perhaps the most sophisticated in the United States. Its layout is traditional: the Ark against the eastern wall and the *bimah* (platform) in the center of the hall. The congregation fell on hard times following the Revolutionary War; but thanks to Isaac de Abraham Touro's two sons, who left money for its maintenance, the congregation has been revitalized.

Touro Synagogue (Congregation Yeshuat Israel), Newport, Rhode Island

Gloria Dei Evangelical Lutheran Church

15 Hayes Street, Providence

ARCHITECT / BUILDER:
Martin Hedmark
CONSTRUCTION / DEDICATION DATE:
1925-1928

S WEDISH IMMIGRANTS arriving in the 1880s formed this congregation in 1890. Quickly outgrowing its first church, the congregation began construction on the present building in 1915. Initially the plan called for a typical Gothic Revival building, but once the basement was completed the members decided to hire a Swedish architect, Martin Hedmark, to design a building reflecting their Swedish heritage. What he produced is a peculiar amalgam of highly stylized elements drawn from Swedish Medieval/Baroque/Rococo sources combined with inventive modern features that reflect current trends in architectural design, including Art Deco elements.

Standing on a high limestone basement, the patterned-brick building displays details recalling traditional Swedish architecture such as the tall centered arch over the main entry, rounded turrets at the corners, and perhaps most reminiscent of their homeland, the tall, stepped-gable side bell tower near the front of the building. The interior reflects a similar marriage of the traditional and modern. The sanctuary is separated from the narthex by a wrought-iron and glass screen. The nave, painted in gray with a white ceiling, culminates at the altar set within an apse. Above the altar is a mural of the Resurrection painted by Newport artist Benny Collins. The octagonal-shaped pulpit recalls similar pulpits found in New England meetinghouses, but other decorative elements, including the chandeliers and radiator screens, are more in the Art Deco style.

Gloria Dei
Evangelical
Lutheran Church,
Providence,
Rhode Island

St. Ann's Roman Catholic Church

82 Cumberland Street, Woonsocket

ARCHITECT / BUILDER:
Walter F. Fontaine

CONSTRUCTION / DEDICATION DATE:
1913-1914

S T. ANN'S, A BUFF-BRICK STRUCTURE with twin, 160-foot towers, is a landmark visible from many parts of Woonsocket. Built by French-Canadians living in tenements and working in nearby mills and factories, St. Ann's still stands in striking contrast to its once-congested surroundings, since cleared for urban renewal. The parish's first building served as a church, school, and convent. It was designed by Walter F. Fontaine, the same architect who designed the present building. The new church made up in grandeur for the plainness of the old parish church. Grand in scale and with borrowings from several revival styles including the Romanesque and Renaissance, the building testifies to the faith and dedication of its congregation. Nowhere is this more visible than in its Renaissance-inspired interior, where every wall and ceiling surface is covered with paintings set within mural panels executed between 1941 and 1953 by Guido Nincheri. Large-scale statues, including figures of the four apostles, and church furnishings carved in white marble, combined with the mural paintings, resulted in an interior of startling scale, elaboration, and richness, considered one of the finest church interiors in Rhode Island.

St. Ann's Roman
Catholic Church,
Woonsocket,
Rhode Island
(interior,
facing page)

NOTES

1. Alexis de Tocqueville, *Democracy in America* (New York: Oxford University Press, 1947), 33.

2. Peter Mallary, *New England Churches and Meeting-houses* (Vendome Press, 1983), 19.

3. George Washington, letter to the Hebrew Congregation in Newport, Rhode Island, 1790 (Morris Morgenstern Foundation, owner).

3

Middle Atlantic Region

New York
New Jersey
Pennsylvania

THE MIDDLE ATLANTIC REGION of the United States comprises the nation's largest and most diverse population. New York was as prominent in the seventeenth century as it is today–the nation that had control of its harbor and trading posts would be able to control much of the New World. In 1664, when New Amsterdam became New York, the change in names reflected the culmination of a power struggle between the Dutch and the British. At first Dutch traders representing the West Indian Company, who had trading posts in Long Island and along the banks of the Hudson River, were in command, only to be usurped by more powerful British forces. Giving up control of the colony, however, did not mean that all Dutch fled the region; many chose to remain, and evidence of their settlements still exists.

Dutch Reformed ministers were the first to express dismay over the region's growing ethnic and religious diversity, a complaint later taken up by the English. In addition to Dutch Reformed congregations, and then the Church of England (later known as Episcopal), there were Presbyterians, Quakers, Anabaptists, and even a settlement of Sephardic Jews fleeing Brazil, all reflecting the population's wide-ranging loyalties. Ethnic groups were equally diverse, including British, Scots-Irish, Flemish, German, French, Spanish, and Italian, as well as free and enslaved Africans. In Pennsylvania, the Quakers' freedom of religion was attracting a variety of Pietist "sects" and other ethnic groups–large contingents of Welsh nonconformists, Scots-Irish Presbyterians, and German and Swedish Lutherans.

If the Dutch thought the region was too diverse in the seventeenth century, they would have been astonished by the changes occurring in the years following. Irish Roman Catholics, followed by massive numbers of immigrants from southern and eastern Europe, all played a part in transforming the region's original predominantly Protestant and northern and western European religious and ethnic character. Over 80 percent of immigrants who arrived between 1890 and 1920, the years of peak immigration, chose to settle in the port cities of New York and Philadelphia, where many found a familiar home in established ethnic enclaves, or if one did not exist, they would form new ones, contributing further to the region's already vibrant multiculturalism.

The dynamic religious and ethnic character of this region continues to be enhanced by the arrival of new immigrants, most recently from the states of the former Soviet Union, Asia, and Caribbean islands. The numberless places of worship built by all these people in major industrial cities, mining and company towns, market centers, and rural areas illustrate the region's rich diversity as well as portray a remarkable variety of ethnic and religious vernacular styles.

PRECEDING PAGE:
Eldridge Street Synagogue (Congregation Kahal Adath Jeshurun with Anshe Lubz), New York City

New York

DUTCH WALLOONS ARRIVING in 1624 were the first permanent European settlers in the region that became New York State. Their first colonies were on Manhattan Island and near the modern city of Albany. **The Old Dutch Reformed Church of Sleepy Hollow,** erected in 1697 in North Tarrytown northwest of White Plains, still stands as evidence of their settlements. The British, who overpowered the Dutch in 1664, were able to retain control of the colony until the Revolutionary War. Although no longer in political control of the region, ample testimony, both physical and cultural, of their presence remains. For example, British forces evacuating New York City in 1783 left undamaged **St. Paul's Chapel,** built between 1764 and 1796, the city's sole surviving religious edifice pre-dating the Revolutionary period. A later example of British influence on religious architecture in the United States is the magnificent **Trinity Church** built in 1847. Designed by Richard Upjohn, an English émigré who arrived in America in 1829 and rose to eminence among a small profession of architects in his day, the church and its widely copied Gothic Revival style were a signal of renewed interest in the Church of England, newly organized in the United States as the Protestant Episcopal Church.

The Shakers represent another British import brought to New York. "Mother" Ann Lee established the first Shaker community in Watervliet, near Albany, in 1776. The present **Watervliet Meeting House** located on the site was erected in 1847 and is one of the last built by the Shakers. By 1826 the Shaker population had grown to 18 communities and 6,000 members, but two decades later it began experiencing an irreversible decline. As of 1995, one community still remained, Sabbathday Lake, Maine, with eight adult members.

Many immigrants disembarking at Castle Garden and later Ellis Island in the years of peak immigration, 1850 to 1920, never left New York City. Settling in ethnic neighborhoods, one of their first acts was to build a place of worship where they could perpetuate their old world language and traditions–a haven of familiarity in the midst of a sea of change. A large number of new immigrants were Roman Catholics; among the first were Irish fleeing their country's potato famine. Impoverished and lacking the means to move beyond the port city, the Irish quickly became one of New York City's largest ethnic groups. The monumental St. Patrick's Cathedral on Fifth Avenue, designed in a Gothic Revival style by James Renwick in 1859, attests to their numbers and important role in the city's development.

A vast majority of people emigrating from eastern and southern Europe were also Roman Catholic. The magnet that drew them to the New World was the promise of jobs opening up in the nation's expanding industries. Like the Irish who preceded them, many stayed in New

York, where each nationality would establish its own parish in order to maintain its old world language and traditions. This resulted in a plethora of Catholic churches being built within one community. The proliferation of ethnic parishes prompted the establishment of the St. Raphael Society in New York City, which lobbied Rome to have the dioceses in the United States set up according to national groups, not geographic units. The Pope denounced this effort, and the "Americanization" of the Roman Catholic church began in earnest.

Seventy percent of all Jewish immigrants arriving in the United States between 1880 and 1924 chose to remain in New York City, transforming it into the world's largest and most diverse Jewish community. Preceding them were Sephardic Jews (initially from Spain and Portugal but now fleeing Catholic-controlled Brazil) who arrived in then New Amsterdam in 1654. Forming a congregation, they worshipped in a storefront before erecting Shearith Israel, the colonies' first synagogue in 1728, located on Mill Street in New York City. The building has since been demolished, but the congregation continues to exist. The Sephardim were soon outnumbered by German-speaking Jews who began arriving in the city in the early nineteenth century. However, by the end of the century, the vast majority of Jews in New York and elsewhere in the nation were from areas of Eastern Europe. Many settled in New York City's teeming Lower East Side, where they built numerous synagogues, including one of the most elaborate to survive, the **Eldridge Street Synagogue,** dedicated in 1886.

Africans, too, were among the city's earliest settlers, arriving prior to the onset of the Revolutionary War. Attesting to their early presence is a document noting the sale in 1826 of the First Colored Presbyterian Church, an early African-American congregation, to Jewish immigrants who converted it into the city's first Ashkenazi (German) synagogue. Harlem, initially settled by the Dutch, evolved into a large and vibrant African-American community, home to numerous congregations. A Mecca for many tourists is the Abyssinian Baptist Church, founded in 1808, which is the oldest black church in New York City. The congregation's present building, erected in 1923, was designed by Charles W. Bolton.

Outside the congested urban area of New York, the completion of the Erie Canal in 1825 and the expansion of railroad lines opened other regions of the state to agriculture and industry. The railroad first brought loggers to upstate New York. Following them came city dwellers, summer tourists seeking temporary relief from congested and polluted cities. Catering to the needs of the loggers and tourists were itinerant Jewish peddlers. As the area became increasingly populated, the peddlers began establishing permanent businesses and homes, and building modest places of worship, such as **Beth Joseph Synagogue** in Tupper Lake.

Another area of Upper New York State is known as the "Burned-Over District," although there seems to be some debate as to why the region received this name. Prior to the Civil War, when the nation was being swept by religious revivalism, this region became the site of a wave of Protestant premillennialism, a view that Christ would come before the millennium. Emerging from this milieu was Joseph Smith, founder of the Church of the Latter-day Saints, and William Miller, founder of the Millerites. Later, after the failure of his prophecies, many of Miller's followers became Seventh-Day Adventists. The **William Miller Chapel,** in Low Hampton, New York, was built by Miller and his followers in 1848 following their dismissal from the Baptist Church.

The Old Dutch Reformed Church of Sleepy Hollow

North Tarrytown

ARCHITECT / BUILDER:
Unknown

CONSTRUCTION / DEDICATION DATE:
1697-1702

FREDERICK AND CATHERINE PHILIPSE of Phillipsborough Manor financed the building of the Dutch Reformed Church of Tarrytown, an excellent example of a typical Dutch Colonial church. Constructed of rubble-stone, the building is nearly rectangular in plan and has a single entry and six windows. The interior is very simple, its focus being the pulpit located opposite the entrance.

During the American Revolution, the church, located in an area known as "Neutral Ground," became an arena where Loyalists–called Cowboys—and Patriots–called Skinners—roamed. It was also during the Revolutionary War that the first significant changes were made to the church's interior, revealing the political change occurring in the colonies. The special pews of the Lords of the Manor and the plain oak tenant benches were removed and replaced by pine pews.

The church went on to gain fame following the publication of Washington Irving's *Sketch Book* in 1820, in which it receives mention as the church in the "Legend of Sleepy Hollow." Partially damaged by fire in 1837, it underwent a series of unfortunate alterations that were later removed when the interior was restored to its original appearance for the 1897 bicentennial observance. The building is well maintained and used for occasional services and special programs.

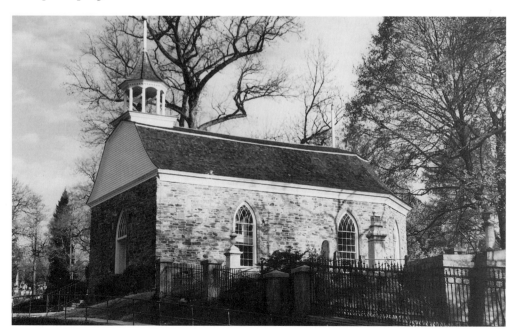

The Old Dutch
Reformed Church
of Sleepy Hollow,
North Tarrytown,
New York

St. Paul's Episcopal Chapel

Broadway between Fulton and Vesey Streets, New York

ARCHITECT / BUILDER:
Thomas McBean; tower: James Crommelin Lawrence
CONSTRUCTION / DEDICATION DATE:
1764-1796

S T. PAUL'S EPISCOPAL CHAPEL, established as a parish of Trinity Episcopal Church, is considered one of the finest examples of Late Georgian church architecture in the United States. Modeled after James Gibbs's St. Martin-in-the-Fields, the chapel at the time of its construction was located in a remote area of the city, facing the river with its back to Broadway. Today, it appears as a small gem set in a surrounding of monumental structures.

The chapel's wineglass pulpit and sounding board are original to the building. The pulpit's carved and gilded decoration reveals the chapel's British heritage–it is surmounted by a coronet and six feathers, an emblem of British nobility. Still hanging in the nave are fourteen Waterford crystal chandeliers installed in 1802.

Religious services following the inauguration of George Washington in 1787 were held in the chapel, and it was also the site of funeral services for two Presidents, James Monroe in 1831 and William McKinley in 1901. Although the chapel's box pews were removed during a later renovation, George Washington's pew has been reconstructed and placed back in its original position.

The church, restored to its Colonial appearance in 1950, has been in continuous service since it opened in 1766.

St. Paul's Episcopal Chapel, New York City, circa 1930s

75

Watervliet Shaker Meeting House

North of intersection of Troy Shaker Road (SR 155) and Albany Shaker Road, Watervliet

ARCHITECT / BUILDER:
Not available

CONSTRUCTION / DEDICATION DATE:
1847

THE SHAKERS, officially known as the United Society of Believers in Christ's Second Appearing, arrived in New York City in 1774 and settled in Watervliet, northwest of Albany, in 1776. Their community is based on religious devotion, celibacy, and communal labor. A meetinghouse constructed in 1791 was replaced in 1847 by the present building.

Shaker meetinghouses are located physically and spiritually in the center of the community. They serve not only as places of communal worship, but also as homes for the ministry. The meetinghouse is a simple, wood-frame building painted according to the Millennial Laws written down in 1821, but in force prior to that time: "Meeting houses should be painted white without, and of a bluish shade within."[1] The Laws also dictate that "no buildings may be painted white, save meeting houses." The three doors on the north façade provide separate entrances for brothers on the left, sisters on the right, and the ministry in the middle.

The interior is as austere as its exterior. The main meeting room consists of a large open space where dances, an important part of Shaker meetings, are performed. New in the 1847 meetinghouse were raised benches along a short wall of the meeting room rather than the usual long wall. The Watervliet Meeting House is a visible reminder of one faith's desire to create the kingdom of heaven on earth.

Watervliet Shaker
Meeting House,
Watervliet,
New York

Synagogue of Congregation Kahal Adath Jeshurun with Anshe Lubz

THE ELDRIDGE STREET SYNAGOGUE

12-16 Eldridge Street, between Division and Canal Streets, New York City

ARCHITECT / BUILDER:
Peter and Francis William Herter
CONSTRUCTION / DEDICATION DATE:
1886-1887

THE SYNAGOGUE, Kahal Adath Jeshurun with Anshe Lubz (Community of the Righteous with the People of Lubz) was designed by two German architects, Peter and Francis William Herter, who should not be confused with the better-known Herter Brothers, cabinet makers and designers to the wealthy. It was dedicated in September 1887, the first Orthodox synagogue built in New York City's Lower East Side, then home to the nation's largest Jewish community, and the first major one built in the United States. Its members were Eastern European immigrants who had achieved a measure of success in the New World, but did not want to identify with their prosperous German co-religionists who were then aligning themselves with the new Reform (liberal) movement.

The synagogue's eclectic mix of Gothic, Romanesque, and Moorish elements is similar to those used by Leopold Eidlitz for his design of the original Reform Temple Emanu-El on Fifth Avenue, erected in 1868 and now demolished. That temple, along with Plum Street Temple in Cincinnati, popularized the Moorish style for synagogues, a style perceived as "non-Christian" and remindful of Jewry's Golden Age in Medieval Muslim Spain.

By the 1920s, Jews were moving out of the Lower East Side and the synagogue's membership declined. The remaining congregants abandoned the large sanctuary and began meeting in a basement chapel. The building was neglected until the 1970s, when a group of concerned citizens began efforts to preserve it. Their work culminated in the formation of the Eldridge Street Project in 1986. This National Historic Landmark is essentially intact, and efforts are under way to return it to its former glory.

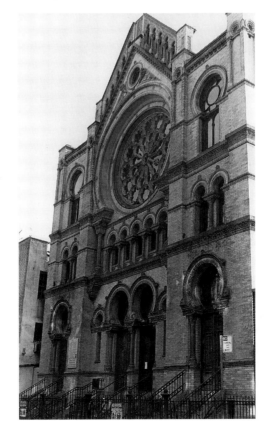

Eldridge Street Synagogue (Congregation Kahal Adath Jeshurun with Anshe Lubz), New York City

Beth Joseph Synagogue

Nake and Mill Streets, Franklin County, Tupper Lake

ARCHITECT / BUILDER:
Not available

CONSTRUCTION / DEDICATION DATE:
1905-1906

THE TUPPER LAKE AREA began to develop in the 1840s, but it was the laying of a spur of the Northern Adirondack Railroad that contributed most to its growth. As the area prospered, itinerant Jewish peddlers who had been selling goods to the lumber camps were joined by their families and began to open permanent stores along the village's main street to service the area's growing tourist population. They helped to form the first Jewish congregation in the Adirondacks in 1881 that in 1906 built a synagogue. The congregation's membership was unique for its time, consisting of two distinct Jewish groups that usually did not associate with one another: Yiddish-speaking Eastern European Jewish immigrant peddlers and merchants and wealthy established German Jews from New York City who summered in the area.

The synagogue's design and execution reflect its unique dual heritage. It displays a combination of elements from nineteenth-century urban synagogue architecture as it was developing in the United States and contemporary resort architecture associated with the Adirondack region.

As the Jewish community began to diminish in size, the synagogue began to be used as a community center and place of prayer for Baptists, finally closing its doors in 1959. Following its restoration in the 1980s the building is once again available for community use, but it does not have regular Jewish services.

Beth Joseph
Synagogue,
Tupper Lake,
New York

William Miller Chapel

County Route 1, vicinity of Fairhaven, Low Hampton

ARCHITECT / BUILDER:
William Miller

CONSTRUCTION / DEDICATION DATE:
1848

THE CHAPEL, located in a small clearing on the edge of the wood in Low Hampton, was built by William Miller and 19 of his followers. Miller, a farmer, was a Bible student who predicted that Christ would return to earth before the millennium. The Baptist Church gave him a license to preach and by 1844 he had given 4,500 sermons and converted thousands of individuals. His followers were known as Millerites and their faith, Millerism. Miller was urged by his followers to make a prediction on what date Christ would arrive. Initially Miller announced the second advent would take place some time between March 21, 1843, and March 21, 1884. The date was later revised to October 22, 1844. When the day passed without incident, it became known among his followers as the Great Disappointment. Many, disenchanted with Miller, abandoned his cause. Others, including Miller and his family, remained faithful but were removed from membership in the Baptist Church. Shortly thereafter, in 1848, Miller and a handful of adherents built a chapel several hundred yards west of the original Baptist church. Miller died in December 1849, but a group of his followers continued to worship in the chapel, later identifying with the Advent Christian Church.

The chapel, dedicated to the memory of William Miller, is a modest white clapboard building featuring Greek Revival elements such as a gable front and corner pilasters. The interior is very much as Miller left it, including an inscription on the wall behind the altar that reads: "For At The Time Appointed The End Shall Be." The chapel was not in use for regular services for several decades, until 1952 when a descendant of William Miller deeded the property to the Advent Christian denomination, with the stipulation that the Seventh-Day Adventists also have the privilege of using it. It is maintained by both denominations and used for special services.

William Miller Chapel,
Low Hampton,
New York

New Jersey

WALLACE N. JAMISON, in his book *Religion in New Jersey: A Brief History*, notes that New Jersey is a "state with many faces, a microcosm of America's religious diversity and an ideal subject for the study of the nation's religious history." New Jersey was an early home to most major Protestant denominations, and, in later years, to large numbers of Roman Catholics and Jews. In addition, many of the notable religious movements and conflicts that occurred in the United States affected New Jersey or took place within its borders. The state's religious diversity is echoed in its ethnic diversity: it is home to over 100 ethnic groups.

New Jersey's diversity is directly related to its location between two great ports, New York City and Philadelphia. As a result it often became the spillover area for immigrants unable or unwilling to move further inland. Initially settled by the Dutch, the British took control of the area in 1664, naming it after the Isle of Jersey. West Jersey was sold to William Penn who opened it to Quakers and a lesser number of Lutherans and Baptists. The Quakers, unwelcomed in most colonies, established meetinghouses where they could openly practice their faith. One of the oldest to survive is **Evesham Friends Meeting House** erected in 1760 in Mount Laurel.

East Jersey, by contrast, welcomed a variety of settlers, as long as they were Protestants. Included were Dutch who remained in the area and worshipped in the **First Reformed Church of Hackensack**, built in 1680. Scots-Irish and Scottish Presbyterians settled throughout Monmouth County, establishing a number of congregations and building churches such as the famed Georgian style Old Tenant Presbyterian Church, built in 1751 on the Monmouth Battlefield. Others who found a haven in East Jersey were African-Americans, whose presence in the area dates back to the late seventeenth century. **Trinity African Methodist Episcopal Church,** built in 1860 in Gouldtown, is the oldest community of free, land-owning African-Americans in the state.

New Jersey's predominantly Protestant identity began to change in the mid-nineteenth century with the arrival of the first Roman Catholics, mainly Irish coming to work in New Jersey's expanding industries. By 1853, the state was home to 33 Roman Catholic churches. It was in an area of Paterson known as "Dublin" that St. John's Roman Catholic Church (now the **Cathedral of St. John the Baptist**) was built in 1865. Like much of the Northeast and Atlantic seaboard, the post–Civil War expansion of the state's manufacturing and industry began attracting numerous new immigrants, including German and Italian Roman Catholics who initially joined the Irish in worshipping in St. John's.

Not all German immigrants, however, were Roman Catholic. The workforce of the developing wool industry in Passaic included many German Lutherans who, after establishing a congregation in 1891, constructed St. John's Lutheran Church in 1891. Designed by a German architect, Ludwig Becker from Mainz, it is modeled after a Gothic Revival church he had built in that city.

Eastern and Southern Europeans continued arriving until the close of immigration in the 1920s. Among them were a number of Russian nationals fleeing from the aftermath of the 1917 Revolution. A Russian Orthodox community, established in the state's Pine Barrens which were reminiscent of their homeland, began erecting two Russian Orthodox churches in 1934, St. Mary's and the more monumental **St. Vladimir's,** which was modeled after Santa Sophia in Kiev, Russia.

The Jewish population of New Jersey grew fivefold between 1880 and 1900; most were Yiddish-speaking Eastern Europeans. Their sheer numbers overwhelmed the older established German-Jewish community, who set out to find ways for the newcomers to become self-supporting. One solution, to establish Jewish agricultural colonies that would be self-supporting, had only mixed success. Woodbine was one colony that survived to the 1940s after changing over to producing soft goods. The colony's brick **Brotherhood Synagogue,** completed in 1896, remains as evidence of a Utopian ideal.

Evesham Friends Meeting House

Northeast corner of junction of Moorestown and Mt. Laurel Road and Hainesport and Mt. Laurel Road, Mount Laurel

ARCHITECT / BUILDER:
Not available

CONSTRUCTION / DEDICATION DATE:
1760

EVESHAM WAS FOUNDED in 1692; six years later the community built its first meetinghouse. The present building, considered one of the most pristine and intact meetinghouses in New Jersey, was constructed in 1760 following the official establishment of the Monthly Meeting of Evesham.

Built of locally quarried stone, the exterior of the building is quite simple. The interior remains virtually unchanged since 1798, when the building was extended westward by half its original length for reasons that remain debatable. Quakers separate into men's and women's meetings for the "wordly," or business, affairs of the church, but it has been suggested the addition was the result of a schism brought on by Edwin Hicks, an anti-evangelical who believed the Quakers should not participate in the revivalism affecting many Protestant faiths in the late eighteenth century. Thus, many meetinghouses, such as this one, found Orthodox Friends meeting in one end of the hall, while the followers of Hicks, called Hicksite Friends, met at the other. A divider of doors hung on weights and pulleys separate the two sections; it can be raised to create one large room.

Although Quakers are pacifists, the meetinghouse and its surrounding land was used on the night of June 19, 1778, as an encampment site by the British Army under the command of General Henry Clinton.

Membership has declined over the years and the meetinghouse is now used only during warm weather. Inadequate heating precludes its use during the winter.

Evesham Friends Meeting House (Mount Laurel Meeting House), Mt. Laurel, New Jersey

First Reformed Church of Hackensack

("CHURCH ON THE GREEN")

42 Court Street, Hackensack

ARCHITECT / BUILDER:
Not available

CONSTRUCTION / DEDICATION DATE:
1791

THE FIRST REFORMED CHURCH of Hackensack, organized in 1686, is the oldest Reformed Dutch congregation in Bergen County, forming the nucleus for the hamlet that became the city of Hackensack. The congregation's present building, its third on the site, is described as representing in stone the principles of American Dutch Calvinism.

The land was given to the congregation in 1696 by John Berry and a stone church, possibly octagonal, was constructed; it was replaced by a similar structure in 1728. The present church, built of local sandstone, is in a style considered typical for Dutch Reformed churches built throughout New Jersey. It is a vernacular interpretation of churches designed by the well-known seventeenth- and eighteenth-century English architects Christopher Wren and James Gibbs. The Gothic arched windows, while typical for late eighteenth- and early nineteenth-century Reformed Dutch churches, may be later additions. The church was lengthened twice: by 10 feet in 1847 and another 20 feet in 1869.

The adjacent Hackensack Green, part of the parcel of land given to the church, is one of the oldest public squares in New Jersey.

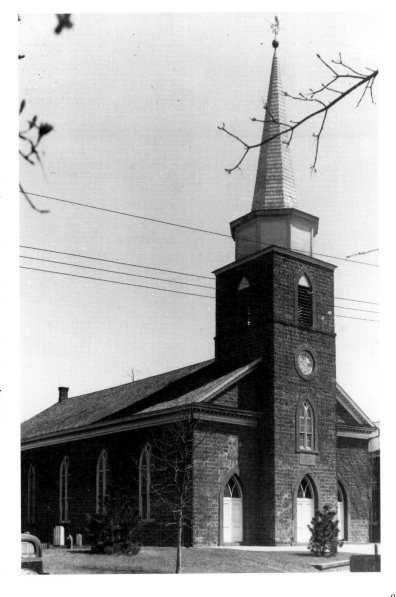

First Reformed (Dutch)
Church of Hackensack,
Hackensack, New Jersey

Trinity African Methodist Episcopal Church

EBENEZER AFRICAN METHODIST EPISCOPAL CHURCH

State Highway 49, Gouldtown, Fairfield Township

ARCHITECT / BUILDER:
Not available

CONSTRUCTION / DEDICATION DATE:
1860

GOULDTOWN IS THE OLDEST community of free, land-owning African-American residents in New Jersey and is among the oldest of such communities in the nation. After the organization of the African Methodist Episcopal (A.M.E.) Church in 1787 by Richard Allen in Philadelphia, African-Americans in Gouldtown began holding a series of meetings. Reverend Reuben Cuff, of Salem County, New Jersey, suggested organizing a society in 1818. Initially members met in private homes and even in a barn before they purchased a vacant school in 1823. A second schoolhouse was purchased in 1834 and moved to Gouldtown where it served as a school and church. The present church was constructed in 1860, immediately prior to the onset of the Civil War. It is possibly the largest surviving pre–Civil War church built by African-Americans in New Jersey.

When built, the church was described as being "meetinghouse" and/or American colonial in design with a clapboard exterior and slate roof. Aluminum siding now sheaths the exterior, the roof has asphalt shingles, and an annex was added in 1959 along the south wall. Characteristic of many African-American churches, on the right of the pulpit there is an "Amen Corner" consisting of two short wooden pews where church officials sit and often say "amen" during the sermon. Gouldtown and Trinity A.M.E. church are of great historic importance to New Jersey, representing a free African-American community dating back to the time of the Revolution.

Trinity A.M.E.
Church of
Gouldtown,
New Jersey

Cathedral of St. John the Baptist

374 Grand Street, Paterson

ARCHITECT / BUILDER:
P. C. Keely

CONSTRUCTION / DEDICATION DATE:
1870

THE CATHEDRAL IS THE OLDEST extant Roman Catholic church in Paterson. Its cornerstone was laid in 1865 and five years later it was ready for use by its mainly Irish members. Its architect, Patrick C. Keely, was trained in Ireland before coming to the United States in 1842. Keely designed some 800 churches in the United States, mainly Roman Catholic, and most in the Gothic Revival style. Twenty of his churches are cathedrals, including St. Patrick's Pro-Cathedral in Newark. St. John's was raised to cathedral status in 1938 when the Diocese of Paterson was formed.

The church was the dream of Father William McNulty (1829–1922), rector of the church until his death, who recognized the importance of having a church where Paterson's growing Irish population could worship. Since then it has welcomed German and Italian Roman Catholic immigrants who began arriving in the latter part of the nineteenth century to work in Paterson's locomotive, silk, and machine shops.

The church, constructed of local brownstone, has retained much of its original appearance, save for changes on the interior to accommodate liturgical reform. The cathedral is now the principal church of the Diocese of Paterson.

Cathedral of St. John the Baptist, Paterson, New Jersey

St. Vladimir's Memorial Russian Orthodox Church

Route 57, north of Route 528, Rova Farms, Cassville, Jackson Township

ARCHITECT/BUILDER:
Roman Verkovsky, Sergei Padukow
CONSTRUCTION / DEDICATION:
Begun 1934

THE ROVA FARMS AREA was first settled in the 1830s when several small grist mills and sawmills were established. Cranberries grown in the area's bogs also provided employment, as did the manufacture of wooden crates to ship the cranberries to market. By 1915 the area began to experience a decline, saved only by the arrival of Russian emigres attracted by the region's pine barrens and rural atmosphere that resembled Russia. Rova Farms, purchased by Russian émigrés in 1934, began as a vacation center for children and families. It has since evolved into a year-round community perpetuating the shared values and ethnic traditions of the earlier Russian settlers.

There are two churches in the area. St. Mary's Russian Orthodox, circa 1934, began as a one-room domed building that has since been expanded eastward and enhanced with three onion domes. The other is St. Vladimir's, begun about the same time and intended to be the greatest and largest Russian Orthodox church in the United States. Modeled after Santa Sophia, built in Kiev in 1037, it is a centrally planned church crowned with a single large golden onion dome set atop a drum. Although still incomplete, its exterior is decorated with three mosaics and the interior displays icons and and an iconostasis created by members of the community. Yet to be completed is an image of Christ Pantocrator in the dome. Rova Farms continues to have the wooded "old world" character that attracted Russians in the first place.

St. Vladimir's
Russian Orthodox
Church, Cassville,
New Jersey

Agudas Achim Anshei Congregation
Woodbine Brotherhood Synagogue

612 Washington Avenue, Woodbine

ARCHITECT / BUILDER:
The Woodbine Brotherhood

CONSTRUCTION / DEDICATION DATE:
1896

THE SYNAGOGUE IS A ONE-STORY red brick rectangular building topped by a simple gable roof. In 1930, a double-stair brick porch was added to the façade. Its design has been described as "American," suggesting that it is not modeled after buildings left behind in the old country by the immigrants. However, its interior retains Orthodox Jewish elements: the Ark (Torah Shrine) to hold the Torah Scrolls against the eastern wall, the *bimah* (platform) in the center of the sanctuary, and a U-shaped balcony for women. The entrance to the building is at the rear, possibly to allow the congregation to face toward the east (Jerusalem), the traditional direction for prayer, while at the same time positioning the building regular to the line of the street.

Woodbine was established in 1891 by 300 Russian and Rumanian Jewish refugees with support from the Baron de Hirsch Fund, an organization named after its founder, a wealthy German-Jewish philanthropist. Their aim was to establish a model agricultural community. However, crop failure resulted in the colony changing over to the production of soft goods.

The synagogue was the community's religious, cultural, and educational center and was built entirely by its members. Woodbine no longer has a Jewish community; the synagogue is used only rarely, but remains in excellent repair.

Woodbine Brotherhood Synagogue (Agudas Achim Anshei Congregation), Woodbine, New Jersey

Pennsylvania

ILLIAM PENN'S "HOLY EXPERIMENT" led Pennsylvania to become one of the most heterogeneous states in the Union. The Dutch first established trading posts in the region, but the first permanent settlers were Swedes who named the territory New Sweden and established two colonies in 1643, New Gottenburg and Upland (near the modern city of Chester). Christ Episcopal Church in Upper Merion was founded as a Lutheran church in 1760 by Swedes from Philadelphia. When the Swedish government withdrew its support of Lutheran churches in the colonies, the congregation voted to affiliate with the Church of England, later becoming Episcopalian. Even so, it is still remembered as "Old Swedes Church."

Penn received a grant from the Crown in 1681 for the colony that came to bear his name. A year later it was home to 2,000 settlers, mainly Quakers emigrating from England who welcomed the opportunity to finally be able to openly worship in their own meetinghouses, such as the one at **Horsham in Montgomery County** established in 1717.

Pennsylvania's reputation as a religious refuge soon attracted additional colonists, all sharing in common a desire for religious freedom—a freedom not readily available in their homelands or in other colonies in the New World, save for Rhode Island and Pennsylvania. Many were members of various Pietist sects. Augustus Lutheran Church in Trappe was built in 1743 by Dr. Heinrich Melchior Muhlenburg, one of four German-speaking Pietist pioneers in the United States. It is the oldest extant Lutheran church building in the country. Mennonites began settling in Lancaster County and portions of Montgomery and Bucks counties, and followers of Jacob Ammann, known as the conservative sect of Amish, founded communities in western Pennsylvania. Moravians from Saxony established Bethlehem in 1742 and the colony of Economy was organized by people from Wurtemberg (later known as "The Harmony Society"). Perhaps the best known Pietist community is the **Ephrata Cloister** founded by a German Pietist mystic, Conrad Beissel, in 1732. Outsiders tend to oversimplify and identify all these groups as Pennsylvania "Dutch," a corruption of the German *deutsch*, although they encompass a heterogeneous mix of German-speaking people from Switzerland, western German states, and areas of eastern Russia. Their cultures and traditions have had a major and lasting impact on the areas in Pennsylvania where they settled and where many of their descendants continue to carry on their traditions.

By the middle of the eighteenth century much of southeast Pennsylvania was urban, populated primarily by British, Welsh, and Quakers. In contrast, areas west and northwest of Philadelphia were over 70 percent German. The cultural and religious differences existing in the two areas of settlement are visible in their places of worship. In stark contrast to the simple, modest places of worship of the German pietist sects is Christ Church in Philadelphia, built between 1727 and 1754 by wealthy Philadelphians of British descent in the grand Georgian Colonial style influenced by Gibbs's London church, St. Martin-in-the-Fields.

The Scots-Irish living in the Cumberland Valley (Franklin County) erected Presbyterian churches, such as **Donegal Presbyterian Church,** built in 1732, and fought on the side of the Patriots during the Revolutionary War. The democratic zeal and the principles of religious freedom upon which the state was founded made its citizens foes of slavery. Their antislavery stance made it possible for free blacks to organize their own congregation in Philadelphia in 1787, **Mother Bethel,** the first church in the newly formed African Methodist Episcopal (A.M.E.) Church. The congregation is now worshipping in its fourth church built on the same site.

Jewish immigrants also found a haven in Pennsylvania; by 1850 the state had seven Jewish congregations, second only to New York. One of the earliest is **Rodef Shalom** established in Pittsburgh during the pre-Revolutionary period; the present building dates to 1906.

The Conewago Chapel near Hanover in Adams County, built in 1785 by Jesuit missionaries on the site of an earlier chapel, is the nation's oldest surviving stone Roman Catholic church. The chapel was primarily a mission site until the 1850s, when it was enlarged to accommodate the many Catholics entering the state to work in its mills and mines. At that time a transept and apse were added and the entire interior was decorated with frescoes.

As industries were established, towns and neighborhoods were laid out to house the immigrant laborers. Such was the case of Cambria City, located just north of Johnstown's central business district. The Cambria Iron Works (later renamed Bethlehem Steel Corporation) opened in 1852; at the same time its Irish and German laborers began to move into the company's housing. The Johnstown Flood of 1889 destroyed two-thirds of Cambria City, but it was quickly rebuilt and was even more congested than before the flood. It was occupied by over 7,000 southern and central Europeans who were sharing the neighborhood with slaughterhouses, breweries, and a lumber yard. The ten churches they erected, nine of them Roman Catholic, were evenly distributed throughout Cambria City with at least one per block between 3rd Avenue and 10th Avenue. They were symbols of faith as well as their parishioners' only oasis; a place of prayer, but also a haven where language and traditions could be perpetuated. Such was the case of **St. Casimir's Polish Roman Catholic Church**, constructed in 1907, the oldest of five major churches in Cambria City.

The "Holy Experiment" initiated by William Penn was an incubator for new denominations. The United Brethren and Evangelical Churches (merged in 1946 into the Evangelical United Brethren) were both founded in the nineteenth century by German-speaking residents of Pennsylvania, Maryland, and Virginia. The importance of religion and education is evident in their buildings. An early example is the Old White Church in rural Schuylkill County. A Lutheran congregation built the original log structure on the site in 1810, but it was acquired by St. Paul's German Reformed Church in 1822. In an early example of ecumenism, the Lutheran congregation continued to share the building with the Reformed church. The log structure razed in 1842 was replaced by the present edifice that was also used by both congregations for another half century.

Horsham Friends Meeting House

Horsham Meeting House and Easton Roads, Horsham Meeting, Montgomery County

ARCHITECT / BUILDER:
Unknown

CONSTRUCTION / DEDICATION DATE:
1804

T HE HORSHAM FRIENDS MEETING is an intact complex of Colonial and Federal era buildings and cemetery that includes a meetinghouse constructed in 1804. The meeting, located at a terminus to several important roads, is on land deeded by William Penn to Samuel Carpenter, a Quaker, who in turn sold it to other Quakers. By 1717 the community was large enough to construct a small, stone meetinghouse that served its needs until 1800, when a larger space was needed.

The new meetinghouse, completed in 1804, is built of carefully cut and squared pink sandstone. It is designed in the standard double meetinghouse style that includes separate entrances for men and women and a large, two-story interior space divided symmetrically into equal men's and women's meeting rooms by a movable central, paneled partition that can be drawn up to create one large, open space. A balcony encircling the entire double room is reached by stairs at its southern corners. The interior has retained virtually all of its original details, including unvarnished woodwork, floorboards, and several benches. A one-story addition added on the east in 1961 accommodates meeting offices and a school.

The Horsham Meeting Quaker complex illustrates the important role that the meeting had in the development of the state's early townships.

Horsham Friends
Meeting House,
Montgomery
County,
Pennsylvania

Ephrata Cloister

632 West Main Street, Ephrata, Lancaster County

ARCHITECT / BUILDER:
Cloister members
CONSTRUCTION / DEDICATION DATE:
1740-1746

THE GROUP OF BUILDINGS known as the Ephrata Cloister, considered among the most medieval of all the Germanic architecture of Pennsylvania, reflects the original members' Rhenish homeland. At its peak in the mid-eighteenth century, the cloister had about 300 members divided into three orders: a brotherhood and a sisterhood, both celibate, and a married order of householders. The three main buildings of the cloister were the *Saal* or chapel, the *Saron* or Sisters' House, and the *Bethania* or Brothers' House. The chapel is a half-timbered five-story building sheathed with split and shaved red-oak clapboards. On the interior, the heavy ceiling beams, great fireplaces, and winding stairs reflect its medieval German ancestry. The chapel has white plastered walls and plain, simple furniture; its only decoration consist of hand-illuminated German scripts hanging on whitewashed walls. The building also contains a meeting hall, community dining room, and small stone kitchen.

The cloister declined after the Revolutionary War and by 1814 the remaining members incorporated the Seventh Day German Baptist Church, which used the buildings until 1934. The site has been maintained and administered by the Pennsylvania Historical and Museum Commission since 1941.

Saal (Meetinghouse),
Ephrata Cloister,
Lancaster, Pennsylvania

Donegal Presbyterian Church

Donegal Springs Road, L. R. 36002, East Donegal Township

ARCHITECT / BUILDER:
Unknown

CONSTRUCTION / DEDICATION DATE:
1732, 1851

S ET ON ROLLING FARMLAND and surrounded by trees, the church is located amid an area of small, rural villages. Built by immigrant Scots-Irish from County Donegal in Ireland, it is one of the earliest Presbyterian church buildings in the area. The congregants' first church, a simple log structure built in 1727, was replaced by the present building in 1732. Constructed of stone gathered from fields or quarried nearby and covered with stucco, the new church resembles other buildings generally found in Irish settlements, while at the same time being similar in layout and size to the church left behind in County Donegal, built in 1674.

The building underwent a major remodeling in 1851 when it was realigned from its original east-west direction to the present north-south arrangement. The pulpit was moved and a narthex added at the same time. In 1958, a wing duplicating the original structure was added; they are connected by an enclosed one-story hallway.

The church functioned as a meetinghouse as well as a place of worship. It became a focal point for military and political discussions at the onset of the Revolutionary War and a gathering place for patriots. Under a white oak, known as the Witness Tree, that still stands outside the church, a group of Scots-Irish patriots pledged their allegiance to the colonists' cause. The tree became a symbol of liberty.

Other than the 1958 addition, the church remains essentially unchanged since its mid-nineteenth-century remodeling.

Donegal
Presbyterian Church,
East Donegal Township,
Franklin County,
Pennsylvania

Mother Bethel A.M.E. Church

Sixth and Lombard Streets, Philadelphia

ARCHITECT / BUILDER:
Edward Hazelhurst

CONSTRUCTION / DEDICATION DATE:
1889-1890

MOTHER BETHEL TRACES its roots to the Free African Society that was founded in 1787 as a mutual aid group. White members of St. George's Methodist Church attempted to segregate black worshippers by forcing them to sit in the galleries, leading to a revolt led by two free blacks, Richard Allen and Absalom Jones, that resulted in the formation of two African-American churches: St. Thomas African Episcopal Church led by Jones and Mother Bethel African Methodist Episcopal Church, established by Allen. Allen purchased an abandoned blacksmith shop and moved it to a plot of ground on Sixth Street and Lombard, making the site of the present church the oldest piece of land in the United States continuously owned by African-Americans. The structure was renovated and the blacksmith anvil became the first pulpit. In 1794, it was dedicated as a church by Bishop Francis A. Asbury of the Methodist Episcopal Church.

In July 1805, the congregation began worshipping in its "Roughcast Church," the first brick church erected in the United States by African-Americans. It was here that the A.M.E. denomination was organized in 1816 and Richard Allen consecrated its first bishop. That building was replaced in 1841 by the "Red Brick Church" that remained in use until the present building was dedicated in 1890.

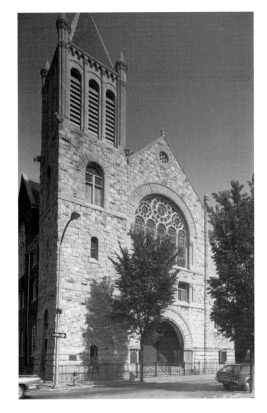

Designed by a white architect whose work was admired by the members, the congregation's present church is a granite three-story Romanesque Revival structure with a four-story tower off to one side. A basement crypt houses a museum and Richard Allen's tomb. The church continues to serve an active congregation.

Mother Bethel
A.M.E.,
Philadelphia,
Pennsylvania

Rodef Shalom Temple

4905 Fifth Avenue, Pittsburgh

ARCHITECT / BUILDER:
Henry Hornbostel
CONSTRUCTION / DEDICATION DATE:
1906

PITTSBURGH'S JEWISH COMMUNITY dates back to pre-Revolutionary times, but the city's first congregation, Rodef Shalom, was not chartered until 1856. The congregation built its first synagogue in 1861 in Pittsburgh's downtown commercial district, but moved to the more elegant Shadyside district in 1906, where they built the present synagogue.

The synagogue's style reflects influences coming from two concurrent sources: the Beaux-Arts and Moorish/Islamic. The Beaux-Arts style embraces a variety of historical styles, but particularly the Renaissance and Baroque, and was a popular choice for religious buildings. The Moorish style began appealing to Jewish congregations in the latter half of the nineteenth century, a time when Jews were seeking an architectural style that would not be confused with Christian church architecture. This synagogue is less exotic in appearance than earlier Moorish style synagogues built in the late nineteenth century, such as the Plum Street Temple in Cincinnati, Ohio.

The synagogue's outstanding features include its square sanctuary capped by a squared dome and its façade dominated by a series of arches, including a grand Syrian style arch framing three sets of double doors. Colorful bands of terra cotta following the lines of the arches and bright green tiles covering the surface of the dome play off the building's cream-colored brick. The two additions made to the building in 1938 and 1956 do not affect its architectural integrity.

**Rodef Shalom
Temple,
Pittsburgh,
Pennsylvania**

St. Casimir's Roman Catholic Church

501 Power Street, Cambria City

ARCHITECT / CONTRACTOR:
Walter Myton
CONSTRUCTION / DEDICATION DATE:
1907

U NSKILLED POLISH LABORERS were among the people who began to crowd into Cambria City in the years following the devastating Johnstown Flood. Living in modest housing cheek to jowl with various industries, they sought beauty and refuge in their church. These were not people of great wealth, but like their neighbors they were people of great faith and a need to retain their distinctive ethnic identity. In addition, St. Casimir's provided them with a refuge from their less than savory surroundings and working conditions.

St. Casimir's was designed by Walter Myton, a prominent local architect who was known for his fashionable designs for prosperous clients. It was built in the Romanesque Revival style, featuring a rough rock-faced stone exterior and round, arched openings. Cruciform in plan it has twin entry towers and an octagonal cupola at the crossing of the nave and transepts; a statue of St. Casimir is set over the entry portal.

Myton also designed the Dom Polski Building at 306 Power Street for the St. Casimir's Society #531 of the Polish Roman Catholic Union. In contrast to the church, it is in the fashionable Arts and Crafts style featuring stucco and half-timbering.

NOTES

1. Julie Nicoletta, *The Architecture of the Shakers* (Woodstock, VT: The Countryman Press, 1995).

St. Casimir's Roman
Catholic Church,
Cambria City,
Pennsylvania

4

East North Central Region

Ohio
Indiana
Michigan
Illinois
Wisconsin

T HIS REGION IS OFTEN referred to as the "Midwest" or the "Middle West." According to the geographer Wilbur Zelinsky, "Everyone within or outside the Middle West knows of its existence, but no one seems sure where it begins or ends."[1] Beginning in the early nineteenth century, the states that comprise this region became home to farms and factories. Crops needed processing, thus mills were erected to produce flour; farm products and other natural resources had to be taken to market, thus transport systems began evolving; and factories were built to manufacture farm machinery and related industrial equipment.

The region's seemingly endless acres of excellent agricultural land attracted land-starved settlers from overpopulated and farmed-out eastern colonies and newcomers arriving directly from central and northwestern Europe. The numerous waterways that led westward into the region made movement there easy, as did the completion of the Cumberland Road (the National Road) in 1840, which provided a direct land route from Cumberland, Maryland, to Vandalia, Illinois. Here, in the flat interior of the nation, diverse people and cultures began to mingle and to create the somewhat romanticized myth of a "midwestern" culture, suggesting a homogeneity that in reality never existed. [2]

The opening of the Great Lakes and the expansion of the nation westward coincided with the first waves of what became a massive human migration from Europe. Germans, among the first to arrive, left a lasting impression on the region. Cincinnati, for example, became a major milling site and transport center. Farm and industry came together in that city when, in 1830, German farmers became involved in pork production, giving Cincinnati its nickname, Porkopolis. Recently the city celebrated its German heritage by decorating its renovated riverfront park with images of flying pigs.

Dutch immigrants arriving in the 1840s were fleeing a potato blight in their homeland. Seeking to stay together, they established colonies in Michigan, Illinois, and Wisconsin. Scandinavians, attracted by cheap land made available following the passage of the Homestead Act in 1862, began homesteading in the region in large numbers, establishing communities and congregations. Not all were Lutheran; many who came were seeking religious freedom, unhappy with their homeland's state church. Also contrary to the stereotype, not all Scandinavians farmed; many chose to settle in urban neighborhoods and work in the region's growing industries. In 1917, the city with the largest number of Scandinavians in the world outside of Stockholm and Oslo was not in Minnesota as one would think, but in Illinois–Chicago.

The growth of industry following the Civil War began attracting many eastern and southern European immigrants, as well as freed blacks and displaced southern whites, all further enriching the region's cultural character. The stockyards and factories of Chicago, the steel mills of neighboring Gary, Indiana, the automobile factories in and around Detroit, Michigan's Upper Peninsula copper mines and those in neighboring Wisconsin, all held out the promise to their laborers of a better life—a promise that was kept until the last decades of the twentieth century.

PRECEDING PAGE:

Congregational
Church,
Atwater, Ohio,
circa 1930s

Ohio

THE FRENCH AND BRITISH fought over control of the territory that became Ohio, each nation refusing to acknowledge the claims of the other. In 1749, George II awarded a royal grant to the Ohio Company, organized by Virginia planters and London merchants, to settle in the Ohio valley. That same year the French laid claim to land along the river banks, precipitating the French and Indian War. The British, emerging victorious in 1774, made the territory part of Canada, thus enraging the American colonists, who added this event to their list of grievances against British rule. Finally, following the end of the War of Independence, the British ceded their rights to the Northwest Territory to the United States. Connecticut retained its claim to an area known as Western Reserve until 1800, and Virginia held onto its Virginia Military District, situated between the Little Miami and Scioto Rivers, until the 1850s.

The area under control of the Connecticut Land Company, known as "New Connecticut," was centered around the village of Cleveland. Even following the transfer of jurisdiction to Ohio the area never lost its New England character, as can be seen in the style of **The Congregational Church** in Atwater, built between 1838 and 1841. At first glance this building looks like many Colonial and Federal churches built throughout New England, such as the Federated Church in Templeton, Massachusetts. However, upon closer examination its pointed windows and doors clearly indicate that its designer was aware of stylistic elements emanating from the Gothic style, which was beginning to enjoy a revival.

In 1833, the completion of a series of canals linking Lake Erie to ports in the East coupled with the invention of the steamboat transformed Cleveland and Cincinnati into major ports. Easy and cheap passage inland and the promise of rich farmland attracted thousands of people. Among the first were numerous German-speaking settlers either fleeing the Napoleonic Wars in Europe or moving west from older settlements in Pennsylvania. Settling on fertile land in the western part of the state they created communities, such as the "Land of the Cross-Tipped Churches," that still retain their German character. The first churches in the area, however, lacked spires. It was only later, after a time of prosperity, that elaborate churches, such as **St. Aloysius Roman Catholic Church** in Carthagena, were built.

Not all Germans were Roman Catholic. Others were Protestant, either members of mainstream Lutheran and German Reform congregations that were accepted denominations in German principalities, or German Baptist and United Brethren, labeled "nonconformists" and "fanatics" in their homeland. In Germany, the government attempted to enforce a permanent union of Lutheran and Reformed congregations; in this nation the union was continued, but now as an economic measure, although services were usually separate. Known as "Union" churches, their efforts were not always successful, as can be seen in the history of **St. Jacob's Lutheran Church** in Miamisburg, constructed in 1861. Other Germans abandoned their Old World denominations and became Methodists, thanks to the assiduous efforts of that denomination's missionaries. A German Methodist society was formed in Cincinnati in 1838, a forerunner to Nast-Trinity United Methodist Church, the first German Methodist Episcopal congregation in the world. In 1958, the congregation merged with Trinity United Methodist and now worships in Trinity's church, dedicated in 1881.

The first Jewish congregation in Cincinnati was formed in 1824 by a small group of English Jews who built the city's first synagogue, Bene Israel, in 1834. They were soon outnumbered by German-speaking Jewish immigrants who erected their own synagogue, B'nai Jeshuran, in 1846. It was replaced following the Civil War by the present building, commonly known as the Plum Street Temple, later renamed the **Isaac Mayer Wise Temple**, to honor the influential rabbi responsible for its erection; Wise had achieved national prominence for his promotion of Reform Judaism in the United States. Built in the Moorish style, it remains one of the city's most prominent buildings, its minarets competing in height with the steeple atop its Greek Revival neighbor across the street, the Cathedral of Saint Peter in Chains, constructed in 1845.

Another minority group who chose to settle in Ohio was the Mormons, led there by Joseph Smith, Sr. Arriving in Kirtland in 1831, Smith and his followers sought to establish a permanent presence by erecting the **Kirtland Temple**, dedicated in March 1836. Their welcome, however, was short-lived; community pressure forced them to abandon their temple only a few months after its completion, and with that they left Ohio to seek a safe haven elsewhere. In 1880 legal title was transferred to the Reorganized Church of Jesus Christ of Latter-day Saints, who maintain the building.

In the years following the Civil War, immigrants from southern and eastern Europe began settling in the state's urban areas. Many were Roman Catholic, but each ethnic group sought to establish its own parish. Built before the Canon Law of 1918 that forbade establishing parishes for non-English-speaking Catholics, many of these churches, such as Cleveland's **St. Stanislaus Polish Roman Catholic Church**, remain in use by descendants of its founders. Others, such as St. Gabriel's Rumanian Greek Catholic Church, built in Dayton in 1916, have been demolished; all that remains of it are brief references in written records.

One of the most influential developments in American Protestant church architecture originated in 1868 in Akron. Lewis Miller, superintendent of the Akron school system, and Jacob Snyder, a local architect, developed an innovative plan for Akron's First Methodist Episcopal Church. Perfected by architect George Kramer, their plan became known as the Akron Plan or Sunday School Plan and was well suited for Protestant denominations whose focus on preaching required good sight lines and acoustics. **Pilgrim Congregational Church**, built in Cleveland in 1897, is a variation of the Akron Plan. A Romanesque Revival structure that retains much of its original appearance, Pilgrim's chancel and pulpit placed in a corner of the sanctuary are reached by two diagonal aisles.

St. Aloysius Roman Catholic Church

Intersection of Route 274 and Route 127, Carthagena

ARCHITECT / BUILDER:
Anton DeCurtins, architect and builder
CONSTRUCTION / DEDICATION DATE:
1875-1878

THE "LAND OF THE CROSS-TIPPED CHURCHES" was established by a Swiss priest, Father Francis de Sales Brunner, who was responsible for the construction of many of the area's Roman Catholic churches. St. Aloysius was designed by Anton DeCurtins, a master architect from Switzerland, and built by its members. It is located north of St. Charles Seminary, which trained priests of the Precious Blood Order. The land upon which it is built was reluctantly sold to the Society of the Precious Blood by freed blacks who attended Emler Institute, a school established for them by Quakers. No longer able to support the school, the blacks departed. Only the town's name, Carthagena, named after the famous city of Carthage in Africa, reflects its heritage.

Anton DeCurtins, the architect, lived in Carthagena and was responsible for the building of many Gothic churches in Mercer County, as well as numerous schools, residences, and rectories.

St. Aloysius Roman
Catholic Church,
Carthagena, Ohio

St. Jacob's Lutheran Church

213 East Central Avenue, Miamisburg

ARCHITECT / BUILDER:
Henry Groby

CONSTRUCTION / DEDICATION DATE:
Dedicated in 1864

MIAMISBURG WAS HOME to a Union congregation, Lutheran and German Reformed, who together built a church in 1833 known as Jacob's Church. In 1861 the congregation split along denominational lines, resulting in the construction of St. Jacob's Lutheran Church. It was designed by one of its members, Henry Groby, and built by church members, including the Reverend Christopher Albrecht, who had migrated westward from eastern Pennsylvania in the first decades of the nineteenth century. Construction began in 1861, but was delayed by the Civil War. Although it was dedicated in 1864, the sanctuary was not entirely completed until about 1873.

The two-story brick Gothic Revival building has been remodeled and added onto over time. Changes including recent embellishment clearly reflect a more affluent and growing congregation. But despite the changes, the original form and style of the building remain visible. The church continues to function both as a place of worship for its congregants and as a reminder of the area's first settlers' efforts to transfer to the New World a tradition enforced upon them in the Old.

St. Jacob's
Lutheran Church,
Miamisburg, Ohio

Isaac Mayer Wise Temple

(PLUM STREET TEMPLE)

Plum and Eighth Streets, Cincinnati

ARCHITECT / BUILDER:
James Keys Wilson, architect
CONSTRUCTION / DEDICATION DATE:
1866

INFLUENCING RABBI WISE'S CHOICE of the Moorish style for his congregation's new synagogue was his awareness of its growing popularity for Reform synagogues in Germany, the home of Reform Judaism. Newly emancipated Jews in central and western Europe, searching for a synagogue style that would reflect their cultural heritage and differentiate their places of worship from those of Christians, latched onto the Moorish style associated with the so-called Golden Age of Jewry in Spain when that nation was under Muslim rule; ironically, no synagogues in Spain survive from this period. The romanticized image of Islamic Spain captured the Jewish people's imagination and Moorish synagogues began to proliferate. This temple is one of the first of many built in variations of this style in the United States. By the early twentieth century the style had become unfashionable due to its increasing association with places of entertainment, such as theaters.

Rabbi Wise called his new synagogue an "Alhambra temple," although upon closer examination its basilica plan and many of its decorative elements are Gothic. Contributing to its outwardly appearing Moorish style are its deeply recessed doors on its front façade, tall slender minarets, horseshoe arches, and arabesque decoration. While many Moorish style synagogues have been destroyed, the Wise Temple, recently restored, remains a Cincinnati landmark and continues to be used by its congregation on special occasions.

Isaac Mayer
Wise Temple
(Plum Street
Temple),
Cincinnati, Ohio
(with steps and
portico of the
Cathedral of
St. Peter in Chains)

The Kirtland Temple

9020 Chillicothe Road, Kirtland

ARCHITECT / BUILDER:
Joseph Bump, master builder
CONSTRUCTION / DEDICATION DATE:
Dedicated 1836

ON JUNE 1, 1833, Joseph Smith, Jr., received a revelation instructing him to build a temple at Kirtland. Included in the revelation were the building's measurements and plan. Its exterior, however, is in an eclectic style revealing Smith's awareness of current architectural trends. Decorative elements borrowed from Georgian, Federal, Greek, and Gothic Revival styles all culminate in a 90-foot belfry. The interior arrangement is what makes the building unique and important. According to Smith's revelation the building was to have two courts: the lower part was for the sacrament offering, preaching, and praying; that is, general church meetings and assemblies. The higher court was a school for apostles–priesthood councils and educational purposes. In each of these courts are eight pulpits, four at each end, one above the other. Those in the west are intended for the Melchizedek Priesthood, and those in the east for the Aaronic Priesthood. The courts each receive natural light from windows located above each pulpit and from five window bays on the side elevations.

Many of the men who worked on the building, including Brigham Young, would be instrumental in designing the Temple in Salt Lake City. The Mormons were forced to abandon the Kirtland Temple soon after it opened. After the death of Joseph Smith, Jr., in 1844, his church split into many factions. In 1880 legal title to this site was given to the Reorganized Church of Jesus Christ of Latter-day Saints. The building was neglected throughout most of the nineteenth century, but has recently been restored and is open to the public.

Kirtland Temple
(House of the Lord),
Kirtland, Ohio
(exterior, facing page)

Polish Roman Catholic Church of St. Stanislaus

Forman and East 65th Streets, Cleveland

ARCHITECT / BUILDER:
William Dunn, architect

CONSTRUCTION / DEDICATION DATE:
Dedicated 1891

Polish Roman
Catholic Church of
St. Stanislaus,
Cleveland, Ohio

ST. STANISLAUS ILLUSTRATES the enormous importance Polish Roman Catholic immigrants attach to their churches as visible proclamations of their dedication to their faith and their ethnic community. This parish was formed in 1877 to serve Cleveland's growing Polish population. The parishioners, although poorly paid in their jobs in the steel mills, were determined to build a monumental church. To that end they purchased land and in 1886 built the foundation for a church measuring 85 feet wide by 200 feet long, the largest church in the diocese. By the time of its dedication in 1891, the building costs were over $250,000.

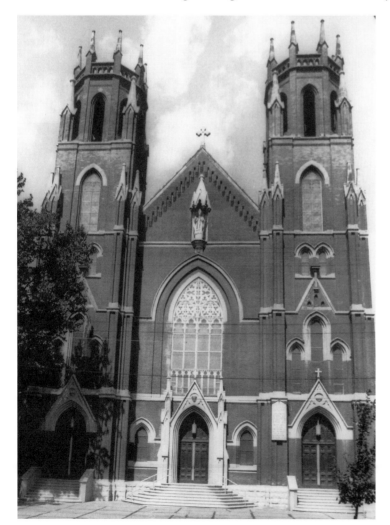

Designed by a well-known Cleveland architect, William Dunn, the church's English High Victorian Gothic style is considered one of the most completely realized in the region. The Gothic style was not unknown to its Polish parishioners. Its ornamental scheme is based on Eastern European prototypes. Examples include the Gothic Cathedral of St. Stanislaus in Krakow and the Warsaw Cathedral that was rebuilt in 1840 in an English Gothic style. The Gothic then became the style of choice for many churches built in Poland's small towns, from which many members in this parish had emigrated.

The church's original steeples, upper parts of the towers, and portions of the nave were destroyed in a cyclone in 1909, but the church was immediately rebuilt. It remains the mother church of the Polish community in northeast Ohio.

Pilgrim Congregational Church

2592 West 14th Street, Cleveland

ARCHITECT / BUILDER:
S. R. Badgeley, architect
CONSTRUCTION / DEDICATION DATE:
1894

T HE FIRST SETTLERS in the Cuyahoga River Valley area known as University Heights were New England farmers who came from Connecticut in 1818. A Sunday school was established in 1854; four years later the University Heights Congregational Church, Pilgrim's precursor, was organized by members representing four Protestant denominations. Sunday school and prayer meetings were held in a small schoolhouse until work began on a church building in 1866. Three years later the auditorium, seating 400 people, was completed. The church served its congregation until 1893, when ground was broken for the present Richardsonian Romanesque structure.

Dedicated in November 1894, Pilgrim Congregational Church is an outstanding example of an innovative plan that began gaining favor among Protestant denominations in the late 1860s. Conceived by Lewis Miller, superintendent of the Akron, Ohio, school system in collaboration with Jacob Snyder, a local architect, for Akron's First Methodist Episcopal Church, the plan was perfected by George Kramer and came to be known as the Akron or Sunday School Plan. The "diagonal plan" selected for Pilgrim is one of its popular variations. The chancel and pulpit, rather than being opposite the main entry, are in a corner reached by two diagonal aisles. Curving rows of pews and a balcony curving gracefully around three sides of the sanctuary provide congregants with outstanding sight lines. The church is famous for its outreach programs, including Cleveland's first library.

Pilgrim
Congregational
Church,
Cleveland, Ohio

Indiana

THE FRENCH WERE THE FIRST to establish a permanent settlement in the territory that became Indiana. Evidence of their presence can be seen in Vincennes where the **Basilica of St. Frances Xavier Church**, also known as the Old Cathedral, still stands. Constructed between 1826 and 1840 in the popular Classical Revival style, it replaced a simple log chapel built by Jesuit missionaries in 1786.

Following the conclusion of the French and Indian Wars, the British acquired the territory and began to actively encourage settlers to move there from the older colonies. Britain then ceded the territory to Canada, fermenting revolt among the settlers who responded by joining the side of the Patriots during the Revolutionary War. Once independence was won, Indiana became part of the Northwest Territory until it achieved statehood in 1816.

Many of Indiana's early settlers who came from southern colonies sought to have slavery legalized in the new state. While their effort failed, laws prohibiting blacks from entering Indiana did remain in force until after the Civil War. The laws, however, were not uniformly enforced. Indianapolis, for example, is home to a black congregation pre-dating the Civil War. Bethel A.M.E. Church, the oldest black Methodist congregation in the state, was established in 1836 by William Paul Quinn. The congregation's present building, built in 1857 by a German Methodist congregation, was purchased by Bethel in 1869.

Settlers of Scots-Irish descent began to arrive in the early years of the nineteenth century, moving along trails partly formed by migrating buffalo, hence the name, Buffalo Trace, a north-south route starting near Owensboro, Kentucky, that cuts through Indiana's Dubois County. Most Scots-Irish were members of the Cumberland Presbyterian Church formed in 1810 following a schism in the Presbyterian Church. Settling in Dubois County they organized the Shiloh Congregation in 1817, and in 1849 erected the Shiloh Meeting House on land donated by one of its founders. The meetinghouse, one of the oldest structures in Dubois County, is no longer in regular use, but it and its cemetery grounds are kept in good repair.

German immigrants who began to arrive in substantial numbers beginning in the mid-nineteenth century quickly outnumbered the Scots-Irish. Sensing there was money to be made and anxious to move on, many Scots-Irish sold their land to the newcomers, but those who chose to stay were able to continue supporting several of their churches. One, **Emmanuel Evangelical Lutheran Church**, organized in 1858, is the second church built for one of the county's oldest German Lutheran congregations. Erected in 1901, it combines elements from the congregation's earlier meetinghouse with fashionable Victorian Gothic detailing.

Franklin County, near Cincinnati, is another pre-statehood county initially settled by Protestants and then Roman Catholics. The area's first significant period of settlement began in 1795 and had ended by the time Indiana became a state. One of the few surviving buildings from this era is **Little Cedar Grove Baptist Church**, constructed in 1812 for a congregation organized in 1806.

The town of Oldenburg, located in the southern portion of Franklin County, was founded by two émigrés from Oldenburg, Germany, who purchased the land in 1837. Advertising for settlers in Cincinnati's German press, they urged recent immigrants to move to a town that was a near replica of the ones they left behind. Indeed, Oldenburg, with its picturesque location in a valley, half-timbered buildings, and a skyline dominated by church spires large and small, is still reminiscent of towns in southern Germany. The town became home to a number of Roman Catholic institutions, including a Franciscan

monastery constructed in 1894 and now demolished, that adjoined **Holy Family Church**, a parish church built by its parishioners in 1862. The town is famous for its Corpus Christi procession that has been an annual community devotion since 1846.

Episcopalians moving westward with the frontier brought with them their plans for Gothic Revival churches. Scores of churches in this style have been built throughout Indiana and the Midwest, but one of the finest in Indiana is **Christ Episcopal Church** in Indianapolis, built in 1857.

In 1919, members of the Church of Christ, Scientist in Huntington erected one of the town's few Neoclassical buildings, a church that served its members for nearly 70 years. The First Church of Christ, Scientist closed its doors as a worship space, but reopened them two years later, following its transformation into the Dan Quayle Center and Museum administered by the Dan Quayle Commemorative Foundation.

Basilica of
St. Francis Xavier
(Old Cathedral),
Vincennes, Indiana

The Basilica of St. Francis Xavier

("OLD CATHEDRAL")

205 Church Street, Vincennes

ARCHITECT / BUILDER:
Not available

CONSTRUCTION / DEDICATION DATE:
1826-1840

THE RED BRICK GREEK REVIVAL church is in the form of a basilica with an apse projecting off its short southern wall and a white frame tower straddling the ridge at the north end of its gable roof. Its style owes much to James Gibbs's famed London church St. Martin-in-the-Fields and its influence on American church architecture during the Colonial and Federal periods. The church has been richly embellished over the years, signifying its importance to its community. Paintings of the Stations of the Cross were executed in France and installed from 1879 to 1890. The Crucifixion behind the main altar was painted on plaster in 1870 by a German artist named Lamprecht. In the 1920s, statues were added of St. Francis Xavier, St. Patrick, and St. Joan of Arc; the latter is thought to be the first one erected following her canonization in 1920.

In front of the cathedral is a statue of Father Pierre Gibault, the individual credited with winning the French civilians of Vincennes to the American cause during the War for Independence. The cathedral, and this statue, remain as symbols of the French Catholic contribution to the capture of the Old Northwest territory for the colonists during the Revolutionary War.

Basilica of
St. Francis Xavier
(Old Cathedral),
Vincennes, Indiana

Emmanuel Evangelical Lutheran Church
(EVANGELISCHE LUTHERISCHE EMANUELS KIRCHE)

County Road 445 East, vicinity of Dubois

ARCHITECT / BUILDER:
Not available

CONSTRUCTION / DEDICATION DATE:
1901

THIS ONE-STORY CLAPBOARD building is considered an excellent example of a gable-front Victorian Gothic rural church. It replaced a similar church built on the site in 1863. Both buildings resemble the nearby Shiloh Meeting House built earlier by the county's Scots-Irish settlers. This is most apparent in the simplicity of their overall design and, in particular, their gable roofs. Emmanuel, however, is distinguished by its introduction of Gothic elements such as lancet windows with mutins in imitation of Gothic tracery. In addition, this church has a large steeple surmounting its roof on the east end.

The interior of the church is austere, consisting of two groups of original wood pews divided by a single aisle. The altar stands on an elevated platform in the center of the west wall. The original elevated octagonal pulpit stands north of the altar along the same wall, and the original lectern is set to the south of the altar.

The church is a significant example of German settlement in Dubois County, although its style reveals influences emanating from the congregants' non-German neighbors. Both its exterior and interior remain virtually unaltered.

Emmanuel Evangelical Lutheran Church, Dubois County, Indiana

Little Cedar Grove Baptist Church

U.S. 52 at Little Cedar Road, vicinity of Brookville

ARCHITECT / BUILDER:
Thomas Carter, carpenter; Thomas Winscott, stonemason
CONSTRUCTION / DEDICATION DATE:
1812-1816

THIS SIMPLE BRICK CHURCH is one of the few buildings of this size and integrity remaining from Indiana's pre-statehood era. The Little Cedar Grove Baptist Church community, formed in 1806, is the first Baptist society in the county. The congregation quickly outgrew its log meetinghouse, and hired Thomas Carter and Thomas Winscott to build a new church of hand-hewn logs and bricks that were molded and baked at the site.

By the 1840s, church membership had begun to decline and in the years following the Civil War the building was used occasionally by several different religious denominations for worship services or revival meetings. The building has undergone two restorations since it was acquired in 1905 by its present owners, the Brookville Historical Society—once in 1912 and again in the 1940s. Thanks to their efforts and those of a number of civic and preservation organizations, the church building has retained most of its original features, including much of its interior, which consists of a large room with a balcony bordered by a cherry wood balustrade and supported by original hand-hewn log beams and pillars (which were covered with walnut boards in the 1940s). Wood pews face a wood pulpit, a replica of the original, that is situated near the rear wall. A walnut stairway on the northwest side provides access to the balcony.

Little Cedar Grove
Baptist Church,
Franklin County,
Indiana

Holy Family Roman Catholic Church

Southeast corner of Main and Pearl Streets, Oldenburg

ARCHITECT / BUILDER:
Dominic Siefert, designer of roof truss system
CONSTRUCTION / DEDICATION DATE:
1862

THE BRICK VICTORIAN GOTHIC CHURCH is part of a complex that consisted of a Victorian Romanesque Franciscan monastery constructed in 1894 at the south side–since demolished–and a school completed in 1932 on the east. The church's founder, Father F. J. Rudolph, is buried in its crypt.

The church's central entrance portal projects from the base of an impressive tower situated in the center of the façade. The tower's spire is topped by a large gilded cross that dominates the skyline. Above the main entry is a niche with a statue of the Holy Family; above the statue is a small rose window and inscription in Latin that includes the building's date, 1861. Much of the church's decoration appears to be carved stone, but in reality is pressed metal, an architectural feature common in Oldenburg.

Up until 1979 the church retained its fine Victorian Gothic interior. Since then much of it has been destroyed. The stained glass windows that survive were made in Munich, Germany, and installed in 1919.

Holy Family Roman
Catholic Church,
Oldenburg, Indiana

Christ Episcopal Church

131 Monument Circle, Indianapolis

ARCHITECT / BUILDER:
William Tinsley, architect

CONSTRUCTION / DEDICATION DATE:
1857-1858; spire added 1869

CHRIST CHURCH, NOW SURROUNDED by large-scale commercial buildings, is built on a beautiful site on the northeast quadrant of Monument Circle. Its location, along with its finely detailed English Gothic Revival style and its tall spire, all proclaim the wealth and success of its founders.

Following its establishment in 1820, Indianapolis was selected as the future site of the state's capital. The following year the town was laid out from plans drawn by Alexander Ralston, a surveyor who had worked with Pierre Charles L'Enfant, the designer of Washington, D.C. Chartered as a city in 1847, the same year the first railroad arrived, Indianapolis began to expand as an important railway terminal and leading commercial and manufacturing center. Many of its leading entrepreneurs came from eastern colonies, bringing with them their Episcopal faith and the Gothic Revival style.

William Tinsley, the church's architect, was born in Ireland in 1804. While still a young man he worked with James Pain, Jr., an architect who had studied under the famed British architect, Sir John Nash, at a time when he was designing several buildings in the Gothic Revival style.

Christ Church is built in the traditional basilica form with slightly projecting transepts and a polyfoil apse off its short end. Its rough-faced ashlar walls are pierced by lancet windows filled with stained glass. Additions made in 1900 include a wooden south porch, rood screen, and reredos.

**Christ Episcopal Church,
Indianapolis, Indiana**

Michigan

THE WATER ROUTE up the Saint Lawrence River and across Lakes Ontario and Erie made access easy for French Canadians entering the territory. Jesuit Father Jacques Marquette established the region's first Catholic mission at Sault Sainte Marie in 1668. Soon to follow were several major French military posts, including one at Detroit founded in 1701 by Antoine de la Mothe Cadillac. A parish established at the same time is the oldest in Detroit and is the second oldest continuously operating Catholic parish in the United States. Its present High Victorian Gothic church, Sainte Anne du Detroit, erected in 1886–1887, was preceded by seven others; it now serves a largely Hispanic congregation.

The British gained control of the territory in 1763, but following the end of the Revolutionary War ceded most of it to the United States. Britain, coveting the area's fur trade, chose not to relinquish its fur trading posts at Detroit and Fort Mackinac until 1796. Following the conclusion of the War of 1812, during which Britain once again occupied Fort Mackinac, the Fort became a trading post for the American Fur Company and the site of a Protestant Indian **Mission Church** erected in 1829 with funds raised by the villagers and traders plus a gift from John Jacob Astor. When the fur trade declined in the 1830s the mission closed, but the church survives as the oldest church building in Michigan.

Detroit's strategic location on the Detroit River contributed to the city's growth and prosperity. It was incorporated as a town in 1802 and named the capital of Michigan Territory in 1805. Lansing, however, was named the state capital in 1847, ten years after Michigan was admitted into the Union. Following a devastating fire in 1805, Augustus B. Woodward, the territory's magistrate, sought to rebuild Detroit along Pierre L'Enfant's 1796 plan for Washington, D.C. His grandiose vision was never fully realized, but some features did survive, including the grand avenue that bears his name. Woodward Avenue was not only an exclusive residential street, it was also home to religious institutions representing nearly every mainstream religious faith and denomination. The Victorian Gothic St. John's Protestant Episcopal Church built in 1860 was the avenue's first church. It was joined six years later by Central Methodist Church, an early example of the use of the auditorium plan, a forerunner to the Akron Plan introduced in Akron, Ohio, in 1868 (see p. 101). Perhaps the avenue's most famous church is the **Cathedral Church of St. Paul** built between 1908 and 1911 and designed by the famed architect, Ralph Adams Cram, a major monument of his early career. Temple Beth El (now Lighthouse Cathedral), one of the last places

Temple Beth El (Lighthouse Cathedral), Detroit, Michigan

of worship built on the avenue, was completed in 1922. Designed by Albert Kahn, an architect who achieved fame for designing automobile factories, its classical exterior, recalling the Lincoln Memorial dedicated in 1922, had an impact on the style of synagogues built elsewhere in the Midwest. In all, between 1859 and 1930 nineteen places of worship were built on Woodward Avenue. Together they are significant landmarks of American religious architecture as it developed in the Midwest.

Detroit's oldest black Baptist congregation, **Second Baptist Church**, was organized in 1836 by former slaves. They purchased their present building in 1857 from a Reformed congregation. Partially destroyed by a fire in 1917, the church has since been reconstructed and an office and educational wing added.

Michigan was the first state to appoint an immigration agent to recruit laborers as they disembarked at the New York docks. Unskilled labor was needed to work in the state's iron and copper mines, the lumber camps in the north, and in the burgeoning industrial complexes of Detroit. Among those who came were Polish immigrants who found work in Detroit's automobile factories. Initially worshipping in German Roman Catholic churches, the Poles were allowed to form their own parish in 1871. As their numbers increased, additional parishes were founded, including St. Stanislaus in 1898. The cornerstone for the parish's fifth church, the current Neo-Baroque St. Stanislaus Bishop and Martyr Roman Catholic Church, was laid in 1911.

The Albion Malleable Iron Company, in Albion, sent its own recruiter to New York to entice immigrants to work in its foundry. Many were Orthodox Christians who, with the help of the foundry's president, were able to build **Holy Ascension of Christ Orthodox Church** in 1916, the oldest Russian Orthodox parish in Michigan outside of Detroit.

The Finnish Evangelical Church (now Glad Tidings Assembly of God Church) in Hancock stands as a reminder of the numerous Finnish immigrants who came to work in Michigan's mines. Hancock was one of the original areas of Finnish settlement in North America, and with the founding of Suomi College in 1896 became an important center for Finnish religion and culture. Another group arriving at the same time were Jewish merchants whose stores on Hancock's main street catered to the needs of the miners. The Jewish families named their place of worship built in 1912 Temple Jacob, after Jacob Gartner, a German immigrant who rose from street peddler to successful merchant, and was an important benefactor to the Jewish community.

Others who came to Michigan saw promise in working the land. These included Dutch settlers who began arriving in 1847, spurred on by potato blights, economic depression, and religious persecution in the Netherlands. Settling in Ottawa County, they recreated their homeland in America, naming their major market town Holland. The town was almost entirely destroyed by fire in 1871, the same day as the Chicago fire, but was quickly rebuilt. One of the buildings destroyed was the **Third Reformed Church of Holland**, which had been recently erected by its congregants. Work began immediately on a new building, but disaster struck again when the partially completed building was destroyed by fire. Not to be discouraged, the congregants set about a third time to complete the present building, dedicated in 1874, that continues in use.

Mission Church

Northeast corner Huron Street and Mission Hill Road, Mackinac Island

ARCHITECT / BUILDER:
Martin Heydenburk, carpenter and builder
CONSTRUCTION / DEDICATION DATE:
1829-1830

FORT MACKINAC ON MACKINAC ISLAND was a military post from 1780 to 1895. Alternately in the possession of the British and Americans, it finally was ceded permanently to the United States by the British following the conclusion of the War of 1812. Transient fur traders also were in the area and the American Fur Company under John Jacob Astor established an important trading post on the island.

William Montague Ferry, a Massachusetts-born minister, established a mission post on Mackinac Island in 1822 to educate Indians and provide religious services and moral guid-

ance for the men at the fort. The mission's simple Classical style wooden church with its square tower and spired belfry resembles the New England churches left behind by its founder. Martin Heydenburk, the carpenter who built the church, was a teacher at the Mission School.

The mission closed in 1837 and the church remained unused for over 50 years. In 1875, Mackinac Island was named a National Park and developed into a popular summer resort. The church was reopened in the 1890s for interfaith services for its residents and tourists. In 1955 it was acquired by the Mackinac Island State Park Commission.

Mission Church,
Mackinac Island,
Michigan

Cathedral Church of St. Paul

4800 Woodward Avenue, Detroit

ARCHITECT / BUILDER:
Ralph Adams Cram
CONSTRUCTION / DEDICATION DATE:
1908-1911

S T. PAUL'S PARISH, founded in 1824, is the pioneer Episcopal parish in Michigan. The present building, the parish's third, was built between 1908 and 1911. It was designed by Ralph Adams Cram of Cram, Goodhue and Ferguson of Boston and New York. Cram, considered the foremost church architect in the United States in the first decades of the twentieth century, firmly believed in the need to search the past for inspiration for new buildings–and for him the past for church architecture was the Gothic period–not the more fanciful interpretations of Gothic that flourished during the preceding Victorian Era, but the "correct" Gothic of the Medieval period. This limestone Gothic cathedral represents an early example of Cram's developing philosophy regarding the adaptation of what he considered a time-honored Christian style for a cathedral.

No expense was spared on the cathedral's interior. Famed artists and artisans contributed various ritual and decorative objects. The famed German woodcarver Joseph Kirchmayer of Oberammergau carved the reredos of the sanctuary, the bishop's seat, the dean's stall, and the lectern. Mary Chase Stratton of the local well-known Pewabic Pottery designed the tile floor. The stained glass windows were designed and executed by Heaton, Butler and Bayne of London and Charles J. Connick of Boston. The cathedral, in all its glory, remains a beacon on a once-proud avenue.

**Cathedral Church
of St. Paul,
Detroit, Michigan
(circa 1920)**

Second Baptist Church

441 Monroe Avenue, Detroit

ARCHITECT / BUILDER:
1968 addition: Sims-Varner and Associates
CONSTRUCTION / DEDICATION DATE:
1857, 1880, 1917, 1968

SECOND BAPTIST CHURCH was organized in 1836 by former slaves who were members of the predominantly white First Baptist Church. After meeting in various halls, the members were able to purchase the former Zion Reformed Evangelical Church in 1857. In 1863, the congregation celebrated Lincoln's Emancipation Proclamation in their own building as free men and women.

Initially the church had only one story, but by 1880 the congregation had grown so large that a second floor was added, transforming the modest building into a two-story structure with an auditorium. The church was partially destroyed by a fire in 1917, but the congregants, determined to remain in their original location, began to construct a new church around the building's 1880 shell. In 1968, a four-story office and educational wing was added, designed by Howard F. Sims and Harold F. Varner, Detroit's major black architectural firm.

Second Baptist
Church,
Detroit, Michigan

Holy Ascension of Christ Orthodox Church

810 Austin Avenue, Albion

ARCHITECT / BUILDER:
O. J. Teller Construction Company
CONSTRUCTION / DEDICATION DATE:
1916

THE BEGINNING OF ALBION'S Orthodox community dates to the recruitment of six Russian immigrants in New York City to work in the town's iron foundry. In an example of chain migration, by 1915 there were 600 immigrants from eastern Europe living in Albion, most Orthodox Christians. At first a visiting priest would come once a month from Detroit to conduct Orthodox services, but in 1915 permission was granted for the congregants to build their own church. The cornerstone was laid in April 1916 and the church was consecrated on Thanksgiving Day the same year.

The church, located near the iron foundry where most of its parishioners worked, is supposedly modeled after the destroyed Saints Peter and Paul Orthodox church in Detroit. According to its members, its style is northern Russian in that it displays less Byzantine influence than churches built in southern Russia. To the observer, however, its white clapboard exterior and Gothic pointed arched windows do not differ greatly from other Gothic Revival churches being built at this time throughout the Midwest. What does differentiate it is its interior where the traditional iconostasis hung with icons separates the altar from the rest of the sanctuary. The church's original iconostasis, destroyed by a fire in 1961 that started in the altar, has been replaced.

Holy Ascension
of Christ
Orthodox Church,
Albion, Michigan

Third Reformed Church of Holland

110 West Twelfth Street, Holland

ARCHITECT / BUILDER:
John R. Kleyn

CONSTRUCTION / DEDICATION DATE:
1873-1874

THE CITY OF HOLLAND was intended to replicate communities in the Netherlands, a country many of its residents had fled because of religious persecution. The settlers arriving with Reverend Albertus Van Raalte established the First Reformed Church. As the community grew, a second Reformed congregation was founded. By the mid-1860s, continued Dutch immigration into the area required yet another congregation, the Third Reformed Church, organized in 1867. One year later the congregation dedicated its new building, only to see it destroyed in a fire on October 8, 1871, that destroyed much of Holland. A second fire destroyed the partially reconstructed building in 1873, but by 1874, the congregation had again rebuilt its church, which was dedicated on November 25, 1874.

The church was designed by John R. Kleyn, a carpenter born in the Netherlands who learned his craft as an architect by studying about it in books. Recently restored to its original appearance, the building has a balloon frame covered with vertical board and batten with buttresses supporting each of the side walls. Its corner tower crowned with a spire rises to a height of 125 feet. On the interior, the "audience room," which seats 700 people, has been returned to its original color scheme of gold walls, walnut wood trim, and dark red, gold, and blue trim colors.

Third Reformed
Church of Holland,
Holland, Michigan

123

Illinois

W HEN THE FRENCH MISSIONARY and explorer Father Jacques Marquette entered the territory that became Illinois, he called it "God's meadow" and claimed it for France. A mission established in 1699 in what is now St. Clair County continued operating even after the territory was transferred to the British in 1763. Holy Family Church, built circa 1790 to replace the mission's earlier church, is considered the oldest religious structure still standing in the Mississippi Valley.

Colonists from New England and the Middle Atlantic regions recognizing the agricultural potential of "God's Meadow" began to arrive, seeking rich farmland and establishing market towns. By 1818, the year Illinois became a state, the town of Cairo was poised to become a major commercial center–a potential it never realized, but one that was to become a reality for another town, Chicago. Contributing to the state's growth was the completion of the Illinois and Michigan Canal in 1848, built primarily by Irish laborers who arrived in Sag Valley in the 1830s to work on the canal. Being Roman Catholic, while their bosses were mainly Protestant, the Irish initially had to worship in a converted cabin until they literally built their own church, St. James at the Sag, completed in 1859, which is the second oldest Catholic church in Cook County.

Illinois' farmlands and industries were a magnet for immigrants; soon a vast spectrum of people were living within its borders, endowing the state with a reputation for "pluralism, dissonance, complexity, and diversity . . ."[3] all made visible in its numerous religious institutions; space allows for only a few to be cited here.

New Englanders brought various Protestant denominations westward with them, including Unitarianism. A Unitarian fellowship was organized in Chicago in 1836 and a modest building, the Old Unitarian Church, was built in Geneva in 1842. Paid for in part by contributions from Unitarians in Massachusetts, it is considered the oldest Unitarian church building west of New York.

Also arriving with New Englanders were their preferences in religious architecture: the fashionable Gothic Revival style popularized by Richard Upjohn in his book, *Rural Architecture* (1852), and preferred by Episcopalians, and the American Church Plan, popularized by buildings designed by architects such as Asher Benjamin and based on James Gibbs's famed London church, St. Martin-in-the-Fields. The Pioneer Gothic Church in Dwight, built by a Presbyterian congregation in 1857, is one of the state's first Gothic Revival churches, whereas the **Benjamin Godfrey Memorial Chapel** in Godfrey, constructed in

1854, is considered one of the most authentic copies of New England church architecture outside of the northeastern United States.

Mormons under the leadership of Joseph Smith, Jr., hoped to find sanctuary in Illinois, but once again tragedy struck and they were forced to flee, but not before a split occurred within the once-cohesive group. Joseph Smith, Jr., was murdered in Carthage, Illinois, in 1844. A break-away group organized by followers of his son formed its own church in Plano, Illinois, the Reorganized Church of Jesus Christ of Latter-day Saints. Plano has a small stone building, begun in 1868, that served as the group's central house of worship until 1881.

Lutherans from Austria disembarking at the Port of New Orleans in 1852 traveled up the Mississippi to southern Illinois where they settled in a valley they named Kornthal, "valley of grain," and built the **Kornthal Church**, completed in 1860. The church is all that remains of what was once a thriving German-speaking culture in southern Illinois.

Danish Lutherans founded their first congregation in America in 1869 in Sheffield. St. Peter's Lutheran Church, a Gothic Revival building constructed in 1880 and modified only slightly since then, is the second Danish Lutheran church built in the United States. The first, in Michigan, has since been demolished.

A Swedish Lutheran church in Andover was founded by a pastor who left Sweden in 1849 and settled in Illinois. In 1851 he built the Jenny Lind Chapel, named after the famous singer known as the "Swedish songbird." Built in the popular Greek Revival style, the chapel is considered the cradle of Swedish-American Lutheranism and the "mother" of the Augustana Lutheran Church, now part of the Evangelical Lutheran Church in America (ELCA).

Contrary to the stereotype, not all Scandinavian immigrants were Lutheran; some were religious dissenters fleeing persecution by their state church. Included were Janssonists, followers of Erik Jansson, a preacher claiming to be a prophet, who established the famed Swedish Bishop Hill community. The community's first permanent building, the **Old Colony Church**, was erected in 1848. Bishop Hill Colony was to have an enormous impact

Holy Cross Lithuanian Roman Catholic Church and St. Joseph's Roman Catholic Church, Chicago, Illinois

on the development of Swedish settlements in Minnesota, Nebraska, Kansas, and as far west as Washington.

Chicago's famed ethnic neighborhoods have undergone dramatic transformations, but the places of worship that have survived the wrecking ball remain as bastions of faith and refuge. It is because of these historic buildings that Chicago is known as a city of churches, and one must add, synagogues, temples, and mosques. An entire book has been written about these buildings, but only a few of these structures can be highlighted here.

Following the drainage of the swamps around Chicago and the completion of a series of transportation systems in the 1850s, including canals and railroads, the city began to experience a population explosion. But in 1871 a devastating fire quickly destroyed over one-third of Chicago, nearly 18,000 buildings. But the city with the motto "I Will" bounced back, and soon became a national hub of transportation, manufacturing, commerce, and the arts.

At the time of the fire Chicago was already home to a variety of religious institutions, many of them Roman Catholic serving the city's burgeoning Irish population. Two of these churches survived the fire, St. Patrick Roman Catholic Church, an early example of the Romanesque style in the Midwest built between 1852 and 1856, and **Holy Family Roman Catholic Church**, begun in 1857. Over the years, Italian, Slavic, Mexican, and African-American people have come to worship in these two historic buildings.

Towers piercing the sky in Chicago's "Back of the Yards" neighborhood belong to **Holy Cross Lithuanian Catholic Church** and **St. Joseph's Polish Roman Catholic Church**. Both structures were built in the years prior to the 1918 passage of Canon Law (see p. 73) to serve the religious needs of immigrants working in the stockyards. Today the neighborhood is nearly all Spanish-speaking.

African-Americans, former slaves active in the abolition movement, organized the city's first black congregation in 1844. In 1891, the congregation built Quinn Chapel of the African Methodist Episcopal Church, a stone Romanesque/Gothic structure that continues to serve its South-side community.

The unique design for **Kehilath Anshe Ma'ariv Synagogue**, now Pilgrim Baptist Church, built in 1890–1891, was by Dankmar Adler of the famed Chicago firm of Adler and Sullivan. The congregation, the oldest in the Midwest, was founded in 1847 by Adler's father-in-law.

Louis Sullivan, Adler's partner and mentor of Frank Lloyd Wright, designed Holy Trinity Orthodox Cathedral, constructed in 1903. Because of the traditional conservatism of Orthodox church architecture, it is the only building designed by Sullivan that is derived from a historic building type.

Sullivan's student, Frank Lloyd Wright, went on to design **Unity Temple**, a church that completely broke with tradition; it was erected in Oak Park in 1906–1907. The temple is distinguished for many reasons beyond its precedent-setting design; for one, it is the first monumental building constructed of reinforced concrete.

Diversity continues to characterize Chicago and its environs. Wilmette is home to the monumental Bahai'i Temple, begun in 1932; an authentic Japanese temple, the Midwest Buddhist Temple, was erected in Chicago's Old Town Triangle District in 1971; and in 1972 a Greek Orthodox Church was transformed into the Elijah Muhammad Mosque #2.

Benjamin Godfrey Memorial Chapel

Illinois Route 67, Godfrey

ARCHITECT / BUILDER:
Not available

CONSTRUCTION / DEDICATION DATE:
1854

THE ONE-STORY WHITE FRAME CHAPEL, originally known as the Church of Christ at Monticello, is significant not only for its Greek Revival style, but also for its unique history. It was organized by Presbyterians, Dutch Reformed, and Congregationalists as a nondenominational church. The chapel was used by townsfolk and women attending the Monticello Female Seminary, founded in 1835 by Captain Benjamin Godfrey, a retired Cape Cod fisherman.

Godfrey's philosophy, "when you educate a woman you educate a family," was unique for its time. The seminary graduated its first class in 1838, and until its final commencement in 1971 educated thousands of women from all over the United States. The chapel was a religious umbrella under which students, teachers, and community members of varying faiths living in what was a sparsely populated area of the country could come together to worship.

The chapel has been renamed and moved across the street to within the Lewis and Clark Community College property.

**Benjamin Godfrey
Memorial Chapel,
Godfrey, Illinois**

Kornthal Church

(KORNTHAL UNION COUNTY MEMORIAL CHURCH;
Originally ST. PAULUS EVANGELISCH LUTHERISCHEN GEMEINDE)

Route Two, Jonesboro

ARCHITECT / BUILDER:
Charles Theodore Fettinger

CONSTRUCTION / DEDICATION DATE:
1860 (completed)

K ORNTHAL CHURCH EMBODIES the cultural influences that shaped its design. Designed by one of its members, Charles Fettinger, the church is built in the *Bet- saal* (House of Prayer) architectural style common in rural village churches of central Europe. It reflects restrictions imposed on Protestant church architecture in Roman Catholic Austria. Entrances could not be built along front streets; thus the church had two side entrances, one for women, the other for men. Protestant churches could not have bells or bell towers; thus this church was originally spireless. In 1889, perhaps after the congregation felt confident about its situation in the new world, a bell was purchased and an 85-foot bell tower and spire added. The tower also provides the structure with a central gable and entrance into the sanctuary.

The interior of the small church is furnished with examples of German woodcarving, including a three-step platform supporting a carved altar. Twelve steps, symbolic of the twelve apostles, on the side of the altar lead to the pulpit, which is capped with a beautifully carved wooden canopy.

Services ended in the church in 1949; in 1960 it was deeded to the State of Illinois and repairs were made. It now belongs to the Kornthal Union County Memorial Board.

Kornthal Church
(Kornthal Union County
Memorial Church),
Jonesboro, Illinois

Old Colony Church

Bishop Hill

ARCHITECT / BUILDER:
Not available
CONSTRUCTION / DEDICATION DATE:
1848

BISHOP HILL, A COMMUNAL SETTLEMENT established by the Jansonnists in 1846, consists of 21 structures built between 1846 and 1861. The colonists first worshipped in a cruciform log and canvas church before they erected Old Colony Church, the first permanent building in Bishop Hill.

The oak-timbered two-story building served as a church on the upper level and as living quarters on the first floor and basement, which was divided into 20 rooms. The second-floor church includes an altar, communion rail, and pews.

Following the assassination of its leader, Erik Jansson, the colony's focus became less on spiritual matters and more on commercial, becoming a major mercantile and industrial center for the developing Midwest. After 1861, land was divided among its original members and newly arriving Swedish immigrants were encouraged to settle in the colony, thereby replenishing it. After flourishing for a century, Bishop Hill went into a decline in the 1960s, only to be revived by the Bishop Hill Heritage Association, which has introduced interpretive programs and other projects that are preserving the site's unique ethnic heritage. The Illinois Historic Preservation Agency owns the Old Colony Church and maintains it as a historic site open to the public.

The Old
Colony Church,
Bishop Hill, Illinois

Holy Family Roman Catholic Church

1019 South May Street, Chicago

ARCHITECT / BUILDER:
John Mills Van Osdel, interior design
CONSTRUCTION / DEDICATION DATE:
Begun 1857

B ECAUSE OF THE DETERMINATION of its parishioners, this historic church will continue to serve its community. Holy Family, while having moments of glory, has been besieged by a series of trials, beginning with its construction in the midst of the depression of 1857, followed by the Civil War, the Chicago fire of 1871, and more recently, the threat of being razed and replaced by a smaller church. Built with pennies, nickels, and dimes donated by impoverished Irish immigrants living on the outskirts of the city, the parish flourished and grew, at one time serving 20,000 people. More recently its membership was down to 130 families; thus its survival was imperiled.

For years, Holy Family's steeple was the tallest structure in Chicago, a landmark in its bustling inner-city neighborhood. But as membership declined, the sanctuary was closed and in 1987 a decision was made to demolish the building. The community protested and in response the parish, the Jesuit owners of the property, and a long list of community leaders formed the Holy Family Preservation Society, a private not-for-profit organization with no religious purpose other than raising funds to preserve the building. Over $3.2 million has been raised, including funds from sources that cannot grant monies to religious bodies. Beautifully restored, this historic structure, a splendid example of Victorian Gothic architecture, continues to serve its community, now consisting of ethnic groups from Mexico and Puerto Rico and African-Americans.

**Holy Family Roman
Catholic Church,
Chicago, Illinois**

Pilgrim Baptist Church

(ORIGINALLY KEHILATH ANSHE MA'ARIV SYNAGOGUE)

3301 South Indiana Avenue, Chicago

ARCHITECT / BUILDER:
Dankmar Adler

CONSTRUCTION / DEDICATION DATE:
1890-1891

ADLER WAS A PARTNER with Louis Sullivan when this synagogue was built, but the design of the building is attributed solely to Adler; Sullivan's contribution was the ornament.

This building represents a dramatic break with tradition in that it borrows little from historic synagogue architecture, or from the currently popular Moorish style exemplified by the Isaac Wise Temple in Cincinnati. Rather, its use of rusticated stone and the large, recessed tunnel-arch at the entrance reflect the influence of Henry Hobson Richardson, the architect of Trinity Church in Boston who developed a version of the Romanesque Revival style that now bears his name–Richardsonian Romanesque.

Perhaps as important as the innovative style used for the exterior of the synagogue is the design of its interior, where a great parabolic vault formed by metal girders reveals Adler's engineering skills. The building is also notable for its acoustical properties, once again the result of Adler's engineering abilities, a skill that brought him considerable fame.

Changes were made to the building when it was transformed into a Baptist church, including the opening of the semi-dome on the east wall for a baptistry and a choir stand covering the pulpit. The building is well maintained and in other respects stands as designed by Adler and decorated by Sullivan.

Kehilath Anshe
Ma'ariv Synagogue
(now Pilgrim
Baptist Church),
Chicago, Illinois

Unity Temple

Lake Street and Kenilworth Avenue, Oak Park

ARCHITECT / BUILDER:
Frank Lloyd Wright
CONSTRUCTION / DEDICATION DATE:
1906-1907

MORE HAS BEEN WRITTEN about this building than any other place of worship in the United States, and rightly so. It remains a landmark in American religious architecture. What is less known by many people is where Wright received his motivation to build such an unusual church.

The American Unitarian Association published a pamphlet in 1903 that set aesthetic standards for Unitarian missions. The designs promoted the unity of secular ethics (the home) with religion (the church). Jenkin Lloyd Jones, Wright's uncle and head of the Western Unitarians, declared there would be no "Gothic pretentiousness" for it was both costly and promoted the sense of individual insignificance; rather, he argued, churches should express Unitarian ideals and be built to human scale. Wright took his uncle's words to heart when he was given the commission to design a church for his own congregation.

Built of reinforced concrete, the function of the building is stated in the inscription above the main entrance: "For the worship of God and the service of man." Using the geometry of the cube and square, Wright created three spaces that are based on Unitarian ideals and the new architectural philosophy that form must fit the function. The two main spaces consisting of the dominating cubical temple or auditorium at the north and the lower, rectangular social hall at the south, are linked by a still lower space, the entrance hall. The unity and harmony of the whole more than fulfill his uncle's expectations..

Unity Temple,
Oak Park, Illinois

Wisconsin

WISCONSIN IS OFTEN identified with beer, cheese, and *gemültlichkeit*, not surprising in a state that by 1860 was home to over 124,000 German-speaking immigrants. Many were "forty-eighters," so called from the failed revolutionary movements against German monarchies of 1848. The economic boom that followed their arrival contributed to Wisconsin entering the Union in 1848.

Germans were not the first Europeans to reach Wisconsin. French explorers led by Jean Nicolet were the first to come ashore near Green Bay in 1634. They were quickly followed by French fur traders and missionaries whose outposts have disappeared, but whose presence remains visible in the lumber town of Ocanto, one of the state's oldest communities, and home to two early Roman Catholic parishes, St. Peter's and St. Joseph. The first parish, organized in 1857, built a small wooden church. It was replaced in 1899 by the present St. Peter's Church, built in a style reminiscent of late French Romanesque churches.

Oconto is also home to the first Christian Science church building. The First Church of Christ, Scientist was organized in Oconto in 1886 and its small Gothic Revival church was dedicated in 1887, seven years before the Mother Church in Boston was completed.

The completion of the Erie Canal provided settlers with easy and cheap access into Wisconsin. What attracted them was cheap land and the discovery of lead and zinc in the state's unglaciated southwest region. Cornish, Welsh, English, and Irish immigrants working in the mines began establishing communities such as the hamlet of Hyde's Mills, described by one resident in 1861 as a "moral waste" in need of a church. The following year a Welsh Methodist minister organized a congregation and a church was built. Dedicated in 1862, **Hyde Chapel (Union Congregational Church)**, an early example of the Greek Revival style in Wisconsin, was jointly used by English and Welsh; thus its name.

Unity Chapel was built in 1886 by religious nonconformists–the Lloyd Jones family, Welsh Unitarians who homesteaded near the present town of Spring Green in the 1840s. The chapel was designed by a Chicago architect, Joseph Lyman Silsbee, with assistance from one of Lloyd Jones's grandsons, Frank Lloyd Wright. The chapel remains essentially unchanged and continues to be used during the summer by the Taliesin group. Unity Chapel represents Wright's earliest work; the **Unitarian Meeting House** in Madison, completed in 1951, is one of his last. Together they illustrate the creative journey taken over the span of three-quarters of a century by one of the nation's most influential architects.

Entrepreneurs from eastern states began acquiring Wisconsin's rich farmland and pristine pine forests, establishing towns and building churches that often resembled those they left behind. White clapboard meetinghouses with octagonal cupolas and spires were built, such as First Baptist Church in Merton, erected in 1845. Gothic Revival structures influenced by Upjohn's *Rural Architecture* began to dot the countryside. One of the finest remaining examples is St. John Chrysostom Episcopal Church in Delafield, built in 1851. Often these first buildings were replaced by more monumental structures, reflecting the increasing prosperity of its members. One example is **Christ Church Cathedral**, an impressive stone Gothic Revival church designed by the famed Minneapolis architecture firm of Purcell, Feick, and Elmslie, begun in 1909 in the thriving lumber town of Eau Claire.

The Yankee influence began to wane with the arrival of large numbers of German immigrants, most of whom chose to live in the eastern third of the state. Second to the Germans were Norwegians who settled mainly on farms where they contributed to the growth of Wisconsin's famous dairy industry. Wisconsin continued to attract nonconformists who were rebelling against state-operated churches in their homeland. Sauk City, for example, was settled by a small number of German humanists who were members of the Union of Free German Congregations (later renamed the Free Thought League of America). The Freie Gemeinde von Sauk County (The Freethinkers Hall), founded in 1868, is one of the largest and most enduring of these organizations. Although now affiliated with the Unitarian Fellowship, it remains a valuable resource in the history of German humanism in America.

Other Germans sought to retain their ties to their homeland, even if it involved much effort and expense, as was the case of the parishioners who had to pay for the building of **St. Anthony Roman Catholic Church** in Milwaukee. Rather than building their church of readily available and inexpensive brick, they chose to have it built of costly limestone because it was customary to build churches of stone in southern Germany, their homeland. Brick was a common building material in Milwaukee; in fact, the city was known as the "Cream City," for the cream-colored locally produced brick that was used for many of its buildings, such as those comprising the St. Francis of Assisi Monastery Complex.

The Milwaukee-Racine-Kenosha area also attracted immigrants from eastern and southern Europe who developed their own enclaves in the late 1880s. Poles were the largest group on Milwaukee's south side, where they built St. Josaphat Basilica, dedicated in 1901, that was elevated to a minor basilica 30 years later. An imposing Renaissance Revival structure, it was constructed of materials salvaged from the Chicago Post Office and Custom House.

As early as the 1830s, southern Wisconsin, and specifically Rock County, was a major Norwegian settlement in America. Arriving in 1839, the Norwegians named the area Luther Valley and modeled their parish after the state Lutheran Church in Norway. The **West Luther Valley Lutheran Church**, built in 1871, is the oldest sanctuary serving the Norwegians of Rock County.

Yiddish-speaking Jewish immigrants settled in Wisconsin's urban areas and small towns. As elsewhere in the nation, many began as peddlers who then opened stores on the main streets of developing towns. One of those communities was Stevens Point, where a group of Jewish immigrants formed a congregation and built Beth Israel, a white clapboard Gothic Revival synagogue minus a steeple, in 1905. This modest building, now used as a community center, reflects the impact of a popular church style on the place of worship of a non-Christian people.

Union Congregational Church

(HYDE CHAPEL, MILL CREEK CHURCH)

County Highway T approximately 1 mile south of County Highway H, Iowa County

ARCHITECT / BUILDER:
Not available

CONSTRUCTION / DEDICATION DATE:
1862

LEAD AND ZINC MINES in the southwest region of Wisconsin attracted early settlers, including many from the British Isles. The tiny settlement of Hydes Mill is named for William Hyde, who built a grist mill in 1856 near the present location of the chapel. A Welsh Methodist minister, Reverend David Jones, held the first services in the area in 1861. At the church's dedication, one of its congregants declared that "no place needed a church and preaching more than did Mill Creek Valley."

The church's Greek Revival style, popular in southern and eastern states in the first decades of the nineteenth century, was the first national style to have a widespread impact on Wisconsin buildings. It probably entered the state in the memories of settlers or in builders' handbooks. Because of its early settlement, Iowa County contains a number of fine examples of Greek Revival buildings. This chapel is considered a representative example of a modest rural vernacular interpretation of the style. The chapel remains essentially intact and since 1966 has been preserved and maintained by the Hyde Community Association.

Hyde Chapel,
Union
Congregational
Church,
Hydes Mill,
Wisconsin

First Unitarian Meeting House

900 University Bay Drive, Madison (Shorewood Hills)

ARCHITECT / BUILDER:
Frank Lloyd Wright
CONSTRUCTION / DEDICATION DATE:
1949-1951

WRIGHT'S FATHER WAS SECRETARY of the Shorewood Hills Unitarian Society when it was organized in 1879, and Wright renewed his affiliation in 1938, so he had a personal investment in the church he was commissioned to design for the Society in 1946. To offset construction costs, Wright accepted only a modest fee for his services, delivered two public lectures, and offered the services of his apprentices. Members contributed by hauling tons of stone from a nearby quarry.

The church, situated on a knoll overlooking Lake Mendota and what was once rural university farmland, is built of local limestone and oak with large expanses of glass. From the exterior, the building's rising green copper roof, romantically described by some as hands held together in prayer, provides an impressive appearance of height without a steeple. Inside the roof line of the auditorium sweeps upward behind the pulpit to a light-filled prow of wood and glass. At the rear of the auditorium is the Hearth Room that features a low ceiling and massive fireplace. Originally it was partitioned from the auditorium by a richly colored drapery, handwoven by women of the parish from a sample woven by Mrs. Wright. Although additions were made in 1964 and 1990 by Taliesin Associated Architects, the basic integrity of the building remains unchanged. In 1960, the American Institute of Architects designated it one of 17 buildings to be retained as an example of Wright's contribution to American culture.

First Unitarian
Society
Meeting House,
Shorewood Hills,
Wisconsin

Christ Church Cathedral

510 South Farwell Street, Eau Claire

ARCHITECT / BUILDER:
Purcell, Feick, and Elmslie, Minneapolis
CONSTRUCTION / DEDICATION DATE:
1909-1910; 1915-1916

T HE CONGREGATION WAS FORMED in the mid-nineteenth century when Eau Claire was entering its prosperous lumber era. A frame church, built in 1875–1877, served until 1908 when a decision was made to build a larger building to be designed by the firm of Purcell, Feick, and Elmslie of Minneapolis, one of the firm's earliest commissions. Purcell and Feick were primarily responsible for the chancel and parish house.

Initially the plan was to construct a parish house and a chancel to be attached to the original frame church. However, in 1915 the frame church was dismantled and the nave was constructed using the firm's design. Purcell, commenting on the building's Gothic design, noted that he tried "to produce in myself the mental attitude with which a master mason architect of 1150 would have come to such a problem." The Bedford stone church reflects his familiarity with English Gothic architecture, particularly notable in the parish house that is reported to be patterned after Benham Abbey in Norfolkshire, England. The cathedral's stained glass windows executed in England are described as the "glory of Christ Church." One was designed by Elmslie. The success of this building led to Purcell and Elmslie receiving other commissions in Eau Claire, including the Community House for the first Congregational Church of Christ, completed in 1914, at the height of the firm's success.

Christ Church was designated a Cathedral in 1931. A chapel, erected in 1935 and added at the southwest corner of the building, was designed by the Chicago firm, Armstrong, Furst & Tilton, in a style compatible with the rest of the church.

Christ Church
Cathedral,
Eau Claire,
Wisconsin

St. Anthony Roman Catholic Church

1711 South Ninth Street, Milwaukee

ARCHITECT / BUILDER:
Fridolin Heer

CONSTRUCTION / DEDICATION DATE:
1877-1886

S T. ANTHONY, THE SECOND PARISH established on the south side of Milwaukee by German immigrants, was founded in 1872 to accommodate the parishioners who were crowding into nearby Holy Trinity Church. Many of the parishioners came from the predominantly Catholic southern area of Germany, where it was customary to build churches of stone. Their desire to replicate the churches of their homeland proved time-consuming and costly; as a result it took nearly 10 years to raise funds and to complete the present building.

Fridolin Heer, the architect, faithfully incorporated into the new church many features that were part of the German tradition. These include the large bell tower centered on the façade, the openwork design used on the belfry and spire, and the beautifully executed rib vaulting and wooden altars and pulpit in the interior.

St. Anthony Roman Catholic Church, Milwaukee, Wisconsin

West Luther Valley Lutheran Church

(BETHANY CHURCH)

West Church Road, Brodhead

ARCHITECT / BUILDER:
Anders Bjornstad, builder
CONSTRUCTION / DEDICATION DATE:
1871-1872

THE CHURCH IS A NEAT VERNACULAR clapboard building surmounted by a square tower and belfry. It was one of two churches built in 1871 to replace earlier buildings that served Norwegians living in Luther Valley. The other, East Luther Valley Church, was destroyed by fire in 1951 and replaced by a third building. West Luther Valley Church is significant both for its association with an influential Norwegian clergyman and for its furnishings.

Reverend Claus Lauritz Clausen (1820–1892) came to Wisconsin in 1843 from what is today Denmark. He was the second Norwegian to be ordained a minister in the United States. He visited Luther Valley in 1844 and two years later accepted a call to be the congregation's first pastor. He pledged half his salary toward the erection of a small stone church that opened in 1847. It was furnished with an altar and reredos, pews, baptismal font, and pulpit that were made by members. All these furnishings were later moved to the present church, where they constitute one of the finest collections of locally made Norwegian folk art in Wisconsin. Clausen went on to become editor of the Norwegian Press Association, which published one of the leading Norwegian-language papers in the United States. He was also closely connected with the organization of the Norwegian Evangelical Lutheran Church in America that occurred following meetings held in East Luther Valley Church in 1851 and 1853.

West Luther Valley
Lutheran Church
(Bethany Church),
Brodhead,
Wisconsin

NOTES

1. Wilbur Zelinsky, *The Cultural Geography of the United States* (Englewood Cliffs, NJ: Prentice-Hall, 1973), 128.

2. James H. Madison, ed. *Heartland* (Bloomington: Indiana University Press, 1988), 3 ff.

3. Cullom Davis, "Illinois: Crossroads and Cross Section" in *Heartland*, ed. by James H. Madison (Bloomington: Indiana University Press, 1988),129.

5

West North Central Region

THIS REGION SUFFERS FROM an identity crisis similar to its eastern neighbor, a reflection of "outsiders' " uncertainty regarding its location and regional characteristics. Described variously as the Middle West, the Upper Midwest, the Northern Heartland, the Northwest, and the Great Plains, it appears the region's most accurate identity is one given to it by a frustrated historian–"muddled." The confusion can be explained in part by the fact that much of what is known about the region comes from popular culture–Mark Twain's stories about life on the Mississippi River; Willa Cather's descriptions of farm and town conflicts in Nebraska; images of Dorothy and Toto blown away by a tornado in Kansas; and Garrison Keillor's tales about Minnesota's long-suffering Scandinavian Lutheran farmers. All these images contribute to a romanticized view of the region as symbolic of "American Pastoralism," a place where "real" American values–hearth, home, and family–are observed. In reality the region is far more complex–in its topography, geography, climate, economy, and culture.

Differences in geography and topography are demonstrable on maps, and the weather and economy can be chartered. Culture, however, is more difficult to illustrate graphically and therefore is easily misunderstood. This "muddled" region is America's salad bowl, having been settled by people representing a vast variety of cultures–its image of homogeneity is quickly dispelled when one examines its settlement patterns.

THIS PAGE:

First Baptist Church, Nicodemus, Kansas, 1943

Visited initially by the ubiquitous French explorers and fur traders, the region's first permanent white settlements were established in the opening decades of the nineteenth century by colonists moving directly westward with the frontier. Thus, Minnesota, North Dakota, and parts of Iowa attracted settlers from New England and Upstate New York; Missouri, from the East South Central Region; and Kansas and Nebraska, as "border" states, from the Northeast and South. The passage of the first homestead law in 1862 allowing anyone over the age of 21 to acquire a tract of federal public land was an incentive not only for eastern farmers and entrepreneurs, but for immigrants, primarily Germans and Scandinavians, who were then flowing into the country in increasing numbers.

The fertile, well-watered soil of Iowa, southern Minnesota, Missouri, and western Nebraska and Kansas was most suitable for agriculture. The Great Plains area, however, comprising most of Nebraska, Kansas, and South and North Dakota, was described by early travelers from the East as an arid, treeless desert, wholly unfit for cultivation or inhabitation. This flat expanse of wind-blown prairie was not the promised land, but an ocean of

PRECEDING PAGE:

St. Martin's Roman Catholic Church, Clay County, Nebraska

143

grass that was crossed over by countless prairie schooners heading west along the famed Oregon Trail to rich farmland opening up along the Pacific coast. But the region became more attractive to settlers because of several important innovations introduced in the years following the Civil War that made farming easier. Perhaps the most important were those that made possible the procurement of much-needed water–the windmill, well-drilling, and the introduction of irrigation. Mennonites from the Ukraine were responsible for the introduction of hard winter wheat adapted to dry growing conditions that transformed the region into the nation's bread basket.

Agriculture, however, was not the region's only attraction. Minnesota's white pine forests harvested by Scandinavian lumberjacks for entrepreneurs from New England built the cities of St. Louis and Chicago. When the forests were gone, iron ore was exposed. Mined by recently arrived immigrants from eastern and southern Europe, the state quickly became the principal supplier of ore for eastern blast furnaces. In Iowa, German farmers established the Amana Colonies, but by the 1930s the colony had developed a reputation for its refrigeration technology and began manufacturing household appliances.

The myth that this region is an agrarian heartland embodying an abstraction called American ideals simplifies its character. What gives the nation's heartland its soul and continued vitality are the contributions made by the many and varied people who chose to accept its challenges of climate, topography, and isolation to carve out for themselves a new life.

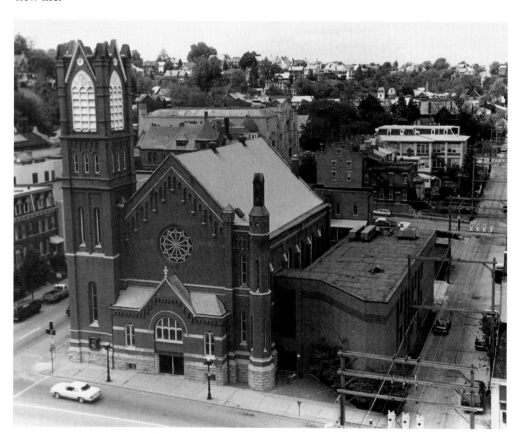

First
Congregational
Church,
Dubuque, Iowa

Minnesota

IN 1680, WHILE TRAVELING ALONG the Mississippi River, the French explorer and missionary Father Louis Hennepin sighted and named the Falls of St. Anthony, that nearly 200 years later became the source of power for Minneapolis's milling industry. But the colonization of the territory did not begin in earnest until the 1850s when Native Americans reluctantly agreed to sign treaties that forced them off their land.

Following the establishment of the Minnesota Territory in 1849, large numbers of New Englanders and "Yorkers" began arriving: lumbermen leaving behind the depleted eastern forests to begin harvesting the state's sought-after white pine, or land speculators who set up town sites and began advertising for settlers. Most who answered their call were immigrants, primarily German and Scandinavian, who quickly outnumbered the New Englanders, but the Yankees had already left their mark on many of the state's major institutions.

Easterners were prominent in territorial politics, and were responsible for St. Paul being named the capital when Minnesota was granted statehood in 1858. Six years earlier these same people supported the organization of the city's first Presbyterian church that received its primary funding from Central Presbyterian Church in Philadelphia–hence its name, **Central Presbyterian Church.**

Other Yankees settled in the timber-rich St. Croix River Valley that for a brief period was the northern white pine center of the world. There they built villages closely resembling the ones they left behind. One, Taylors Falls, has a neighborhood known as Angel's Hill because of the houses clustered around the **First Methodist Church**, a wood frame structure considered one of the finest examples of Greek Revival architecture in the state.

Episcopalians settling in Northfield, a small market center and college town south of Minneapolis, constructed All Saints Episcopal Church in 1866. It is an example of the small Gothic Revival churches constructed in the state under the guidance of Episcopal Bishop Henry Whipple, who had in his possession a copy of Richard Upjohn's 1852 book, *Rural Architecture.*

Beginning in the 1850s the state began to receive a large number of Roman Catholic immigrants, mainly from Ireland and German-speaking states of central Europe. They were encouraged by the efforts of several Catholic immigration societies. Evidence of their numbers and influence can be seen by the positioning of St. Paul's Cathedral on a prominent hillside, overlooking not only the city, but also the state capitol. Erected at great expense between 1906 and 1915 and designed by the well-known French architect Emmanuel Masqueray, who had gained fame as the architect of the St. Louis World Fair in 1904, it was built at the behest of Archbishop John Ireland, one of the primary forces behind Catholic immigration to the United States. Ireland had also commissioned Masqueray to design the Basilica of St. Mary (1907-1925) in Minneapolis as a means of establishing a visible Catholic presence in a city that was overwhelmingly Protestant.

Ireland was not the first Catholic clergy to try to make Minnesota a haven for Catholics. Father Francis X. Pierz, a missionary to Indians in central Minnesota, published a series of articles in 1851 in German Catholic newspapers advocating Catholic settlement in central Minnesota. Large numbers of immigrants, mainly German, but also Slovenian and Polish, responded. Over 20 parishes were formed in what is now Stearns County, each centered on a church-oriented hamlet. As the farmers prospered, the small frame churches were replaced by more substantial and permanent buildings of brick or stone such as St. Mary's Help of Christians, a Gothic Revival stone structure built in 1873. Stearns County retains its German character and is still home to one of the largest rural Catholic populations in Anglo-America.

Another large enclave of Germans can be found in Dakota County located south of the Twin Cities where, in a town named New Trier, you will find the small, elegant German Baroque **Church of Saint Mary**, built in 1909, which would look equally at home in the hills of Bavaria.

Thanks to the growth of the milling industry, the area around St. Anthony Falls soon surpassed St. Paul in size and economy. Renamed Minneapolis, the city retained its Yankee character well into the twentieth century, even following the arrival of large numbers of Scandinavians. Wesley Methodist Church, a large Richardsonian Romanesque Akron plan church designed by Warren H. Hayes and dedicated in 1890, was founded by wealthy Yankee businessmen including the parents of J. Paul Getty. Its active congregation remains dedicated to the needs of its members, many of whom live in its aging urban neighborhood.

Thanks to Garrison Keillor's popular radio show and books, Minnesota has a reputation of being populated by long-suffering Scandinavian Lutherans. But not all Scandinavians are Lutheran. Minnesota has its share of dissenters, including the founders of Nora Free Church, a liberal Norwegian Unitarian congregation, built in 1883 in Brown County. The congregation meets in a white clapboard Gothic Revival church typical of those built by other Scandinavian congregations, such as the **Cross of Christ Lutheran Church** in Goodhue County, a Swedish congregation that was organized in 1873 by the Reverend Eric Norelius, considered the father of the Swedish Lutheran Church in Minnesota.

Northeastern Minnesota, known as the Iron Range, has an ethnic flavor far different from the rest of the state, as a result of the eastern and southern Europeans who arrived to work in the iron mines that opened in the last decade of the nineteenth century. The mining companies had two compelling reasons for supporting the construction of places of worship for the various ethnic and religious groups laboring in their mines. One was to establish a moral order, as many of the miners were bachelors, bereft of families. The other was to encourage separateness. The mining companies feared that if the miners joined together, under whatever pretenses, they would be empowered to strike for higher wages and better working conditions. Saints Peter and Paul Ukrainian Catholic Church was built in 1914 for one of the last ethnic groups to settle on the Range. Among the first to arrive were Jewish merchants who began opening shops on the Main Streets of the expanding mining towns. The Jewish community in Virginia, the city considered the Range's "capital," built what was described in the local newspaper at the time of its construction in 1908 as "the Range's finest church [sic]." After serving its community for nearly 90 years, **B'nai Abraham Synagogue**'s future is uncertain.

Scattered groups of eastern Europeans settled elsewhere in the state, including a group of Orthodox Christians recruited by the railroad to settle on cutover land it owned in north central Minnesota. There they erected **St. Mary's Russian Orthodox Church** in 1897, a small white Gothic Revival building crowned with a tin onion dome, a rare sight on the edge of a cornfield in Minnesota.

African-Americans fleeing slavery arrived in the state in the midst of the Civil War. Settling in St. Paul they organized several congregations, including Pilgrim Baptist Church, founded in 1866. The construction of the congregation's present church, its third, was completed in 1928.

Central Presbyterian Church

500 Cedar Street, St. Paul

ARCHITECT / BUILDER:
Warren H. Hayes

CONSTRUCTION / DEDICATION DATE:
1889 (cornerstone)

FOUNDED IN 1852, the congregation initially met in a variety of places, including the First Baptist Church and the Territory's Supreme Court Room. The congregation's first church, built in 1854, was partially destroyed by a fire in the late 1880s and replaced on the same site by the present building.

The Romanesque Revival church built of Lake Superior brownstone was designed by

Warren H. Hayes, a well-known local architect responsible for the design of several other prominent churches in the Twin Cities, including Wesley Methodist in Minneapolis. Like Wesley, it uses the diagonal Akron Plan (see p. 101), then gaining in popularity for nonliturgical Protestant churches. Changes have been made to the building's interior over the years, including replacing with a solid wall the glass doors that opened vertically to permit an overflow section, known as the Lecture Room, to view the sanctuary. The sanctuary retains its original pulpit, main floor pews, and theater-style seating in the balcony.

Central Presbyterian Church continues to occupy its prominent site in the heart of downtown Saint Paul and is home to an active congregation.

**Central Presbyterian Church,
St. Paul, Minnesota**

First Methodist Church

Corner of Government and Basil Streets, Taylors Falls

ARCHITECT / BUILDER:
J. L. Bullard, carpenter-builder

CONSTRUCTION / DEDICATION DATE:
1861

THIS SMALL WHITE WOOD FRAME structure is typical of the small meeting-houses left behind by its New England born founders. Clapboarded on the sides and rear elevation, wider, flat horizontal boards are used on the front façade, giving the illusion of stone. They are interrupted by four pilasters, tapered so they are wider at the base than at the top, and two entries, possibly one for women and the other for men. Topping the structure is a small domed bell tower. Essentially unaltered since its construction, and beautifully maintained, the church is an example of the transfer of a popular style from the eastern seaboard into the nation's expanding heartland.

The houses of Angel's Hill, while displaying variety in detail, are almost all built of local white pine frame covered with white clapboard, highlighted by green or black painted sash and shutters. The church, while in harmony with its neighbors, dominates the district, not only physically, but also socially and spiritually. It was the focal point for the wealthy lumber barons who built their homes surrounding it.

**First Methodist
Church,
Taylors Falls,
Minnesota**

Church of St. Mary Roman Catholic Church

8433 239th Street, 3 miles east of Hampton on Highway 52, New Trier, Dakota County

ARCHITECT / BUILDER:
George J. Ries, architect

CONSTRUCTION / DEDICATION DATE:
Begun 1909

LOCATED IN WHAT IS DESCRIBED as the "most ethnically homogeneous population in the county and surrounding communities," the Church of St. Mary was founded by the first German Roman Catholic families that began to arrive in this area in the 1850s soon after it was opened up for white settlement. Religious services were first held in 1855 and the following year a parish was organized and a small log church built that was soon replaced by a frame church that seated about 200 people. As the parish prospered, a cornerstone for a larger and more elaborate limestone church was laid in 1864; it served the growing parish until plans were drawn for the present building.

Built prior to World War I when there was still pride in things German, the church, beautifully situated on a hill, was designed in a German Baroque Revival style by George J. Ries, an architect from St. Paul. Ries is also responsible for the design of St. Agnes Roman Catholic Church in St. Paul, a large, elaborate structure that is also clearly indebted to Bavarian prototypes. Incorporated into the new building from the 1864 church are its cornerstone and a statue of the Virgin and Child located in the arch window over the main entry. The church is beautifully maintained and remains an important indicator of the ethnic pride of Minnesota's German settlers.

Church of St. Mary
Roman Catholic
Church, New Trier,
Minnesota

The Cross of Christ Lutheran Church

Intersection of U.S. Route 61 and County 7, Goodhue County

ARCHITECT / BUILDER:
Charles E. Johnson
CONSTRUCTION / DEDICATION DATE:
1878

CROSS OF CHRIST IS TYPICAL of the white frame Gothic Revival churches built by Swedish settlers in southeastern Minnesota once their settlements had passed through their pioneer stage. Swedish immigrants arriving in the mid-nineteenth century often headed for agricultural settlements in Illinois (see Bishop Hill, p. 129), but as land became scarce in Illinois and available further north and west, many took the relatively short journey by steamboat to southern Minnesota. Among those who came was the Reverend Eric Norelius, who organized this church in 1873 in one of the most solidly Swedish districts in the state. Norelius is considered the father of the Swedish Lutheran Church in Minnesota and was the founder in 1862 of Gustavus Adolphus College, now located in St. Peter.

The church, located on its prominent site, remains essentially unchanged and continues to serve as its community's religious and cultural center, and as a visible reminder of the state's Swedish pioneers. In appearance it relates more to the Gothic Revival style being popularized in the United States than to the churches the immigrants left behind in the Old World.

Cross of Christ
Lutheran Church,
Welsh, Minnesota

B'nai Abraham Synagogue

328 South Fifth Street, Virginia

ARCHITECT / BUILDER:
Not available

CONSTRUCTION / DEDICATION DATE:
1908-1909

JEWISH IMMIGRANTS, mainly from eastern Europe, began settling on the Iron Range in the late 1890s, establishing stores to cater to the needs of the miners. Virginia was considered the Range's "Queen City," because of the relative wealth of its citizens and its position as the Range's market center. Its churches and synagogue are, indeed, among the finest built on the Range.

The Range was home to four Jewish synagogues; only this one survives. The synagogues in Hibbing and Eveleth were former churches, their steeples carefully removed and otherwise adapted to be used as synagogues. Chisholm's synagogue, based on people's recollections and photographs taken at the time of its demolition, was a white frame building, distinguished by its Star of David set into an oculus window on its façade. Virginia's structure is by far the finest of the four, and the most visible due to its corner site and its distinctive red brick Romanesque design. The building's nonfigurative stained glass windows display the usual Jewish symbols, plus several others that clearly have Masonic associations.

The building has undergone some unfortunate changes, including an unsightly wooden addition on the front and glass block windows on the lower level. The interior has been paneled with plywood, but retains its Ark and other ritual accoutrements. The congregation has diminished in number and the building's future is uncertain.

B'nai Abraham
Synagogue,
Virginia, Minnesota

St. Mary's Russian Orthodox Church

One mile south on county 21; four miles southwest of Bowlus,
Two Rivers Township, Morrison County

ARCHITECT / BUILDER:
Not available

CONSTRUCTION / DEDICATION DATE:
1897

I N A REMOTE CORNER of Morrison County on the edge of a cornfield there stands a small, white Gothic Revival church, distinguished from others that dot the countryside by its tin onion dome and Greek cross. It was founded by Russian Orthodox Christians who had immigrated to the area from central Europe, possibly Rusyns, although this is uncertain. At first they worshipped in a German Roman Catholic church, until the Soo Railroad offered them land upon which they could build a church. According to tradition, the beautiful crystal chandelier, unelectrified, that still hangs in the church was a gift of the Russian Czar. The interior of the church remains intact, including its iconostasis hung with icons, and behind its royal doors, the altar table and all necessary ritual objects. Although it is no longer used on a regular basis, rather primarily for funerals and burial in the nearby Orthodox cemetery, the building is being maintained by a Russian Orthodox congregation in Minneapolis. It remains an important monument attesting to the diversity of the state's settlers.

St. Mary's Russian
Orthodox Church,
Morrison County,
Minnesota

Iowa

W HAT IS GENERALLY KNOWN about Iowa comes from artists, writers, and, more recently, films. Grant Wood's paintings portray the state's rich farm lands, picturesque towns, and hard-working folks. Popular books and films have convinced many people that Iowa is, indeed, the pastoral "heart of America." Confirming this image is the state's presidential primary which attracts all serious candidates for the office. Ethnically Iowa is considered the most homogeneous of all the states in the region–primarily white, Anglo-Saxon, and Protestant. But upon closer inspection it becomes apparent that it is actually home to a wide range of ethnic and religious groups.

Iowa's first permanent settlement was established by Julien Dubuque, a French Canadian, in 1788 near the town that bears his name. His interest was in mining the area's lead deposits and fur trading, not agriculture. But it was rich farmland, not furs or lead, that made the area attractive following its opening to settlement in the 1830s. By the time Iowa was admitted into the Union in 1846, land speculators, entrepreneurs, and religious groups had already laid claim to much of its rich land.

Dubuque, described in the 1850s as one of the state's largest cities, is endowed with many fine buildings, including a number of churches built by New Englanders who by then had begun to displace the Roman Catholics who founded the city. With them came their Congregational faith and the denomination's newly published text, *A Book of Plans for Churches and Parsonages.* One example of the Romanesque Revival style advocated in the publication is the **First Congregational Church**, designed by local architect David Jones and built between 1857 and 1860. Together with the Gothic Revival **Saint Raphael's Roman Catholic Cathedral**, built at the same time, the churches illustrate the impact of mid-century Romanticism in a region then far removed from the nation's mainstream.

German and Austrian immigrants founded farming communities in eastern Iowa including New Vienna, where the French Gothic Revival St. Boniface Roman Catholic Church, built between 1884 and 1887, continues to dominate the surrounding countryside. Other German communities were founded farther to the west in Audubon and Shelby counties, including one of the largest, the Westphalia Colony named after the hometown of its founders, two brothers who were devout Roman Catholics. Their goal in the New World was to establish self-sufficient German communities centered around a church where their faith and traditions could be maintained. St. Boniface Roman

Catholic Church in Westphalia, begun in 1881, became the mother church for other parishes founded in the area.

Another well-known religious colony was established by the Amana Society, a German Christian utopian communitarian society known as the Community of True Inspiration. It was founded by immigrants from southwestern Germany who had settled near Buffalo, New York, in 1842, before migrating westward and purchasing 18,000 acres of land in Iowa County. Between 1855 and 1883, they built six villages centered around a communal meetinghouse, such as the one in Amana, a simple, unadorned worship space.

Perhaps the Quakers' best-known community in the state is at West Branch, the birthplace and grave site of President Herbert Hoover. The Friends Meeting House, built in 1857, where Hoover attended meetings as a boy, is similar to those in the Eastern Colonies built a century earlier.

Other ethnic groups in the state include Dutch near Pella, Norwegians in Decorah, where Luther College testifies to their presence, and Danes in Audubon County. Many of the Danish immigrants were religious dissenters who had left the state Lutheran Church. But even among those who chose to remain Lutheran there was dissension resulting in a split among the followers of the Danish bishop N.S.F. Grundtvig, known as Grundtvigians, and the more pietistic Lutherans who formed the Danish Evangelical Lutheran Church Society. Although the groups have since united, **Bethany Danish Evangelical Lutheran Church**, built in 1898, remains as a representation of this historic period in the Danish Lutheran Church in Iowa.

Southwest of Decorah is a small town known for its association with a famous Czech composer, Antonín Dvořák. Spillville, where Dvořák spent the summer of 1893, is a small Czech community on the Turkey River. As early as 1849, a mill and dam had been built on the river and in 1860, the town's Czech population built a handsome church, **Saint Wenceslaus Roman Catholic Church**, modeled after Saint Barbara's Church in Kutna-Hora, in the Czech Republic.

Des Moines, founded as a fort in 1843, and Cedar Rapids, located on a wide bend of the Cedar River, platted in 1841, are both well known for being in the forefront of city planning and architectural development. Each is home to many handsome places of worship, including two in Des Moines: the First Church of Christ Scientist, built in 1931, and Central Presbyterian Church, built in 1936, both considered exercises in modernizing Romanesque and Gothic architecture. In 1910, a competition was held in Cedar Rapids for a design for **Saint Paul's Methodist Episcopal Church**. Louis Sullivan won the competition, but the building as it now stands was based on compromise; while remaining an interesting and unique structure, it pales next to Sullivan's original plan.

Perhaps one of the most important, and certainly most unique, places of worship in Cedar Rapids is its **Islamic Center and Mosque** built in 1925 as a community center for Muslims from Syria; it was converted into a mosque nine years later. Although replaced in recent years by a new mosque, the original building, the oldest mosque in the United States, has been preserved as a symbol of one minority group's journey to Middle America and its effort to maintain and transmit its traditions and its faith.

St. Raphael's Roman Catholic Cathedral

231 Bluff Street, Dubuque

ARCHITECT / BUILDER:
John Mullany

CONSTRUCTION / DEDICATION DATE:
1857-1859; 1878, tower

T HE PARISH'S FIRST CHURCH, built in 1835, was a simple Greek Revival structure with a low pitched roof and round arched windows. The present Gothic Revival building, the third cathedral church with this name, is in a far different style, illustrating the changing taste in religious architecture taking place at the time of its construction. It was designed by an Irish architect, John Mullany, who was trained in the London office of the great English exponent for the revival of Gothic architecture, Augustus Welby Pugin. Stained glass windows imported from England were added in 1866 and interior walls are decorated with murals painted by an artist known only as Gregori.

The building's site, at the west end of a wide street, coupled with its 243-foot-high square central tower, added in 1878, make it a town landmark.

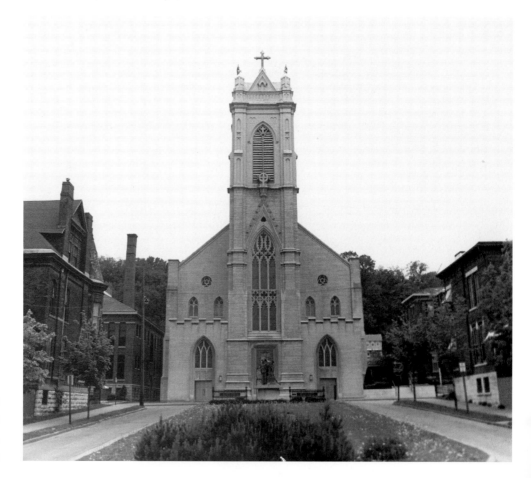

St. Raphael's
Roman Catholic
Cathedral,
Dubuque, Iowa

Bethany Danish Evangelical Lutheran Church

One and one half miles north of Highway 44 and one mile east of Highway 68,
vicinity of Kimballton, Audubon County

ARCHITECT / BUILDER:
Nils P. Hjuler, carpenter
CONSTRUCTION/DEDICATION DATE:
1898

THE CHURCH WAS ORGANIZED prior to the Danish Lutheran Church split into two synods in 1894. Following the split, some of its members left to join the Grundtvigians. Those who remained became affiliated with the newly formed United Danish Evangelical Lutheran Church, also known as the "United Church." The present building, constructed following the destruction of the congregation's first building by fire in 1898, is the only one of nine United churches in Shelby and Audubon counties to retain a substantial measure of its architectural integrity.

Much of the work on the one-story frame church was done by Nis P. Hjuler, a founding member of the congregation. Hjuler was born in Denmark and had settled in Seattle, Washington, before migrating to Audubon County. He was a carpenter and blacksmith by trade and was responsible for much of the interior work that has remained relatively intact since the building's construction. The painted enamel wood graining on the pulpit, wainscoting, and window and door surrounds, and the original pews with decorative applied woodwork, constitute a rare surviving example of Danish decorative arts.

Bethany Danish
Evangelical
Lutheran Church,
Audubon County,
Iowa

St. Wenceslaus Roman Catholic Church

Spillville

ARCHITECT / BUILDER:
Not available

CONSTRUCTION / DEDICATION DATE:
1860-1870

SPILLVILLE IS A SMALL CZECH COMMUNITY in central Iowa made famous by its association with the composer Antonín Dvořák, who spent a summer there, and memorialized in the book *Spillville*, written by Patricia Hampl (Minneapolis: Milkweed Editions, 1987). The Italianate two-story building where Dvořák spent the summer of 1893 is in the center of town and now is home to the House of Clocks. But the town's most outstanding building remains St. Wenceslaus Roman Catholic Church located on a hilltop site. According to tradition the church is modeled after Saint Barbara's Church in Kutna-Hora, the Czech Republic. St. Wenceslaus displays an interesting combination of Classical and Gothic elements perhaps best seen in its small chapel in the form of a classical temple set in its chevet (east end of the apse) and the sanctuary's pointed Gothic windows.

St. Wenceslaus Roman Catholic Church, Spillville, Iowa

St. Paul's United Methodist Episcopal Church

1340 Third Avenue SE, Cedar Rapids

ARCHITECT / BUILDER:
Louis H. Sullivan, George Grant Elmslie, W. C. Jones
CONSTRUCTION / DEDICATION DATE:
1910-1914

C EDAR RAPIDS IS PROBABLY BEST KNOWN as the home of the Quaker Oats Company, founded in 1873. But it is also home to a rare example of a church designed by the great Chicago architect, Louis H. Sullivan (see p. 129, Holy Trinity Orthodox Church, Chicago).

The story of the design of this church is complicated, involving three architects and a congregation's attempt to cut costs. The congregation's building committee held a design competition in 1910 for a new church. Two designs stood out: Sullivan's and another by the firm of Purcell, Feick, and Elmslie. Sullivan's was selected but its construction as designed was too costly, so he submitted a second, simpler version that was also rejected. The committee then engaged George Grant Elmslie to rework Sullivan's design. Elmslie attempted to be true to Sullivan's second plan, but eliminated many of its distinctive (and costly) interior and exterior features. Still deemed too costly, a third architect was then engaged, W. C. Jones of Chicago, whose only contribution was to eliminate much of Sullivan's distinctive ornamentation. Finally Elmslie was brought back in an effort to restore some of the building's unique features. Although badly compromised, the building presents a unique profile for a church retaining Sullivan's three basic parts: a semicircular auditorium that relates back to the mid-nineteenth-century Akron plan preferred by Methodists, next to a rectangular space for classrooms, and capped by a high tower with hipped roof to the rear.

St. Paul's United Methodist
Episcopal Church,
Cedar Rapids, Iowa

Islamic Center and Mosque

1335 Ninth Street NW (original location), Cedar Rapids

ARCHITECT / BUILDER:
Not available

CONSTRUCTION / DEDICATION DATE:
1925-1934

IN THE LATE 1890s, Arab immigrants, mainly Christians from areas of greater Syria, began immigrating to the United States pushing westward with the expanding frontier. Cedar Rapids became home to a small Arab community comprised of peddlers catering to the needs of farmers living on isolated farms. A second group of Arabs, this time Muslims from the same region, began to arrive about 1910. Although their numbers were small, about 20 in all, the Muslims rented a small building to serve as a temporary mosque and in 1925 formed a society known as "The Rose of Fraternity Lodge," to maintain their religious and cultural traditions. Plans were made in 1929 to build a mosque, but the onset of the Depression prevented its completion until 1934. It is the first place of worship specifically designed and built as a mosque in North America. (Another mosque, founded in 1929 in Ross, North Dakota, was recently bulldozed.) Referred to as the "Mother Mosque in North America," the small white clapboard building reflects its ancient heritage and its new

home in America. What distinguishes it from its neighbors is its single minaret, the tower from which the faithful are called, and its onion-shaped blue dome surmounted by the distinctive Islamic symbol, the crescent moon.

By the late 1960s the community had outgrown the Mosque and plans were drawn for a new Islamic Center and Mosque. Completed in 1972 and partially funded by grants from Saudi Arabia and Kuwait, the building's style reflects its Islamic heritage.

Islamic Center
and Mosque,
Cedar Rapids, Iowa

Missouri

M ISSOURI HAS BEEN DESCRIBED as a southern culture in a middle-western latitude–literally and figuratively a state in the middle.[1] Missouri does indeed straddle the nation geographically and culturally. Geographically, Missouri is defined by its two major waterways, the Missouri and the Mississippi rivers, that provided French explorers, fur traders, and missionaries access to vast areas of the continent's interior. First claimed by France in the seventeenth century, Missouri passed into Spanish hands, then back to the French, who sold it to the United States as part of the Louisiana Purchase of 1803. The following year, at the bidding of Thomas Jefferson, Lewis and Clark set out on their voyage of discovery, journeying from present-day St. Louis in search of the Northwest Passage. Although they never discovered the fabled passage, their explorations did lead to St. Louis, a French trading post located at the confluence of the Missouri and Mississippi rivers, becoming the "Gateway to the West," the jumping off point for countless wagon trains journeying westward along the Santa Fe and Oregon Trails.[2]

St. Genevieve, the region's first white settlement, was established by the French about 1750, but major migration into the area didn't occur until after 1815, when the first steamboats began to arrive in St. Louis laden with settlers from Kentucky, Tennessee, and Virginia. Settling in Platte County, the fertile Boonslick area of central Missouri, the southerners reestablished their plantation system, including slavery, which was to sow the seeds of future conflict. The debate over slavery stalled Missouri's efforts to become a state until 1821 and had an impact as well on the state's settlement. Anti-slavery organizations recruited potential settlers in northern and eastern states and from northern and central Europe, knowing they would support the Abolitionist movement. Because of their efforts Missouri remained in the Union during the Civil War.

Following the end of the war, freed slaves who had worked in the hemp industry in Platte County began to drift into Parkville seeking work. Many found employment as laborers at Park College, a newly established Presbyterian school. The college's proposed "Negro Annex" was never completed, but the related **Washington Chapel C.M.E.** was dedicated in 1907.

St. Louis was not only the nation's major gateway to the West, but it was also Missouri's exit to the East–a prime commercial outlet for farm products heading to eastern markets. The city's expanding industries attracted numerous immigrants from southern and eastern Europe, including a group of Czechs who founded the first Czech parish in the United

States. **St. John Nepomuk Roman Catholic Church**, the parish's second church, was constructed in 1870. The brick Romanesque–Gothic Revival structure stands as a visual reminder of a once-thriving ethnic community.

The heavy German immigration in the mid-nineteenth century produced a network of German settlements–Catholic, Protestant, and Freethinkers–in counties located along the Missouri and Mississippi rivers. The county of Cape Girardeau, located about 100 miles south of St. Louis, is overwhelmingly Lutheran, with many of its settlers coming from a region around Hanover, Germany. As early as 1803, an itinerant Lutheran pastor was ministering to a few German families, but it was not until 1846 that a Lutheran congregation was formally organized. As was often the case, the congregation initially worshipped in a log church until they were able to erect a more elaborate place of worship, a goal that was realized in 1887 when the red brick **Hanover Lutheran Church**, picturesquely sited at the crest of a gently sloping hill, was constructed.

Morgan County in central Missouri was once home to Osage Indians who were converted to Christianity by Catholic missionaries in the 1820s. It is thought that the early Catholic presence in the county was one reason Irish immigrants chose to settle there; another factor was cheap land. Settling near Gravois Mills, and with the help of a German-Catholic neighbor and a Protestant Scotsman, the Irish immigrants were able to acquire land and build **St. Patrick's Roman Catholic Church**, completed in 1870, the oldest stone church in the three counties surrounding the Lake of the Ozarks.

The majority of people settling in the Ozarks came from Tennessee where their southern and Appalachian cultural characteristics blended together, creating what is viewed by many as a true Missouri identity. In reality, the Ozarks is a region of great ethnic diversity. After the Civil War, railroads, eager to dispose of large land grants, began to encourage immigrants to settle on their holdings in the Ozarks. One group was the Waldensians, Protestants from France who had settled in Italy and then Uruguay prior to their arrival in Missouri in 1875. A small frame church erected in 1877 in Monnett served its congregation until 1908, when the present **Waldensian Presbyterian Church** was constructed.

Washington Chapel C.M.E. Church

1137 West Street, Parkville

ARCHITECT / BUILDER:
Charles Patrick Breen, builder
CONSTRUCTION / DEDICATION DATE:
1907

THIS TWO-STORY LIMESTONE church located high on a hill overlooking the town of Parkville is associated with the town's historic African-American community. Its founders were former slaves who ventured into the nearby town of Parkville in search of work. Parkville, founded on slavery and river traffic, was searching for new ways to survive, first by securing a railroad, and second, by establishing a Presbyterian college. The college hired the African-Americans to clear land and construct buildings. The founder of the college, Dr. John A. McAfee, had the idea of adding a "Negro Annex" to the college where blacks could receive a separate but equal education. The Annex never became a reality, but the chapel did.

Blacks living in northern states established the African Methodist Episcopal Church in 1816 which remained affiliated with the Methodist Episcopal Church (see p. 93). However, in the South, blacks were not allowed to organize their own Methodist congregations, forcing them to continue worshipping in the churches of their masters. Following Emancipation, the few African-American Methodists remaining in the South were permitted to organize a separate church, the Colored Methodist Episcopal Church, formed in 1870. This chapel was organized the same year, possibly the second C.M.E. church in Missouri. It is possible that the chapel was designed by Charles Patrick Breen, the college's superintendent of construction.

Washington Chapel
C.M.E. Church,
Parkville, Missouri

St. John Nepomuk Roman Catholic Church

Lafayette and Eleventh Streets, St. Louis

ARCHITECT / BUILDER:
Not available

CONSTRUCTION / DEDICATION DATE:
1870, 1896

DOMINATING THE FRONT FAÇADE of the church is its central belfry and steeple, rising high above its entrance. Constructed entirely of red bricks in a combined Romanesque and Gothic Revival style, St. John Nepomuk was almost totally destroyed by a tornado in 1896, but was reconstructed in its original form in subsequent years. It has not undergone any significant alterations since then, although the community has declined with many members moving to the suburbs.

The parish was organized to minister to the city's expanding Czech (Bohemian) population that had begun to congregate in the neighborhood in the late 1840s. By 1854, the Czechs began to demand an independent church and school, not only to function as a place of worship, but also to provide a gathering place where they could continue to worship in their mother tongue and maintain their traditions. Facing increasing hostility from the city's old-stock pioneer families, the church was a haven in an alien and unwelcoming environment. The church also served other eastern European ethnic groups in the city–Croatian, Slovak, Polish, Lithuanian, and Ukrainian–until each was able to establish its own national church.

Although the neighborhood has been destroyed by housing developments and freeways, St. John Nepomuk continues to survive as testimony to St. Louis's diverse ethnic heritage.

St. John Nepomuk Roman Catholic Church (circa 1900), St. Louis, Missouri

Hanover Lutheran Church

2949 Perryville Road, Cape Girardeau

ARCHITECT / BUILDER:
William Regenhardet, builder
CONSTRUCTION / DEDICATION DATE:
1887

T HE CONGREGATION'S LOG CHURCH, constructed in 1846 and since demolished, served as a parish school and parsonage. By the mid-1870s, plans were under discussion for relocating the church so it could better serve its growing congregation. Land was purchased in 1875 and a frame parsonage and school were completed the following year. In 1887, work began on a new church directly across the street. Its material, styling, and meticulous craftsmanship, as well as its siting in a wooded area at the crest of gently sloping ground, are all considered characteristic of rural German traditions in Missouri. Solidly constructed of red brick preferred by German builders, its only architectural features are its round-arched windows and slender frame bell tower sheathed with galvanized tin. The interior is equally simple.

Hanover Lutheran was the mother church of numerous county congregations, but it is the only church associated with the German Lutheran heritage in Cape Girardeau from this period to survive. Although a new church was constructed in 1969, the congregation decided to preserve this historic building.

Hanover
Lutheran Church,
Cape Girardeau,
Missouri

St. Patrick's Roman Catholic Church

One and one tenth miles east of Missouri Hwy. 5 on SR 5, Gravois Mills

ARCHITECT / BUILDER:
Tom Fitzpatrick, builder
CONSTRUCTION / DEDICATION DATE:
1868-1870

TOM FITZPATRICK ARRIVED in Morgan County in 1850 from the county of Fermanagh, Ireland. He squatted on some land before returning to Ireland for his family. By 1863, Fitzpatrick had returned to Missouri and began to make plans for a church. Land was donated, stone was quarried on nearby land, and a simple practical stone church was erected. Completed in 1870, it wasn't dedicated until 1883.

The rectangular one-story church has an L-shaped addition adjoining its southwest corner. Its exterior is austere, made of thick, roughly dressed, coarsed rubble of native limestone. Its only decorative element is a Latin cross surmounting the east main façade's gable roof. The interior, however, displays Gothic features, including a tripartite arrangement of plaster Gothic arches, a large central arch over the altar, flanked by two smaller ones framing statues of the Virgin and Joseph.

Perhaps what is most intriguing about the church is its early demonstration of ecumenism. Its builders were Irish and German Catholics and one Scottish Protestant. Henry Purvis, the Scot, was buried in the church's cemetery, but after protest by some Roman Catholics his body was exhumed and moved to a local Protestant cemetery.

The stone
St. Patrick's Roman
Catholic Church,
Gravois Mills,
Missouri

The Waldensian Presbyterian Church

Route 2, Monett

ARCHITECT / BUILDER:
Not available

CONSTRUCTION / DEDICATION DATE:
Dedicated 1908

THIS BUILDING ILLUSTRATES the Americanization process of one small persecuted minority group who found a safe haven in the United States. Founded in the
twelfth century in Lyons, France, in defiance of the Roman Catholic Church, the
persecuted Protestant Waldensians fled to the mountain fastness of the Cottian Alps of Italy.
In 1526, they allied with the Calvinist Reformation, but continued to suffer brutal attempts
by the Catholics to exterminate them. Finally granted freedom of worship in 1848, they
were forced to leave Italy because of over-
crowded conditions and sought refuge in
Uruguay. It was from Uruguay that a small
group departed for the United States in 1875,
purchasing land in Missouri from the
Atlantic and Pacific Railroad. Few in number, they established a Presbyterian congregation, but had to rely on others to support
their church. In time, due to the process of
dilution and assimilation, and the lack of
persecution that had previously forced them
into a cohesive and closed society, the group's
ethnic identity began to weaken. Perhaps
this is most clearly seen in the congregation's
new church, constructed in 1907. As was the
case with many other ethnic groups
throughout the nation, the style selected was
one perceived as being "American," a vernacular interpretation of the Gothic Revival
style found throughout the Midwest.

The church has been remodeled, but
remains the vital center of the Waldensian
heritage of Monett; it is only one of three
Waldensian churches remaining in the
United States.

Waldensian
Presbyterian
Church, vicinity of
Monett, Missouri

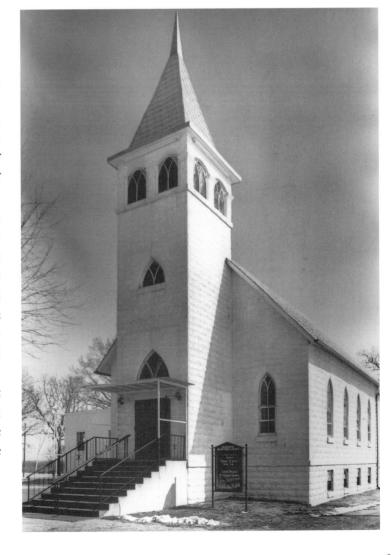

Kansas

WHEN THE SPANISH EXPLORER CORONADO ventured into this territory, he commented upon its fertile soil, but quickly departed when he did not find the gold he was seeking. Coronado left no commentary on the area's weather, perhaps because he was not there long enough to experience its unpredictability. The endless acres of grassland and the alternate periods of drought and downpours, punctuated by tornadoes, caused visitors who arrived centuries later to classify it as the "Great American Desert." Even Dorothy, in *The Wizard of Oz*, describes her home to the Scarecrow as gray and dry, but, she assures him, no matter how dreary it is, there is no place like home.

Kansas eventually did become home to many Americans and immigrants from distant shores, all in search of productive farmlands. Its unpredictable weather, like its grasshoppers, was just one more challenge to be overcome, like the prolonged drought coupled with a related economic depression that lasted from 1887 until 1897. Anyone who survived this difficult era was viewed as being a typical Kansan, a person, according to one historian, who ". . . finds exhilarating the challenge of extreme difficulty." [3]

It was the signing of the Kansas-Nebraska Act on May 30, 1854, that first opened the territory up for white settlement. Settlers began arriving from neighboring states and a lesser number from New England. Missouri's slave-operated hemp-producing plantations located near the state's eastern border precipitated clashes between settlers from northern and eastern states who were seeking to have Kansas declared a free state and those from the Upland South and Missouri who wanted Kansans to support slavery. The issue was finally put to a vote, and, as a result of the arrival of numerous northerners, the Abolitionists won and Kansas entered the Union in 1861, on the eve of the Civil War, as a free state.

Emigrant Aid Societies organized by Protestant religious institutions in Massachusetts, Connecticut, and New York were responsible for recruiting northerners to settle in Kansas. Most of their early settlements were located in northeastern Kansas in areas along the Kansas River and its tributaries that were easily reached by steamboat. Since many of these colonies were church-sponsored, it is not too surprising that one of the first buildings erected in a town was a church. The Christian and Congregational Church in Eureka, built in 1888, is the second church built by the Congregational Church Home Missionary Society that came to Kansas in 1854 to support the Free State Movement. The **Beecher Bible and Rifle Church**, in Wabaunsee, was organized by settlers from New Haven, Connecticut, who arrived in Kansas in 1856. The congregation's unusual name comes from a speech made by Henry Ward Beecher upon their departure from Connecticut urging that money be given to the pioneers so they could purchase rifles to defend themselves.

Although Roman Catholics were not recruited as settlers, their missionaries were active in the area, attempting to convert the Indians. One mission was established as early as 1858 in the area that became Kansas City. By 1903, when the parish dedicated its third building, **St. Mary's Roman Catholic Church**, located in the city's historic "Strawberry Hill" neighborhood, its members were primarily immigrants from eastern and southern Europe who were working in the city's meat-packing companies in the nearby West Bottoms area.

The Homestead Act of 1862 and the completion of railroad lines crossing the state encouraged further settlement. The railroad companies, in an effort to settle the vast acreage they owned, began a systematic recruiting drive in Europe. Their targets were Protestant

Immaculate Heart of Mary Roman Catholic Church, Windthorst, Kansas

northern and western Europeans who were perceived as being productive workers. Germans were preferred, not only those coming directly from Germany, Bohemia, or Russia, but also farmers living in eastern states. Scandinavians, English, Scots, and Welsh were also acceptable, but not Irish. As a result of this recruitment pattern, people of German heritage ultimately became the largest European group to settle the rich agricultural plains of central Kansas; most, as it turned out, were Roman Catholic.

Among the first to arrive were German Catholics from the Volga region of Russia who were fleeing persecution and seeking a place to safely practice their faith and traditions. They found a haven in central Kansas, where they established towns with names like Liebenthal, Pfeifer, Schoenches, Antonio, Munjor, and Catherine. Each community was centered around its church, often constructed by its members from native limestone they had quarried. One beautiful example is St. Catherine's Roman Catholic Church, built in 1890 and named after Katherinestadt in Russia, the town they fled in 1876. Another is **St. Fidelis Roman Catholic Church** at Victoria, dedicated in 1911 and known as the "Cathedral of the Plains."

Windthorst was settled in 1878 by members of the Cincinnati-based German Catholic Aurora Homestead Association. The **Immaculate Heart of Mary Roman Catholic Church** was described at its dedication in 1913 as a "landmark that can be seen many miles in every direction."

Railroad recruiters had less success convincing Scandinavians to move to Kansas; they preferred settling in already established enclaves in Iowa, Minnesota, or Nebraska. But one Danish community did take up the offer, establishing a town appropriately named Denmark, where they erected the **Danske Evangelist Lutheran Kirke (Denmark Evangelical Lutheran Church)** in 1880.

Jews fleeing religious persecution at the hands of the Russians, and blacks fleeing racism in southern states, both established agricultural colonies in Kansas. The Jewish ones failed, but one black colony, Nicodemus, survives, thanks to the efforts of its residents and other supporters. Formed on April 18, 1877, by seven people—one white and six black—who were attracted by promotional literature handed out by its two promoters, one black the other white, the town in one year grew to nearly 700 residents. When the railroad bypassed Nicodemus in 1888, the majority of its population relocated; however, a small number remained. Life was difficult, but relief was to be found in their churches—one African Methodist Episcopal and two Baptist. Until the **First Baptist Church** was built in 1880, worship took place in dugouts or sod buildings. In 1975, a new church was constructed north of the existing church. Although only a few people now reside in Nicodemus, the town remains a historic landmark, a reminder of the dedication and perseverance of its founders and their descendants.

Beecher Bible and
Rifle Church,
Wabaunsee, Kansas

Beecher Bible and Rifle Church

Chapel Street and Elm Street, Wabaunsee

ARCHITECT / BUILDER:
Not available

CONSTRUCTION / DEDICATION DATE:
1862

ABOUT 70 MEN FROM CONNECTICUT arrived in Kansas in April 1856 and organized the town of Wabaunsee. A church established the following year was, according to its organizing papers, "Congregational in form but not in name and in fact as unsectarian as possible"; it was to be known as the First Church of Christ in Wabaunsee. However, two years later the congregation voted to affiliate with the Congregational fellowship in Kansas, and erected a small frame church. It was replaced in 1862 by the present building that was built, according to the congregation's history, after four years of effort and much personal sacrifice on the part of members.

Constructed of native limestone laid in a random pattern, the church remained in use for 50 years before the town's declining population forced it to close. Restored in 1948 by the Old Timers Association, it remains standing as one of the oldest permanent church buildings in the state and as a reminder of the efforts of early settlers to see that Kansas entered the Union as a free state.

Beecher Bible and
Rifle Church,
Wabaunsee, Kansas

St. Mary's Roman Catholic Church

800 North Fifth Street, Kansas City

ARCHITECT / BUILDER:
Not available

CONSTRUCTION / DEDICATION DATE:
1890-1903

SITUATED IN THE HISTORIC AREA of Kansas City called "Strawberry Hill," St. Mary's accommodated the needs of the vast number of predominantly Roman Catholic immigrants who came to work in the city's meat packing plants. St. Mary's Church is a pioneer Catholic church in Kansas, the oldest Catholic parish in Kansas City, and as such has played a major role in the city's religious and community history. The parish, established in the wilderness as a mission to the Indians in 1858, moved to the city in 1864 under the leadership of Father Anton Kuhls, the parish pastor for 44 years.

The arrival of new immigrants from eastern and southern Europe was the impetus for the construction of a new church in 1903. The architecture of the church is less significant than its history. It is a simplified Romanesque Revival structure constructed of native limestone. Its interior housed three outstanding carved oak altars and beautiful stained glass windows. The church was closed in 1980, but although vacant it is still being maintained. It has survived poverty, hard times, and debts, remaining a symbol of a people's determination to make a new life in a new world, while maintaining their faith and traditions, thanks in great part to the efforts of Father Anton Kuhls.

St. Mary's Roman Catholic Church, Kansas City, Kansas

St. Fidelis Roman Catholic Church

St. Anthony Street and Delaware, Victoria

ARCHITECT / BUILDER:
John T. Comes, John Marshall
CONSTRUCTION / DEDICATION DATE:
1908-1911

S
T. FIDELIS SHARES WITH Immaculate Heart of Mary in Windthorst the appellation of the "Cathedral of the Plains." Built by German-Russians who came to Kansas in 1876, the congregation worshipped in two older small frame churches until a decision was made in 1900 to build a large church that would serve its present and future needs. To that end they hired John T. Comes of Pittsburgh, Pennsylvania, a well-known church architect, to design a building. Apparently not completely satisfied with his plans, the congregation had the plans modified by John Marshall, a Topeka architect.

Constructed primarily of local limestone with Bedford stone from Indiana and Vermont granite used for pillars and ornamental details, at the time of its construction the Romanesque style church was the largest Catholic church west of the Mississippi River. Its stained glass windows made in Munich are considered among the outstanding church windows of their type in the United States. William Jennings Bryan, after seeing the church with its twin spires dominating the countryside, proclaimed it the "Cathedral of the Prairies." However, more often it is called "Cathedral of the Plains."

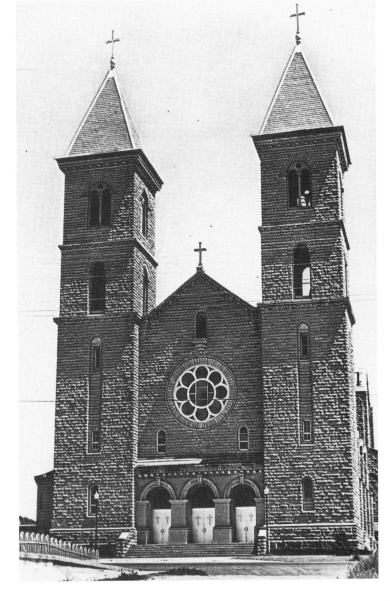

St. Fidelis Roman
Catholic Church,
Victoria, Kansas

Immaculate Heart of Mary Roman Catholic Church
Windthorst

ARCHITECT / BUILDER:
Preuss and Aimes, Co. Architects
CONSTRUCTION / DEDICATION DATE:
1912-1913

THE CHURCH IS THE CORE of a religious complex that includes a school, rectory, and teacher's house. Its Gothic-Romanesque style is considered a striking example of early twentieth-century church design. Constructed of red brick and decorated with yellow brick striations, and standing on a yellow brick and limestone block foundation, the church's centrally located tower on its front façade is visible for miles, contributing to it being referred to by locals as the "Cathedral of the Plains," an identity it shares with St. Fidelis.

Windthorst, in Wheatland Township, was settled mainly by Germans; some were immigrants, others had migrated westward from neighboring states. They formed three churches: two were Catholic, this one and St. Joseph's, and one Lutheran, Zion. As the population of the township grew and prospered in the years between 1900 and 1915, St. Mary's parish was in a position to build a new, more elaborate church. An architectural firm from St. Louis was commissioned to design the building and the Emil Frei Studios in St. Louis was selected to design the stained glass windows. The period of prosperity was short-lived and the number of parishioners began to decline in the years following World War I. The future of the church is uncertain; however, it remains in use and its interior maintains much of its original appearance.

Immaculate Heart
of Mary Roman
Catholic Church,
Windthorst, Kansas

Danske Evangelist Lutheran Kirke

(DANISH EVANGELICAL LUTHERAN COMMUNITY CHURCH, DENMARK EVANGELIST LUTHERAN CHURCH)

Denmark

ARCHITECT / BUILDER:
James Morgansen, mason; Anders Rasmussen, carpenter
CONSTRUCTION / DEDICATION DATE:
1875-1880, 1901

T HE CORNERSTONE FOR THE CHURCH was laid in 1875, but theological disputes among members delayed its construction for five years. The one-story, one-room vernacular style church constructed of locally quarried stone stands at the crossroads of Denmark. Its bell tower and entry were added on the south in 1901. If it were not for the tower and the Gothic detailing of the doors and windows, it would resemble many secular buildings in Kansas built at this time.

Disputes continued to plague the congregation as it tried to make adjustments to life in a new world. Among its members were several Swedes and Norwegians who left the church in 1876 when the Danish members voted to join the Danish Synod of the Lutheran Churches. The exclusive use of the Danish language introduced in 1884 for services and in the school caused other members to leave. Yet another schism occurring in 1895 resulted in dissatisfied Danes forming the Free Mission Church one mile away.

The construction of the Salina and Northwestern line of the Atchison, Topeka, and Santa Fe Railroad in 1915 caused the town to experience a temporary boom. The Depression and drought of the 1930s had a severe impact on the community; many people moved on, leaving behind the church, community hall, and grain elevator. The church survives, maintaining a high degree of its architectural and structural integrity.

Danish Evangelical Lutheran Community Church, vicinity of Denmark, Kansas

Nebraska

NEBRASKA STRADDLES MUCH of the Great Plains, but its physical environment changes dramatically as one journeys westward. This is particularly visible upon reaching the Sand Hills in the north central portion of the state, a sparsely populated, grass-covered area. Its cultural character, too, changes. This may have its origin in the Kansas-Nebraska Act passed by Congress in 1854 which created two territorial governments in the Great Plains. Among other things, the act allowed people living in the territories to decide whether they wanted to legalize slavery, and it permitted railroads to lay tracks across the land leading westward to California. In the minds of many people the two territories blended into one–a vast treeless and arid land; an ocean of uninhabitable grasslands. By the 1880s, after the territories achieved statehood (Nebraska in 1867), the region came to be identified as the Middle West to distinguish it from the Northwest, Minnesota and the Dakotas, and the Southwest, consisting of Texas and Indian Territory. Kansas and Nebraska, according to writers of the period, even shared similar cultural characteristics acquired through the challenges settlers faced in attempting to survive on arid, treeless grasslands.

Spanish and French explorers passing through the area in the seventeenth and eighteenth centuries described it as "inhospitable," a view shared by others who followed in the early nineteenth century. Once steamboats began plying the Missouri River, towns began to develop as jumping off points for pioneers starting their arduous trek westward. With the settlers came missionaries intent on taming the rapidly growing towns by establishing congregations and building churches, such as the Congregational Church (later Methodist) built in 1859 in Brownsville and **St. Benedict's Roman Catholic Church**, built two years later in Nebraska City.

Not all the "overlanders" continued westward; some chose to settle along the fertile banks of the Platte River, Nebraska's important east-west river "highway." Passage of the 1862 Homestead Act transformed the state; it was no longer viewed as a passageway west, but rather as a destination point for immigrants as well as Americans from neighboring states, all of whom were seeking cheap, rich farmlands. The first pioneers settled along the Missouri River; others then began moving westward following the rivers, particularly the Platte, searching for land. Railroad interests were given acres of land as right-of-ways and Civil War veterans and Irish laborers were hired to lay track. Parishes, such as Holy Family in Omaha, were formed as a means of providing religious and moral guidance for the Irish workers.

The state also became a destination for people seeking a safe haven where they could continue to practice unimpeded their religious and cultural traditions. Their communities and churches soon became a prominent feature of Nebraska's landscape. It is the heterogeneous character of these settlers that one author claims makes Nebraska unique–that separates it from its neighbors, and in particular, from Kansas. Nebraska's unique history can be summed up in its interaction between place–the Great Plains the state straddles–and people, its mix of immigrants and Americans.[4]

People of German heritage comprise the state's largest ethnic group. Arriving either directly from Germany or moving westward from older German settlements in the United States, many settled in the state's northeast quadrant, where St. John's Lutheran Church in Burt County was built in 1902 for a congregation formed in 1874 by German immigrants who had first settled in Minnesota. German Catholic families settling in Cedar County built **St. Boniface Roman Catholic Church** in 1886, utilizing a highly decorative combination of native chalk rock and brickwork in its construction.

Czech immigrants, Catholic and Protestant, settling in Colfax County along the Platte River, were memorialized in Willa Cather's book *My Antonia*. Their presence remains visible in Our Lady of Perpetual Help Catholic Church, also known as Wilson Church, a Gothic Revival structure, constructed in the vicinity of Schuyler in 1918 for a parish that originated in the 1870s. Nearby in the vicinity of Clarkson is Zion Presbyterian Church,

Pilgrim
Holiness Church,
Sand Hills, Nebraska

the first Czech Presbyterian church in the state, which was designed in 1887 by a Czech architect, M. D. Flechor. Further south in Clay County, Moravian immigrants from Czechoslovakia founded a small Catholic parish in the late 1880s and built the Gothic Revival **St. Martin's Roman Catholic Church** in 1907–1908. The building is now owned by the Clay County Historical Society.

Swedes, second only to Germans in numbers, settled mainly in the state's Central Plains region. Most were Lutherans, including the founders of *En Torv Katedral*, the Sod Cathedral built in Kearney County in 1878. An organizational dispute in 1879, however, caused a number of members to leave. By 1884 they had formed an officially sanctioned congregation, **Salem Swedish Methodist Episcopal Church** in rural Axtell, and the following year built a frame church that was replaced by the present building in 1898. Other Scandinavians who settled in Nebraska were Danish followers of N.F.S. Grundtvig (see Iowa, p. 155), who established the town of Kronborg and built St. John's Evangelical Lutheran Church in 1899.

As Nebraska's settlement moved westward so did the Methodist circuit-riding preachers. St. Paul's Methodist Protestant Church in Hitchcock County near the Kansas/Colorado borders was built in 1900 to replace a sod building used by the congregation since its organization in 1892. Sod has been called "Nebraska marble," as the lack of trees made it the most readily available and cheapest local building material.

Nebraska's uniqueness extends beyond people and place; it is seen too in its religious architecture. **Pilgrim Holiness Church**, built in 1928 in the state's sparsely populated Sand Hills region, is the only known church built of baled straw, a building material used throughout the treeless Sand Hills. The First Congregational Church in Naponee, built in 1887, and **People's Unitarian Church** in Ord, are rare examples of octagonal buildings in the state. **Keystone Community Church** in Keith County was built in 1908 to accommodate Protestant and Catholic services; thus, apses protrude from both ends of the building.

Due to lack of in-migration during the past century, many of Nebraska's original ethnic and religious settlements remain relatively intact, testifying to the fortitude of the state's original settlers and their descendants.

People's
Unitarian Church,
Ord, Nebraska

St. Benedict's Roman Catholic Church

411 Fifth Rue, Nebraska City

ARCHITECT / BUILDER:
Not available

CONSTRUCTION / DEDICATION DATE:
1861

S T. BENEDICT'S IS LOCATED at the summit of Kearney Hill, a subdivision of Nebraska City. The city, sited on high ground near the Missouri River, was a major river port and a jumping off center for ox-drawn wagons carrying commercial freight or settlers heading westward. The town's historic district still contains many excellent examples of buildings built by its most prominent residents, mainly eastern entrepreneurs involved in commercial and freighting ventures.

But not all of the town's early settlers came from the East. Father Emmanuel Hartig, a missionary and Benedictine priest from Germany, was responsible for the erection of six Catholic churches, including St. Benedict's, and for the establishment of several parishes in southeastern Nebraska and northwestern Missouri. St. Benedict's, believed to be the oldest brick Catholic church in Nebraska, is built in a simplified version of the Romanesque Revival style. Although an addition has been added to the rear of the structure, and changes made to the interior, it still retains its 1890s oak high altar and walnut pews cut in 1861 from local trees.

St. Benedict's
Roman Catholic
Church, Nebraska
City, Nebraska

St. Boniface Roman Catholic Church

Main Street, Menominee, Cedar County

ARCHITECT / BUILDER:
Franz Zavadil, contractor
CONSTRUCTION / DEDICATION DATE:
1886, 1902

GERMAN CATHOLIC FAMILIES settling in Antelope Valley in the 1860s built a small frame church, but it was destroyed by a storm before it could be completed. Work began immediately on a second church that was then replaced in 1886 by one built of native chalk rock. Once again, disaster struck when all but the rock walls of the church were destroyed in a fire in 1900. Again the congregants set out to rebuild their church that was dedicated two years later. Franz Zavadil, a native of Bohemia, is thought to be responsible for its construction. Zavadil established a homestead in the vicinity in the 1870s, erecting a chalk rock and glacial rock dwelling that is considered an important example of folk architecture.

St. Boniface is a handsome Gothic Revival church constructed of chalk rock and brickwork. Its impressive façade, highly decorated with designs formed of chalk rock and brickwork that look back at medieval Czech churches, reflects Zavadil's masonry skills using readily available materials. The church remains in use by descendants of its original founders.

FACING PAGE:
St. Boniface Roman
Catholic Church,
Cedar County,
Nebraska

Salem Swedish Methodist Episcopal Church
(JOHN FLETCHER CHRISTIAN COLLEGE CHAPEL)

Southwest of Axtell, Kearney County

ARCHITECT / BUILDER:
Not available

CONSTRUCTION / DEDICATION DATE:
1883, 1898, 1910

THE CONGREGATION QUICKLY OUTGREW its 1884 church building and replaced it in 1898 with the present building. Thanks to securing subscriptions from neighborhood farmers, the church was built nearly debt-free. The building's design merges two popular styles: the exterior is in the Carpenter Gothic style, sided in white clapboard with green trim, similar to many Lutheran churches built throughout the Midwest, while the interior is a modified Akron plan favored by preaching denominations, and introduced by the Methodists (see p. 101). Here, the Sunday School rooms are adjacent to the nave instead of classrooms off a central Sunday School area.

The church has been restored for the most part to its 1898 condition, retaining original pews, altar rail, pulpit, and 1914 pressed tin walls and ceiling covering.

PRECEDING PAGE:
Salem Swedish Methodist Episcopal Church (now John Fletcher Christian College Chapel), Wakefield County, Nebraska

Keystone Community Church

("THE LITTLE CHURCH")

McGinley Street, Keystone

ARCHITECT / BUILDER:
Ed Casey, carpenter

CONSTRUCTION / DEDICATION DATE:
1908

LOCATED IN A SPARSELY POPULATED AREA near the border with Colorado is the small unincorporated village of Keystone. People of diverse faiths settled in the town, but due to their few numbers they remained without a place of worship until the erection of this "little church." Mrs. William Paxton, Jr., the wife of a wealthy rancher whose father opened the Union Stock Yard Company in Omaha in 1884, and members of "King's Daughters," a teenage girls' club, were the inspiration behind the construction. The church was built by Ed Casey, a carpenter from Red Oak, Iowa, as a one-story board and batten church designed to accommodate Catholic and Protestant services.

Known as "The Little Church," it is unique for having apses protruding from both ends of the building: a Catholic altar at the north and a Protestant lectern at the south. The backs of the pews are hinged so that the seating can be reversed. It is the only known building of this type in Nebraska, and one of the few such structures in the United States.

The last regular services were conducted by Lutherans in 1949. The church remained unoccupied until about 1953 when the Keystone Extension Club took over maintaining and preserving it. Since then it has become a tourist attraction and can be reserved for special occasions.

Keystone
Community
Church, Keystone,
Nebraska

South Dakota

F OR PEOPLE LIVING along the eastern seaboard, the region west of the Mississippi River was considered as exotic and unknown as China. Intrepid French
explorers and fur traders entering the area known as "Dakota" as early as 1743
established friendly relations with the Indians, providing them with trade goods,
horses, and smallpox. But it wasn't until the Dakotas were acquired as part of the Louisiana
Purchase and information about Lewis and Clark's voyage of discovery became known that
the region began to attract attention.

Many of the fur traders of French descent came from St. Louis, Missouri, and Montreal,
Canada. They established small settlements, including one near present-day Jefferson.
Although the fur trade began to decline in the mid-nineteenth century, several families
remained in Jefferson, and in 1862, the year after the Dakota Territory was organized, they
formed St. Peter's parish and erected a log Catholic church. Grasshopper infestations were
threatening many rural communities in 1869, the year the congregation dedicated a new
church. St. Peter's priest organized a pilgrimage around the parish perimeter chanting
prayers that, according to local tradition, saved their crops from destruction. The parish
prospered, and erected its present church in 1892. The liturgy was conducted in French until
1939, and many of the parish's current members are descendants of its founders.

The history of St. Peter's is one that is repeated throughout South Dakota and is, perhaps, the state's most unique characteristic–the retention of ethnic identity. Living in isolated areas in ethnic enclaves, immigrants and their descendants were able to maintain
many of their cultural and religious traditions without interference. Churches, denominational primary schools, academies, and even colleges allowed South Dakota's ethnic patch-
work to remain essentially unchanged for nearly a century. But these ethnic communities
came at a cost to the native peoples who occupied the land.

South Dakota was settled in two sections–east and west of the Missouri River. Settlement
of the east began in the 1860s but was slowed by the Civil War, bad weather, grasshoppers,
and hostile Indians who were forced into the area. Their hunting grounds, the fertile Yankton Triangle or Delta region in southeastern South Dakota, were coveted by white settlers.
Finally in 1858, to avoid further bloodshed, the Dakota Indians ceded the area and were
moved to a reservation, the first of many concessions Indians were forced to make, concluding with the Great Sioux Agreement of 1889, ordering all Indians to be confined to nine
reservations. That same year South Dakota was admitted into the Union.[5]

Rather than agree to move onto a reservation, some Indians chose instead to surrender their tribal affiliation in exchange for homestead privileges. Santee Sioux took up home-steaders' rights in Grant County, on the border with Minnesota and on the edge of the Sis-seton Reservation, where a Presbyterian minister organized a congregation serving Indians and, later, white settlers. **Brown Earth Presbyterian Church**, built in 1877, one of the few surviving log churches in South Dakota, served both groups until 1884 when most of the Indian families moved back to the Sisseton Reservation.

The Czech Agricultural Society, formed in Chicago in 1868, sent several members to north central Nebraska with the express purpose of locating land for Czech immigrants. The Sand Hills held little promise for agriculture, so they ventured northward, finally arriving in the fertile Yankton area, now free of Indians, where land was purchased and Czech set-tlements were quickly established. One group founded Tabor, named after a Hussite rad-ical capital in Bohemia, where they worshipped initially in a simple chalkrock edifice before building **St. Wenceslaus Roman Catholic Church** in 1898.

Germans, including German Russians from the Volga River area, were the largest eth-nic group to settle in eastern South Dakota. Bishop Martin Marty, a missionary to the Indians, also ministered to the newcomers, establishing a convent and school in Zell in 1883. The parish's present church, St. Mary's, begun in 1884 but not completed until 1905, is a frame Victorian Gothic Revival structure with a corner tower.

Hutterite Brethren migrated from Ukraine to Bon Homme County in eastern South Dakota in 1874, where over a period of a century they established 46 colonies; only half survive. The Wolf Creek Colonies include (Old) Tschetter, founded in 1890 and resettled in 1942. Despite repeated persecution because of their communal nature and German heritage, many Hutterites have chosen to remain in South Dakota, worshipping in sim-ple frame buildings similar to the **Church Building** in the Tschetter Colony, erected between 1903 and 1910.

Norwegians were second in numbers of immigrants to Germans, but unlike many other ethnic groups in South Dakota that chose to cluster in certain areas, Norwegian commu-nities are scattered throughout the state. Their small wood frame churches surrounded by cemeteries, such as **Telemarken Lutheran Church**, built in 1894 in Codington County, are primarily based on widely available pattern books, such as Richard Upjohn's plans for rural Gothic Revival churches. But the interiors are more traditionally Norwegian, generally with the emphasis placed on the altar, pulpit, and baptismal font.

Two factors had an impact on the settlement of western South Dakota: a steamboat and an artist who traveled on one. The first steamboat headed up the Missouri River from St. Louis to Fort Pierre in 1831. The following year, traveling by steamboat, came the artist George Catlin, born in Wilkes-Barre, Pennsylvania, whose scenes of the exotic West found a receptive audience in the East. Exhibitions of his paintings stimulated the beginnings of South Dakota's tourist industry, augmented by the arrival of the railroad. One town that became a popular health resort was Hot Springs in the southwestern corner of the state. By the turn of the century, it had a college, five public baths, and ten hotels, including one modeled after the famed King David Hotel in Jerusalem. Almost all the town's public buildings were built of the local pink Lakota limestone, including **St. Luke's Episcopal**

Church, constructed in 1902 by a congregation founded in 1896.

In the 1870s, the discovery of precious minerals in the Black Hills brought in prospectors and soon mining towns like Deadwood, Lead, and Rapid City began to develop, as did the myth of the "Wild West." With the westward expansion of the railroad and the Homestead Act came farmers and ranchers, but the area's arid conditions limited farming mainly to livestock ranching. Railroad cars not only brought in settlers and carried out livestock to eastern markets, they also served as places of worship for ranchers living in sparsely populated areas of the state. Only three of these cars survive, including Chapel Emmanuel now located in Prairie Village in Madison, built in 1893 by the Baptist Church, and in service until 1942.

Brown Earth Presbyterian Church

Vicinity of Stockholm, Grant County

ARCHITECT / BUILDER:
Not available

CONSTRUCTION / DEDICATION DATE:
1877

A DIRT PATH THROUGH tall prairie grass and scattered pine trees leads to the Brown Earth Presbyterian Church, one of the best-preserved log churches in South Dakota. Constructed of hand-hewn logs with dovetail notching, the exterior's only embellishment is its frame open belfry. A group of Santee Indians homesteaded the area under the aegis of the American Board of Commissioners for Foreign Missions. The church was built in 1877 to serve Indian families, but many of the area's first white settlers often joined in worship. This ended when the Indian families decided to move back to the Sisseton Reservation. The building was used by several other denominations before it was given to an American Legion Post in 1931.

The building has undergone few changes, appearing today much as it did when it was built over 100 years ago.

Brown Earth Presbyterian Church, vicinity of Stockholm, South Dakota

St. Wenceslaus Roman Catholic Church

Northwest corner of Yankton and Lidice Streets, Tabor

ARCHITECT / BUILDER:
Augustus O. Goetz, Yankton, South Dakota
CONSTRUCTION / DEDICATION DATE:
1898

L OCATED ABOUT 20 MILES SOUTH of Yankton, Tabor is in the heart of an area homesteaded by Czech immigrants, the majority of whom were Roman Catholic. The parish's first church completed in 1874 was constructed of chalkrock quarried near the Missouri River. It was razed in 1898, the same year the present church was constructed on the same site.

St. Wenceslaus is constructed of brick in the Gothic Revival style similar to many Catholic churches built in the state. Its interior is decorated with captioned Stations of the Cross and stained glass windows with biblical passages written in Czech script. A rectory built in 1910 lies adjacent to it, a cemetery extends to the north and east, and across the street is the old parish house built in 1878. Together with the church, whose tall bell tower and steeple dominate the skyline of the small town, this complex illustrates the central role the Catholic religion played in the life of Czech immigrants who settled in Tabor.

St. Wenceslaus
Roman Catholic
Church,
Tabor, South
Dakota

Church Building

Tschetter Hutterite Colony, Hutchinson County

ARCHITECT / BUILDER:
Not available

CONSTRUCTION / DEDICATION DATE:
1903-1910

THE HUTTERITES WHO FORMED the original Tschetter colony originated in a small village, Hutterdorf, on the west side of the Dnieper River, northwest of the city of Odessa. Named the Dariusleut after their minister and founder Darius, they were known in South Dakota as the Wolf Creek Colonists, the second Hutterite colony in the state. It was one of the colonies that moved to more hospitable Canada in 1918 to escape the harsh treatment many of its members received from suspicious neighbors. However, they returned and resettled in the area in the 1940s, a time when South Dakota, suffering from the aftereffects of the Dust Bowl and the Depression, welcomed new settlements.

The colony's physical layout closely conforms to the traditional Hutterite courtyard square arrangement–buildings built around a central courtyard often aligned with their long walls in a north-south direction. The church often forms either the north or south boundary of the courtyard. As with other Hutterite buildings, this simple one-story frame church has its main entrance on its broad front façade, contrary to the practice found in most basilica plan churches. It is one of only four buildings remaining from the early colony. The others are two dwellings and a dining hall.

Church Building,
Tschetter Colony,
South Dakota

Telemarken Lutheran Church

Half mile west and one mile north of Wallace

ARCHITECT / BUILDER:
Edward E. Holvig; Halvor Markrud
CONSTRUCTION / DEDICATION DATE:
1894

THE ROLLING AND FERTILE PLAINS of northeastern South Dakota where Telemarken Lutheran Church is located were settled by Norwegian immigrants in the 1880s. The congregation was founded in 1887 and this small wood frame Gothic Revival church was built in 1894. Although the exterior of the building is quite plain, the interior retains all the elements associated with Norwegian Lutheran worship, where the focus is on the altar, pulpit, and baptismal font.

Besides regular worship services, the church was also the focal point for the Norwegian community's social and cultural activities. However, as the community declined, the congregation merged with Calvary Lutheran in nearby Wallace. Telemarken recently has been completely restored with funds raised from former members and stands today as a reminder of the Norwegian immigrants who were among the first settlers in the area.

Telemarken Lutheran Church, Wallace, South Dakota

St. Luke's Episcopal Church

Between Hammond and Minnekahta Avenues, Hot Springs

ARCHITECT / BUILDER:
Gus Knorr, stonemason
CONSTRUCTION / DEDICATION DATE:
1902

S T. LUKE'S BEGAN AS A MISSION CHURCH organized in 1896, a time when Hot Springs was becoming a favorite tourist destination. At first the congregation met in a small building purchased from the Congregational Society until the present church was constructed in 1902. Fred T. Evans, owner of Evans Plunge, a favorite health resort in town, traded the land plus the stone used to construct the church in exchange for a lot owned by the parish on River Street, the town's main avenue. The following year an expert stone cutter named Gus Knorr was put in charge of constructing a new Episcopal church that was consecrated in 1907.

The pink sandstone Gothic Revival church is built on a lot that is literally cut out of a hill. It has a commanding view of the town whose main street is lined with buildings made of similar stone. The church's ten stained glass windows are all gifts, including one decorated with Masonic symbols, a gift of Masonic lodges throughout the Black Hills. Hot Springs no longer is a tourist Mecca, but its citizens, recognizing the historic importance of their stone buildings, have pursued their restoration. The church was closed in 1968 but following its restoration in 1975 as a Bicentennial Project, it is once again housing an active congregation.

St. Luke's
Episcopal Church,
Hot Springs,
South Dakota

North Dakota

NORTH DAKOTA HAS BEEN DESCRIBED as a state where the trees are few and the grass is often short. A dry, flat, featureless land, it became known to outsiders as "America's Siberia."[6] But this did not discourage settlement. As a result of the efforts of the railroads that crossed the state, publicity generated by settlement agencies, and an increasing demand for hard spring wheat, North Dakota began to attract numerous settlers in the boom years of the 1870s and 1880s. Some were Americans moving westward with the frontier, but the vast majority were immigrants. By 1910, 70 percent of the state's population was either immigrants or the children of immigrants, and 80 percent of the population was farmers.

By the time the immigrants began arriving in the 1870s, the territory already had an infrastructure, thanks to Yankee entrepreneurs–railroad magnates, bankers, and land speculators–who saw it as a "colony" ripe for exploitation. They invested capital, but most chose to live elsewhere. Regardless, as good Yankees who were concerned about the moral well-being of the people inhabiting their colony, they underwrote the building of churches, such as **St. Stephen's Episcopal Church**, in Casselton just west of Fargo, built with a donation from General George W. Cass, an Ohio-born civil engineer and president of the Northern Pacific Railroad. At the time of its construction, the church had only eight members, but it was free of debt. The church continued to struggle for members until it was sold to a Mennonite congregation in 1951.

North Dakota entered the Union in 1889, but by that time its ethnic mosaic was in place, one that remains highly visible today. Most settlers came from central and northern Europe; some were members of Pietist groups seeking isolated areas of land where they could continue to practice their faith and traditions without interference. North Dakota was able to provide them land in abundance, but often that land was inhospitable, forcing many to leave. Those who stayed had to adapt their farming methods to accommodate the weather and terrain and their lives to living often miles from their closest neighbor. Churches became the center of the settlers' lives; as one author states, "they fixed one's position in the universe."[7]

Norwegians, the predominant Scandinavian group in the state, homesteaded in the Red River Valley area. A fairly sizable number living in Wild Rice Township organized the **South Wild Rice Lutheran Church** in 1872, building their church in 1883 and engaging the state's first resident Lutheran pastor.

Arriving in the 1880s were Black Sea Germans, known as German-Russians, who settled within a roughly triangular area of the state encompassing its south and north central parts and an area to the southwest across the Missouri River. The oldest continuous German-Russian parish in North Dakota is near Hague in Emmons County, where the spire of **St. Mary's Roman Catholic Church**, built in 1929, still dominates the prairie.

Not all Black Sea Germans were Roman Catholic; some were of the Evangelical faith, including a group of Lutherans who settled in the vicinity of Zeeland, in McIntosh County, in the midst of a large settlement of Catholic German-Russians. Religious services were initially held in homes, until 1893 when the newly chartered **St. Andrew's Evangelical German Lutheran Church** was built. That structure, along with the congregation's second church built in 1906, survive as intact examples of the vernacular building methods employed by German-Russians on the Dakota prairie.

A small group of Ukrainians from Galicia migrated to North Dakota in 1897 via Canada and settled in the Winton area where they homesteaded or worked in the nearby lignite mines. By 1913, there were enough Ukrainians living in the area to build **Holy Trinity Ukrainian Greek Orthodox Church**, one of three Ukrainian Orthodox churches in North Dakota.

Polish immigrants began arriving in the area of the Red River Valley in 1873, creating one of the state's most cohesive and persistent ethnic settlements. Settling in a town they named Warsaw, the community built its first Roman Catholic church in 1884; it was replaced in 1901 by the present **St. Stanislaus Roman Catholic Church**. The immigrant community was justifiably proud of the fact that when the building was dedicated it was free of debt.

North Dakota's ethnic mosaic was further enhanced by the arrival of Syrian (Lebanese) and Jewish homesteaders. Records indicate that over 350 Syrian immigrants settled on the state's free land in the 1890s where they erected the first Arabic Christian church in the United States, and what is believed to be one of the nation's first mosques, located on a farm in Ross. Built in 1929, the mosque has subsequently been destroyed.

German-speaking Jews were early arrivals in North Dakota, settling in the opening market towns of Fargo, Bismarck, and Grand Forks, but they were soon outnumbered by eastern European Jewish immigrants who were sent to North Dakota by Jewish settlement agencies in the east. Their reasoning was that in order to avoid an anti-Semitic backlash, it was necessary for Jews to move out of overcrowded ghettos into the nation's heartland. At one time North Dakota was home to five major and two minor Jewish homestead colonies. All ultimately failed and the Jews moved elsewhere, primarily to towns and cities where many became merchants. Grand Forks has the distinction of having the state's first resident rabbi and first synagogue. The city still has a synagogue, B'nai Israel, built in 1937, as does Fargo.

The drought and Great Depression of the 1930s had an enormous impact on North Dakota, but these events did not discourage people from building new places of worship. Two of the more outstanding are United Lutheran Church in Grand Forks, completed in 1932, and the Cathedral of the Holy Spirit in Fargo, begun in 1942. Both are monumental structures built in the Art Deco style, signifying that although outsiders may see the state as America's Siberia, its residents are more than aware of current architectural styles.

St. Stephen's Episcopal Church

Southeast corner of Third Avenue and Fifth Street, Casselton

ARCHITECT / BUILDER:
George Hancock (see below)
CONSTRUCTION / DEDICATION DATE:
1886

S T. STEPHEN'S, CONSIDERED AMONG the most distinctive churches in North Dakota, is remarkably similar to Christ Church in Medway, Massachusetts, designed by Stephen Earle. What is most distinctive about the building is its material, particularly the quality of stonework, notable in its unique entry tower with soaring turret. Unlike most churches built in the state dating to this period, this one does not have wood shingles in the gable ends nor is its tower open and primarily of wood. The plans for the

St. Stephen's Episcopal Church, Casselton, North Dakota

stone Gothic Revival building may have been brought to North Dakota by an Episcopal missionary who, along with the English-born architect George Hancock, served on the Church Building Committee of the Episcopal Diocese of North Dakota.

The church was constructed during the first Dakota Boom, which began in 1878 when the Northern Pacific Railroad began to lay tracks across the state. The state's first bonanza farm was established near Casselton and by 1885, the town had a population of over 1,300. The town was named after General George W. Cass, who was president of the Northern Pacific Railroad and developer of land along the line. He donated the church as part of the Episcopal Church's home missionary movement to "save the west." At the time of its construction, the church had only eight members. It continued to struggle for members and rectors and by 1943 there was no congregation and the building stood vacant until it was purchased by a Mennonite congregation.

The South Wild Rice Lutheran Church

(ST. JOHN'S LUTHERAN)

Rural Galchutt, Richland County

ARCHITECT / BUILDER:
Not available

CONSTRUCTION / DEDICATION DATE:
1883

SITUATED IN A RURAL AREA, the South Wild Rice Lutheran Church, although small in size, can still be seen for miles because its steeple, added in 1897, rises to a height of approximately 50 feet. The steeple was struck by lightning in 1995 but was restored the following year.

Settlement of southeastern North Dakota began in earnest in the 1870s when the St. Paul, Minneapolis, and Manitoba Railroad reached Breckenridge, Minnesota, on the border with North Dakota. The fertile Red River Valley was now within easy reach of the large number of immigrants arriving from Norway. With their arrival came mission efforts on behalf of various Norwegian Lutheran synodical bodies in the United States. One minister from Goodhue County in southeastern Minnesota was successful in organizing a Lutheran church in Richland County in December 1872. After meeting in homes and a log schoolhouse, a decision was made in October 1881, with only $6.50 in the treasury, to construct a church. The simple, white clapboard building was completed in 1883. Much effort was expended on the sanctuary, which is dominated by an imposing wooden altar, altar screen with a painting of Christ on the Cross, and pulpit. Regular services ceased in 1956, and the church is now used only occasionally for baptisms and marriages. However, it retains an extraordinarily high degree of integrity, particularly in comparison with similar rural churches in North Dakota. The church bell is still rung on Christmas Eve and for the death of a pioneer from the community.

South Wild Rice Lutheran Church, Richland County, North Dakota

St. Mary's Roman Catholic Church

Off ND 11, Hague

ARCHITECT / BUILDER:
Charles A. Hausler

CONSTRUCTION / DEDICATION DATE:
1929

GERMAN RUSSIANS BEGAN TO SETTLE in Emmons County in 1885, converging in Hague, which was incorporated as a village in 1908. Early church services were held in private homes until a small church was constructed west of town in 1890. It was replaced in 1906 by a new building that was destroyed by fire in 1929. Despite the Depression, parishioners raised money to build yet another church, duplicating the exterior style and interior opulence of the one that was destroyed. Much of the labor for excavating the building's foundation and laying brick was contributed by members; work on the church's interior continued until the 1950s.

By far the most prominent structure in the small community, the church is an excellent example of Romanesque Revival architecture coupled with Byzantine features, including the use of polychromatic ceramic tile, brick, and sandstone banding that contribute to the structure's appearance of massiveness. Along with its cemetery, located one and a half miles west of Hague, which is celebrated for its wrought-iron grave crosses and a grotto fashioned from the entrance of the 1906 church, St. Mary's remains a viable expression of the state's oldest continuous German-Russian Catholic parish.

St. Mary's Roman
Catholic Church,
Hague,
North Dakota

St. Andrews Evangelical German Lutheran Church

Vicinity of Zeeland

ARCHITECT / BUILDER:
Not available

CONSTRUCTION / DEDICATION DATE:
Church A: 1893; Church B: 1906

IN 1884, SEVERAL FAMILIES from the Black Sea area of South Russia migrated to McIntosh County, where they formed a Lutheran colony in the midst of a region predominated by German-Russian Roman Catholics. In the first years of settlement they worshiped in their homes, until 1892 when the decision was made to build a church, Church A, dedicated in 1893. The church is a highly intact example of a building style and technology transported from the Old World to the plains of North Dakota. Based on a German-Russian domestic building type, it is constructed primarily of native sandstone rubble held together by mortar of clay, straw, and water. Interior and exterior walls were originally finished with a render composed of the same mortar mixture used to bond the stone, but more recently were overlain with a cement mixture that is whitewashed every spring. The original hand–made pulpit is still in place at the north end of the room.

In 1906 a second, larger frame church was built in a style that reveals the congregation's awareness of American church architecture. The design is a simplified version of the classically inspired Colonial churches of New England, complete with tower, except for its polygonal apse. In addition, the interior retains the white painted walls and the sky blue ceiling associated with German-Russian tradition. The two churches, located next to one another, provide visual evidence of the transition within one ethnic community from the use of traditional building styles and methods to those acquired in the New World.

St. Andrew's
Evangelical German
Lutheran Church,
vicinity of Zeeland,
North Dakota

Holy Trinity Ukrainian Greek Orthodox Church

Bismarck Avenue and Sixth Street North, Wilton

ARCHITECT / BUILDER:
John Krivatski and John Schowchuk, carpenters
CONSTRUCTION / DEDICATION DATE:
1913

I N 1897 A SMALL GROUP of Ukrainians from Galicia migrated to the Wilton area to homestead or to work in the nearby lignite mines. In 1913, when enough money was available, the community engaged two carpenters, John Krivatski and John Schowchuk, to supervise the building of a small white frame clapboard church. Designed in the traditional Orthodox fashion, the church is divided in three parts: an entry bell tower, sanctuary or nave, and apse. Each is crowned with an octagonal drum, onion dome, and distinctive Orthodox cross.

The church interior is original, consisting of a few benches around the nave perimeter. An elaborate iconostasis, painted white with gilt trim, separates the nave from the altar in the apse. The icon screen and tabernacle were carved by the carpenters. Members of the church contributed icons they carried from their homes in Galicia. The church is one of three Ukrainian Greek Orthodox churches in the state that are now used only for special occasions.

Holy Trinity
Ukrainian Greek
Orthodox Church,
Wilton,
North Dakota

St. Stanislaus Roman Catholic Church

Off I-29, Warsaw

ARCHITECT / BUILDER:
John W. Ross

CONSTRUCTION / DEDICATION DATE:
dedicated 1901

S T. STANISLAUS HAS BEEN THE CENTER of organized activity of one of the state's most cohesive and persistent ethnic settlements. The area around Warsaw was settled by Polish immigrants who began arriving in 1872. The first Roman Catholic church, built in 1884, was replaced by the present brick Gothic Revival church, dedicated in 1901. The building's size and predominance in its small community and the fact that at the time of its dedication the $50,000 building was free of debt, indicates its importance to its immigrant community.

The church's architect, John W. Ross from Grand Forks, designed many commercial and government buildings in eastern North Dakota. His design may have been influenced in part by the Polish-born and educated parish priest who had the plans drawn. St. Stanislaus is considered an excellent example of Gothic Revival construction in brick, and is one of the premier turn-of-the-century churches of the region. Because of its size and towering spire, it is a local landmark visible for miles in every direction. The interior of the church was not finished until some years after the exterior but was badly damaged in a 1978 fire. It has since been restored to its original appearance, including inscriptions in Polish and Latin. St. Anthony Academy was built across from the church in 1920 as a school that would help preserve the native language and customs of the Polish community; it served that purpose for 50 years.

St. Stanislaus
Roman Catholic
Church, Warsaw,
North Dakota

NOTES

1. James R. Shortridge, *The Middle West: Its Meaning in American Culture* (University Press of Kansas, 1989), 118 ff.

2. Lawrence O. Christensen, "Missouri: The Heart of the Nation," in *Heartland,* James H. Madison, ed., 86 ff.

3. Quoted in Leo E. Oliva, "Kansas: A Hard Land in the Heartland," in *Heartland,* James H. Madison, ed., 268.

4. Frederick C. Luebke, "Nebraska: Time, Place, and Culture," in *Heartland,* James H. Madison, ed., 235 ff.

5. Herbert T. Hoover, "South Dakota: An Expression of Regional Heritage," in *Heartland,* James H. Madison, ed., 190 ff.

6. David B. Danbom, "North Dakota: The Most Midwestern State," in *Heartland,* James H. Madison, ed., 107.

7. Ibid., 122.

CHAPTER

6

South Atlantic Region

Delaware
District of Columbia
Maryland
Virginia
West Virginia
North Carolina
South Carolina
Georgia
Florida

Coffin Point
Community
Praise House,
St. Helena Island,
South Carolina

S TRETCHING FROM DELAWARE SOUTH to Florida and encompassing the nation's entire southeast coastline, this large expanse of land, known popularly as "The South," has historically been described as standing apart from the rest of the nation. Its settlement pattern did differ from that of other areas of the nation, resulting in the region having a relatively high incidence of certain Protestant denominations, especially Baptist, and a scarcity of Roman Catholics and Jews.

The vast area of fertile land south of the Chesapeake Bay with its ideal growing climate was one of the first to be colonized by the British. The region's numerous navigable rivers made expansion and settlement in some areas relatively easy, as was the case for the Scots-Irish who moved south along a route running inland from the Delaware River ports. Although the region's first settlers did not differ culturally from their counterparts in the northern colonies, the society that developed did, mainly due to the arrival of colonists from Barbados who maintained direct links with the West Indies and introduced African culture and slavery into the region.

While to "outsiders" the "South" may appear to be homogeneous, in reality its composition is far more complex and diffuse. As Mills Lane has observed in his book, *Architecture of the Old South,* "It is a region of regions–the aristocrats of the Tidewater, the new-rich planters of the Piedmont, the small farmers of the trans-Appalachian 'West.' Tobacco was raised in Virginia and Maryland, rice in coastal Georgia and the Carolinas, cotton across the Piedmont. There were few slaveholders in western North Carolina, Virginia, and Maryland, or northern Georgia, but great plantations with numerous slaves were along the coast and in central Georgia and South Carolina."

Except for areas of Delaware and Florida, the region is essentially rural, with few large cities other than ports like Norfolk, Wilmington, Baltimore, Charleston, Savannah, or cities along major rivers, such as Richmond, Columbia, and Augusta, and more recently, Atlanta and Miami. The plantation form of enterprise imported from the Caribbean spread throughout much of the region, bringing with it a need for cheap imported labor–African slaves.

The first Africans arrived in Virginia in 1619, but the large-scale importation of slave labor did not commence until after the establishment of the Royal African Slave Company in 1662. By 1790, blacks comprised almost 40 percent of Virginia's population, 43 percent of South Carolina's, and 25-35 percent of the populations of North Carolina, Georgia, and Maryland. The use of slave labor led to the development of other characteristics considered uniquely southern. A scarcity of blue-collar jobs due to a lack of industry resulted in few eastern and southern European immigrants entering the region. Thus, the majority of southern whites are Protestants of English and Scots-Irish descent.

Small, modest churches dot much of the region's countryside, drawing members from isolated farms, villages, and small towns. Most are Baptist, but small pockets of other religious and ethnic groups provide variety: the Austrian Salzburgers in Georgia, Swiss and French Huguenots in South Carolina, Greeks in Florida, Roman Catholics in Maryland, and a sprinkling of Jews in many of the region's cities and market towns.

Delaware

N AMED AFTER LORD DE LA WARR, governor of the colony of Virginia, Delaware's first white settlement was a trading post established by the Dutch West Indian Company in 1631. Destroyed by hostile Indians, a second, more successful colonization project was organized in 1638 by Swedes who settled on the site of what is now Wilmington. Naming their colony Fort Christina, in honor of the daughter of the founder of the corporation sponsoring the colony, the area around it soon became known as New Sweden. Its centerpiece is **Holy Trinity (Old Swede's) Church** in Wilmington, built in 1698 on the site of the settlement's first burial ground. When the Swedish government withdrew its support of New World churches in 1791, the congregation voted to become Episcopalian, changing its name to Holy Trinity Episcopal Church.

Although founded by Swedes, it was Pennsylvania Quaker families who built up Wilmington's economy and gave the town its name. In 1738, two years after Wilmington was incorporated, the Quakers built their first meetinghouse in an area known as Quaker Hill. As their membership grew, increasingly larger meetinghouses were built, concluding with the **Friends Meeting House**, completed in 1817.

Known as the "Territories of Three Lower Counties on the Delaware," the area was deeded to William Penn in 1682 and remained under the control of the colonial governor of Pennsylvania until 1776 when it became Delaware State. Dutch settlements initially established by Peter Stuyvesant, governor of New Netherlands, continued to be maintained on the site of present-day New Castle. The Dutch settlers, mostly members of the Reformed Church, purchased land near Odessa and built a meetinghouse in 1711. It was replaced in 1773 by **Old Drawyers Church**, which remained in use until 1861 when a new church was built. Abandoned and allowed to decay, the building was restored by a group of concerned citizens, the Friends of Old Drawyers, who continue to maintain it.

Baptists were among the first dissenters to answer Penn's invitation to religious minorities to settle in his new colony. A Baptist congregation, which arrived in 1703, had organized in Wales in 1701 with the purpose of establishing a colony on a 30,000-acre grant in western New Castle County. The Welsh Tract Congregation, as it was known, was the parent of other Baptist congregations in Delaware, including Cow Marsh/Mount Moriah, the fourth Baptist church in Delaware. The congregation's first church, erected in 1796, was replaced by the present frame unadorned chapel, completed in 1872.

As elsewhere in the colonies, the British authorities attempted to impose the practices of the Church of England on the colonists. Immanuel Episcopal Church in New Castle,

Frienc

Fourth ar

A
house. In
began or
the type
nineteen

The n
midst of
ple, feat
supporte
areas ha
once wa:

founded in 1689, has the distinction of being Delaware's first Anglican parish. The parish's brick church, picturesquely located on the village green, was built in 1703. Ultimately, it was another faith imported from Great Britain that was to have the greatest impact in Delaware–Methodism.

Barratt's Chapel, located in Kent County, was built in 1780, the first church in the county erected especially for Methodist worship. The two-story brick meetinghouse is known as the "Cradle of American Methodism," as it was the site where Dr. Thomas Coke and the Reverend Francis Asbury met to make preliminary arrangements for the formation of the Methodist Episcopal Church in America (see Lovely Lane, Baltimore, and Trinity Methodist, Savannah, pp. 225, 260).

During the last half of the nineteenth century, Methodist camp meetings became popular throughout the region, but especially in Delaware and on the eastern shore of Maryland. The camp established at Rehoboth in 1872 had a dual purpose–it was to be a resort, but also a religious retreat. Yearly meetings were held there for nearly ten years, until the coming of the railroad transformed the area into a popular secular resort.

Delaware was home to a free black community that pre-dates the Civil War. Camden, a traditional Quaker community, is said to have been a stop for slaves fleeing northward on the Underground Railroad. **Zion African Episcopal Methodist Church** was organized in 1845 by free blacks living in a rural area outside of Camden. Their one-story Classical Revival church, damaged by a fire and rebuilt in 1889, is one of the few surviving rural African-American churches from this era in Delaware.

Like other states in this region, Delaware's economy was initially based on agriculture, but this changed in the years following the Civil War, when a period of intensive industrialization began, particularly in New Castle County, located near Pennsylvania's coal and iron fields. The industries attracted new immigrants, mainly Roman Catholics, who settled in Wilmington and its environs. Among those arriving were Poles from the province of Posen who established a parish and erected a modest red brick church in 1891. The present St. Hedwig's Roman Catholic Church, a brick and limestone structure built in 1904, was designed in the more elaborate Victorian Gothic Revival style by A. Brilmaier, an architect from Milwaukee, Wisconsin. It continues to serve as the centerpiece of the Wilmington Polish community.

Zion African Methodist Episcopal Church

Center Street, Camden

ARCHITECT / BUILDER:
Not available

CONSTRUCTION / DEDICATION DATE:
1889

THE CONGREGATION WAS ORGANIZED and built its first church in 1845. It was destroyed by fire and replaced by the present church, constructed in 1889. When it was built, the church was located in a rural area of Camden, on the edge of a traditionally African-American section of town. Since then the city has expanded around it.

The one-story Classical Revival structure covered with white-painted weatherboard is very similar in style to other rural churches in Delaware. On the interior, an elaborate painted mural covering the apse behind the altar depicts a shepherd carrying a staff, herding his sheep. A needlepoint depiction of the Last Supper hangs on the wall near the choir box.

Many small rural churches contemporary to Zion have been demolished. Although this congregation has diminished in size, the church remains in use, thanks to the efforts of its members, many of whom are related to the congregation's original trustees.

Zion A.M.E.
Church,
Camden, Delaware

District of Columbia

W ASHINGTON, D.C., IS COEXTENSIVE with the District of Columbia, the Federal District of the United States designated by Congress as the new national capital in 1790. The city has since expanded into the district's rural areas, as new neighborhoods began to develop beyond L'Enfant's original layout of the city. Washington's major government buildings and monuments are well known. Their designers read like a roll call of the nation's most famed architects. These same architects were often called upon to design religious buildings; thus, Washington became a showcase for many dominant architectural styles favored by Americans for their places of worship.

One of the city's most famous churches, renowned as "the church of the Presidents," is Benjamin Latrobe's **St. John's Episcopal Church** built in 1816. The neoclassical structure has undergone many transformations over the course of its history, but it remains one of the few original structures around Lafayette Park.

James Renwick, the designer of Grace Church and St. Patrick's Cathedral in New York City, left his mark on Washington, D.C., in his design for the Smithsonian Institution, completed in 1851, which is a fusion of Romanesque and Renaissance styles. Renwick also designed several important churches in the district, including enlarging Latrobe's St. John's Episcopal Church. One of his lesser known commissions is St. Mary's Episcopal Church, a red brick Gothic Revival structure built in 1886 in Foggy Bottom, a low-lying marshy area along the Potomac River, for an African-American congregation.

Built on high ground are three of Washington's most visible places of worship: the Cathedral of St. Peter and St. Paul, known as the National Cathedral, begun in 1906; the National Shrine of the Immaculate Conception, begun in 1919 and completed 40 years later; and the most recent addition, the **Islamic Center**, built between 1949 and 1957. These three buildings, like so many others in Washington, were planned and built to serve the city's transient population and its many visitors.

But Washington is also a city of neighborhoods where, as elsewhere throughout the nation, places of worship are centers of community. However, unlike many other large cities, Washington did not develop distinct ethnic enclaves. People generally chose to live close to where they worked rather than in isolated ghettos. Thus, one finds mixed congregations like the one that built St. Theresa of Avila in 1879, whose members were German, Irish, and African-American Roman Catholics.

Washington's openness was also extended to its black citizens, at least until the early twentieth century, when segregation became more common. **Mount Zion United Methodist Church**, formed in 1814 by blacks objecting to the treatment they were receiving from white worshippers in the Montgomery Street Methodist Church, is the oldest black congregation in the district and the first black Methodist church in the area. The congregation built its first church in 1816 in Georgetown, replacing it with the present church in 1888. The church continues to be an integral part of Georgetown, serving the religious, educational, and social needs of its members.

Meridian Hill, initially a rural area that began to develop in the 1880s, was incorporated within the city's limits in 1903. Home to mansions, embassies, and apartment buildings, it was also the site of a number of churches, including **St. Luke's Episcopal Church**, once home of the district's oldest black Episcopal congregation. All that remains standing of the congregation's historic Gothic Revival church built in 1879 is its front façade. The building was destroyed by arson in 1970.

Three other religious institutions moved to Meridian Hill in the 1920s, where their towers and spires continue to compete for attention. They are: the National Baptist Memorial Church, completed in 1926; the Unification Church (Washington Chapel), Church of Jesus Christ of Latter-day Saints, built in 1932; and All Souls Church, completed in 1924.

Other ethnic groups spread throughout the city, including people of German descent who established one of the city's first settlements, known as Funkstown or Hamburg, prior to the founding of the national capital. A congregation, Concordian German Evangelical Lutheran Church, was established in 1833. The present church, built in 1891–92 and renamed **Concordia United Church of Christ**, is the second on the site. The land on which it stands has been in continuous ownership of the congregation since the late eighteenth century.

Many of the Jewish people who began to settle in the district in the 1840s had ties with their co-religionists in Baltimore. The district's first Jewish institution, Washington Hebrew Congregation established in 1852, was affiliated with the Reform Movement and initially met in a church remodeled for use as a synagogue. An Orthodox congregation, **Adas Israel**, was formed in 1869. Their building, erected in 1876, which was the first synagogue built in Washington, D.C., has been restored and now serves as a Jewish museum.

St. John's Episcopal Church

Lafayette Square, Washington, D.C.

ARCHITECT / BUILDER:
Benjamin Latrobe; James Renwick; McKim, Mead, White
CONSTRUCTION / DEDICATION DATE:
1816; 1820; 1883; 1919

KNOWN AS "THE CHURCH OF THE PRESIDENTS," with a special pew, number 28, set aside for the chief executive, St. John's Episcopal Church was established in 1809, but its construction was delayed by the War of 1812. Following the war, Benjamin Henry Latrobe, famous for his work on the Capitol, the White House, and other Washington buildings, volunteered to design a church to be located across the meadow from the White House. The church, completed in 1816, has undergone many alterations.

Latrobe's plan was for a Greek Cross church with a cupola set atop a shallow dome, but in 1820 the west transept arm was lengthened, turning it into a Latin cross fronted with a Roman style portico. Two years later, a 40-foot steeple was erected over the west transept.

St. John's Episcopal Church, Washington, D.C.

Together the additions create an exterior remindful of James Gibbs's St. Martin-in-the-Fields in London, built in 1722–26. Initially, clear glass windows flooded the interior with light, but they were later replaced by large stained glass windows. Latrobe designed the interior to have an open preaching space focused on a wine-glass pulpit on a movable iron rail positioned so it projected into the circle of pews under the dome. The gallery rested on 12 columns. Changes made in 1883 under the direction of James Renwick, Jr., included lengthening the east end, one- and two-story additions on the north and south, and a Palladian window over the altar. Alterations made in 1919 by the firm of McKim, Mead, and White further obscure Latrobe's original design.

Islamic Center

2551 Massachusetts Avenue, NW

ARCHITECT / BUILDER:
Irwin S. Porter and Sons; Egyptian Ministry of Works
CONSTRUCTION / DEDICATION DATE:
1949-1957

BUILT ON MASSACHUSETTS AVENUE'S "Embassy Row," and not far from the Egyptian Embassy at 2301 Massachusetts Avenue, the Islamic Center is located on one of the city's higher sites, allowing its minaret to be visible for miles around. The distinctive building, occupying nearly a city block, contains a mosque and offices. Approaching it from the street, its front façade appears to parallel that of the street. However, upon entering the central arcade that opens onto a courtyard, it becomes apparent that the front façade of the mosque itself is skewed so its *mihrab* or niche, the focus of prayer, is facing toward the city of Mecca.

The building's decorative elements, although exhibiting modern influences, nevertheless are rendered in the Islamic style. Besides the distinctive minaret, other elements include the use of the horseshoe arch, corbeling, roof crenelations, and blue and gold mosaic trim. The domed interior is lavishly decorated with tiles displaying nonfigurative motifs and sayings from the *Qur'an* rendered in beautiful Arabic script. The floor is covered with prayer rugs.

Islamic Center,
Washington, D.C.

Mount Zion United Episcopal Church

1334 Twenty-ninth Street, NW

ARCHITECT / BUILDER:
Reverend Alexander Dennis, carpenter
CONSTRUCTION / DEDICATION DATE:
1884

THIS CONGREGATION EMBODIES an important part of the history of Washington. A Methodist congregation was organized in Washington in 1772, one of the oldest in the nation. Known later as the Montgomery Street Church (now Dumbarton United Methodist), in 1801 it counted 37 blacks among its 95 members. Dissatisfied with the treatment they received from white congregants, the blacks formed their own congregation in 1814. Purchasing land, they built a small church known both as "The Meeting House" and the "Ark." A church register for the years 1820–1850 provides chilling evidence of the congregants' lives: notations indicate that some had "run away," were "lost," or were "sold."

In 1844 the congregation changed its name to Mount Zion. As its membership steadily increased in the years following the Civil War, it became evident that a new, larger church was needed. The present site in Georgetown was purchased and the foundations dug in 1876. Work began on the building in 1880, much of it being done by members working under the supervision of Reverend Alexander Dennis, a Virginia carpenter, and his associate pastor Edgar Murphy. As the congregation continued to grow, additions were made to the church; however, it remains a simple two-story brick structure with Gothic detailing. The congregation continues to play an important role in its neighborhood, ministering to the needs of all people, regardless of color.

Mount Zion United Episcopal Church, Georgetown, Washington, D.C.

St. Luke's Episcopal Church

Fifteenth and Church Streets, NW

ARCHITECT / BUILDER:
Calvin T. S. Brent (?)

CONSTRUCTION / DEDICATION DATE:
1879 (first services)

ALL THAT IS LEFT OF St. Luke's Episcopal Church, the oldest African-American Episcopal congregation in the city, is its front façade that faces a small park, dedicated in memory of this historic church that was destroyed by arsonists in 1970. Although the church no longer stands, the story of its founding and construction is an important part of the history of Washington.

The congregation developed out of St. Mary's Episcopal Church's mission among Washington's black community. The impetus for building the church came from one of the nation's most distinguished African-American intellectuals, Dr. Alexander Crummell, born free in 1819, and educated in the United States and Queen's College, Cambridge, England. While in England, Dr. Crummell attended services in many small parish Gothic churches and was impressed with their architecture. Upon his return to Washington, D.C., in 1873 to be vice-rector at St. Mary's serving the city's black community, he made the decision to form a separate black parish. He resolved to build a Gothic Revival church that would be the

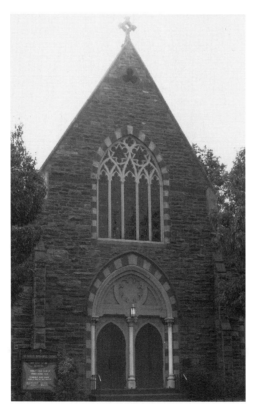

St. Luke's Episcopal
Church, ruins,
Washington, D.C.

physical embodiment of his belief in the role the Episcopal Church must play as an advocate for social change, education, and self-help within the African-American community.

The architect for the church may have been Calvin T. S. Brent working in collaboration with Dr. Crummell. Brent is the first known African-American architect in the District of Columbia. Crummell's recollections of England's parish churches provided Brent with many of the Gothic design elements that appeared in St. Luke's. While the church lacked the towering grandeur of many Gothic Revival churches built at this time, its fine proportions and excellent craftsmanship more than compensated for its modest size.

Adas Israel Synagogue

Third and G Streets, NW; originally located at 619 Sixth Street, NW

ARCHITECT / BUILDER:
Not available

CONSTRUCTION / DEDICATION DATE:
1876

ADAS ISRAEL WAS ORIGINALLY in the center of a Jewish community that was located above Pennsylvania Avenue. The simple two-story red brick synagogue hosted President Ulysses S. Grant at its dedication ceremony in 1876. It served its congregation until 1907 when a larger synagogue was constructed several blocks away. The building was then transformed into a Greek Orthodox church, and in the 1940s became a carry-out deli. For over 60 years the synagogue was forgotten until it was threatened with demolition to make room for a new subway line. The thought of losing Washington's first synagogue mobilized citizens to see that it was preserved. The Jewish Historical Society of Greater Washington purchased the building and, in 1969, moved it three blocks to a new site.

The synagogue, now restored, houses a museum of Jewish heritage on the first floor, and the former sanctuary upstairs is used for cultural events.

Adas Israel Synagogue
(now Lillian and Albert Small
Jewish Museum),
Washington, D.C.

Concordia United Church of Christ

Twentieth and G Streets, NW

ARCHITECT / BUILDER:
Paul Schulze, Albert Goenner
CONSTRUCTION / DEDICATION DATE:
1892

THE CONCORDIA UNITED CHURCH OF CHRIST, originally known as the Concordia Lutheran Evangelical Church, was built in 1892 and is considered one of the finest Victorian eclectic churches still standing in Washington, D.C. It is the congregation's third church, built on a site that has been in the continuous ownership of the German congregation since the late eighteenth century. At that time the area now known as Foggy Bottom was called Hamburg or Funkstown. Jacob Funk, a German immigrant, established a small German settlement there that pre-dates the founding of the Federal City.

The present church was designed by two local architects. The details of its design are essentially Gothic Revival. The building's most distinctive feature is its four-story tower on its northwest corner. The interior retains its German and somewhat Baroque character. Only the area around the altar has been modernized.

The congregation that built this church played an important role in Washington's German community throughout the nineteenth and much of the twentieth centuries. The church and its rectory remain important architectural landmarks in their neighborhood.

FACING PAGE:

Concordia United
Church of Christ
(Concordia Lutheran
Evangelical Church),
Washington, D.C.

Maryland

ARYLAND WAS THE LAST NEW WORLD COLONY established by England before the events of the 1640s that witnessed the beheading of King Charles I and the establishment of Oliver Cromwell's protectorate. The colony was given to George Calvert, first Baron Baltimore, by Charles I in 1632. Baltimore was Roman Catholic and saw the need for a separate colony where Catholics could worship free of the persecution they experienced in England and its colonies. Ironically, nearly 50 percent of Maryland's first settlers were Protestant, including Scots-Irish indentured servants who organized **Rock Presbyterian Church, Elkton**, in 1720, and constructed the present building in 1761.

The Act of Establishment of 1692 that made the Church of England the state-supported religion resulted in the formation of many Anglican parishes in Maryland. One of the earliest, Christ Church in Calvert County, specifically mentioned in the Act, was founded in 1671. The church, erected in 1772, is still in use. Although the Anglicans tried to impose their faith on all who settled in the colony, this did not discourage others from attempting to establish communities. Among those who achieved limited success were Moravians, German-speaking Protestants, migrating south from Pennsylvania who established Maryland's only Moravian settlement in 1746. The Graceham Moravian Church at Graceham, built in 1822, was added onto the eastern end of the settlement's meetinghouse and parsonage built 25 years earlier.

Methodist missionaries also were operating in the colony. A Methodist conference was held at the Lovely Lane Meetinghouse in Baltimore in December 1784 to organize the Methodist Episcopal Church of the United States and to ordain Reverend Francis Asbury as its first bishop. **Lovely Lane United Methodist Church**, constructed in 1884 and designed by the well-known architect Stanford White is known as the mother church of American Methodism.

The fifth Lord Baltimore was a Protestant, and a colony founded as a haven for Roman Catholics no longer tolerated their presence and forbade them from worshiping in public. But a minority Roman Catholic population survived and became a vital center for Catholicism in the colonies. In 1806, Baltimore's large, ethnically diverse Roman Catholic population–French, Irish, Belgian, German, Italian–dedicated the first Roman Catholic cathedral built in the United States. Designed by the famed architect Benjamin Henry Latrobe, the designer of St. John's Episcopal Church in Washington, D.C., plus many other major buildings in the capital, the **Minor Basilica of the Assumption of the Blessed**

Virgin Mary, is considered one of the most distinguished buildings ever erected in the United States.

Following Maryland's passage of the "Jew Bill" in 1826 allowing Jews to hold public office without submitting to a Christian oath, German-speaking Jewish immigrants began arriving in Baltimore, where they incorporated the Baltimore Hebrew Congregation in 1830. In 1845, the congregation built the first synagogue in the state, the **Lloyd Street Synagogue**, considered Baltimore's last Greek Revival building. In 1891, the synagogue was sold to a Lithuanian Roman Catholic congregation and renamed St. John the Baptist. In 1876, Orthodox Jewish immigrants built the city's second synagogue, Chizuk Amuno (later renamed **B'nai Israel**), right down the street from the Lloyd Street Synagogue; it is still in use, and with the Lloyd Street Synagogue, forms part of the Jewish Historical Society of Maryland's complex.

For well over a century and a half, a church has stood on Orchard Street in Baltimore's Seton Hill, a historic African-American neighborhood. The congregation, founded in 1839 by a former slave, Trueman Le Pratt, erected the state's first black church. It was replaced in 1882 by the grand Renaissance Revival **Orchard Street Church** that served its congregation until the 1970s. Today it is headquarters for the Baltimore Urban League.

Free blacks in Cumberland established the African Methodist Episcopal Church in 1847. The congregation's first church, a modest frame structure built in 1848, was replaced in 1892 by a more monumental two-story brick building that is still in use.

Lloyd Street Synagogue (now Jewish Historical Society of Maryland, Inc.), Baltimore, Maryland

Rock United Presbyterian Church

MD 273 at Rock Church Road, vicinity of Elkton

ARCHITECT / BUILDER:
1900 renovations by architect W. L. Plack
CONSTRUCTION / DEDICATION DATE:
1761

SCOTS-IRISH IMMIGRANTS began settling in northeastern Maryland not far from the Pennsylvania and Delaware lines in the first quarter of the eighteenth century. Presbyterianism was then enjoying a tremendous growth resulting in the building of a number of new churches, including Rock United Presbyterian Church, organized in 1720. The congregation's first meetinghouse was a simple log building later replaced by a more substantial frame and clapboard one. Finally, in 1761, the members were prosperous enough to build an impressive stone church that has been in continuous use since its construction. The church's appearance, however, reflects the series of renovations it has undergone in response to the changing needs and tastes of the congregation. In its present form it is a mid-eighteenth century vernacular church building with Victorian Gothic elements grafted onto it, including a stained glass rose window inserted above the arched entrances and lancet windows of colored or etched glass with Gothic tracery along the side walls.

Rock United
Presbyterian
Church,
Elkton, Maryland

Lovely Lane United Methodist Church

2700 St. Paul Street, Baltimore

ARCHITECT / BUILDER:
Stanford White

CONSTRUCTION / DEDICATION DATE:
1884

L OVELY LANE METHODIST CHURCH, known as the mother church of American Methodism, is one of Baltimore's architectural gems. It was designed by the noted architect Stanford White, who liberally borrowed elements from several well-known churches built between the sixth and twelfth centuries, mainly in Ravenna, Italy. For example, the church's most commanding feature, its monumental square bell tower situated in the southeast corner, is modeled after the campanile of a twelfth-century church near Ravenna. The pulpit is a reproduction of that in another Ravenna church, and its stained glass windows are reproductions of mosaics from a fifth-century church, now preserved in a museum in Rome. The dome over the sanctuary is patterned after the sixth-century Hagia Sophia in Constantinople (Istanbul, Turkey). A clever element is the dome's interior decoration. The firmament is represented in blue and gold, with every visible star in the position it occupied at 3 A.M. on the day of the church's dedication, allegedly the same arrangement of the heavens as that over Judea at the time of the birth of Christ, except for the Star of Bethlehem.

The congregation had taken the name First Methodist in 1872, but in 1954 it decided to return to its original name, Lovely Lane. The following year the Baltimore Conference Historical Society opened the Lovely Lane Museum in the church building where priceless treasures of early Methodist history are exhibited.

Lovely Lane United Methodist Church, Baltimore, Maryland

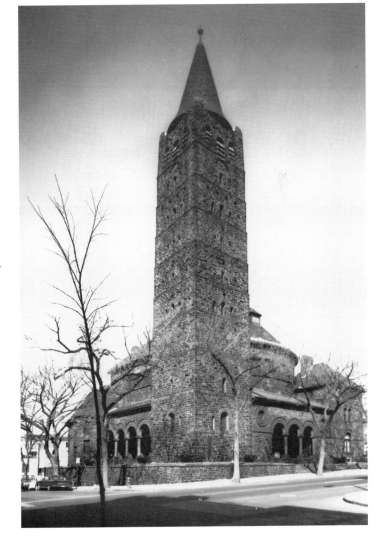

Minor Basilica of the Assumption of the Blessed Virgin Mary

Cathedral and Mulberry Streets, Baltimore

ARCHITECT / BUILDER:
Benjamin Henry Latrobe

CONSTRUCTION / DEDICATION DATE:
1806

THIS IS THE FIRST ROMAN CATHOLIC CATHEDRAL built in the United States and is one of the nation's most important and original buildings. It was designed by the architect Benjamin Henry Latrobe, who was born in England, the son of a Moravian minister. He trained there and in Germany to be an architect and engineer before immigrating to the United States in 1795. The Baltimore cathedral is considered among his greatest works.

At the time of the cathedral's construction, America's religious architecture was dominated by styles originating in England and being disseminated through pattern books. Churches, frame or brick, were oblong with a temple-front portico and a steeple rising from the ridge of the roof. Through the influence of the Anglican Church in the colonies, the style swiftly became associated with American Protestant theology. Latrobe was the first in the United States to borrow elements from this Neoclassical lexicon for a Roman Catholic church, but he also added to that vocabulary.

The cathedral's plan, so unlike contemporary Protestant churches, looks back to the grandeur of imperial Rome for its models. It is in the form of a Latin cross, but its circular nave, reminiscent of the Pantheon in Rome and capped by a similar shallow dome, and its highly sophisticated system of masonry barrel vaults are of a structural design never before used in this manner in the United States.

Minor Basilica
of the Assumption of
the Blessed Virgin Mary,
Baltimore, Maryland

Lloyd Street Synagogue

11 Lloyd Street, Baltimore

ARCHITECT / BUILDER:
Robert Cary Long, Jr.
CONSTRUCTION / DEDICATION DATE:
1845

THE BALTIMORE HEBREW CONGREGATION, organized by German-speaking Jews, worshipped in several second-floor storefronts before its members were able to build the state's first synagogue in 1845. The Greek Revival building was designed by Robert Carey Long, Jr., an architect who had already designed three churches in Baltimore. The synagogue underwent renovations in 1860 that included extending the hall 30 feet and adding two smaller doorways in the west façade. A large gas chandelier and an elaborate new Ark for the Torah Scrolls were also added.

In 1891, the congregation built a larger synagogue uptown, and this building was sold to a Lithuanian Roman Catholic congregation who renamed it the Church of St. John the Baptist. After considerable effort it was acquired and restored by the Jewish Historical Society of Maryland and, along with its neighbor, the Chizuk Amuno Synagogue, now forms part of the Society's museum complex in east Baltimore.

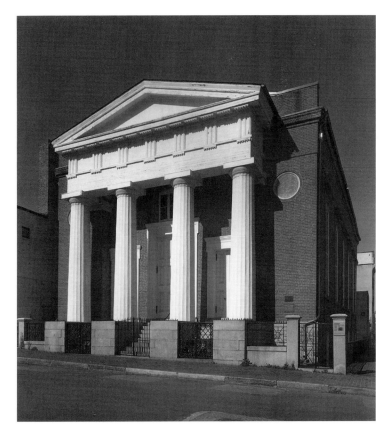

**Lloyd Street Synagogue
(now Jewish Historical
Society of Maryland, Inc.),
Baltimore, Maryland**

Chizuk Amuno Synagogue

(B'NAI ISRAEL)

27-35 Lloyd Street, Baltimore

ARCHITECT / BUILDER:
Henry Burge
CONSTRUCTION / DEDICATION DATE:
1876

CHIZUK AMUNO (STRENGTHENING THE FAITH) founded this synagogue; B'nai Israel (Children of Israel) currently uses the building. The Chizuk Amuno congregation was organized to protest the reforms introduced into the religious practice of the Lloyd Street Synagogue. Those opposed resigned from the congregation and in 1870 formed the Chizuk Amuno congregation. The congregation grew and in 1874 purchased a lot just south of the Lloyd Street Synagogue. The synagogue was designed by the amateur architect Henry Burge, a recent non-Jewish immigrant from Bavaria. Its eclectic style, combining Gothic, Romanesque, and Moorish elements, is quite different from its Greek Revival neighbor, the Lloyd Street Synagogue. Horseshoe arches frame this synagogue's three entrances while Gothic pointed arches are used for its windows. A large rose window dominates its façade.

The focal point of the interior is the Ark set in an apse projecting from the eastern wall. A *bimah*, a raised reading platform, is set in the center of the hall.

The synagogue was sold to B'nai Israel in 1895. Known as the Russian Synagogue to distinguish it from the earlier German congregation, its members were Polish and Russian Jews who began to arrive in the city in the 1870s and moved into neighborhoods being vacated by German Jews. It continues to be used as a synagogue and is part of the complex that comprises the Jewish Historical Society of Maryland.

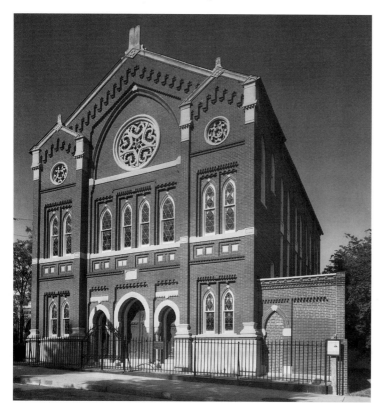

B'nai Israel Synagogue
(formerly Chizuk
Amuno Synagogue),
Baltimore, Maryland
(interior, facing page)

Orchard Street Church

(BALTIMORE URBAN LEAGUE)

512 Orchard Street, Baltimore

ARCHITECT / BUILDER:
Frank E. Davis, architect
CONSTRUCTION / DEDICATION DATE:
1882

ACCORDING TO LEGEND, this African-American congregation's first church was painstakingly constructed over a period of ten years by slaves and freedmen who laid the bricks by torchlight. As the first black church in Maryland, it reputedly was part of the Underground Railroad during the Civil War.

The present building, designed by Frank E. Davis, was constructed in 1882 and served the congregation until the 1970s, when it relocated to the suburbs. The building stood vacant for two decades and was scheduled for demolition until it was saved by preservationists who had it listed in the National Register. In 1988, the Baltimore Urban League, a not-for-profit organization, needed larger headquarters to house its social services. The League's president concluded that the spacious, centrally located Orchard Street Church, with its many historic ties to the community, was the ideal building. The League funded the building's $4 million restoration with city and state monies and a grant from the Maryland Historical Trust. In addition, a $600,000 construction loan was obtained from NationsBank's Community Development Lending Group, an innovative program that provides crucial support to inner-city revitalization projects. The local African-American community donated more than half a million dollars. The restored church and Sunday School building now house offices, a community service center, and a museum of African-American history and culture. The building again plays an important role in its community.

Orchard Street Church (now Baltimore Urban League), Baltimore, Maryland

Virginia

V IRGINIA IS THE OLDEST AND WEALTHIEST of all the English colonies in the South. The area, explored by Walter Raleigh in 1584, was given its name by Queen Elizabeth I. By 1632, the colony had 15,000 settlers, mainly English loyal to the Anglican Church. In the late seventeenth century, Scots-Irish indentured servants began to arrive, raising concern among the English that they would soon be outnumbered by the Scots-Irish Presbyterians. To prevent this from happening, the English colonists put a limit on the number who could settle in the colony.

The Anglican Church in America, established in Jamestown in 1607, was formally adopted as the Church of the Virginia Colony in 1619. The only early Anglican church building dating to this period is **St. Luke's Episcopal Church**, also known as Benns Chapel, in Isle of Wight County, built between 1632 and 1682. This remarkable building is considered an outstanding example of early Anglican Gothic architecture in America.

Not all Anglicans favored the Gothic style; others preferred churches built in the "new" style introduced by Christopher Wren and exemplified by St. Martin-in-the-Fields in London designed by Wren's student, James Gibbs. **Aquia Episcopal Church** in Stafford County, constructed in 1757, is an essentially intact example of a rural Georgian Colonial church built in this style. Its sophisticated design–a Greek cross plan–and its fine masonry details and richly detailed woodwork reflect the wealth and substance of the colony's rural plantation society.

Many Scots-Irish Presbyterians traveling through the Cumberland Valley of Pennsylvania settled in Virginia's Shenandoah Valley. Old Stone Church in Winchester, built in 1788, is a surviving example of their austere religious architecture. In 1834, the Presbyterians merged with another congregation and the building was transformed into a Baptist church, but they regained control of it again in the 1930s, restoring it to its original appearance.

Due to the shortage of trained Presbyterian ministers and the inevitable loosening of ties to the homeland, a number of Scots-Irish Presbyterians began to join Methodist and Baptist congregations. The greatest period of growth for the two denominations was the Colonial period, when increasing numbers of Baptists from Maryland and New England and colonists from England began to settle in the area. Between 1760 and 1780, 67 Baptist churches were formed in Virginia alone. One of the early rural congregations is **Frying Pan Meeting House** located near the town of Floris, built by its members between 1783 and 1791.

Richmond is home to the sixth Jewish congregation formed in the United States. In 1789, a small group of Jews living in Richmond organized a congregation, Kahal Kadosh Beth Shalome, that followed the Sephardic rite of Jews who had fled persecution in Spain and Portugal. German-speaking Jews who began arriving in the early nineteenth century were uncomfortable with the Sephardic ritual and as a result decided to form their own congregation, **Beth Ahabah**, incorporated in 1841. Seven years later the congregation built a synagogue that was replaced by a larger building in 1880, which in turn was replaced by a yet larger and more impressive Greek Revival style building in 1904.

Scots-Irish Presbyterians' exposure to Methodism came from the ubiquitous itinerant Methodist preachers who were traveling throughout the nation's rural areas holding outdoor revival meetings that attracted large crowds. As the revivals began to lose their spontaneity and became more institutionalized, the campgrounds gave way to more permanent quarters. Shelters, essentially pavilions, were erected on the campgrounds to house the speaker's platform, choir tiers, and "mourners" bench. The **Methodist Tabernacle** in the vicinity of Mathews, erected in 1922, is one the state's few remaining permanent revival shelters.

At the other end of the scale in the design of Protestant worship spaces is the 1812 Neoclassic Monumental Church in Richmond, displaying a Doric portico and octagonal plan. Its architect, Robert Mills, a student of Thomas Jefferson and Benjamin H. Latrobe, referred to himself as the first native American who directed his studies to architecture. The church is a memorial to 71 people killed in a fire at a theater that had stood on that site.

Virginia, a border state during the Civil War, had a difficult time deciding where it stood regarding its large African-American population–slavery or freedom. Initially Virginia was a slave state, but by 1778 it had a statute on the books prohibiting the importation of slave labor. However, slavery continued to be part of its culture. The state's dilemma remains visible in two surviving churches.

The simple Gothic Revival **Bremo Slave Chapel** constructed in 1835 still stands as a reminder of the status of many of the blacks in Virginia in the years leading up to the Civil War. Third Street Bethel African Methodist Episcopal Church in Richmond, on the other hand, was built about 1857 by the city's large free black population, one of the first congregations in the state to join the newly organized African Methodist Episcopal denomination.

As early as 1780, German Lutherans had nine churches in the colony of Virginia. Sharon Lutheran Church in Wythe County, built in 1821, is part of a large-scale German settlement. The present church, built about 1893, is in an Eastlake Revival style popularized by the English architect Charles Eastlake. Its interior remains essentially intact. Lutherans shared their church with a Presbyterian congregation until 1911 when the Presbyterians were able to build their own structure.

Virginia, like all of the South, had a very minuscule Roman Catholic population. Irish immigrants recruited to work on the construction of the Orange and Alexandria Railroad formed one of the state's earliest Roman Catholic parishes. St. Mary's Roman Catholic Church in Fairfax Station, built in 1858, is a simple rural Gothic Revival style building that achieved fame through its association with Clara Barton, first president of the American Red Cross, who used it during the Civil War as a field hospital.

St. Luke's Episcopal Church

(BENNS CHAPEL)

State Route 10, Isle of Wight County

ARCHITECT / BUILDER:
Not available

CONSTRUCTION / DEDICATION DATE:
1632 (?)

S T. LUKE'S, ALSO KNOWN AS BENNS CHAPEL, "Old Brick," or "Newport Parish" Church, is generally considered the finest surviving example of seventeenth-century Gothic (note: not Gothic Revival) architecture in the United States. Except for its Flemish bond brickwork, it is similar to rural medieval Gothic churches in England. Its construction date of 1632, however, is not accepted by all authorities. Some believe it probably was built later in the seventeenth century when the colonists began to erect more substantial buildings.

Although it is an outstanding example of the English colonists' link with their homeland, the disestablishment of the Anglican Church in Virginia in 1785 caused it to go into decline. It stood in more or less ruinous condition throughout the nineteenth century, except for a brief period of rehabilitation in the 1820s, when there was a renewal of interest in the Anglican Church, reborn in the United States as the Protestant Episcopal Church. Some repairs were begun in the 1890s, but a far more thorough restoration was completed in 1957 when the church was restored to its seventeenth-century condition. It was also embellished with several rare items, including chancel furnishings of seventeenth-century cut-velvet, a seventeenth-century Bernard Smith organ, and a font made from a tree trunk.

No longer a parish church, St. Luke's is officially designated a historic shrine of the Episcopal Diocese of Southern Virginia and is open to the public.

St. Luke's
Episcopal Church
(Benns Chapel),
Isle of Wight,
Virginia

Aquia Episcopal Church

U.S. 1 and State Route 676, Stafford County

ARCHITECT / BUILDER:
William Copein, stonemason; Mourning Richards, contractor
CONSTRUCTION / DEDICATION DATE:
1751-1757

AQUIA EPISCOPAL CHURCH IS A RARE southern example of rural Georgian colonial church architecture that has survived essentially intact. Its once isolated rural location is one of the church's distinguishing characteristics and reflects the isolated plantations where most of its members lived. The church is now surrounded by suburban sprawl, but thanks to mature trees remains reasonably screened from modern intrusions. Like other Anglican churches in Virginia, the church was abandoned following the disestablishment of the Church of England in 1786. However, the resurgence of interest in the Episcopal Church in the years prior to the Civil War resulted in its repair.

The church's sophisticated Georgian design and fine craftsmanship reflect the wealth and substance of the colony's plantation society. Although modest in scale, as were most rural churches in Virginia, it reveals its builders' knowledge of contemporary styles, probably available to them through English pattern books of famous architects such as James Gibbs, the designer of St. Martin-in-the-Fields. Its Georgian elements include its Greek cross plan, rusticated stone doorways, and richly detailed woodwork, including original box pews and a rare three-tiered pulpit.

Aquia
Episcopal Church,
Stafford County,
Virginia

Frying Pan Meeting House

2615 Centreville Road, Floris

ARCHITECT / BUILDER:
Not available
CONSTRUCTION / DEDICATION DATE:
1783-1791

T HE FRYING PAN MEETING HOUSE takes its unusual name from nearby Frying Pan Run. Originally in an isolated rural area, it is now surrounded by suburban development. The area was settled in the 1720s by workers in a copper mine on Frying Pan Run. The mine failed, but a few settlers chose to remain and formed a Baptist congregation. They built their own church in 1783, the only church in Floris until the late nineteenth century.

The Frying Pan Meeting House is a simple one-room, one-and-a-half-story nearly square white weatherboard structure. It has had no major structural changes or alterations since it was built except for the addition of a balcony and stair along its back interior wall.

From 1791 until 1867, free blacks as well as slaves were members of Frying Pan. By 1840 the church had 29 black members and 33 white. Following the Civil War, blacks in the area organized their own Baptist congregation and in 1882 constructed Mount Pleasant Baptist Church nearby.

The meetinghouse and cemetery remain intact. In 1984, the congregation's last member deeded the church and property to the Fairfax County Park Authority.

Frying Pan
Meeting House,
Floris, Virginia

Beth Ahabah Synagogue

1117 West Franklin Street, Richmond

ARCHITECT / BUILDER:
Nolan and Baskervill

CONSTRUCTION / DEDICATION DATE:
1904

AFTER WORSHIPPING IN TWO prior buildings built on the same site in the downtown area of Richmond, the congregation moved into its new building located west of downtown. The stunning neoclassical synagogue was designed by two noted local architects, Nolan and Baskervill, who had designed a number of other religious buildings. It is unclear why the congregation selected this style, but it is similar to the earlier synagogue built in Charleston (see p. 255) and perhaps relates back to the congregation's founding in the Federal era when the Classical Revival style was popular.

Other than the addition of a two-story religious school on the west, the synagogue has remained essentially intact and is still in use by descendants of its original members.

Congregation
Beth Ahabah
Synagogue,
Richmond, Virginia

Bremo Slave Chapel

Bremo Bluff, Fluvanna County

ARCHITECT / BUILDER:
Not available

CONSTRUCTION / DEDICATION DATE:
1835

B REMO SLAVE CHAPEL, built in 1835, is located up the hill from the James River in the village of Bremo Bluff. It was moved from its original site, part of the Bremo plantation owned by General John Hartwell Cocke, sometime between 1882 and 1884. After being remodeled it was moved again in 1924 to its present location, where it is in use as a parish hall for Grace Episcopal Church. A simple Gothic Revival building set on a brick foundation, its wood frame is covered with board-and-batten siding.

Cocke apparently built the chapel so his slaves could be taught to read and receive religious instruction, activities that were illegal at the time. He would frequently conduct the services himself. The chapel fell into disuse following the Civil War. Cocke died in 1866, leaving the plantation to his sons, who then offered the chapel to the community of Bremo Bluff. It was consecrated as Grace Episcopal Church in 1884 and served in that capacity until 1924, when a new brick church was built to replace it. Fortunately the building has not been destroyed; it remains Virginia's only known slave chapel.

Bremo Slave
Chapel, vicinity
of Bremo Bluff,
Virginia

West Virginia

W EST VIRGINIA IS THE ONLY STATE situated entirely within the Appalachian Uplands that stretch from New York to Alabama. Mountains and deep valleys characterize its geography. Rich in mineral resources, especially bituminous coal, the state also has many small farms settled by people moving westward through the valleys that cut through the region. Topography and demography contributed to the formation of West Virginia as a separate state. Until 1863 the region was part of Virginia, but culturally it was quite different. Rural, with isolated settlements populated by proudly independent people who did not sympathize with the wealthy slave-holding plantation owners to the east, it was inevitable that the issues that precipitated the Civil War would divide Virginia. Much of the population in Virginia's western mountain area chose to withdraw from the state when it voted to secede from the Union. Thus in 1863, in the midst of the Civil War, the State of West Virginia was established.

Scots-Irish, Welsh, and German settlers began arriving in the 1730s. Many were freed indentured servants who in the years prior to the Revolutionary War were able to establish at least 30 Presbyterian churches in the colony. One of the oldest in continuous use west of the Allegheny Mountains is the **Old Stone Presbyterian Church** in Lewisburg, constructed in 1796. Its simple yet massive architecture is typical of buildings in this area.

A break-away group of Presbyterians, later known as the Disciples of Christ, was founded by Alexander Campbell, an Irish immigrant who had differences about the interpretation of doctrine. Campbell moved to western Virginia in 1811, and by 1829, had a large enough group of followers to establish a congregation known today as **Bethany Church of Christ**. Built in 1850, the church replaced an earlier meetinghouse built in 1830.

Circuit-riding Methodist preachers found a receptive audience in the independent isolated rural population of West Virginia; by 1906, the state numbered more Methodists than Baptists. One of the first regular Methodist Societies formed on Virginia's western frontier is in an area known locally as the "Sinks" of Greenbrier County (now Monroe County). The society's first meetings were held either in members' homes or in widely scattered schoolhouses until 1786, the year the congregation engaged their first full-time minister and built **Rehoboth Methodist Episcopal Church**.

Many Baptists were African-American, including those who erected the **African Zion Baptist Church** in Malden about 1872. Organized in 1863, the year West Virginia became a state, it is the first organization in the state completely owned and controlled by African-

Americans. Zion is recognized as the mother church of African-American Baptists in West Virginia.

Irish immigrants began to arrive in Lewis County in central West Virginia in the years prior to the Civil War to work on the network of roads and turnpikes that were then being built. One hundred acres of land were donated by a local real estate company to the Diocese of Richmond for the purpose of building a Roman Catholic church, rectory, and cemetery. The aim was to encourage further settlement and land sales in the area. St. Bernard's Roman Catholic Church in Camden, built in 1909, the parish's third church on the site, is a simple one-room clapboard Gothic Revival structure known locally as the "Little Cathedral of the Wilderness."

The increasing demand for coal following the Civil War and the concurrent opening of factories began to attract eastern European immigrants seeking employment. One of the factories, the American Sheet and Tin Plate Company in Morgantown, employed immigrants from the Carpathian mountains and Ruthenia who were the founders of St. Michael the Archangel, later renamed **St. Mary's Orthodox Church**, one of the few Orthodox churches in West Virginia.

Old Stone Presbyterian Church

Church and Foster Streets, Lewisburg

ARCHITECT / BUILDER:
Not available

CONSTRUCTION / DEDICATION DATE:
1796; 1830

THE TWO-STORY LIMESTONE CHURCH was built in what has been described as the "Old Virginia Style." Originally 44 feet square, an extension was added to the west end in 1830 that enlarged the building to 75 x 44 feet. At the same time the main entrance was moved from the east to the west wall where it is marked by double doors. Over the doorway of the original building is a polished stone with an engraving that reads: "This building was erected in the year 1796 at the expense of a few of the first inhabitants of this land to commemorate their affection and esteem for the gospel of Jesus Christ reader if you are inclined to applaud their virtues give God the Glory."

Also marking the exterior is an open cupola belfry set in the center of the roof. A balcony on the interior was built to accommodate slaves of the worshippers. An education building added to the northeast corner of the building does not detract from its original appearance. This simple but massive building is the oldest church in continuous use in this region west of the Allegheny Mountains. Its cemetery is the first west of the mountains and contains the graves of many prominent West Virginians, including Governor Henry Mathews (1877-1881).

Old Stone
Presbyterian
Church,
Lewisburg,
West Virginia

Old Bethany Church

(BETHANY CHURCH OF CHRIST)

Main and Church Streets, Bethany

ARCHITECT / BUILDER:
Not available

CONSTRUCTION / DEDICATION DATE:
circa 1830

THIS SIMPLE, UNADORNED CHURCH is important for its role in the development of the Disciples of Christ, a denomination established in Bethany by Alexander Campbell, who was born in Ireland and immigrated to the United States in 1809. Originally a Presbyterian, he then became a Baptist prior to establishing a separate congregation, known as a Church of Christ. The Baptist association responding to Campbell's different interpretation of doctrine withdrew support of his congregations, now known as Disciples, resulting in his decision in 1829 to form a separate denomination. A year later a Disciples meetinghouse was built in Bethany that was replaced by the present building in 1850. However, the first meetinghouse was retained because of its symbolic importance to the denomination. It was used regularly until 1915; currently it is used once a year for the ordination of ministers or for special events or tours.

The simplicity of design and lack of ornamentation of the meetinghouse reflect the teachings of its founder. The only decorative detail on the exterior is a semi-circular stone plaque in the west gable added after the building's construction that is inscribed: "Bethany Church of Christ: 1831–1852."

The interior is equally plain, consisting of simple straight-backed, wooden box pews separated by a partition, one side for women and the other for men, and a raised pulpit.

The meetinghouse has undergone few alterations since it was built, and stands today much as it did in 1852.

Old Meetinghouse
of the Bethany
Church of Christ,
Bethany,
West Virginia

Rehoboth Methodist Episcopal Church

("OLD REHOBOTH")

Two miles east of Union off State Road 3, Monroe County

ARCHITECT / BUILDER:
Not available

CONSTRUCTION / DEDICATION DATE:
1786

REHOBOTH CHURCH IS ONE OF TEN Methodist Shrines in America. It was constructed only two years after the founding of the Methodist Society in America in 1784 in Baltimore. According to tradition, Francis Asbury, the first Methodist bishop in America, preached the dedication sermon to an overflowing crowd.

At the time the church was built, Rehoboth, "broad place" (Gen. 26:22), was on the western frontier. The site was selected because it was a broad place, an open space that provided few hiding places for attacking Indians. The building's design reflects its use as a haven against attacks. A small structure built of medium-size logs, the building's only door is in the middle of the south side. There is one window on the east end, and another larger window high on the church's north side. A deep gallery extends along three sides at the height of the door. A high, rough-hewn walnut and poplar board pulpit stands against the east wall. Some of the split-log backless benches are still in place.

The building has undergone repairs over the years, but its rough-hewn appearance has remained essentially unchanged. It is one of the state's few remaining log churches, a reminder of the early days of religion in America's expanding western frontier.

Rehoboth
Methodist
Episcopal Church
(Old Rehoboth),
Union,
West Virginia

African Zion Baptist Church

4104 Malden Drive, Malden

ARCHITECT / BUILDER:
Not available

CONSTRUCTION / DEDICATION DATE:
circa 1872

A FRAME STRUCTURE BUILT ATOP a stone foundation, African Zion Baptist Church remains essentially unchanged since the time of its construction. One addition, a small storage facility, was added in 1940. A wooden bell tower crowns its gable roof. The importance of this building, however, is not its architecture, but its history as the mother church of African-American Baptists in West Virginia. Among its members were Booker T. Washington and "Father" Lewis Rice, founder of the church and a leader of the early black community in the Kanawha Valley, a few miles east of Charleston, West Viriginia.

Slaves were brought to the area to work in salt processing plants. By 1863, they had organized a Baptist church and began holding meetings in the home of Reverend Rice. The congregation's first church was built in 1865 with the aid of General Lewis Ruffner, a local salt entrepreneur. Following the Civil War, freed slaves remaining in the area now found work in coal mining, which was replacing the salt industry. The demands for coal resulted in the congregation relocating in Malden, where the present sanctuary was constructed sometime around 1872.

African Zion
Baptist Church,
Malden,
West Virginia

St. Mary's Orthodox Church

Corner of West Park and Holland Avenues, Westover

ARCHITECT / BUILDER:
Not available

CONSTRUCTION / DEDICATION DATE:
1923

THE SMALL YELLOW BRICK ORTHODOX CHURCH set on a high foundation of textured concrete block has changed little since its construction in 1923. The projecting square tower on the east façade and a smaller one at the west end of the church are capped with distinctive onion-shaped domes covered with gold leaf and supporting the traditional orthodox cross. The interior, too, has remained essentially unchanged. The iconostasis, or altar screen, closes off the sanctuary area in the apse where the altar is located. The iconostasis, as well as the walls of the church, are covered with icons created in the 1940s and 1970s.

The congregation has a complex history. It was formed in 1919 by Uniate immigrants from the Carpathian Mountains and Ruthenia who for political reasons decided to break away from the existing Orthodox church. They built this church in 1923 and named it St. Michael the Archangel, but it was forced to close ten years later during the Depression. It reopened again in 1937 with a new name, St. Mary's, and a different affiliation, the newly created Carpatho-Russian Orthodox Greek Catholic diocese under the patriarch of Constantinople, with headquarters and cathedral in Johnstown, Pennsylvania.

St. Mary's remains one of a very few Orthodox churches in West Virginia.

St. Mary's
Orthodox Church,
Westover,
West Virginia

North Carolina

I N 1663, THE BRITISH KING, Charles II, granted territory in the new world to eight proprietors, who divided it into two sections they named North and South Carolina. North Carolina's rugged coastline and mountainous terrain attracted only the most hardy of settlers, mainly English dissidents who were fiercely independent and in constant rebellion against British authorities. For a time Quakers moving south down the Great Wagon Road from Pennsylvania were the only organized religious body in the colony. Responding to their unwelcome presence, British authorities launched an all-out effort to make the Church of England the colony's official religion. But despite the Crown's efforts, by 1750 there were only nine Anglican churches in the colony.

The unrelenting attempts by the British to impose the Anglican faith on the colonists resulted in Piedmont farmers forming "The Regulation" in 1766. The "Regulators," as its members were known, were protesting against the Crown's efforts to tax them for the building of Anglican churches. The erection of St. John's Episcopal Church in Williamsboro in 1771 set off an insurrection that was violently suppressed by the British. The church was built, a visible symbol of the victory of the Crown and the established church and a thorn in the side of the colonists. Thus, it is not too surprising that North Carolina was the first colony to vote for independence from Britain.

By the time of the Revolutionary War, many of the colony's first settlers were moving westward, settling in scattered isolated areas that came to characterize the western portion of the state. Meanwhile the expanding plantation system in the state's eastern sector began requiring the importation of increasingly large numbers of slaves. By 1790, enslaved blacks comprised 25 percent of the state's total population.

Others, too, began to find the colony inviting. Included were Germans moving south from Pennsylvania who were settling in the central portion of the state, establishing communities and building churches, such as the simple but elegant St. Paul's Lutheran Church in the Catawba River Valley, built in 1818. German-speaking Moravians were also leaving older settlements in Georgia and Pennsylvania. They were far more organized than most ethnic or religious groups in the area thanks to the guidance they received from Moravian authorities in Europe and Pennsylvania on the building of their new settlements, including housing and churches. The beautiful stucco over stone **Bethabara Moravian Church**, also known as the **Gemein Haus**, built in Bethabara in 1788 by Moravians who arrived from Pennsylvania in 1753, is typical of many of their places of worship. The building encompasses two functions: it contains both the *Saal* or meeting room and a residence for the minister.

The first Baptist church in the colony was established in 1727, and in spite of efforts by the Anglicans to banish it, the denomination experienced its greatest expansion in the latter part of the eighteenth century. By the end of the colonial period there were 55 Baptist churches in North Carolina compared to 23 Anglican. However, a Baptist schism in the early nineteenth century resulted in several congregations in eastern North Carolina forming a separate entity, the conservative Primitive Baptist Church. Although Baptist architecture in general is conservative, that of the Primitive Baptist church is even more so, as exemplified by **Bear Grass Primitive Baptist Church** in Martin County, a simple, unadorned building that was begun in 1829.

The frontier spirit of Methodism spread by itinerant preachers at open-air camp meetings that were part religious revival and part social gatherings attracted many followers, particularly among people living in isolated rural areas. Rock Springs Camp Meeting Ground, in Lincoln County, is one of the oldest and most nearly intact meeting grounds in the Piedmont. Its first meeting, held in 1794, attracted over 300 converts.

Many African-Americans were also attracted to Methodism and formed or joined congregations affiliated with the newly formed African Methodist Episcopal Church (A.M.E). By the end of the Civil War, the A.M.E. Church had a membership of 53,670. Poplar Run A.M.E. Zion Church in Perquimans County is typical of many small frame Gothic Revival African-American Methodist churches built by freed blacks following the Civil War.

Other African-Americans chose to affiliate with the Presbyterian church. **Murkland Presbyterian Church** in Charlotte, organized following the Civil War by ex-slaves and freedmen, is named after its first pastor, Reverend Sidney Murkland. Reverend Murkland was instrumental in forming the first all-black Presbytery in the Presbyterian Church U.S.A. in 1887. Designated a historic property by the Charlotte-Mecklenburg Historic Landmarks Commission, Murkland Presbyterian Church was destroyed by an arsonist on June 7, 1996.

The Anglican Church, under its new name, the Protestant Episcopal Church, experienced a rebirth in the years prior to the Civil War, and began to attract members from the prospering middle class. Soon, grand Gothic Revival Episcopal churches began to appear in the state's prospering urban areas, such as **Christ Episcopal Church** in Raleigh, built in 1848, one of the first in the South. Its architect was Richard Upjohn, the designer of Trinity Church in New York.

New industries developing in the state following the Civil War were a magnet for a small number of Roman Catholics. The Church of St. Lawrence in Asheville, built in 1907, is considered one of the finest Roman Catholic churches in the state. Its architect, Rafael Guastavino, was in Asheville to work on the extravagant Biltmore Mansion being built for the Vanderbilt family. While there he undertook the additional task of designing and building a beautiful edifice for the city's Roman Catholics.

North Carolina's Jewish population was minuscule in the years preceding the Civil War, but began to grow with the expansion of the state's textile industry. Wilmington is home to the state's oldest Jewish institutions, including a Jewish burial society established in 1852 and a cemetery opened in 1855. The first permanent congregation organized in 1872 by Reform German Jews broke ground for a Moorish style synagogue, **Temple of Israel**, in 1875.

Bethabara Moravian Church

(GEMEIN HAUS)

2147 Bethabara Road, Winston-Salem

ARCHITECT / BUILDER:
Frederic William Marshall, designer; Abraham Loesch, master mason
CONSTRUCTION / DEDICATION DATE:
1788

F REDERICK WILLIAM MARSHALL planned a building for the small congregation that would serve two functions: a *Saal* or meeting room and a residence for the minister. The two functions are differentiated in the building's design by their window treatments and the shift in the roof line. A narrow window set into the rake of the *Saal*'s higher roof sheds light into its organ loft. Set on the ridge line of the *Saal* is a small, arcaded octagonal tower similar to church towers found in the members' homeland in central Europe.

The pastor's residence has its rooms arranged around a center chimney. There is a cooking hearth in a second chimney at the gable end. The spare interior of the *Saal* is typical of Moravian meetinghouses. Tall windows surmounted by shallow, arched openings with clear glass light the interior. Plain backless wooden benches, separated by a center aisle, face the table and chair placed beneath the windows. The entire effect is one of tranquillity and simplicity.

Bethabara
Moravian Church
(Gemein Haus),
Bethabara,
North Carolina

Bear Grass Primitive Baptist Church

*Northwest side of NC Highway 1001, one-tenth mile north of junction
with State Road 1106, Martin County*

ARCHITECT / BUILDER:
Not available
CONSTRUCTION / DEDICATION DATE:
1829

GENERAL BAPTIST CHURCHES, at least by the mid-nineteenth century, could be picturesque, with simple Gothic Revival details. Separated from the General Baptists by doctrinal differences, Primitive Baptists maintained a conservative form of architecture bereft of decoration or symbolism in keeping with the strict tenets of the faith, not surprising for a people who were at times referred to as "hard shell" or "foot-washing" Baptists.

The exterior of this white clapboard building is relieved only by its two entrances on the broad gable end, one for men and one for women, and large plain windows along the sides. The interior is equally stark. Two aisles flanking rows of wooden benches set in the middle of the hall and separated by a narrow board rail, one side for women, the other for men, lead to the pulpit set on a raised platform. On either side of the pulpit is the "Amen corner" reserved for church leaders.

The church, in its simple and unadorned appearance, continues to symbolize the original congregants' strict interpretations of predestination theology.

Bear Grass
Primitive
Baptist Church,
Martin County,
North Carolina

Murkland Presbyterian Church

7001 Old Providence Road, Charlotte

ARCHITECT / BUILDER:
Billy Stewart and Charlie Jarman (or Yarmouth)
CONSTRUCTION / DEDICATION DATE:
circa 1912

THE AFRICAN-AMERICAN CONGREGATION'S first church was destroyed in a brush fire, but its bell was saved and installed in the new church built by members of the congregation who were assisted by Stewart and Jarman.

The building was quite impressive considering it was built by generally unskilled volunteers. Its stained glass windows were a gift from members of nearby Matthews Presbyterian Church who were in the process of building a new church and no longer needed them. The design and style of the building are somewhat unusual for this area. A vernacular interpretation of the Gothic Revival style, the frame building with its two entry towers on the west façade was for many years a landmark on the Old Providence Road.

The congregation built a new church in 1976 on an adjoining lot, but continued to maintain and occupy this building until this "enduring landmark" was destroyed by an arsonist.

Murkland
Presbyterian
Church, vicinity of
Charlotte,
North Carolina

Christ Episcopal Church

120 East Edenton Street, Raleigh

ARCHITECT / BUILDER:
Richard Upjohn

CONSTRUCTION / DEDICATION DATE:
1848, completed 1852; tower built 1859-1861

CHRIST CHURCH PARISH WAS FORMED in 1821 and its first church was built in 1829. It served the parish until the present building was completed in 1852. Richard Upjohn, the English architect who gained fame in the United States for his Gothic Revival design of Trinity Church in New York City, was asked by the parish's bishop to provide a design for a "neat Gothic church" modeled after St. Mary's Episcopal Church in Burlington, New Jersey, which in turn was based on an English model, St. John's in Shottesbrooke. Upjohn's Christ Church is one of the first Gothic Revival churches in the South and had an enormous impact on the region's religious architecture.

Based on English parish churches, Christ Church is built of locally quarried stone worked by Scottish masons imported from New York. The tower and spire were completed in 1861. A parish house and chapel completed in 1921 were designed by Upjohn's grandson, Hobart Upjohn.

**Christ Episcopal Church,
Raleigh, North Carolina**

Temple of Israel Synagogue

1 South Fourth Street, Wilmington

ARCHITECT / BUILDER:
Alex Strausz

CONSTRUCTION / DEDICATION DATE:
1876

SEPHARDIC JEWS BEGAN TO ARRIVE in North Carolina in the early eighteenth century. By the end of the century a Jewish community was established in the port of Wilmington. A Jewish Burial Society was formed in 1852 and an Orthodox Jewish congregation in 1867. The congregation did not succeed and a second more successful effort was made in 1872, this time by German-speaking Jews under the auspices of the Reform Movement. The synagogue, dedicated in 1876, is one of the earliest Reform synagogues in the South.

The building's Moorish style is unique in Wilmington, but not unique for synagogues built in the latter half of the nineteenth century. The emancipation of most European Jews and the freedom of worship in the United States provided Jewish people with the impetus to seek a style of architecture that would distinguish their places of worship from those of Christians. They adapted a style from Medieval Spain inspired by the period known as the Golden Age of Jewry when Jews lived in relative peace under the Muslim Moors.

Moorish synagogues remained in vogue for only a short period; by the beginning of the twentieth century they were viewed as being too exotic, too foreign for American Jewry. This stuccoed masonry synagogue's twin towered façade is a common feature of Gothic Revival buildings; however, the horseshoe arches and golden onion domes capping the towers are Moorish.

Temple of Israel Synagogue,
Wilmington, North Carolina

South Carolina

A SPANISH EXPEDITION EXPLORING the coast of South Carolina in 1521 was unsuccessful in its attempt to establish a permanent colony in the region. British colonists from Barbados eager to find new lands on which to establish their plantations were far more successful with the colony they established on the Ashley River in 1670. Ten years later the settlement moved and was given the name Charles Towne, later changed to Charleston. By 1700, the city was booming, with a population of over 5,500.

Charleston is home to some of the nation's most beautiful and historic places of worship. These buildings document the city's history and settlement pattern. Perhaps one of the most historic congregations is now housed in the **Circular Congregational Church**, a Richardsonian Romanesque structure built in 1890. Its founding, however, dates back to 1681, when colonists–English Congregationalists, Scots Presbyterians, and French Huguenots–set aside their differences to form a congregation and in 1685 built their first meetinghouse.

St. Michael's Episcopal Church, the oldest religious structure in Charleston, reflects the wealth of the city's founders. Organized in 1751, the church was built and opened for services 10 years later. Its architect remains unknown, but its design is clearly derived from James Gibbs's famed London church, St. Martin-in-the-Fields, Ironically, the church became the focal point of colonial resistance to British rule.

It was more than Charleston's prosperity that attracted settlers; they were also drawn by its leaders' liberal attitude toward religion. This is what motivated Sephardic Jews from Amsterdam and London to settle in Charleston, where they established a profitable trade in indigo. By 1749, their numbers were sufficient to organize a congregation, **Kahal Kadosh Beth Elohim** (Holy Congregation, House of God). The congregation's present Greek Revival synagogue, constructed in 1840-1841, is its second and is the second oldest synagogue in the United States (Touro Synagogue in Newport, Rhode Island, is the oldest; see p. 64) and the oldest in continuous use.

French Protestants, known as Huguenots, also sought refuge in Charleston. Fleeing persecution in their homeland, they established a small community in the city and erected a church in 1687. Although their numbers began to decrease in the eighteenth century, the congregation was able to build a new church on the same site in 1845. The French Huguenot Church at the corner of Church and Queen Streets is the city's first Gothic Revival structure.

Additional evidence of the city's liberal attitude toward religion is the establishment in 1789 of one of the earliest Roman Catholic parishes in a southern state, St. Mary's. The parish's original founders were Irish, but their numbers were greatly augmented with the arrival in 1793 of French refugees fleeing the insurrection in St. Domingo. The parish's first church built in 1801 was destroyed by fire; replacing it is the present structure, built in 1839.

South Carolina's rural areas and coastal islands were home to many small churches built by white and black congregations. A charming example is **Christ Episcopal Church** located about five miles north of Mount Pleasant in Charleston County. Construction of the church began in 1701, and although it was destroyed or damaged three times it was always rebuilt in its original form by its intrepid congregation. **St. James Episcopal Church**, built between 1708 and 1719 in Goose Creek, is more ornate, possibly due to the taste of its builders, wealthy Barbadian planters.

Slaves, whose labor allowed for the building of churches such as St. James and Christ Episcopal, had to be content to worship in far more modest buildings known as Praise Houses. The earliest ones have long since disappeared, but the **Coffin Point Community Praise House** constructed in 1900 remained in use until about the mid-1930s, an important example of a vernacular architectural form that predates the Civil War.

The frontier's relentless movement westward in the latter half of the eighteenth century witnessed the arrival of new settlers into the colony. People representing a wide variety of faiths began populating the midlands, Piedmont, and upcountry areas of South Carolina. One community attracting new settlers was Camden, a town settled prior to the Revolutionary War. A small Presbyterian church built in 1790 soon proved inadequate, and a new church was built. **Bethesda Presbyterian** was designed by Robert Mills, the architect of the Circular Church in Charleston, and dedicated in 1822.

Abbeville, located deep in the rural Piedmont region, was the market town for surrounding plantations whose wealthy owners contributed to its antebellum prosperity. One of the city's best-known landmarks is Trinity Episcopal Church, completed in 1861. The Gothic Revival church, one of the town's grandest structures and a reminder of its prosperous past, is sorely in need of restoration.

St. James
Episcopal Church,
Goose Creek,
South Carolina

Circular Congregational Church

150 Meeting Street, Charleston

ARCHITECT / BUILDER:
Robert S. Stephenson and Ernest S. Greene of New York (see below)
CONSTRUCTION / DEDICATION DATE:
1890

T HE PRESENT CHURCH OCCUPIES THE SITE of the congregation's first meetinghouse, erected about 1685. Because of the congregation's independent spirit, the church soon became a center for revolutionary sentiment. When the British gained control of the city, many of the church members were forced to leave, but as soon as the British were defeated, they returned and rebuilt the meetinghouse. As the congregation grew, plans were made for a much larger building. According to the congregation's history, a circular plan proposed by a female member was given to the noted architect Robert Mills who drew up the plans. The design, based on the Pantheon in Rome, consisted of a large circular space covered with a dome. It was argued that the people who built the church were largely Calvinists and thus had built a "meetinghouse" rather than a "church" in the Anglican/Episcopal sense. A 182-foot steeple added in 1838 was intended to satisfy those members who believed a church was not a church without a steeple.

The Circular Church was destroyed by fire in 1861, at the onset of the Civil War. It wasn't until 1890 that the devastated congregation was able to erect a new building. Once again the congregation decided to create a church that was a departure from Charleston's traditional architecture. According to the congregation's history the new church was designed by New York architects Stephenson and Greene in a Romanesque style inspired by Henry Hobart Richardson, who designed the trend-setting Trinity Church in Boston. The design combines two forms: the circle for the exterior plan as a reminder of the former church, and the Greek cross on the interior. The sanctuary was restored in 1987.

Circular Congregational
Church, Charleston,
South Carolina

Temple Kahal Kadosh Beth Elohim Synagogue
(HOLY CONGREGATION HOUSE OF GOD)

90 Hassell Street, Charleston

ARCHITECT / BUILDER:
Cyrus L. Warner, architect; David Lopez, builder
CONSTRUCTION / DEDICATION DATE:
Dedicated in 1841

JEWISH SETTLERS, MOST SEPHARDIC DESCENDANTS of Spanish and Portuguese Jews who fled the Inquisition, began to arrive in Charleston in the early eighteenth century. They were followed by German-speaking Jews. Together the two groups organized a congregation in 1749 that followed Sephardic rituals. Construction began on a synagogue in 1792 and two years later it was dedicated. The Georgian style building resembled contemporary colonial churches, including its handsome arcaded bell tower. It was destroyed in the great Charleston fire of 1838 and was replaced three years later by the present building.

At the time of this building's construction a split occurred in the congregation along Orthodox and Reform lines. The Reform, supported by German Jews, ultimately gained control and the first service in the new building followed the new Reform liturgy, including music. This was the first time an organ was used in a synagogue in the United States.

The synagogue is considered one of the finest examples of Greek Revival architecture in the United States. The exterior remains virtually unchanged, but the interior has been reconfigured to accommodate changes in liturgy. Initially the *bimah*, or platform, for the reading table was in the center of the sanctuary; later it was moved to its present position against the wall where the Ark, made of Santo Domingo mahogany, stands. The iron fence surrounding the building dates to the 1794 building. The synagogue is beautifully maintained and remains in use.

Kahol Kadosh Beth
Elohim Synagogue,
Charleston,
South Carolina

soon became the colony's dominant religions. The first Baptist congregation organized in Georgia was founded in 1772 near Kiokee Creek in Columbia County. The congregation's first church built that same year was replaced in 1807 by the present Kiokee Baptist Church, a simple, austere, well-preserved one-story brick structure that is still used for special occasions.

Later Baptist churches are less austere, possibly due to the influence of Greek Revival architecture that came into vogue during Georgia's period of antebellum prosperity. **Hopeful Baptist Church**, built in 1851 near Keysville, is a notable example of a rural interpretation of this style. The congregation was unique during this era for it was one of the few that permitted whites and blacks to worship together.

Two African-American Baptist congregations in Savannah lay claim to being the first African-American congregation in the United States: First Bryan Baptist Church, built in 1873, and First African Baptist Church, built in 1859. Both trace their founding to 1788, when four black men were converted by a Virginia slave, George Liele, who had been ordained a Baptist minister in 1775. The two congregations were the result of a doctrinal dispute in 1832 occasioned by the preaching of a white minister, Alexander Campbell, founder of the Disciples of Christ (see p. 238).

St. Bartholomew's Episcopal Church in Burroughs, built in 1896, is a relatively rare example of an African-American Episcopal congregation in Georgia. The Episcopal Church began to evangelize slaves working on Georgia's rice plantations in the 1830s. Following the Civil War many former slaves chose to remain in Georgia, working land given or purchased from former plantation owners. St. Bartholomew's Church in New York gave a gift of $400 to the Mission that built the present church.

Trinity United Methodist Church in Savannah refers to itself as the "mother church of Methodism." (Apparently the Methodist Church in America had three "mothers." Lovely Lane Meeting House in Baltimore, Maryland, and Barratt's Chapel in Frederica, Delaware, also lay claim to this honor; see pp. 225 and 211.) In 1736, John Wesley and three other students of Christ College in Oxford, England, came to Savannah at the urging of John Oglethorpe to establish "societies" of worship. A chapel was built in Savannah in 1813 and named after Wesley. Membership steadily increased and a larger church was constructed in 1848. Its Classical Revival style is modeled after the Wesley Chapel in London.

The state's largest city is Atlanta, known as the "Gate City," and is located at the terminus of the Georgia Railroad, completed in 1845. Devastated by Sherman's campaign during the Civil War, the city made an amazing recovery and became the state's capital. Among those attracted to Atlanta during its period of post-war prosperity were blue-collar workers, mainly Presbyterians, seeking employment in the city's expanding industries. They settled in a small village that has since been swallowed up by the city of Atlanta. Their church, **Rock Spring Presbyterian Church**, built in 1936 on the site of their earlier church, is all that remains of the community.

Temple Mickve Israel Synagogue

20 East Gordon Street, Savannah

ARCHITECT / BUILDER:
Henry G. Harrison
CONSTRUCTION / DEDICATION DATE:
1878

THE FIRST SYNAGOGUE IN GEORGIA was built in 1818 by descendants of Spanish and Portuguese Jews who landed in Savannah in 1733. The congregation's present building, the third on the site, was begun in 1876 and consecrated two years later. Its style and plan are somewhat unusual for a synagogue.

The synagogue is in the prevailing Gothic Revival style, including its plan–a Latin cross–a longitudinal basilica with projecting transepts. It has all the expected decorative elements–pointed arches over the entries and traceried stained glass windows, pinnacles decorating the façade, buttresses between the bays, and even a two-stage tower. Rather than a steeple rising from the tower there is a rather unusual Islamic appearing cupola. Outwardly the building could be mistaken for a church, but its interior has all the accoutrements for Jewish worship–an Ark for the Torah Scrolls and a *bimah*, or platform, supporting the reading desk and pulpit. The choice of the Gothic style by a Jewish congregation is rare but not unknown. Several prominent synagogues were built in the 1850s in this style, including one in New York, now destroyed, that was allegedly modeled after the Cathedral of Cologne. Mickve Israel is considered the only surviving example in the United States of a synagogue modeled after the great Gothic cathedrals of Europe.

Temple Mickve
Israel Synagogue,
Savannah, Georgia,
circa 1930s

Jerusalem Lutheran Church

GA Highway 275, New Ebenezer

ARCHITECT / BUILDER:
Not available

CONSTRUCTION / DEDICATION DATE:
1767

NEW EBENEZER WAS LAID OUT by James Oglethorpe in a plan similar to Savannah's. It was surrounded by a wooden fence separating the farms and mills from the houses and gardens. One occupation in which the Salzburgers were active was silk production, which was promoted by the colony's trustees and supported by the British government. Mulberry bushes were planted and the colonists became involved with silk-making. The enterprise came to an end when the Revolutionary War began and the British withdrew their support.

The congregation, formed by the Salzburgers in 1734, was known as the Ebenezer German Evangelical Lutheran Church. Their loyalty was to their home church in Germany, which sent them pastors and covered the costs for their new church. The labor and material were provided by the congregants, including the bricks formed from clay taken from deposits by the Savannah River. The one-story brick building topped by a square wooden belfry is very austere, but the symmetry and simplicity of its design and its excellent craftsmanship provide it with a sense of elegance.

The church has been in continuous use since its founding, except for a period during the Revolutionary War when British troops occupied the town and used the church first as a hospital, then as a stable. The community went into decline following the war, and by the mid-nineteenth century had only a few residents.

Jerusalem
Lutheran Church,
New Ebenezer, Georgia

Hopeful Baptist Church

Winter Road east of junction with Blythe Road, near Keysville

ARCHITECT / BUILDER:
Not available

CONSTRUCTION / DEDICATION DATE:
circa 1851

HOPEFUL BAPTIST CHURCH IS AN EXAMPLE of a southern church built by black slaves for their white masters who in turn allowed them to worship with them in the church. Churches were one of the few places in the antebellum South where blacks and whites could gather together, albeit in segregated seating. Perhaps what is unique here is that black members were allowed to have their own preacher once a month.

The church is a one-story frame Greek Revival structure built in a rural area near the community of Keysville. Georgia began to develop during the early nineteenth century, the same time that the Greek Revival style was becoming popular in the United States. Thus, it is not unusual to find a Greek Revival building in a relatively remote rural setting. Its appearance is reminiscent of a miniature Greek temple, symmetrical in plan, with broad granite steps leading up to a portico along its façade supporting an oversized pediment. The building's original hand-crafted pews, doors, and other details are intact.

Following the Civil War the congregation's African-American members left and established their own congregation, Second Hopeful Baptist Church, on land donated by Hopeful Baptist. They continued to worship in Hopeful until their building was completed.

Hopeful Baptist Church, vicinity of Keysville, Georgia

St. Bartholomew's Episcopal Church

Cheves Road, Burroughs, Chatham County

ARCHITECT / BUILDER:
Not available

CONSTRUCTION / DEDICATION:
1896

S T. BARTHOLOMEW'S IS THE OLDEST ACTIVE African-American congregation in the Episcopal Diocese of Georgia, and also one of only a few in a state where the Methodist and Baptist denominations predominate. The congregation grew out of efforts by the Episcopal Church to evangelize slaves. Beginning in the 1830s, Episcopal missions established on plantations were teaching slaves to read and write. The Ogeechee Mission serviced the plantations in Chatham County. Its success was such that following the Civil War the blacks who remained in the area formed a community called Burroughs, and with the help of a gift of $400 from St. Bartholomew's Church in New York City, were able to build a school and church.

St. Batholomew's is an excellent example of an intact Victorian-Eclectic style church built by a rural black Episcopal congregation. Its builders had little formal training, and little money, but they still were able to build an attractive structure. The roof is steeply gabled and a bell tower at the northeast corner provides the building with an interesting silhouette. Triangular framing is repeated throughout, unifying all the elements.

The building has undergone little alteration since it was constructed and continues to play an important religious and educational role in its community.

St. Bartholomew's
Episcopal Church,
Savannah, Georgia

Rock Spring Presbyterian Church

1824 Piedmont Avenue NE, Atlanta

ARCHITECT / BUILDER:
Charles Henry Hopson
CONSTRUCTION / DEDICATION DATE:
1923

T HE CHURCH IS UNIQUE IN SEVERAL RESPECTS. It is one of a small number of Presbyterian churches in a state where Methodists and Baptists predominate, and it is a rare Atlanta example of a religious building in the half-timbered, stone-and-stucco English Tudor Revival style.

The Rock Spring community was established in what was a rural area outside of Atlanta for blue-collar workers moving into the area during the era of prosperity following the Civil War. As a minority, the Presbyterians recognized the importance of establishing a congregation, which they did in 1870.

The present church was begun in 1923, but the chancel area was not completed until 10 years later. The architect, Charles Henry Hopson, was born in Reading, England, where he studied architecture. He settled first in Nova Scotia, then in Washington, D.C., and Selma, Alabama, before coming to Atlanta in about 1914, where he spent the rest of his life designing various types of buildings; however, he considered churches to be his specialty.

Additions have been made to the church, but it retains its original Tudor character. It remains in use, although the original Rock Spring village has been absorbed into the urban fabric of the city.

Rock Spring
Presbyterian
Church,
Atlanta, Georgia

Florida

ALTHOUGH PENINSULAR FLORIDA is one of the most southern territories of the United States, it is not usually thought of as being part of the deep South. However, the panhandle region, the first area to be permanently settled, did have plantations and a slave culture similar to other areas of the deep South. The character of the rest of the state was and remains quite different.

The Spanish navigator Juan Ponce de Leon, landing near the mouth of what is now known as the St. Johns River, claimed the land for Spain, naming it *La Florida*, "the flower." Efforts by the Spanish to colonize Florida were doomed by the native people's refusal to capitulate. Ultimately, the French, Spanish, and English all fought at different times for control of the peninsula. St. Augustine, established by the Spanish, was repeatedly burned and plundered by the British, but Spain held on to it, continuing in its effort to control and Christianize the native Americans. As part of that effort, the Parish of St. Augustine was established and in 1593 plans for a church were drawn; the building, however, was not completed for two centuries. The church was renamed the Cathedral of St. Augustine in 1870 when the Diocese of St. Augustine was established. The original church gutted by a fire in 1887 was subsequently enlarged and partially restored by James Renwick, a New York architect. Only the façade and portions of each side of the original structure were retained.

The territory's almost constant turmoil did not discourage its settlement. As a result of its growth and prosperity, Florida was accepted into the Union in 1845. As most of its settlers came from southern states, it is not too surprising that Florida joined with its southern neighbors to support the cause of the Rebels during the Civil War, voting to secede from the Union. Like elsewhere in the South, the state's growth was stalled during the period of hostilities, but following the war it once again began to experience an era of growth and prosperity spearheaded by the arrival of the railroad and the building of new roads that made seemingly remote areas accessible for settlement. The Everglades were drained, opening them to agriculture, and the refashioning of barren wastes and mangrove swamps produced a popular winter resort–Miami Beach–known for its beaches and pleasant weather.

As early as the eighteenth century, Florida's mild climate attracted enterprising entrepreneurs. One of the first was a Scottish physician, Andrew Turnbull, who in 1763 received from the British a grant of land 75 miles south of St. Augustine to be used for a plantation. Rather than using slaves, Turnbull recruited Greeks who he believed were well suited to work in a hot climate. Over 1,000 impoverished and desperate Greeks escaping the ravages of war in their homeland accepted his offer to work as indentured servants. After arriving in St. Augustine in 1768 and establishing a colony, New Smyrna, they found the combination of heat and labor to be deadly–over half the colonists perished in the first year. In 1777, the survivors left New Smyrna and walked to St. Augustine, then under Spanish control, where they joined the Roman Catholic Church. A building in St. Augustine dated to the Spanish Colonial era honors these early Greek settlers. This building, the Avero House or St. Photios Greek Orthodox National Shrine, was built between 1735 and 1743, and is one of the oldest structures in the state. Acquired by the Greek Orthodox Diocese of North and South America in 1966, the building underwent extensive restoration and reconstruction before it reopened in 1979 as a shrine dedicated to St. Photios.

Other Greeks began arriving in Florida in the early twentieth century to work in the sponge industry that was developing in Tarpon Springs, a former winter resort and health center. As the demand for sponges increased, so did the town's Greek population. By 1910, the community was able to build a simple wood frame Greek Orthodox church that remained in use until World War II when the community began to prosper as European sponge centers were closing. During the war, the parish built **St. Nicholas Greek Orthodox Cathedral**, one of the most beautiful Orthodox churches in the United States.

Mt. Pilgrim African Baptist Church in Milton was founded in 1866 by freed slaves who chose to remain near the plantations where they had worked. Initially the congregation met in an arbor, then in a small frame church, before the present building, designed by W. A. Rayfield, an African-American architect from Birmingham, Alabama, was built in 1916.

Florida's mild weather, lush vegetation, and untouched wilderness areas began luring wealthy New Englanders seeking escape from the north's cold, inhospitable winters. With them came their Episcopal faith and plans for Gothic Revival churches, such as **St. Mary's Episcopal Church** erected in Green Cove Springs in 1878. The church continues in use, a visible reminder of its northern heritage in a southern environment.

Other northerners were religious visionaries seeking "Gardens of Eden," where they could relocate religious movements founded in the "Burned Over" district of New York State in the mid-nineteenth century (see p. 73). One group, the Southern Cassadaga Spiritualists, established a camp in east central Florida, 30 miles north of Orlando, in 1895. It was part of the American Spiritualist Movement, founded in the 1840s by the Cassadaga community in Chautauqua County, New York. After initial opposition, Spiritualism gained members in Florida in the years following the Civil War. Colby Memorial Temple, constructed in 1923 and named after the man who sold the land, was used for religious and secular purposes and is considered one of the most striking buildings in the district.

Henry Flagler, considered Florida's "empire builder," played an important role in transforming Florida into a major winter tourist destination. He was responsible for building 642 miles of railway and a system of luxury hotels stretching from Jacksonville to the Bahamas. Miami is one of his success stories. The extension of the railway into what was a swampy, isolated town in 1896 signaled the beginning of its boom years. Among the first to arrive were Jewish merchants who opened shops on the city's main streets and in 1912 organized a Conservative congregation, B'nai Zion (later renamed Beth David). A schism between Conservative and Reform Jews in the 1920s gave rise to a second congregation, **Temple Israel**. Its members, followers of the liberal Reform Movement, built a synagogue in 1927 that is the core of an enlarged complex.

St. Nicholas Greek Orthodox Cathedral

44 North Pinellas Avenue, Tarpon Springs

ARCHITECT / BUILDER:
Not available
CONSTRUCTION / DEDICATION DATE:
1943

THE BYZANTINE REVIVAL CHURCH was built by Tarpon Springs' Greek community at the height of its economic success in the sponge industry. Prior to its construction, the congregants met in a small, simple frame building constructed in 1910, five years after their arrival in Tarpon Springs. As the sponge industry grew, the Greek community prospered, reaching its apogee during World War II when European sponges were no longer available. At that time the congregation decided that a new, more elaborate church was needed. Wealthy members guaranteed its financing. Although it was in the middle of World War II, the congregants went about obtaining the finest material available. Marble was shipped from New York, chandeliers made from Czechoslovakian glass were imported, and 23 stained glass windows were donated. Although the sponge industry went into a decline following World War II, the cathedral, considered one of the best known in the United States, remains in use by its community and is the site of the largest and most elaborate Epiphany rituals in the nation.

St. Nicholas
Greek Orthodox
Cathedral,
Tarpon Springs,
Florida

Mount Pilgrim African Baptist Church

Corner of Alice and Clara Streets, Milton

ARCHITECT / BUILDER:
Wallace A. Rayfield
CONSTRUCTION / DEDICATION DATE:
1916

A 46-FOOT BELL TOWER is the dominant feature of the façade of this red brick Gothic Revival church. It is the only building in Florida known to have been designed by Wallace A. Rayfield of Birmingham, Alabama, one of the most important African-American architects in the South in the early twentieth century. It is also one of the few Gothic Revival buildings in Milton. The church was actually constructed by its members, first- and second-generation descendants of its original founders.

Mount Pilgrim was organized in 1866 by freed blacks who had been members of the white First Baptist Church of Milton, established in 1845. The Mount Pilgrim congregation first met in an arbor until land was bought from a member of First Baptist Church in 1880 and a modest frame church was constructed. In 1911, the congregation was able to purchase another parcel of land and began to make plans to build a new church. It was a good thing because their frame church was destroyed by fire in March 1916, and the present building was able to open for worship just five months later.

The church remains a focal point in the social, civic, and religious life of Milton's African-American community.

Mount Pilgrim
African Baptist
Church,
Milton, Florida

St. Mary's Episcopal Church

St. John's Avenue, Green Cove Springs

ARCHITECT / BUILDER:
Lawrence Lewis of Philadelphia, and M. T. Adams of Boston, architects
CONSTRUCTION / DEDICATION DATE:
1878

THIS CHURCH IS ONE OF THE BEST EXAMPLES in Florida of the Carpenter Gothic style advocated by Richard Upjohn, the architect of New York's Trinity Church. John Freeman Young, the bishop of Florida, had served as the assistant rector at Trinity Church in the 1860s and was in sympathy with the Episcopal Church's ecclesiological movement that advocated a return to the Gothic style. Young had an important influence on the appearance of many churches built in Florida in the 1870s and 1880s. There he found a responsive audience in the wealthy northerners, many Episcopalian, who were making the state a popular winter resort. The snowbirds who vacationed in Green Cove Springs soon became involved in forming an Episcopal congregation and eventually erecting a church. The architects Bishop Young asked to assist with the plans designed a frame church along the lines of those depicted in Upjohn's popular and well-traveled book on rural church architecture.

St. Mary's remains as a legacy to the important role northern tourists played in the growth of the Episcopal Church in Florida during the nineteenth century.

St. Mary's
Episcopal Church,
Green Cove Springs,
Florida

Temple Israel

137 NE Nineteenth Street, Miami

ARCHITECT / BUILDER:
L. R. Patterson, M. L. Robertson
CONSTRUCTION / DEDICATION DATE:
1927

THE FIRST JEWISH CONGREGATION ORGANIZED in Miami in 1912 was B'nai Zion, a member of the Conservative Movement. Following World War I, the congregation, renamed Beth David, purchased a former church and transformed it into a synagogue, the first in south Florida. The state began to experience a real estate boom in the 1920s that brought more Jews to south Florida. Some were members of the more liberal Reform Movement who expressed dissatisfaction with the more traditional services conducted in Beth David. A schism occurred and Temple Israel, a new Reform congregation, was established. A lot was purchased and in 1927 ground was broken for a new synagogue designed by E. L. Robertson and L. R. Patterson, Miami architects. The basilica plan synagogue is in the Moorish Revival style, which had gained popularity in the late nineteenth century, but by the time this building was constructed had all but been abandoned by Jews as too exotic and foreign. However, it may have been seen as appropriate for a synagogue in a state that had such close associations with Spanish culture.

The Temple Israel complex now includes a community center, religious school, and chapel.

**Temple Israel,
Miami, Florida**

7

East South Central Region

Alabama
Mississippi
Tennessee
Kentucky

THE FOUR STATES COMPRISING THIS REGION share several characteristics in common: areas of rugged topography with limited access, large rural populations, and few large cities, but each maintains an independent identity. This is notable, for example, in the musical traditions that developed in neighboring Tennessee and Kentucky. Bluegrass gets its name from the Bluegrass Basin of Kentucky, whereas Nashville is the home of country and Memphis is where the blues were born. Geography shaped the region's settlement patterns. The barrier formed by the Appalachian Mountains stretching from the Mohawk River in New York southward to northern Alabama made movement in and out of the area difficult, contributing to the region historically having the nation's smallest percentage of foreign-born population, peaking in 1870 at 2.4 percent.

The Cumberland Gap is a winding and difficult trail discovered by explorers in 1750. In the aftermath of the Revolutionary War, hardy frontiersmen from Virginia and the Carolinas, like Daniel Boone, were hired by eastern land speculators to bring in settlers from Virginia, Maryland, and the Carolinas. Their destinations were the fertile Nashville Basin and loess plains in Tennessee and the Bluegrass Basin of Kentucky. Among the migrants were tobacco plantation owners who introduced into the area the Anglican Church and slavery. The majority of the pioneers, however, were Scots-Irish, English, and Germans, many of whom were freed indentured servants seeking small parcels of land where they could establish subsistence farms.

The Mississippi Territory, created in 1798 by land ceded to the United States by Spain in 1795, includes most of present-day Mississippi and Alabama except for a strip along the Gulf of Mexico. Standing in the new nation's way of control of the entire region were three Indian tribes: the Creek, Choctaw, and Chickasaw. By 1838, all the Indian nations had either been crushed or forcibly removed, opening up millions of acres of rich land for speculation, thereby initiating another period of mass migration from the old colonies, including New England. The region's cultural character, however, was firmly established by its first settlers from the South Atlantic Region.

The Civil War tore the region asunder. Kentucky, Tennessee, and surprisingly, Alabama, had soldiers fighting on both sides. But following the war, differences were set aside and the region began to experience a slow but steady recovery thanks in great measure to the introduction of industry into what had been basically an agricultural economy founded on a single crop–cotton. A large deposit of high-quality coking coal discovered near Birmingham, Alabama, in 1870 transformed Birmingham and nearby Chattanooga, Tennessee, into industrial centers for the production of iron and steel. At about the same time, New Englanders attracted by cheap labor began establishing textile mills to process the cotton grown on nearby fields. The booming economy contributed to the area's economic and demographic expansion in the last decades of the nineteenth century continuing into the new century.

PRECEDING PAGE:

**Mother of God
Roman Catholic
Church,
Covington,
Kentucky**

Alabama

LTHOUGH ALABAMA WAS SPARSELY SETTLED in the years prior to the Revolutionary War, Mobile, its only seaport, was already in operation, having been laid out by the French in 1711. The port was variously under the control of France, Great Britain, and Spain until 1817 when it was annexed by the United States and became part of the territory of Alabama. Two years later Alabama entered the Union with its first capital located at Tuscaloosa; it was moved to more prosperous Montgomery in 1845.

A Catholic church was built on a broad avenue in Mobile known as "Promenade Iglese" at the time the city was under French control. When Mobile was transferred to the United States in 1822, the promenade was renamed Church Street and the Catholic church was replaced by Christ Episcopal Church, a brick edifice erected in 1840 and modeled after James Gibbs's St. Martin-in-the-Fields.

Mobile prospered in the years prior to the Civil War, becoming a market center for Yankee merchants servicing the needs of the area's wealthy plantation owners. This era of success coincided with the emergence of the Greek Revival style. Appearing fully matured in Mobile soon after 1835, the style spread rapidly, finding a ready and wealthy audience in the rich Black Belt counties of central Alabama.

The **Government Street Presbyterian Church**, built in Mobile in 1836-1837, is one of the oldest and least-altered Greek Revival churches in the nation. Built of a combination of local brick and imported granite (from New York) and by local talent (the bricklayer) and imported talent (the joiner from New York), it was, at the time of completion, considered the most impressive church in the city.

Evidence of the spread of the Greek Revival style beyond the confines of the wealthy is found in the small rural Greek Revival meetinghouses, such as the Baptist Church in Orion, built in 1858, or **Mount Sterling Methodist Church**, built in 1859 in what was once a thriving antebellum cotton and timber center.

Alabama is essentially a rural state. Many early pioneers were subsistence farmers from Tennessee and Kentucky who were abandoning their overworked fields for the promise of more fertile land in Alabama. The places of worship they erected are similar to the modest buildings they left behind. A surviving example of one of their early churches is **Andrews Methodist Chapel**, also known as the McIntosh Log Church, constructed in 1860. It is one of the few remaining log churches in the state and is a poignant reminder of a building type that once blanketed the state.

Montgomery's prosperity is directly linked to the huge cotton plantations in the Black Belt prairie lands. The city standing on the east bank of the Alabama River was founded in the years prior to the Civil War. Originally it was given the name New Philadelphia and nicknamed "Yankee Town," reflecting the origin of many of its original settlers–transplanted Yankees who were opening up textile mills near the cotton fields. As elsewhere in the South, the Yankees brought their Episcopal faith and their preference for the Gothic Revival style. St. John's Episcopal Church in Montgomery is one of three Episcopal churches in the state designed by Frank Wills and Henry Dudley, nationally known architects, who along with Richard Upjohn were major proponents of the Gothic style.

Like the popular Greek Revival style, the Gothic, too, was not restricted to urban churches. At least 12 Gothic Revival churches were built in Alabama in the decade prior to the onset of the Civil War, including the three designed by Wills and Dudley. All are small wooden structures whose plans were based on Upjohn's *Rural Architecture*, including **St. Andrews Episcopal Church**, built near Prairieville in 1853–1854 by slaves of Captain Henry A. Tayloe, a prominent member of the congregation and an acquaintance of Upjohn. St. John's-in-the-Wilderness located nearby actually replicates the design of a rural chapel appearing in Upjohn's book.

Alabama ranked second in the Union in the number of cotton bales its fields yielded at the onset of the Civil War, but hostilities brought this period of prosperity to an end. Alabama came to recognize that it could no longer base its economy on a single commodity, cotton, that was dependent upon slave labor. A solution was reached in the discovery of coal and iron ore deposits. Alabama now entered its second era of prosperity, known as the "Iron Decade." The area around Birmingham has vast deposits of high-quality bituminous coal, iron ore, and limestone, which are the three principal ingredients in steel. By the 1870s, Birmingham, along with nearby Chattanooga, Tennessee, became an important steel-making center. The steel industry, in turn, attracted other manufacturers dependent upon steel.

Birmingham's era of prosperity coincided with the popularity of Henry Hobson Richardson's Romanesque style, known as Richardsonian Romanesque. The United States Post Office and Federal Courthouse built in Birmingham in 1889–1890 were both in that style, as was the Union Depot. But some of the best examples of the Richardsonian Romanesque style in the city are churches, including First Methodist built in 1890–1891. Its interior, designed by the Akron-based architectural firm of Weary and Kramer, features the new Akron plan that was gaining favor for denominations whose focus was on preaching (see p. 101). The plan features a broad auditorium-type hall with ranks of curving pews that all have clear views of the pulpit, and whose acoustics assure that the preacher will be heard.

Birmingham's best-known church is famous both for its architecture and its important role as the center of local civil rights activities during the early 1960s. **Sixteenth Street Baptist Church**, constructed in 1909–1911, was designed by Wallace A. Rayfield, an African-American architect who was the official architect for the A.M.E. Zion denomination. The tragic incident of September 15, 1963, when a bomb exploded in the basement of the church taking the lives of four children, was a turning point in the Civil Rights Movement. The church is now part of Birmingham's Civil Rights District.

Government Street Presbyterian Church

Government and Jackson Streets, Mobile

ARCHITECT / BUILDER:
James Gallier, James Dakin, Charles Dakin
CONSTRUCTION / DEDICATION DATE:
1836-1837

THE DESIGNERS OF THE GOVERNMENT STREET Presbyterian Church were trained in New York City under three famed architects who pioneered the Greek Revival style in the United States: Ithiel Town, Alexander Jackson Davis, and Minard Lafever. Hearing of the deep South's booming prosperity, Gallier and the Dakins moved south in 1834, where they introduced the fashionable Greek Revival style into southern architecture and made their reputations in New Orleans and Mobile.

The Government Street Presbyterian congregation was formally organized in 1831. Much of the funds for building the church came from Henry Hitchcock, a local millionaire who served on the building committee. The resulting building has been described as one of the most beautiful surviving Greek Revival churches in the United States. It remains remarkably intact even though it has undergone several changes, including the loss of its steeple, blown down in an 1852 hurricane, and rear additions in 1904 and 1912 that gave the building a T-shape. The church's distyle-in-antis (two columns between pilasters) portico is one of the earliest surviving examples in the United States of a usage that was to become widespread for religious architecture. Its interior, too, remains well preserved and little altered, revealing Greek Revival details borrowed from books of famous architects, such as Lefever's *The Beauties of Modern Architecture*, published in 1835.

Government Street
Presbyterian Church,
Mobile, Alabama,
circa 1930

Mount Sterling Methodist Church

Mount Sterling, Choctaw County

ARCHITECT / BUILDER:
Not available

CONSTRUCTION / DEDICATION DATE:
1859

MOUNT STERLING WAS ONCE A THRIVING antebellum cotton and timber community that has seen its prosperity and population diminish over the years. Only a few houses remain; the church is by far the most notable structure of any kind to survive. The Methodist church was erected in the popular Greek Revival style during the town's heyday. A small one-story frame structure with two doors on its front façade, one for men the other for women, illustrates a puritanical streak that existed in the South at this time.

In the 1970s, after the church's congregation could no longer maintain the building, it was deeded to the Choctaw County Historical Society. With only 49 members and a small budget, the Society spent over 15 years raising money and completing emergency repairs to the structure so it could be used as a community hall. Most of the work has been completed, allowing this historic building that has withstood so much over the years, including a war and tornadoes, to continue to have an active existence in its community and to serve as a reminder of the town's past.

Mount Sterling
Methodist Church,
Mount Sterling,
Alabama

Andrews Methodist Chapel

(McIntosh Log Church)

U.S. Highway 43, vicinity of McIntosh, Washington County

ARCHITECT / BUILDER:
Not available

CONSTRUCTION / DEDICATION DATE:
1860

Andrews Methodist Chapel (McIntosh Log Church), vicinity of McIntosh, Alabama

ANDREWS METHODIST CHAPEL, also known as the McIntosh Log Church, is one of the few remaining log churches in Alabama. The origins of the church date back to the arrival of the first Methodist preacher in southwest Alabama, Lorenzo Dow. Dow recorded in his diary that he found a "thick settlement" of people in McIntosh who had little interest in religion. He spent several years preaching in the area. His success is evidenced by the fact that after he left, the residents filed petitions for a preacher. The location of the congregation's first church is not known. The present church is built on land donated in 1860 by John G. Rush and his wife. The church remains essentially intact and retains its original wooden pews and pulpit furniture. It was used by its congregation until 1952, when a new church was built adjoining the earlier structure.

St. Andrew's Episcopal Church

U.S. Route 80, Prairieville

ARCHITECT / BUILDER:
Possibly based on a Richard Upjohn design
CONSTRUCTION / DEDICATION DATE:
1853-1854

THIS SMALL FRAME GOTHIC REVIVAL CHURCH reveals the widespread impact of Richard Upjohn's publication, *Rural Architecture*. A variation of Upjohn's published plans, it has been suggested that Upjohn, an acquaintance of Captain Henry A. Tayloe, an influential member of the congregation and an avid Episcopalian, may have actually provided a design for the church. It was consecrated in 1858 by Bishop Nicholas Homner Cobbs, the first Episcopal bishop of Alabama.

The church was built by slaves belonging to members of the congregation working under the direction of two master carpenters, Peter Lee and Joe Glasgow, slaves of Captain Henry A. Tayloe. The church's fine craftsmanship is a testimony to their ability.

The first Episcopal services were conducted in Prairieville in 1834. The Prairieville congregation was then formally organized and land was acquired for a church and cemetery. The church served the planters of surrounding counties of the Canebrake area, but after the Civil War when the plantation era came to an end the number of parishioners steadily decreased. The building, however, is maintained thanks to a trust fund left by two women, including one who was a granddaughter of Captain Tayloe. Services are conducted on occasion, usually concluding with a picnic lunch on the beautiful grounds surrounding the church.

St. Andrews
Episcopal Church,
Prairieville,
Alabama

Sixteenth Street Baptist Church

Downtown Birmingham

ARCHITECT / BUILDER:
Wallace A. Rayfield
CONSTRUCTION / DEDICATION DATE:
1909-1911

WALLACE A. RAYFIELD GRADUATED from Howard University before attending Pratt Institute, Brooklyn, and Columbia University where he received a B.Arch. degree in 1899. After teaching at Tuskegee Normal and Industrial Institute, he moved to Birmingham and set up an architectural practice. In about 1909, Rayfield was selected as the official architect for the A.M.E. Zion denomination throughout the United States and Africa. The Sixteenth Street Baptist Church was one of his first commissions. At the time of its construction, Birmingham had a prospering African-American community of professionals and white-collar workers. Rayfield was responsible for the design of several large African-American churches being built in the city at this time.

Sixteenth Street Baptist stands out, not so much for its Romanesque style architecture, but for its role as the center of Civil Rights activities in Birmingham in the early 1960s. The bomb that exploded in its basement on September 15, 1963, taking the lives of four young girls, marks a turning point in the struggle for Civil Rights in Birmingham, and elsewhere in the South.

Since the bombing, the church has undergone a complete restoration and with Kelly Ingram Park and the new Birmingham Civil Rights Institute forms part of Birmingham's Civil Rights District.

Sixteenth Street
Baptist Church,
Birmingham, Alabama

Mississippi

THE TERRITORY OF MISSISSIPPI, formed in 1798, was officially admitted to the Union in 1817. In the years following the Revolutionary War settlers from Virginia, the Carolinas, Kentucky, and Tennessee searching for new land began migrating into the area, traveling along the Natchez Trace, a 600-mile Indian path leading from Nashville, Tennessee, to Natchez on the Mississippi River. However, it wasn't until 1838, following the forcible removal of all the area's Native Americans, that millions of acres of fertile farmland became available for exploitation.

Natchez and its surrounding area had a population of about 2,200 people in 1820, making it the largest and wealthiest town between New Orleans and St. Louis. Although the city never became a large metropolis, its proximity to the rich cotton lands along the Mississippi River transformed it into a social and economic center. Natchez's period of greatest growth, occurring between 1820 and the onset of the Civil War, coincided with the flourishing of the Greek Revival style that quickly became the style of choice for homes of many wealthy plantation owners and for churches that were then being built in the state.

The style cut across denominational and economic lines. Scots-Irish farmers from Alabama and the Carolinas erected **Bethel Presbyterian Church** in Lowndes County in 1845. This small wood-frame church is considered the finest surviving example of Greek Revival religious architecture in the Black Prairie Region of Mississippi.

Methodist preachers began riding regular circuits in Mississippi in 1800, preaching to the unchurched and holding camp meetings. Their success can be seen in the number of churches they established–454 by the 1850s, many of which were built in the Greek Revival style, including **Kingston Methodist Church** in the vicinity of Natchez, built in 1856 to serve the needs of a rural, plantation community.

By 1850, Baptist churches were only second in number to Methodist. Mashulaville Baptist Church is one of the few dating to the antebellum era to survive. Built in 1855 in Mashulaville, Noxubee County in eastern Mississippi, it is a simple vernacular interpretation of the popular Greek Revival style.

Although the Episcopal Church never gained many adherents in Mississippi, it did begin to experience a revival among prosperous Mississippians during the antebellum period, when 14 Episcopal churches were established. Arriving with Episcopal missionaries was Richard Upjohn's pattern book, *Rural Architecture*, featuring the Gothic Revival style. This soon became the style of choice for religious architecture. An intact example of this style is the **Church of Our Saviour, Episcopal** in Iuka, consecrated in 1873.

Although Catholicism is rare in most southern states, nine Catholic parishes were scattered around Mississippi by the mid-nineteenth century. One, Annunciation Parish, founded in Columbus in 1854, prospered during the early years of the Civil War when the town was a center of industry for the Confederacy. This prompted the parish's pastor to design and begin construction on a brick Gothic Revival church. The church was unfinished when the tide of war turned, so the pastor, in desperation, sent out a call for help in its completion, arguing that the Catholics in Columbus were "few and very poor." Apparently his call was answered, for the church was finally completed and dedicated in 1868.

Catholic missionaries were also active on plantations. Prior to the outbreak of hostilities in 1861, over 50 percent of the people living in many of Mississippi's counties were slaves. The priests received a warm welcome from plantation owners who hoped that by caring for the "spiritual" needs of their slaves they could allay many of the abolitionists' criticisms. Separation of the races, however, was to be maintained: Black Catholics had to sit in the back of churches and were the last to receive communion. Twenty years after the end of the Civil War, the Third Plenary Council of the Catholic Church meeting in Baltimore called for the establishment of separate black parishes as a way to evangelize blacks more effectively. One of the first of these parishes was established in Natchez where **Holy Family**, the first African-American Roman Catholic church in the state, was constructed in 1894 with money raised in northern and eastern states.

Far more blacks, however, chose to join the African Methodist Episcopal Church. Bethel A.M.E. is the first A.M.E. congregation organized in Mississippi. It was founded in Vicksburg in 1864 by a pastor from Indiana. The congregation's present Romanesque Revival building, constructed in 1912, has an auditorium plan favored by the Methodists for its sight lines and acoustics.

Jewish settlers in Mississippi who arrived early in the nineteenth century had by 1830 established cemeteries in Biloxi and Natchez. Others following them included immigrants from Germany and Alsace who became peddlers and small shopkeepers in many of the state's isolated small towns. By 1860 Mississippi had at least six Jewish congregations, including **Gemiluth Chassed** in Port Gibson, established in 1859. The congregation's Moorish-Byzantine synagogue, erected in 1891, is one of the state's most exotic structures. No longer in use as a synagogue, it has been preserved by its private owner and is now the oldest extant synagogue building in the state.

Bethel Presbyterian Church

Off U.S. Highway 45, south of Columbus, Lowndes County

ARCHITECT / BUILDER:
Not available

CONSTRUCTION / DEDICATION DATE:
1844-1845

BETHEL CHURCH, A SMALL, WOOD-FRAME Greek Revival building, is located in a rural area of the Black Prairie Region of northern Mississippi. Its nearest community, a small hamlet, is four miles away. The church was erected to house a Presbyterian congregation founded in 1834 by Scots-Irish settlers from Alabama and the Carolinas. Although the Greek Revival style was popular in Mississippi, few churches were built in this style in the Black Prairie Region. Bethel is considered the finest surviving example.

The church is said to have been built by members of the congregation and neighbors; the designer, however, remains unknown. What is apparent is that the builders were fully aware of current architectural styles, possibly from architects' pattern books, as can be seen by the Greek Revival elements featured in this building. Most prominent is the façade that features a distyle-in-antis (two columns between pilasters) portico surmounted by a pedimented gable. The architectural integrity of the interior and exterior have largely been maintained. The pews are original to the building, except the doors that enclosed the ends have been removed. The gallery along the east wall, supported by a single column, remains intact. Its only access is from the exterior.

Bethel Presbyterian Church, vicinity of Columbus, Mississippi

Kingston Methodist Church

Kingston-Hutchins Landing Road, vicinity of Natchez, Adam County

ARCHITECT / BUILDER:
Not available

CONSTRUCTION / DEDICATION DATE:
1856-1857

Kingston
Methodist Church,
vicinity of Natchez,
Mississippi

LOCATED ABOUT 15 MILES SOUTHEAST OF NATCHEZ, Kingston Methodist Church is a small, simple but elegant Greek Revival building designed to serve the needs of a rural, plantation community. The stucco is scored in imitation of stone, but the church's most dramatic exterior feature is its portico supported by two large columns and surmounted by a pediment that shelters the central entrance. The most dramatic element of the interior is a wooden Greek Revival frontispiece behind the pulpit. It consists of an entablature (moldings) supported by paired pilasters. There is a gallery for slaves at the northern end of the sanctuary, as well as an interior stairway. The church's setting and the building as a whole maintain their integrity, illustrating the ability of a small, rural congregation to build a church in the latest style on a small scale.

Church of Our Saviour, Episcopal

East Eastport Street, Iuka

ARCHITECT / BUILDER:
James B. Cook, architect
CONSTRUCTION / DEDICATION DATE:
1873

T HE CHURCH IS TYPICAL OF HUNDREDS of Carpenter style Gothic Revival churches built throughout the nation's rural areas in the latter half of the nineteenth century. It is, however, one of only a handful of surviving board-and-batten Gothic Revival churches left in Mississippi. Although James B. Cook, an English-born architect who moved to Memphis in 1854, is given credit for giving the church its Gothic door, its plan appears to be based on those depicted in Richard Upjohn's book on rural church architecture that was directed toward small, Episcopal congregations.

This small church has maintained all of the features associated with the Carpenter Gothic style, except it lacks a tower. Instead it has a small, square belfry with a gabled cap placed at the peak of the roof gable. The congregation no longer owns the building; it is now in the possession of a community organization that completely restored it to its original condition.

Church of Our
Savior, Episcopal,
Iuka, Mississippi

Holy Family Roman Catholic Church

16 Orange Avenue, Natchez

ARCHITECT / BUILDER:
Not available
CONSTRUCTION / DEDICATION DATE:
1894

AT THE TIME THIS CHURCH WAS BUILT there were only about 150,000 African-American Roman Catholics in the United States. Up until 1885 black and white Roman Catholics worshipped together, although blacks were relegated to the gallery or rear of the church and were the last to receive communion. This changed following the Plenary Council meeting held in Baltimore in 1885, at which it was determined that the establishment of separate black parishes was a more effective way to evangelize blacks.

Holy Family Parish, organized in 1889, is the oldest black parish in Mississippi. A small church and school constructed in 1890 served the parish for several years until its priest received permission to seek funds for a larger and more impressive building. He succeeded and the present brick Gothic Revival church was constructed in 1894. One of its parishioners remarked that erecting this building in a state where nearly all other Catholic churches were small and built of wood was equivalent to building St. Patrick's Cathedral in New York City.

The congregation continues to worship in its historic building.

**Holy Family
Roman Catholic
Church, Natchez,
Mississippi**

Gemiluth Chassed Synagogue

Church Street (U.S. Highway 61 South), Port Gibson

ARCHITECT / BUILDER:
Bartlett and Budemeyer
CONSTRUCTION / DEDICATION DATE:
1891

T HE CONGREGATION, GEMILUTH CHASSED, was organized in 1859 by the city's small Jewish community. As more Jews began moving into the Delta Region, primarily from eastern Europe, the congregation was finally able to construct a synagogue in 1891. It now has the distinction of being the oldest surviving synagogue building in the state.

Little is known of the building's two architects, except that it appears they chose to design a synagogue that they thought was similar to those in Russia, a country from which many of the members had fled. It is unlikely, however, that the congregants held any warm memories of Russia. The repeated use of the horseshoe arch both on the exterior and interior comes from Moorish architecture, a popular style for synagogue architecture in the late nineteenth century.

The congregation has disbanded and the synagogue is now the property of a private owner who saved it from being demolished for a parking lot. It is in the process of being restored and preserved.

Gemiluth Chassed Synagogue, Port Gibson, Mississippi

Tennessee

P ERMANENT WHITE SETTLEMENT BEGAN in the territory's northeast sector in about 1769 when English, Scots-Irish, and German settlers began arriving from Virginia. Nashville, established in 1779 on the Cumberland River, became the northern terminus of the Natchez Trace, a 600-mile Indian path leading to Natchez, Mississippi. Nashville was named the state's capital in 1843.

Tennessee voted against secession at the start of the Civil War, but later chose to join the Confederacy, making it the last state to secede from the Union. Tennesseans, however, remained divided in their loyalty during the conflict, serving in both armies. The last to leave the Union, Tennessee was the first Confederate state to rejoin it following the close of hostilities. The state then began to experience a boom as its cotton industry began expanding and its natural resources were developed.

The vast majority of the state's early settlers were white, Anglo-Saxon, and Protestant, primarily Presbyterian. Following on the heels of the settlers were circuit-riding Methodist preachers who began conducting camp meetings that were part religious revival and part social outing. However, their success in attracting adherents was short-lived; they were soon replaced by Baptists who found a fertile field for their beliefs in the expanding southern frontier.

The state's oldest Presbyterian congregation, **Salem Presbyterian Church** in Washington County, was founded in 1780 by a pioneer Scots-Irish minister, Samuel Doak, considered the "apostle" of Presbyterianism in the state. The congregation's present building, erected in 1894–1895, is a memorial to Doak.

Another historic Presbyterian church, but in a totally different style, can be found in Nashville. Popularly known as "Karnak on the Cumberland," the **Old First Presbyterian Church**, erected in 1851, is one of the few places of worship in the United States built in the Egyptian Revival style–a reflection of nineteenth-century Romanticism and, perhaps, its congregants' knowledge of recent archaeological discoveries in Egypt. The church was designed by William Strickland at the same time he was involved in the design and construction of the state's capitol.

Lawrence County on the Alabama border was settled by German Catholics from Ohio who were seeking relief from the financial depression affecting the Ohio Valley in the years following the Civil War. A German Catholic priest from Cincinnati formed the German Catholic Homestead Society that purchased 15,000 acres of land in the county in 1869–1870. Families immediately began arriving; ironically, considering who recruited them, many lacked farming experience. Most were artisans and craftsmen who found employment in the state's expanding industries. These new settlers brought with them a religious and ethnic diversity that is unique in rural Tennessee, which remains predominantly Protestant and Anglo-Saxon. The Germans established four churches and two cemeteries. **Sacred Heart of Jesus** built in Lawrenceburg, the county seat, in 1887, is in the *hallenkirchen* Gothic Revival style that reflects the ethnic origins of its parishioners.

The Church of God in Christ (Mason Temple) was incorporated in Memphis in 1897. It was founded by Charles Harrison Mason, an African-American preacher who converted the congregation's doctrine to Pentacostalism in 1907. The denomination's first National Temple, large enough to hold 5,000 worshippers, was constructed in Memphis in 1924. Destroyed by fire in 1936, it was replaced by a new Temple complex built between 1940 and 1945. While the Temple's design is important, its congregation's role in the Civil Rights Movement, and in particular, in the life of Dr. Martin Luther King, Jr., is vastly more important.

A group of German-speaking Jews settled in the small town of Brownsville in eastern Tennessee, where they formed a congregation in 1867. Religious services were held in a private home before **Adas Israel Synagogue** was built circa 1882. The synagogue, a single-story frame Gothic Revival structure, is similar to contemporary churches built in the area. For a time, it even had a small steeple that was removed in the 1920s. As the Jewish community declined, the building was sold to a Christian congregation.

Salem Presbyterian Church

147 Washington College Road, Limestone, Washington County

ARCHITECT / BUILDER:
A. Page Brown

CONSTRUCTION / DEDICATION DATE:
1894-1895

L OCATED IN THE STATE'S OLDEST COUNTY, Salem is also the oldest Presbyterian congregation in the state. It was established at the same time and on the same land donated for a school, Martin Academy, now Washington College Academy. The congregation's first log church was the site of the organization of the first western Presbytery (Abingdon) in 1785. Demonstrating the ambivalence many Tennesseans felt during the Civil War, the congregation refused to join the denomination's Southern Assembly.

The congregation erected a more substantial brick church in 1825, but by the end of the century an even larger one was needed. Funds for the new church were donated by Mrs. Nettie Fowler McCormick, who, along with her husband Cyrus, were major supporters of Presbyterian churches and church colleges. Mrs. McCormick was apparently very involved in the design of the building, mainly due to her concern about costs, that were kept to a minimum by using the labor of members and Academy students. The brick was burnt on the premises and the logs for the beams in the sanctuary were donated by members. It was through Mrs. McCormick's efforts that the architect, A. Page Brown, was hired to design the Richardsonian Romanesque building. Brown, who was then residing in California, was trained at Cornell University and worked in Minnesota before designing Fowler Hall, now part of McCormick Seminary in Chicago.

Salem Presbyterian Church, Limestone, Tennessee

Old First Presbyterian Church

(DOWNTOWN PRESBYTERIAN CHURCH)

154 Fifth Avenue North, Nashville

ARCHITECT / BUILDER:
William Strickland, architect
CONSTRUCTION / DEDICATION DATE:
1851

WILLIAM STRICKLAND BEGAN his architectural career as an apprentice to Benjamin Henry Latrobe, known for his design of the Minor Basilica of the Assumption of the Blessed Virgin Mary in Baltimore. Strickland went on to become one of the foremost architects in the nation. This church was designed late in his career, at the same time he was designing the state's capitol. The interest in Egyptian architecture was part of the Romantic Classicism of the nineteenth century. It was stimulated by the extensive archaeological excavations being undertaken in Egypt and the dissemination of profusely illustrated publications describing the discoveries. It is unclear why Presbyterians in Nashville selected this style for their new church, but it has been argued that the so-called "severity" of Egyptian architecture was very appealing to Calvinistic Presbyterians.

The outside of the church was not completed until 1880, when the two portico pillars with lotus blossom capitals and the classic winged disc on the pediment were added. At about the same time the interior, designed to resemble the interior of an Egyptian temple—especially the Temple at Karnak on the Nile, was extensively remodeled. Initially drab in color, it was transformed to a brilliantly colored space decorated with both Christian and Egyptian symbols and echoing the Egyptian style. In 1887, stained glass windows replaced the original clear glass ones. The new windows also include a similar symbolic Egyptian/Christian vocabulary.

Old First Presbyterian Church (Downtown Presbyterian, Karnak on Cumberland), Nashville, Tennessee

Sacred Heart of Jesus Roman Catholic Church

Berger Street, Lawrenceburg, Lawrence County

ARCHITECT / BUILDER:
Not available

CONSTRUCTION / DEDICATION DATE:
1887

THE MAJORITY OF SETTLERS ARRIVING in Lawrence County at the urging of the Cincinnati German Catholic Homestead Society were Alsatian, but there were also a number of Poles. The first Mass was celebrated in Lawrenceburg in October 1870. Two years later the congregants constructed a wooden church, St. Joseph, and the following year established a convent.

The present church was constructed by members of the parish, many of whom were skilled artisans. It is a massive brick structure with a square bell tower and a tall copper steeple centered on the façade. This style is reminiscent of the *hallenkirchen* Gothic churches of Germany which are so named because their nave and aisles are all of equal height. The church is one of the most impressive landmarks in Lawrenceburg and the only surviving Catholic church in the county seat.

Sacred Heart of
Jesus Roman
Catholic Church,
Lawrenceburg,
Tennessee

Church of God in Christ, Mason Temple

958 Mason Street, Memphis

ARCHITECT / BUILDER:
W. H. Taylor

CONSTRUCTION / DEDICATION DATE:
1945 (dedicated)

THE MASON TEMPLE, and its surrounding World Headquarters complex for the Church of God in Christ, were constructed in phases between 1940 and circa 1960; the Temple was dedicated in 1945. COGIC, the acronym by which the denomination is known, is second only to the National Baptist Convention, U.S.A., as the largest denomination of African-Americans in the United States. The complex is significant for its association with Charles H. Mason, the founder of the Church of God in Christ, who oversaw the construction of the entire complex. It is equally important for its association with the ministry of Dr. Martin Luther King, Jr. It was in this temple that Dr. King delivered his famous "Mountaintop" speech, his final public speech before his assassination.

Between 1907 and 1914, COGIC was the only body to which white Pentecostal congregations could go to have their ministers ordained. With Mason's blessings, a group of white COGIC ministers formed the Assemblies of God denomination in 1914.

The original National Temple was destroyed by fire in 1936. Convocations were held in Bishop Mason's own church until the new Temple was completed. W. H. Taylor, an Elder in the church, was selected as its architect. Lack of funds and supplies, however, dragged out its construction for nearly six years. At the time of its dedication, the Temple was described as the "largest convention hall owned by any Negro church group in America."

Church of God in Christ (Mason Temple), Memphis, Tennessee

Mother of God Roman Catholic Church

("MUTTER GOTTES")

119 West Sixth Street, Covington

ARCHITECT / BUILDER:
Father Ferdinand Kuhr, drawings; Walter & Stuart, architects
CONSTRUCTION / DEDICATION DATE:
1869-1871; 1890

THE OLDEST GERMAN PARISH in Covington, Mother of God Roman Catholic Church was founded in 1841 by a Prussian priest, Father Ferdinand Kuhr. The parish's first church was constructed in 1842, but as more German immigrants arrived and the parish grew, its members began to agitate for a larger and more impressive building. The Cincinnati architectural firm, Walter & Stuart, was hired to draw up plans based on Father Kuhr's drawings. The firm had already designed several Protestant churches in the area; this was its first Roman Catholic commission. The church was dedicated in 1871, but its embellishment continued for many decades.

The monumental Beaux-Arts Renaissance basilica underwent a complete restoration in 1890 in honor of the parish's Golden Jubilee. Stained glass windows from Munich were installed, a wood-carved communion table and pulpit commissioned, and frescoes were painted by Johann Schmitt, a parish member who has been called the "first Christian painter in America."

Restoration and repairs continued throughout the nineteenth and well into the twentieth century, both in response to need–damages due to fire and tornadoes–and the members' desire to preserve and embellish the church's artistic heritage.

FACING PAGE:
Mother of God Roman Catholic Church, Covington, Kentucky

8

West South Central Region

Louisiana
Arkansas
Oklahoma
Texas

THE STATES COMPRISING THIS REGION are culturally and geographically diverse. Oklahoma and parts of western and northern Texas share characteristics with the South and West, whereas East Texas, Louisiana, and southern Arkansas are most similar to the deep South. The latter area's plantation culture dates back to the arrival in the first half of the nineteenth century of plantation owners moving westward from the Carolinas and Georgia. Most were of English and Scots-Irish descent, members of various evangelical religions, especially Baptist, and slave owners. Their culture was in vivid contrast to that of the three long-term resident populations of the region: Mexican, Cajun, and Native American.

People of Mexican ancestry, many of whom are able to trace their families back for generations, reside primarily in an area south of a line running diagonally through Texas from the northwest to the southeast. Mexico recognized the American annexation of Texas at the signing of the Treaty of Guadalupe Hidalgo in 1848. The treaty also guaranteed that all Mexican citizens would retain their property and traditions and, after a year of residency, be accorded American citizenship with all its rights and privileges.

The name Cajun, derived from Acadian, refers to the Catholic, French-speaking population of southern Louisiana that came from Acadia, now Nova Scotia and New Brunswick. The French-speaking Acadians were expelled from Canada in 1755 and found a haven in the Spanish Roman Catholic coastal region along the Gulf of Mexico.

While southern Arkansas is identified with the deep South, its northern region takes on a far different identity. It lies in the Ozarks, an irregular, hilly area of eroded plateaus similar to Appalachia. The similarity extends to its settlers: white, Anglo-Saxon, Protestant, and fiercely independent.

Oklahoma became the government's "dumping ground" for all the Indian groups displaced from regions to the East. It was established formally as Indian Territory in 1854 with a provision forbidding white people by law from settling there. However, the white man's ongoing search for new land caused the law to be rescinded in 1889, when unoccupied tracts of land were opened for settlement resulting in the famed land runs that brought immigrants and easterners into the Territory.

Texas has the region's most complex settlement patterns, which is not too surprising given its size. Scholars still argue about how to divide its cultural areas. Mexicans, as noted, were long-term residents of the area; later settlers came from older areas of the South, bringing with them the plantation culture and slaves. They were followed by other immigrant groups, including German and later French and Alsatian settlers.

PRECEDING PAGE:

Boston Avenue
United Methodist,
Tulsa, Oklahoma

Louisiana

L OUISIANA, DESCRIBED BY ONE HISTORIAN as the most "foreign" of all southern states, was named in 1682 in honor of Louis XIV of France by the French explorer Robert Cavalier de La Salle. Among the first colonists in the area were immigrants from Germany and Alsace who settled along the Arkansas and Red Rivers. New Orleans was founded by the French, but in 1763, France decided to rid itself of the city and the territory west of the Mississippi River, by ceding them to Spain, and, at the same time, transferring control of the region east of the river to England. In 1800, Spain returned its part of the territory to France, who then sold it to the United States as part of the Louisiana Purchase, concluded in 1803.

Louisiana was admitted to the Union in 1812 on the eve of war with Great Britain. Three years later New Orleans became the site of a crucial battle with the British for control of its port. The city withstood the assault, and in the years following the war, the port ranked second only to New York City's in volume. However, this era of prosperity came to an abrupt end with the start of the Civil War.

One of the legacies of French occupation was the infamous Louisiana Black Code, promulgated in Paris in 1724, prohibiting the practice of any religion other than Catholicism. However, it would appear that Jews were living in New Orleans in the eighteenth century, as documents reveal that nine were expelled from the city in 1769. The situation began to change once Louisiana entered the Union. German Jews organized a congregation in New Orleans in 1828, followed by one founded by Sephardic (Spanish-Portuguese) Jews in 1846. The congregations merged in 1881 to become the **Touro Synagogue**, named for Judah Touro, a descendant of the Touro family of Newport, Rhode Island (see p. 64). The congregation's present Byzantine style synagogue was constructed in 1909.

French influence still prevails in Louisiana, particularly in New Orleans and along the lower reaches of the Mississippi River. It was reinforced by the continued importation of French culture either through immigration, such as the arrival of refugees from the French island of Santo Domingo, or directly from France in the person of architects and artisans commissioned to design and construct buildings in the growing city of New Orleans. The only confirmed building dating to the period of French domination, however, is the former Ursuline Convent built in 1745 to replace an earlier one. It remained in use as a convent until 1824, when it became the residence for bishops and archbishops. Restored in 1973 it is the archival repository for the Archdiocese of New Orleans. The adjacent chapel is now designated Our Lady of Victory Roman Catholic Church.

German-speaking immigrants were among the first to settle in Louisiana. By mid-nineteenth century, New Orleans was home to the largest German colony in the South, numbering nearly 20,000 people. Many were artisans and builders fleeing Europe. Three, Charles Lewis Hillger, William Drews, and William Fitzner, designed and built many places of worship in New Orleans and in the area of Lafayette City known as "Little Saxony." Neither faith nor style mattered to them. Hillger, for example, in 1871 designed Zion Evangelical Church on St. Charles Street in New Orleans in a Gothic Revival style, added Romanesque detailing to the German Protestant church in "Little Saxony," and combined both styles in Temple Sinai (now demolished), built for a German-Jewish congregation.

Roman Catholics comprise 80 percent of the population of southern Louisiana. The **Cathedral of St. Louis** in New Orleans, the third church constructed on the site, is, perhaps, the state's most famed religious edifice. The parish's first church, erected in 1724, was destroyed by fire and replaced in 1794, the same year it was raised to the rank of cathedral. A half century later the cathedral was in need of repair or replacement. Designs for a new building submitted by the French architect Jacques Nicholas Bussiere dePouilly included a Neoclassical façade and an intricate Gothic steeple of cast iron and wood. Unfortunately the tower collapsed, bringing down part of the roof and walls. DePouilly and his builder were dismissed, and the finished cathedral retains little of the original design.

Irish and German Catholics began settling in Lafayette, now part of New Orleans, in the mid-1840s. Soon each group began agitating for its own ethnic parish where traditions and language could be maintained. The **Church of St. Alphonsus** was built in 1857 for the English-speaking Irish Catholics living in an area known as the "Irish Channel." The church is important both for its excellent craftsmanship and for the Redemptorist priests who ministered to the people. One, Father Seelos, is being investigated for possible canonization.

Protestants, mainly planters migrating westward, were always a minority in the state. The few churches constructed in Louisiana in the Greek Revival style were built for Protestant congregations. Three of the seven are in Keachi. One, **Keachi Presbyterian Church**, built in 1858, is considered the finest surviving example. The other two, built 20 years later, Keachi United Methodist Church and Keachi Baptist Church, are in a Greek Revival–Gothic Revival style, revealing a transition in taste toward the increasingly popular Gothic Revival style. A far less pretentious building tradition exists in northern Louisiana, where **Walnut Creek Baptist Church**, a remote descendant of the Greek Revival style, is typical of many churches built for rural and small-town Methodist and Baptist congregations.

Most of the state's African-American churches are also unpretentious structures with little or no style. That certainly describes Rosedown Baptist Church located on the Rosedown Plantation in St. Francisville. Founded in the mid-1800s by the plantation's slaves, it was recently saved from demolition thanks to the intercession of blacks and whites living in the area. A more monumental example of an African-American church is the brick Romanesque Revival **Antioch Baptist Church** in Shreveport, built in 1903 for a congregation organized in 1866 by 73 newly freed blacks. The church was designed by N. S. Allen, a white man and Louisiana's first Fellow of the American Institute of Architects.

Touro Synagogue

St. Charles Avenue at General Pershing, New Orleans

ARCHITECT / BUILDER:
Emil Weil

CONSTRUCTION / DEDICATION DATE:
1908

TOURO SYNAGOGUE, THE OLDEST JEWISH congregation in the Mississippi Valley, was formed by the merger in 1881 of a German-Jewish congregation and one that was composed of Spanish-Portuguese Jews who had emigrated from South America and the Caribbean. It is named after a community leader, Judah Touro, the son of a rabbi who was born in Newport, Rhode Island, and was a generous contributor to both congregations. The present synagogue, completed in 1908 at a cost of $100,000, was designed by a well-known local architect, Emil Weil, who won the congregation's design competition.

The Byzantine style brick structure, decorated throughout with polychromatic terra-cotta, is crowned with a large dome. At the top of the dome in its exact center is a blue stained glass representing the Heaven of Heavens. An addition on Pershing Avenue has a Moorish style entryway consisting of three arches framed within a larger arch. A chapel has been added on St. Charles. On the interior, the pulpit and Ark, removed from the earlier synagogue, were donated by Judah Touro. The pillars supporting the Ark were crafted in the Middle East from Cedars of Lebanon.

Touro Synagogue,
New Orleans,
Louisiana

Church of St. Alphonsus

(ROMAN CATHOLIC)

2029 Constance Street, Lafayette (New Orleans)

ARCHITECT / BUILDER:
Louis L. Long
CONSTRUCTION / DEDICATION DATE:
1857

S T. ALPHONSUS WAS ERECTED TO SERVE the Irish Catholic population that settled in an area of Lafayette known as the Irish Channel. A temporary frame church
erected in 1851 was used until the present building was completed. It is the first of
three large ethnic Roman Catholic churches built in Lafayette. The design was obtained
from the Baltimore architect, Louis Long, who was then completing the construction of a
large Jesuit church, St. Ignatius, in Baltimore that apparently served as a model for St.
Alphonsus. The building displays many elements from the Renaissance Revival style that
first appeared in the United States in about 1850 in R. G. Hatfield's design for the Sun
Building in Baltimore. Long was apparently familiar with that building, as can be seen in

the design and decoration of the church's
exterior that includes a similar symmetry of
design, arched windows, pilasters, and bold
moldings. The interior of the church is
impressive in its size and scale. Its decoration, including the millwork, wood carvings, paintings, and pews, all display a high
quality of craftsmanship.

St. Alphonsus was closed in 1976 and is
currently undergoing restoration. It still
belongs to the Redemptorist order, but a
nonprofit Friends of St. Alphonsus is raising
funds for its restoration and plans to reopen
the building as a community center.

**Church of
St. Alphonsus
(Roman Catholic),
Lafayette, Louisiana**

Keachi Presbyterian Church

LA Highway 5, Keachi

ARCHITECT / BUILDER:
Not available

CONSTRUCTION / DEDICATION DATE:
1858

KEACHI PRESBYTERIAN IS CONSIDERED the finest rural Greek Revival church in Louisiana. Only seven churches were built in this style in Louisiana; three are in Keachi, a center for the Greek Revival style. This may be due to DeSoto Parish's settlement in the first half of the nineteenth century that coincided with the spread of the Greek Revival style. Although many examples in the Parish dating from this period have been lost, including Keachi Female College, a number still survive, including the temple-fronted Keachi Presbyterian Church. Its pedimented front portico was enclosed with clap-boarding in the 1890s, but it was placed behind the columns so no original features were lost or damaged. Also added in the 1890s were a cupola, several windows, and a lean-to at the rear. The principal feature on the interior is the aedicule or shrine framed by two columns supporting an entablature that is set behind the raised platform altar.

Keachi
Presbyterian
Church,
Keachi, Louisiana

Walnut Creek Baptist Church

One and one half miles northwest of Simsboro on Lincoln Parish Rd. 3

ARCHITECT / BUILDER:
Not available

CONSTRUCTION / DEDICATION DATE:
circa 1870; 1918

T HE CHURCH IS A RARE SURVIVING EXAMPLE of an important North Louisiana building type, a remote descendant of provincial Greek Revival style churches such as the ones built in Keachi. Generally associated with the Methodists and Baptists, these buildings are simple gable-roofed, wooden meeting halls with two doorways on the front façade, one for women, the other for men. What makes this particular church significant, other than the fact that it remains essentially unchanged, is the embellishment found on its interior. In about 1900, a polygonal, stepped platform, known as the "pulpit," was moved from the north end of the building to the south. It features three richly paneled and molded lecterns that in 1918 were decorated with a false marbling treatment in gray and blue. This embellishment is considered an important and unusual example of a local folk art tradition.

Walnut Creek Baptist Church, vicinity of Simsboro, Louisiana

Antioch Baptist Church

1057 Texas Avenue, Shreveport

ARCHITECT / BUILDER:
N. S. Allen
CONSTRUCTION / DEDICATION DATE:
1901–1903

A LARGE BRICK ROMANESQUE REVIVAL STRUCTURE, Antioch Baptist was designed by one of Louisiana's preeminent architects, N. S. Allen, F.A.I.A. Allen, who was white, came to Shreveport in 1870 to practice architecture. Over the course of the next 30 years he designed over 300 buildings in the city, but only two, besides this church, survive.

The Antioch Baptist Church was organized in 1866 by 73 newly freed blacks. Initially known as the First Colored Baptist Church, its name was changed in 1871 to Antioch Baptist. Completed in 1903, the church is located along the once fashionable Texas Avenue just outside the Shreveport central business district. Its location, design, and architect all make it one of Louisiana's most important churches. That an African-American congregation was able to purchase land, hire a prominent white architect, and build a large brick church in the latest architectural style illustrates the congregants' unique position in a southern urban area at the turn of the century. Most African-American churches in Louisiana in the late nineteenth and twentieth centuries are modest, frame structures, similar to Rosedown Baptist Church in St. Francisville.

Antioch
Baptist Church,
Shreveport,
Louisiana

Arkansas

RKANSAS' TOPOGRAPHY RANGES from the Ozark Mountains in the north-west, the delta region of the Mississippi Valley, to the low, gulf coastal plain. Arkansas Post, a trading station, was established near the confluence of the Arkansas and Mississippi rivers in 1686 by a French explorer who claimed the territory for France. It was ceded to Spain in 1762, but France, after regaining control in 1801, sold the land to the United States as part of the Louisiana Purchase. At the time of the sale the territory had a population of about 500.

A French priest established a Roman Catholic parish at Arkansas Post in 1796. A second parish was formed in Little Rock, the state's capital, in 1838, two years after Arkansas entered the Union. **St. Andrew's Roman Catholic Cathedral**, completed in 1881, is the oldest extant church building in the state.

The end of the War of 1812 signaled the beginning of migration into the state. Many who came were war veterans, while others were cotton farmers and their slaves. Presbyterians who began settling in an area incorporated in 1848 as Augusta established a congregation in 1861, but had to delay the building of a church because of the onset of the Civil War. **Augusta Presbyterian Church**, completed in 1871, is a small, elegant building designed in the now popular Gothic Revival style.

Arkansas had at least 168 Methodist churches by 1850, attesting to the successful efforts of itinerant preachers who were following the nation's frontier south and westward, conducting well-attended religious revival meetings. The **Ebenezer Camp Ground** in Howard County is one of the oldest religious encampments in the west south central region of the country. The camp's first meeting was held in 1837 about where the present-day Center Point Cemetery is located. The present site was purchased in 1857, but most of the buildings were destroyed during the Civil War. Camp meetings were resumed about 1874.

By the time of the Civil War, the state's population had increased to nearly 550,000, over 20 percent of whom were slaves. Slave owners had considerable political clout, but there were those in Arkansas who opposed the Confederate cause during the Civil War. Although the state voted to secede, over 8,000 men chose to fight on the side of the Union. Many were descendants of German Lutheran farmers who arrived in the late eighteenth century and were vehemently opposed to slavery.

Arkansas had a difficult time recovering from the War. Its agrarian economy was disrupted with the abolition of slavery, but a recovery of sorts began with the exploitation of its natural resources. In the 1880s, land speculators, taking advantage of the state's natural hot springs, established a resort industry that flourished well into the twentieth century. One of those resorts was Winona Springs, just south of Eureka Springs, where the Greek Revival style **Winona Church and School** was erected. The church, the center for all of the small community's social and religious activities, is an example of a typical "country church" that was built throughout the state.

Further contributing to the state's recovery was its growth in industry, which began to lure new settlers, including German and Swiss Catholics who immigrated to Franklin County in the late nineteenth century to work in the area's coal mines. A parish was established in 1879, and a frame church built two years later was replaced in 1902 by the Romanesque style **Our Lady of Perpetual Help**, one of Arkansas' most architecturally significant churches.

St. Andrew's Roman Catholic Cathedral

617 Louisiana Street, Little Rock

ARCHITECT / BUILDER:
Thomas Harding

CONSTRUCTION / DEDICATION DATE:
1878-1881

THE CATHEDRAL, AN EXCELLENT EXAMPLE of the Gothic Revival style that became popular for religious architecture in the latter half of the nineteenth century, is notable for its use of stone from nearby Fourche Mountain, the first building in Arkansas constructed entirely out of this native stone. Its most dramatic feature is its steeple, completed in 1887 and measuring 231 feet, considered at the time of its completion to be the tallest steeple in the South.

Although the interior of the building has undergone modernization, its stained glass windows brought from Chicago at the time of its construction remain intact, as do most of its exterior features.

St. Andrew's
Roman Catholic
Cathedral,
Little Rock,
Arkansas

Augusta Presbyterian Church

Third and Walnut Streets, Augusta

ARCHITECT / BUILDER:
Thomas Hough
CONSTRUCTION / DEDICATION DATE:
1871

THE CHURCH'S STYLE AND DECORATION reflect the determination of its founders to establish a place of worship in a rural community worthy of their faith. Built during the difficult postwar years, its congregation was composed of many civic leaders, including the founder of the town's first school. Carrie Nation visited the church during a local temperance crusade, and a young Woodrow Wilson frequently attended services during the tenure of his brother-in-law as pastor.

The Gothic Revival structure was designed by one of its members, Thomas Hough, who also donated the land. Built of hand-made bricks shaped from local clay, the small church displays a number of refined Gothic Revival details not usually associated with small town churches, including lancet windows set in recessed bays. A steeple-like belfry has been removed as well as an interior balcony.

The congregation has disbanded and the church is no longer in use. A small group of local women, recognizing the historic and aesthetic importance of the building, have raised funds to restore the exterior. The interior has not been touched, but the building and its grounds are being maintained until funds are available to complete the work. They are also seeking an appropriate use for the building.

Augusta
Presbyterian
Church,
Augusta, Arkansas

Ebenezer Camp Ground

North of Center Point off AR 4, Center Point

ARCHITECT / BUILDER:
Not available

CONSTRUCTION / DEDICATION DATE:
Post–Civil War

WIND AND FIRE DOMINATE the history of this campground. Evolving out of the circuit ministry of John Henry, the first Methodist minister to preach in southwest Arkansas, the campground provided a permanent site for religious worship and social gathering along the Arkansas frontier.

The first camp meeting was held in 1837 where the present day Center Point Cemetery is located. The meeting was later moved to the top of Red Hill, but was destroyed by a forest fire in 1856. The present site, purchased in 1857, saw its buildings destroyed during the Civil War. The tenacious Methodists once again rebuilt the camp in 1874 and it continued in use until fires destroyed several of its buildings in 1942 and again in 1956.

Seven rustic buildings remain standing, including three dormitories, two small ministers' cabins, and a small ancillary structure. All are arranged along the perimeter of a square forest clearing. In the center of the clearing is a large tabernacle composed of a tin gabled roof set on squared log supports.

The campground is a reminder of the nation's rural past, when settlers living in remote areas would eagerly journey to a camp meeting that was a combined religious, social, and recreational experience.

Ebenezer Camp Ground, vicinity of Center Point, Howard County, Arkansas

Winona Church and School

Rockhouse Road, Winona Springs

ARCHITECT / BUILDER:
George Pinkley, Joe Clark (builders)
CONSTRUCTION / DEDICATION DATE:
circa 1893

THE WOOD-FRAME WINONA CHURCH and school building is considered the best example locally of the rural building type known as the "country church," popular among smaller, relatively isolated communities. It is a simplified version of the Greek Revival style that became popular throughout much of Arkansas in the mid-nineteenth century and remained popular in many areas into the twentieth century. The building is notable for its use of symmetry throughout, visible in window and door placements. The most significant alteration on the exterior was the removal of a small, pyramidal belfry that sat on the roof ridge near the front of the building. The interior retains much of its original appearance. It is a single rectangular room that served as the sanctuary and classroom. Rising through the center of the room is the original brick flue that vents a large wood stove.

Built by George Pinkley and Joe Clark, it illustrates the ability of local craftsmen to adapt a sophisticated popular building style to the needs of a small community congregation.

Winona Church,
Winona Springs,
Arkansas

Church of Our Lady of Perpetual Help

(CHURCH OF ST. MARY'S)

Route 1, vicinity of Altus, Franklin County

ARCHITECT / BUILDER:
John Riedt, stonemason
CONSTRUCTION / DEDICATION DATE:
1901-1902

OUR LADY OF PERPETUAL HELP is situated atop Pond Creek Mountain overlooking the Arkansas River Valley. The Romanesque style church, with its 120-foot bell tower rising next to the apse, was built of hard white sandstone cut from a nearby quarry. Parish members were German and Swiss Catholics who immigrated to Franklin County in the late nineteenth century. The first priest arrived in the area in 1879, and two years later a frame church was built. As the coal mining industry expanded, additional German and Swiss workers arrived and by 1900 a new church was needed.

The local parish priest and a stonemason from St. Louis, John Riedt, supervised the construction of the new church. Much of the labor was done by parishioners. Perhaps the church's most significant features are the murals painted by Fridolin Fuchs, a German artist. Between January 1915 and April 1916, Fuchs painted 12 stations of the cross similar to those found in German churches. Each station was inscribed with a German text, which was replaced with English in 1964. It is noteworthy that the faces of several church members, plus the artist's and that of the priest, are included in the murals. Fuchs also painted images of saints on the walls and stenciled the domed ceiling above the altar.

The church's architectural style, reminiscent of parish churches in Germany and Switzerland, and its mural paintings by a German artist remain unique in Arkansas.

Church of Our Lady of Perpetual Help (Church of St. Mary's), vicinity of Altus, Arkansas

Oklahoma

EXCEPT FOR ITS EXTREME WESTERN panhandle portion, Oklahoma became part of the United States as a result of the Louisiana Purchase in 1803. Fourteen years later the territory was divided among the Five Civilized Nations, Indian tribes being displaced from the South and Southeast: Creek, Cherokee, Chickasaw, Choctaw, and Seminole. When it became Indian Territory in 1834, it was administered by tribal authority. The government punished tribes that were slaveholders and supporters of the Confederacy by giving permission to loyal Indian tribes to settle in the territory's western portion.

Although white settlers were forbidden by law from settling on these lands, many violations occurred. Ultimately, the government capitulated to the white settlers' demand for more land, which set off one of the most significant events in the settlement of the territory, the land runs of 1889 and 1893. The first run brought 50,000 people into the territory—farmers and would-be ranchers from throughout the Midwest and South. With their arrival came the development of small rural market towns and the establishment of Oklahoma as a territory in 1890. After much debate, Oklahoma and the remaining Indian Territory were admitted into the Union in 1907.

Missionaries were in the region long before Oklahoma became a territory or state. **Wheelock Mission Presbyterian Church**, located in McCurtain County in the far southeastern corner of Indian Territory, was established in 1832 as a Presbyterian mission to the Choctaw Indians who had survived the tragic journey along the "trail of tears" from their ancestral home in Mississippi. Built of hand-chiseled stone in 1846, it is the oldest church building in Oklahoma.

Four Carpenter Gothic churches located in north central Oklahoma represent the oldest and best examples that remain of religious structures constructed in small towns. They represent the three major Protestant denominations in the state: Methodist, Baptist, and Presbyterian—Marshall Methodist Church, built in 1898; Morrison Baptist Church, completed in 1903; Blackburn Methodist Church, constructed in 1904; and the First Presbyterian Church of Chandler, constructed in 1894. Each church played a vital role in its community, providing a place for worship as well as a social outlet.

St. Joseph's Catholic Church in Krebs in Pittsburg County is the oldest church in the eastern Oklahoma Diocese. The parish was founded three years before Oklahoma Territory was opened to white settlement. Those involved in the construction of the parish's first church illustrate the county's ethnic mix. It was planned by a French priest and built by

Irish, Italian, and German miners. As coal mining expanded, more southeastern European immigrants arrived, and by 1910, over 7 percent of the county's population was foreign born.

Roman Catholics were not the only ones attracted to Pittsburg County by the promise of work in the coal mines. Ukrainian miners, followers of the Orthodox Church, also came. **Saints Cyril and Methodius Russian Orthodox Greek Catholic Church** in Hartshorne is the only Russian Orthodox church in Oklahoma. The Byzantine style brick church was built in 1916 by Ukrainian immigrants from the province of Galicia.

Blacks first entered Indian Territory as slaves owned by Indians; others arrived later, as participants in the land runs. The five tribes freed about 7,000 black slaves in 1863, and an additional 7,800 blacks homesteaded. The freedmen remaining in Indian Territory were given farms of up to 100 acres. Other blacks came because of the promise held out to them by Edwin P. McCabe, who believed that this so-called "dumping ground" for Indians could be transformed into a haven for freed blacks. McCabe arrived in Oklahoma Territory in 1869 to promote the establishment of an all-black state. When that failed, he lowered his sights and sought to promote the founding of all-black towns. Twenty-nine were established, most located in Indian Territory. All became rural market centers for blacks living in and around them, and each supported a church. Methodist and Baptist missionaries were active in Indian Territory, with the result that most blacks chose to affiliate with these denominations.

Oklahoma still has 12 historic all-black towns that were founded prior to 1907. Four have Protestant churches constructed between 1915 and 1930—Tatums, Summit, Taft, and Lima. One congregation is A.M.E., the others are Baptist. All the churches are one- or two-story, relatively unadorned, detached buildings, and all have held continuous services since their founding. The oldest, Mount Zion A.M.E., located in Lima, was built in 1915. It is a two-story, rectangular building constructed of randomly laid native sandstone.

African-Americans from Tennessee chose to settle in Oklahoma City, where they organized a congregation. After merging with several other African-American congregations, **Calvary Baptist Church** was established as the primary institution for the city's black community. The church, constructed in 1916, was designed by an African-American architect, Russell Benton Bingham, who was a graduate of the school of architecture at Tuskegee Institute. It is one of the few churches in the central part of the United States to be designed by a black architect for a black congregation.

The **Boston Avenue United Methodist Church**, built in Tulsa in 1929 just before the onset of the Depression, is described as "a religious expression of the modern spirit." It is also an expression of the new-found wealth and confidence of Tulsa's citizens resulting from the oil boom. Designed by a well-known architect, Bruce Goff, with symbolic decorative motifs by Adah Robinson, the church is one of the more prominent buildings in the city.

Wheelock Mission Presbyterian Church

Two miles northeast of Millerton, McCurtain County

ARCHITECT / BUILDER:
Not available
CONSTRUCTION / DEDICATION DATE:
1846; 1883

REVEREND ALFRED WRIGHT, the congregation's founder, started his work among the Choctaw in Mississippi in 1820. He accompanied them on the "trail of tears" that led to their resettlement in Indian Territory, later Oklahoma, and the establishment of the Wheelock Mission in 1832. Their first worship space was under a towering oak, where a few benches made of split logs were assembled along with a pulpit made from a wooden box. Log buildings were quickly constructed, but by 1845 the congregation wanted a more suitable place of worship.

The present church, the oldest church building in Oklahoma, was completed in 1846. Labor and funds were provided by congregants, with additional money donated by established Presbyterian churches in the north and east. The building's 20-inch thick walls are constructed from local stone hand chiseled into shape; its wooden steeple over the front entrance is 35 feet high. The interior has a vaulted ceiling over the main floor and balcony, and hand-carved pews and pulpit.

The church suffered during the Civil War and again following a fire in 1866 which only left standing its thick stone walls, but no roof. The Choctaw Council voted in 1883 to obtain and use funds for the erection of new mission buildings and the restoration of the church. In the 1970s, the church and nearby cemetery were purchased by the Presbyterian Church, U.S. (South), for preservation as a tribute to the Presbyterian missionary effort among the Indians and as a memorial to Reverend Wright.

Wheelock Mission
Presbyterian
Church, McCurtain
County, Oklahoma

St. Joseph's Roman Catholic Church

Off OK 31, Krebs, Pittsburg County

ARCHITECT / BUILDER:
Not available
CONSTRUCTION / DEDICATION DATE:
1903

T HE PARISH WAS FOUNDED BY PIONEER Roman Catholics who arrived in Indian Territory in 1886. A French priest, Dom Isidore Robot, O.S.B., planned the parish's first wooden church which was then built by its members. It was destroyed by fire and replaced by the present building in 1903. The church became the spiritual focus for the large number of southern and eastern European immigrants arriving in Pittsburg County in the late nineteenth and early twentieth centuries to work in the coal mines. In 1916, the county was home to over 5,000 Roman Catholics, the heaviest concentration in the state.

The Romanesque Revival red brick church is entered through doors placed in its tower. The exterior remains virtually unaltered from its original state, but the interior has been extensively remodeled to conform to liturgical changes. The original stained glass windows are intact; several are inscribed in the languages of their donors.

St. Joseph's Roman Catholic Church, vicinity of Krebs, Oklahoma

Saints Cyril and Methodius
Russian Orthodox Greek Catholic Church

South Third Street, Hartshorne, Pittsburg County

ARCHITECT / BUILDER:
Not available

CONSTRUCTION / DEDICATION DATE:
1916

A MINE DISASTER IN 1887 led to the establishment of Oklahoma's only Russian Orthodox church. Several Ukrainian immigrants who had arrived in the area in the late nineteenth century to work in the coal mines were killed in the disaster. The mining company had to send to Galveston for a priest to conduct funeral services. Recognizing the need for an Orthodox church, the priest set about immediately to organize a parish. The first services were conducted in a building now in use as a residence. With the

arrival of another group of Ukrainians in 1894, many of whom were miners from Pennsylvania, came the need for a new church building. A small wooden church built in 1897 was replaced by the present building in 1916.

Built of locally produced brick by the Ukrainian miners it served, the church is composed of three sections: the narthex, or vestibule, for the unbaptized; the sanctuary for baptized members; and the altar area behind the iconostasis reserved for the priests. It is crowned with the traditional Orthodox three domes representing the Trinity.

Although the congregation has diminished in size, the church continues to function and remains an Oklahoma landmark.

Saints Cyril and
Methodius Russian
Orthodox Greek
Catholic Church,
Hartshorne, Oklahoma

Calvary Baptist Church

300 North Walnut, Oklahoma City

ARCHITECT / BUILDER:
Russell Benton Bingham
CONSTRUCTION / DEDICATION DATE:
1921-1923

THE CONGREGATION WAS ORGANIZED in 1890 by Baptist African-American settlers from Tennessee who moved to Oklahoma City, Oklahoma Territory, where they established the Second Street Baptist Church in a small store building. In 1900, they merged with another group of black Baptists, moved to 308 West California, and named their church Calvary Baptist Church. Calvary quickly became the primary social and religious center for the city's African-American community.

The present church building was designed by Russell Benton Bingham, a church trustee and superintendent of its Sunday school for two years. Bingham, a graduate of Tuskegee Institute with a certificate in architecture, designed an auditorium-style red brick building composed of a large two-story square sanctuary surrounded by two-level seating on three sides. Few changes have been made to the building's interior or exterior. It is remarkable as an example of a church designed by an African-American for an African-American congregation.

The church is also important for its role in the Civil Rights Movement. In 1957, the church was the site of a locally authored play based on Martin Luther King, Jr.'s civil rights activities. Invited by an NAACP executive to perform in New York, the young cast members experienced their first meal at an integrated lunch counter. Upon their return these young members of the congregation instituted a "sit-down" demonstration in August 1958, to protest against their exclusion from eating in the city's restaurants. For several years they staged protest marches that finally yielded change in mid-1961, when most of the city's restaurants opened their doors to African-Americans.

Calvary
Baptist Church,
Oklahoma City,
Oklahoma

Boston Avenue United Methodist Church

1301 South Boston, Tulsa

ARCHITECT / BUILDER:
Bruce Goff, architect; Adah Robinson, decoration
CONSTRUCTION / DEDICATION DATE:
1926-1927

THIS CHURCH IS ONE OF TULSA'S MOST significant monuments. Designed by Bruce Goff early in his career, it was widely seen as exemplifying the modern American church, responding to the needs for worshipping, educating, and socializing in one building. The inspiration for the design according to Goff was Louis Sullivan's design for Saint Paul's Methodist Church in Cedar Rapids, Iowa. Unfortunately, Sullivan's church was never built as planned; Goff's was.

The church is composed of three components: a half-circular auditorium-style sanctuary on the west; a rectangular four-story education wing on the east; and a 200-foot tower joining the two. The different activities of the church are clearly separated and accommodated by the design. A lobby behind the sanctuary gives parishioners a place to socialize.

Adah Robinson, the art advisor for the church, developed the symbolism of the decorative motifs used throughout the building that were then executed by artist Robert Garrison. Sculptures on the exterior pay tribute to the founders of Methodism, circuit riders, and attributes of the church, such as brotherly love. Another unusual design theme is the repeated use of the Tritoma, a native Oklahoma flower known for its ability to thrive under adverse conditions.

**Boston Avenue
United Methodist,
Tulsa, Oklahoma**

Texas

TEXAS COMPRISES MANY CULTURAL AREAS, ranging from the deep South character of eastern Texas with its cotton plantations to the dry and dusty "cowboy" west, with a richness and variety of topographies and heritages in the midst and between them. Spain's first colony was established in 1682 at Isleta, near El Paso. A French colony organized three years later at Matagorda Bay failed. The Spanish, naming the territory Texas after the Texas Indians, strengthened its hold by founding numerous missions along the San Antonio River and in the lower Rio Grande Valley, including **Mission de Corpus Christi de la Ysleta** in El Paso. Erected in 1744 to serve the Indians and 18 Spanish families living in the area, a devastating fire in 1907 destroyed the nave, tower-belfry, and transepts. The Mission was rebuilt the following year and continues to serve the Tigua Indian community.

Nuestra Senora de la Purisima Concepcion de Acuna in San Antonio, dedicated in 1755, is thought to be the oldest church still in use in Texas. Built of porous limestone, its design reveals Spanish and Moorish influences. At one time its façade was painted with frescoes in vivid colors, long since faded.

American attempts to wrest the territory away from Spain failed, but the signing of the Louisiana Purchase in 1803 provided justification for their continued attacks on the Spaniards. Finally, in an attempt to eliminate hostilities, the Spanish government gave Moses Austin permission to establish an American colony. Austin died before he could accomplish this goal, but his son Stephen, dealing now with the Mexican government that superseded the Spanish, succeeded. Promising the Americans land and citizenship in return for swearing allegiance to the Mexican Constitution and Roman Catholicism, the Mexican government gambled that in return the Americans would pledge loyalty to Mexico, thus providing a buffer to American expansionist ideas. It was a gamble Mexico lost.

Many of the settlers were Protestants who had no intention of converting to Roman Catholicism. Soon they began agitating for religious freedom and for restrictions to be lifted on the numbers of American settlements. Hostilities climaxed on April 21, 1836, when the Texan army under Sam Houston defeated the Mexican army at San Jacinto, capturing its commander, Santa Anna. Texas achieved independence and Sam Houston was named president of the Republic of Texas. Continued unrest and financial disaster, however, led to the young Republic accepting admittance into the Union in 1845. The boundary dispute with Mexico was finally resolved in 1848 by the Treaty of Guadalupe Hidalgo that established the Rio Grande as the state's southern boundary.

The Society for the Protection of German Immigrants, an agency that assisted German settlement in Texas, was also responsible for the building of churches. One of the Society's settlements was Round Top, founded in 1852 and located at the site of an important cross-road in Fayette County. The town, a trading and social center for both German and Anglo-American farmers, is also the site of a German Lutheran congregation formed in 1855, and its church, **Bethlehem Lutheran**, built in 1866.

Many German-speaking settlers were Roman Catholic. The small painted "Churches of Schulenburg" they erected and decorated replicate ones left behind in the Old Country, introducing a bit of German culture into the Texas heartland. The churches are well known and popular tourist attractions. One of the most sophisticated is **The Nativity of Mary, Blessed Virgin Catholic Church (St. Mary's)** in High Hill, built and decorated in 1906 by German and Moravian Czech settlers, and known as a "Baroque jewel box."

Circuit-riding Methodist missionaries, who found the new state to be fertile ground, established the Methodist Texas Conference in 1840. Other Protestant denominations soon followed: the first Episcopal Diocese was organized in 1845; a Baptist State Convention in 1848; and two Presbyterian synods, the Cumberland in 1843 and another in 1851. Many of the early Protestant churches were quite modest, similar in appearance to the First Baptist Church in Amarillo, built in 1899. As the settlers prospered, they built more elaborate structures, often in the latest revival styles gaining popularity in the East. First Baptist Church in Beaumont, designed by A. N. Dawson and built in 1903, combines Gothic and Romanesque Revival forms. The building now houses the Tyrrel Historical Library.

Texas, a slave-holding state, seceded from the Union at the onset of the Civil War. Its economy suffered as a result, but the expansion of agriculture and manufacturing, and most importantly, the discovery of oil at the beginning of the twentieth century, saw a reversal in its financial fortunes. African-Americans living in the state also benefited from the boom. A black itinerant preacher in Fort Worth organized Tarrant County's first African Methodist Episcopal Congregation in 1870. Its members, all former slaves, began to prosper and by 1878, they were able to acquire land to build a church named in honor of Bishop Richard Allen of Philadelphia, the former slave who founded the African Methodist Episcopal movement. **Allen Chapel A.M.E.**, the congregation's present building, erected in 1914, was designed by William Sidney Pittman, one of the few trained black architects in Texas.

There are those who argue that Jews fleeing the Inquisition in Mexico were in Texas possibly as early as the seventeenth and eighteenth centuries, but no evidence of their existence survives. More certain is the story of Henri de Castro, a French Jew, who helped colonize the area west of the Medina River. In the 1840s, he convinced over 5,000 Alsatians to settle there. Castro's name and fame are reflected in the county in the Panhandle south of Amarillo, as well as the town of Castroville, both of which are named after him. Other Jews began settling in the small towns opening up in Texas due to the arrival of the railroad. The completion of the Houston and Texas Central Railroad to Corsicana made that town an important market center. A cemetery association and congregation were organized in 1887 and a new synagogue, **Temple Beth-El**, dedicated in 1900, was built in the Moorish Revival style then in vogue for synagogues.

Mission de Corpus Christi de la Ysleta

U.S. Highway 80, Ysleta

ARCHITECT / BUILDER:
Not available

CONSTRUCTION / DEDICATION DATE:
1744; rebuilt 1908

I N THE LATE SEVENTEENTH CENTURY, the Rio Grande Valley south of El Paso was part of the range lands of the Sumas and Manos Indians. Later, other Indians, including the Pueblo tribe the Tiguas, were forced into the area and it soon became a refugee camp dominated by the Tiguas. In 1684, the camp was formally organized into the village of Sacramento de los Tiguas de Ysleta. The mission church as it stands today is primarily the result of the reconstruction following the 1907 fire. Parts of the walls of the original building were reused; therefore, its basic size and shape are similar to the church constructed in 1744. Changes made in its appearance include the entrance façade and tower. On the interior, all furnishings are in a late Classical Revival style dating from the 1908 reconstruction. Remaining from the original building are its old mission bell and a statue of Christ which had been brought from Spain.

Also on the plaza is the Ysleta del Sur Pueblo community building, which, according to records, was established between 1682 and 1690.

Mission de Corpus
Christi de la Ysleta,
Ysleta, Texas

Bethlehem Lutheran Church

Northwest corner of White Street, Round Top

ARCHITECT / BUILDER:
Carl Siegismund Bauer, stonemason
CONSTRUCTION / DEDICATION DATE:
1866

THE CONGREGATION ESTABLISHED IN 1855 began to build a church in 1861, but the onset of the Civil War delayed their effort until the war's conclusion. Then an experienced stonemason originally from Saxony was persuaded to oversee construction. Carl Siegismund Bauer and his kinfolks plus other townspeople all volunteered to assist in constructing the building. Another native of Germany, John Traugott Wantke, built the cedar pipe organ that is still used occasionally.

The one-story rectangular stuccoed building was built of sandstone quarried from the banks of nearby Cummins Creek. Its cedar framing timbers were cut from trees growing in the Creek bottom and hand-hewn into beams. Except for four stone buttresses added to the southwest side of the building in 1881, no other major additions or changes have been made to the exterior. The original altar and pulpit were replaced by a modern altar in the 1960s.

Bethlehem
Lutheran Church,
Round Top, Texas

The Nativity of Mary,
Blessed Virgin Roman Catholic Church

(ST. MARY'S)

FM Road 2672, High Hill, Fayette County

ARCHITECT / BUILDER:
Leo M. J. Dielmann, architect; Frank Bohlmann, builder
CONSTRUCTION / DEDICATION DATE:
1906

DESIGNED BY SAN ANTONIO ARCHITECT Leo M. J. Dielmann and built by Frank Bohlmann of Schulenburg, St. Mary's is the most prominent structure in the rural community of High Hill located southeast of Austin. It is the third church to be built on the site, and is partly constructed of materials from the second building, a wooden structure erected in 1875. These include 18 stained glass windows installed between 1884 and 1889.

The first church, a log structure with clapboard siding, was founded by German Catholic settlers who had arrived in 1844 and by Moravian Czech settlers who followed in 1860. The present building constructed of red brick is in the Gothic Revival style. Its most outstanding feature is its interior, which is one of the most elaborate and sophisticated uses of decorative painting found in any Texas church. Canvas was painted or stenciled, then attached to the ceilings and walls in all of the sanctuary's major spaces. Its carved wooden columns are painted to look like marble, as is the altar. Two San Antonio artists, Ferdinand Stockert and Hermann Kern, executed the painting in 1912.

The Painted Churches of Schulenburg, of which this is the most elaborate, remain important visual reminders of the town's Czech and German heritage.

The Nativity of Mary, Blessed Virgin Roman Catholic Church, High Hill, Texas

Allen Chapel A.M.E. Church

116 Elm Street, Fort Worth

ARCHITECT / BUILDER:
William Sidney Pittman
CONSTRUCTION / DEDICATION DATE:
1914

ORGANIZED IN 1870 by a circuit-riding black Methodist minister, the small congregation—all former slaves—purchased land in 1878 on which to build a church. A modest red brick chapel was constructed on the site and served the congregation until 1912. A dynamic new pastor, Reverend S. R. Jenkins, persuaded the congregation to build a new church and to hire the well-known and respected black architect, William Sidney Pittman, to design the building. Pittman was trained at Tuskegee Institute and Drexel Institute in Philadelphia and married Portia Washington, daughter of Dr. Booker T. Washington, before moving to Dallas in 1910.

Pittman's design for Allen Chapel differs dramatically from the modest, single-story churches then being built for most African-American congregations in Texas. It is a monumental yellow brick building with a three-and-a-half story tower on the southeast (the one on the northeast is truncated), fine art glass windows, and sophisticated Gothic Revival detailing. Its plan is unusual in that the entrances located in the base of the two towers emerge on the sides of the main altar. It shares several basic features with Mother Bethel A.M.E. Church in Philadelphia, notably its tower on the southeast and Gothic detailing.

The blacksmith's anvil located at the front of the church symbolizes the anvil that served as Allen's first pulpit.

**Allen Chapel
A.M.E. Church,
Fort Worth, Texas**

Temple Beth-El

208 South Fifteenth Street, Corsicana

ARCHITECT / BUILDER:
Not available

CONSTRUCTION / DEDICATION DATE:
1898-1900

THE SYNAGOGUE REMAINS A MONUMENT to what was once a thriving and active Jewish community. It served its congregation for over 80 years before it was disbanded. The building has been preserved and is now only one of a few surviving historic synagogues in Texas.

Temple Beth-El is distinctive not only for its historic association with Corsicana's Jewish community that at one time numbered about 200 families, but also for its architectural Moorish Revival style. It reflects the widespread popularity of a style that had gained favor for synagogue architecture in the latter half of the nineteenth century. Onion domes sheathed with sheet metal and horseshoe arches are two features of the style used for this structure. For Jewish people, the Moorish style was reminiscent of the Golden Age of Jewry in Spain during the Middle Ages when that country was under Muslim control.

The Navarro County Historical Society acquired the building in 1982 for use as a community center.

Temple Beth-El
Synagogue,
Corsicana, Texas

CHAPTER

9

Mountain Region

New Mexico
Colorado
Wyoming
Montana
Idaho
Utah
Arizona
Nevada

St. Stephen's Roman
Catholic Church,
Wild River
Reservation,
Wyoming

R EACHING FROM THE BORDER of Canada southward to Mexico, the Mountain Region of the United States encompasses nearly one-third of the nation's land mass. It is literally where the amber waves of grain of the plains and prairie meet the nation's purple mountain majesties. Thanks to the writings of authors like Zane Grey and Louis L'Amour, the region has been immortalized as simply "the West," a rugged and demanding area of mountains and deserts that is home to cowboys, Indians, and cattle. In reality, the region is far more complex, both in its geography and demography. In fact, the Mountain Region comprises two distinct areas: the Southwest consisting of Arizona, New Mexico, and a portion of Colorado; and "the West," described in one geography book as "the Empty Interior," that includes all of Nevada, Utah, and Idaho and much of Colorado, Wyoming, and Montana.[1]

Perhaps the most dramatic illustration of the differences in the two areas can be seen in their settlement patterns. The ancestors of the Navajo and Pueblo peoples occupied the Southwest for centuries prior to the arrival, in 1540, of the Spanish explorer Francisco Coronado, whose quest was gold and riches. Instead he found an arid land bereft of gold but occupied by small agricultural colonies of native people. With the explorers came Roman Catholic missionaries whose objective was not gold, but to convert the Indians to Christianity and to establish Spanish dominance in religion, culture, and government. Indian, Spanish, and Mexican cultures coexisted for 250 years after the arrival of the Spanish, mingling and producing a distinctive Spanish-speaking population referred to both as Hispanic and Chicano.

American and European settlers found little to attract them to the Southwest, but that was to change dramatically in the mid-nineteenth century, when Coronado's vision of great riches became a reality with the discovery of the region's enormous reserve of gold, silver, and copper. Soon, hordes of eastern entrepreneurs, miners, and assorted adventurers began arriving, quickly outnumbering those of Spanish and Indian descent. Boomtowns blossomed, infusing the region with Anglo culture. However, unlike elsewhere in the country, evidence of the region's earlier culture did not completely disappear and still remains visible, particularly notable in the appearance of its places of worship.

The awesome mountains and deep canyons of northern Arizona and southern Utah visited by thousands of tourists each year were barriers for Spanish expansion northward. This vast rugged area stretching north to Canada was virtually unoccupied until the mid-nineteenth century. Nomadic Indian tribes traversed its broad expanse in search of game and furs, but few permanent settlements were established. A few hardy Europeans and Americans, including French-Canadian fur trappers and missionaries, and the famed American duo Lewis and Clark, traveled through the wilderness in search of souls, furs, and the Northwest Passage to the Pacific Ocean. In their view this was a region to exploit or to pass through quickly on the way to somewhere else. Congress's passage of the Donation Land Act in 1850, giving free land to settlers in Oregon, coupled with the dramatic discovery of gold in California the previous year, prompted the largest peaceful migration of people in history. Over a quarter of a million pioneers began the journey along the Santa Fe and

Oregon Trails to reach the promised land on the West Coast. One group, however, had the vision that part of this inhospitable area was Zion–the Mormons, members of the Church of Jesus Christ of Latter-day Saints.

It was a long and dangerous trek for the followers of Joseph Smith, Jr., who set out from New York in 1831 for a place where they could safely practice their faith. Following Smith's death in 1844, Brigham Young became their leader. In 1847, after facing challenges and hazards that would discourage all but the most faithful, the group arrived at the Salt Lake Valley where Young proclaimed, "This is the place." It has been said that the miracle of gulls in 1848 that rescued the Mormons' first crops and the discovery of gold the following year saved the isolated community from extinction. Miners rushing to California transformed Salt Lake City into an important stopping off point and market center. As the Mormons became more efficient in dry agricultural methods and missionary work, their numbers grew, until by 1870, more than 86,000 people lived in Utah, 95 percent of whom were Mormons.

Utah is unique in the central and northern expanse of the region in that much of its land is privately held. The government is the major land owner elsewhere in the region due to its scenic beauty and lack of agricultural potential. Tourism and ranching became major attractions until irrigation was introduced and farmers began arriving to plow the now-watered fields. The West then became an area of conflict romanticized in fiction and film. Ranchers fought with sheepherders and farmers; miners battled over claims; railroads, which began to transverse the region in the 1860s, were marked for robbery. But there were positive developments as well. Cattle raised for eastern markets were shipped out on railroads that brought in settlers and tourists eager to experience the beauty and challenges of "the West." Tourism was further encouraged by the establishment of Yellowstone as the nation's first national park in 1872 and the others that soon followed. As the economy and population expanded, market towns began to develop to service miners, lumberjacks, ranchers, and tourists. Yet when the Bureau of the Census proclaimed the end of the settlement frontier in 1890, much of this area remained unsettled. Even today, the region retains much of its original character–awesome and empty.

NOTES

1. Stephen S. Birdsall and John W. Florin, *Regional Landscapes of the United States and Canada*, 4th ed. (New York: John Wiley & Sons, 1992), 341.

New Mexico

ENTURIES BEFORE THE FIRST WHITE PERSON arrived, the region that
became New Mexico was home to a technologically advanced civilization
known as the Anasazi, the direct ancestors of the Pueblo people. Ruins of their
civilization that flourished during the eleventh and twelfth centuries remain
visible within the walls of Chaco Canyon in northwestern New Mexico. Now a source of
inspiration for artists and writers and a mecca for tourists, the colorful buttes, mesas, and
deserts of New Mexico were viewed as an enormous challenge by its earliest inhabitants.
In order to survive, the Anasazi developed sophisticated irrigation systems allowing them
to grow crops and engage in trade with people as far away as Central America. The Navajo,
arriving several centuries later, also raised crops and herded animals.

Rumors of an advanced civilization to the north with cities of gold attracted the attention of Spaniards in Mexico who were seeking wealth for their nation and souls for the
Roman Catholic Church. Spanish expeditions, composed of explorers and soldiers, and
including Franciscan priests, began to travel north in search of these fabled cities; instead
they found small agricultural communities of the Pueblo people. The Spanish may not
have found gold, but they did find thousands of souls in need of saving. By 1660, it is esti-
mated there were at least 45 Franciscan churches in New Mexico.

The **Chapel of San Miguel**, near the Rio Grande north of present-day Santa Fe, is one
of the first churches constructed by Spanish colonists in the United States. Portions of the
chapel possibly predate the Pueblo Revolt of 1680, and most of it was reconstructed in 1710
following the Spanish Reconquest of the region in 1693.

Following Mexico's declaration of independence in 1821, the area became a province of
Mexico until it was ceded to the United States in 1848. A year later it became a territory,
but attracted few settlers, mainly because of its rugged and arid terrain, but also because of
ongoing warfare. The territory was briefly occupied by Confederate forces during the Civil
War, and following the war there were ongoing skirmishes with Indians that did not end
until 1886, when they were confined on reservations.

The coming of the railroad in the late 1870s gave the territory a needed economic boost, doubling its white population and leading to its entry into the Union in 1912. By this time the Spanish and Pueblo people had co-existed for nearly two and a half centuries, developing what has
become a unique and identifiable southwestern culture clearly visible in the state's famed adobe
churches. San Francisco De Asis, constructed in 1815 at Rancho de Taos, is perhaps the most
well known of the small village churches, largely because it has been the subject of paintings
and photographs by artists such as Georgia O'Keeffe, Ansel Adams, and Paul Strand.

Not all the clergy who arrived in New Mexico were enamored with the local adobe churches. One, in particular, was Bishop Jean-Baptist Lamy, who arrived in Santa Fe in 1850. He had the old adobe Church of Saint Francis of Assisi, the Parroquia, dismantled and began plans to replace it with a new building reflecting his personal preference for the contemporary architecture of his native France, the Napoleonic Second Empire style. It has been suggested that **The Cathedral of St. Francis of Assisi** is neither Spanish nor French in style, but rather a unique design reflecting the personality of Archbishop Lamy.

The cathedral and smaller churches such as San Miguel are assured of preservation because of their fame. But hundreds of other adobe churches located in small, often impoverished, villages are in danger of slowly melting back into the earth. The Cornerstones Community Partnerships, a not-for-profit preservation organization working with volunteers and professionals, recognizes the historic and communal value of these structures. This group is in the process of preserving many of the state's historic adobe churches, such as the **San Jose Mission of Upper Rociada**. Another Cornerstones project, **San Rafael Roman Catholic Church** in La Cueva, constructed in 1862, is a unique adobe Gothic Revival structure abandoned since 1951. Recent restoration efforts have enabled this early example of European influence in New Mexico to remain part of its community.

Protestant denominations, forbidden in New Mexico while it was under the control of Spain and Mexico, viewed the new territory as a promising missionary field. Presbyterians began to establish churches and schools in the Santa Fe, Taos, and Las Vegas areas and later in Albuquerque following the arrival of the railroad in 1880. When the school in Albuquerque was taken over by the government in 1886, a second Presbyterian school, named Menaul after its founder James Menaul, was formed to educate Hispanic boys from Presbyterian mission schools in northern New Mexico. Menaul served as minister of the First Presbyterian Church and was the founder of the Second Presbyterian Church (La Segunda Iglesia Presbiteriana Unida) in Martineztown. The congregation's present church, completed in 1922, is one of Albuquerque's few Mission style buildings.

A Methodist congregation was also established in Albuquerque in 1880; the same year foundations were laid for its first church, a simple adobe structure. It was replaced in 1905 by a larger, more impressive building, First Methodist Episcopal Church, that was to symbolize the growth of Methodism in New Mexico. The new church resembles the countless Gothic Revival structures built throughout the United States.

The first Episcopal church service in New Mexico was conducted in June 1863 at Fort Union, a frontier United States Army post 30 miles north of Las Vegas, New Mexico, a town that was beginning to boom following the arrival of the railroad in 1879. A decision was made to extend missionary services into Las Vegas, believing that the arrival of the railroad would make the town New Mexico's most important city. Land was purchased and a small adobe church was built in 1879; it was the first Episcopal church building in New Mexico. As the congregation grew, plans were made to erect a larger and grander church that was to serve as New Mexico's Episcopal cathedral. Erection began on the red sandstone Gothic Revival **St. Paul's Memorial Episcopal Church** in 1886, but its sanctuary and chancel were not completed until 1950. Las Vegas never lived up to its expectations, and in 1927, Albuquerque was permanently established as the cathedral city.

The Chapel of San Miguel

Old Santa Fe Trail and East De Vargas Street, Santa Fe

ARCHITECT / BUILDER:
Not available

CONSTRUCTION / DEDICATION DATE:
circa 1640; reconstructed 1710

RECORDS OF THE EARLY HISTORY of the chapel were destroyed during the Pueblo Rebellion of 1680, but it is believed that the thick adobe walls of the present building may pre-date the rebellion. Following the rebellion, stone buttresses were added to strengthen the walls, and the tower and façade were remodeled. An inscription on the beam supporting the choir loft records that the building was erected by Royal Ensign Don Augustin Flores de Vergara in 1710 with contributions from the Spanish Marquis of Penuela.

Adobe was the traditional material used for building the pueblos. The entire community participated in the building process. The adobe mud was packed on top of the wall being constructed and left to dry, and the procedure was repeated until the wall was the desired height. The Spaniards modified this technique by using formed adobe bricks, which contributed to a faster and more efficient building process.

The interior of the chapel is adorned with a reredos, a beautiful screen made by a *santero*, a layman who paints images of saints. The altar screen also holds paintings on canvas executed in Mexico, including one at the top of St. Michael, and *bultos*, carved and brightly painted wooden statues made by local artisans.

The chapel, cared for by the Christian Brothers, remains in use, is well maintained, and is open to visitors.

**Chapel of San Miguel,
Santa Fe, New Mexico**

Cathedral of St. Francis of Assisi

East end of San Francisco Street, Santa Fe

ARCHITECT / BUILDER:
Original plans: Antoine and Projectus Moulay; second set of plans:
Francois Mallet, architect; Monier and Machebeuf, builders

CONSTRUCTION / DEDICATION DATE:
Cornerstone laid in 1867; not completed until 1967; refurbished in 1986

BUILT OF LOCALLY QUARRIED STONE, the building is considered an anomaly, an amalgam of influences emanating from contemporary French architecture and other sources as recalled and interpreted by its patron, Archbishop Jean-Baptiste Lamy, born in the region of Auvergne in south central France.

Although begun well over a century ago, the cathedral remains incomplete, its twin towers unfinished. According to Carl D. Sheppard, the author of a provocative book on the cathedral, the lack of pinnacles and towers allows the building to fit into the scale of the present-day Santa Fe cityscape. Furthermore, he argues, the decorative and architectural elements selected by the archbishop for the front façade are autobiographical: the polychromy recalls the architecture of his homeland; the unfinished towers are similar to the tower crowning the Cathedral of St. Peter-in-Chains in Cincinnati where he was made bishop; and the Gothic elements are similar to those found at St. Francis at Assisi, the thirteenth-century church in Italy, the first to honor the Saint, to whom this cathedral is dedicated.

The adobe Chapel of La Conquistadora that adjoins the sanctuary to the north escaped Lamy's destruction. It was restored in the 1950s and renamed Our Lady of Peace. The sanctuary, transepts, and contiguous chapels were completed in 1967, and the complete church was refurbished in 1986.

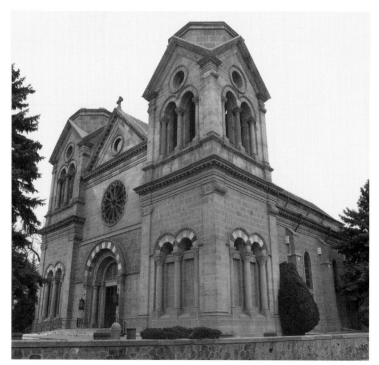

The Cathedral of
St. Francis of Assisi,
Santa Fe,
New Mexico

San Jose Mission

Upper Rociada, near Mora

ARCHITECT / BUILDER:
Not available

CONSTRUCTION / DEDICATION DATE:
circa 1867

THE PICTURESQUE SAN JOSE MISSION of Upper Rociada is located on the eastern slopes of the Sangre de Cristo Mountains, a beautiful but impoverished area of New Mexico. The small community of about 30 families had been trying valiantly to save its endangered, moisture-laden church, but lacking funds and restoration skills, the church appeared doomed. An indigenous interpretation of the more famed Spanish mission churches such as the one at Acoma, small rural adobe churches like San Jose had been ignored by preservationists and were slowly melting back into the mud from which they were built. With their disappearance went an important part of our nation's cultural history. The New Mexico Community Foundation, recognizing that these small churches are the vital centers of their communities, determined that in order to "fix" the communities it was necessary to "fix" their churches. Thus was born the organization known as Cornerstones Community Partnerships that works with small congregations, providing technical assistance and training for volunteers to restore the state's decaying historic adobe churches.

Thanks to Cornerstones, the residents of Upper Rociada have completed the repair work to the once-sodden adobe walls of their church, guaranteeing that it will continue to serve as a symbol of their community.

San Jose Mission
of Upper Rociada,
New Mexico

San Rafael Roman Catholic Church

La Cueva, Mora County

ARCHITECT / BUILDER:
Not available

CONSTRUCTION / DEDICATION DATE:
circa 1865

A BEAUTIFUL EXAMPLE of the Gothic Revival style executed in adobe, San Rafael was abandoned in 1951. The church was vandalized, its windows destroyed and its walls covered with graffiti. Since it was inactive, the Archdiocese of Santa Fe gave it a low priority and funds were not available for its restoration. Father Walter Cassidy, the pastor who had said the last mass in the church, along with former majordomo Jose Gurule, heard of the Cornerstones project and set about raising community support for restoring the church. The archdiocese approved their effort and funds were raised from various sources, local and national. Local residents and skilled volunteers working under professional supervision carried out the restoration project, which included restoring the Gothic windows and the cedar shingle roof. New adobes have been laid and literally hundreds of people applied fresh coats of mud plaster throughout the entire building. The mission's original bell, thought lost, was recovered and placed in the tower, and the four-foot statue of the patron saint, San Rafael, salvaged from the church in the 1960s, has resumed its place next to the altar.

On July 4, 1992, while still under restoration, Father Walter Cassidy celebrated the first mass in 40 years at San Rafael Church. On June 30, 1996, Archbishop Michael Sheehan celebrated the mass of rededication commemorating the completion of the church's restoration.

San Rafael Roman
Catholic Church,
La Cueva,
New Mexico

St. Paul's Memorial Episcopal Church

714-716 National Avenue, Las Vegas

ARCHITECT / BUILDER:
1950 addition: John Gaw Meem

CONSTRUCTION / DEDICATION DATE:
Begun 1886-1888; sanctuary and chancel added in 1950

L AS VEGAS WAS ENVISIONED as a growing city, soon to become the largest city in New Mexico. It didn't happen, but the Episcopalians who began to build St. Paul's in 1886 didn't know that. The congregation that included the families of many important New Mexico businessmen and political leaders soon outgrew its small adobe church consecrated in 1879, and plans were made to replace it with a new building that would become the cathedral church of the missionary district. Built of red sandstone in what has been described as a folk-Gothic style, also known in New Mexico as "territorial architecture," the building was to remain incomplete for 62 years. Financial difficulties led to the decision to enclose the north end of the structure by a "temporary" lath and plaster wall. Although the church was consecrated in 1890, it wasn't until 1950 that the congregation was able to purchase sufficient sandstone from the recently razed San Miguel County Courthouse to enclose the sanctuary and replace the "temporary" wall which had swayed back and forth on windy days for over half a century. Plans were drawn by John Gaw Meem and the building was finally completed, but by then Albuquerque had become the site of the cathedral.

To the east of the church stands a small pitched-roof adobe building, the original chapel of the congregation now known as the Guild Hall.

St. Paul's Memorial
Episcopal Church,
Las Vegas,
New Mexico

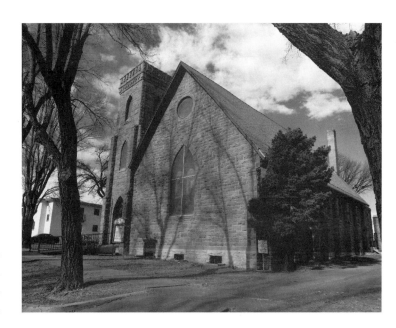

Colorado

COLORADO'S NAME CAME from Spanish explorers traveling through its southern reaches in search of gold and silver. While their quest for riches went unfulfilled, their description of the region's awesome reddish-brown landscape was immortalized in its name, Colorado, "color red." The state has also been immortalized in song. It was while viewing Pike's Peak that Kathryn Lee Bates wrote the words "purple mountain majesties" in her patriotic composition, "America the Beautiful."

Long before the arrival of the white man, Colorado was occupied by the Anasazi Indians, an agricultural people whose elaborate dwellings built into cliffs are reminders of their presence. Finding that the Anasazi dwellings were not built of gold, the Spanish left, but traces of their presence remain in names such as La Junta, a major fur-trading post located at the junction of the old Navajo and Santa Fe trails. It wasn't gold, but the popularity of beaver hats in Europe that attracted fur trappers, and the Louisiana Purchase that inspired explorers such as Colonel Zebulon Pike to mount expeditions. But settlers did not follow, mainly because of another explorer, Major Steven H. Long's description of the area as uninhabitable.

Colonel Pike went on to achieve immortality by giving his name to a mountain he never scaled, a name that later became the rallying cry for miners setting out to make their fortune. "Pike's Peak or Bust," echoed throughout the nation and abroad following the discovery of gold near Denver in 1858. As elsewhere in the West, when a prospector shouted the magic word "gold," thousands would respond, staking claims and establishing boom towns consisting of tents and shanties. One of those towns was Fairplay, an ironic reference to the lack of fairplay its founders found at a nearby mining town where they had been cheated out of their claims. Traveling preachers would visit these shanty towns in hopes of introducing a modicum of morality into what was essentially a lawless society. They would preach anywhere–saloons and brothels not excluded. As towns prospered a permanent church would be built, often a modest building such as the Sheldon Jackson Memorial Chapel built in Fairplay in 1874, whose Gothic Revival design and decoration came directly out of Richard Upjohn's well-traveled book *Rural Architecture* (1852).

The United States government's response to the discovery of gold was the establishment of the new Colorado Territory in 1861. Denver, bolstered by the gold strike on nearby Clear Creek, was named its capital. With tales of its riches proven, Colorado entered the Union in 1876. But following the boom years came the inevitable bust; two years after achieving statehood the gold mines were depleted and the economy collapsed. Once bustling mining towns were abandoned. The state did survive thanks to the coming of the railroad, the discovery of silver and lead deposits, and a new major gold deposit at Cripple Creek. This boom lasted until 1893, when the federal government abruptly stopped buying silver. But by that time thousands of immigrants had entered the state–some in search of gold, others to work in the smelters, brickyards, and packing houses developing around Denver.

Globeville is one of Denver's largest ethnic enclaves. Between 1880 and 1924, thousands of immigrants representing every major European ethnic group settled in this community that was absorbed by Denver in 1903. Polish immigrants were numerous enough to lay the cornerstone for **St. Joseph's Polish Roman Catholic Church** in 1902.

A parish for Irish immigrants settling in northwest Denver was formed in 1881 by Bishop Joseph Projectus Machebeuf, known as the "Apostle of the Rockies." **St. Patrick's Mission Church** received its name and architectural style from the vision of its second pastor, Joseph Carrigan, who wanted a church that would serve as a "mission" to all people living in the area. To make his vision visible he had his new church, dedicated in 1907, built in the style of early California missions he had visited. Over the years St. Patrick's has served many ethnic groups other than Irish–including Italians who came to farm in the Platte Valley and more recently, Hispanics.

According to legend, the first religious services conducted in Denver were held by ten Jews on the Jewish New Year in 1859. The following year a Jewish burial society was formed, and in 1874 a Reform congregation, Temple Emanuel, was founded. Many Jewish settlers were merchants, including the founders of May Shoe and Clothing Company in Denver, the nation's oldest department store. The congregation's first building, erected in the 1870s, was demolished, but the second, built in 1882, still stands. Although it was rebuilt following a fire in 1897, its Moorish and Romanesque features remain visible. Similar stylistic features were used in **Temple Emanuel**'s third building, dedicated in 1899.

Colorado is not all mountains and mines. Its eastern one-third consists of plains, some well watered, others semi-arid. Those who settled in this area were not seeking gold, but cheap farmland. Longmont in the fertile St. Vrain Valley was named, rather ironically, after Steven H. Long, the explorer who pronounced Colorado uninhabitable. A farming community established there in 1871 attracted a group of Dunkards from Pella, Iowa, who were of German descent. Arriving in 1874, they organized the First Church of the Brethren in 1877. The church, built in 1880 and in use by its congregation until 1910, is now a community center, wedding chapel, and the site for annual meetings of the Northern Colorado Church of the Brethren.

In 1870, over 300 German Lutherans from Chicago arrived in Westcliffe located in the fertile Wet Mountain Valley. Two years later they organized one of Colorado's first Lutheran congregations and erected a simple shelter to use as a church. The **Hope Lutheran Church**, built in 1917, is the congregation's fourth building.

Swedish Lutherans settling in rural Boulder County in 1869 named their community Ryssby after their parish in Sweden. The **Swedish Evangelical Lutheran Church**, built in 1882, is similar to the one they left behind in the Old World.

St. Joseph's Polish Roman Catholic Church

517 East 46th Avenue, Denver

ARCHITECT / BUILDER:
Frank Kirchof, builder

CONSTRUCTION / DEDICATION DATE:
1902

ST. JOSEPH'S WAS BUILT by Polish immigrants who settled in Globeville, an ethnic community that was absorbed into the city of Denver in 1903. Although it was intended to be used solely by "Polanders," Croatians and Slovenians also attended mass, but formed their own societies separate from the Polish. The handsome Gothic Revival brick church with its central entrance tower announces its Polish heritage in its name inscribed in Polish above the doorway.

The church continues to serve as a focal point for Denver's Polish community even though the construction of Valley Highway (I-25) and I-70 in the early 1950s destroyed the Polish enclave surrounding it. Second- and third-generation Poles who have moved to the suburbs still belong to the parish, providing it with ongoing vitality as a visible reminder of the city's first Polish settlers.

St. Joseph's
Polish Roman
Catholic Church,
Denver, Colorado

St. Patrick's Mission Church

3325 Pecos Street, Denver

ARCHITECT / BUILDER:
Wagner and Manning
CONSTRUCTION / DEDICATION DATE:
1907-1910

LOCATED ON A BLUFF overlooking the Platte River, this mission style church dominates the skyline of northwest Denver, a neighborhood initially settled by Irish immigrants. The Roman Catholic parish, Denver's first, was established in 1881, and a church was built three years later. In 1907, the parish's second pastor, Reverend Joseph P. Carrigan, decided a new church was needed to make visual his dream of the parish serving as a mission to people of all faiths. He traveled to California to study the design of early missions there, and returned with ideas that he then gave to the Denver architectural firm of Wagner and Manning. The building they designed is in the traditional Franciscan mission style, the only building of this style in Denver at the time of its construction.

St. Patrick's continues to serve as the center of community life in what has now become an inner-city neighborhood. First were the Irish, whose presence is reflected in the parish's name, followed by Italians, and, beginning in the 1930s, those of Hispanic heritage. Each cultural group in turn has left a significant mark on the area and parish.

St. Patrick's
Mission Church,
Denver, Colorado

Temple Emanuel Synagogue

1595 Pearl Street, Denver

ARCHITECT / BUILDER:
1899: John Humphreys, architect; 1924 addition: Robert T. Wieger, architect
CONSTRUCTION / DEDICATION DATE:
1899, 1924

TEMPLE EMANUEL, the oldest Reform Jewish congregation in Denver, was established in 1874. Little is known of the congregation's first synagogue, but its second at 2400 Curtis Street, constructed in 1882 and designed by Frank E. Edbrooke, still stands and remains a dominant feature in its neighborhood. It was damaged by fire in 1897 and rebuilt in 1902 in its original form; however, the congregation had already moved into its new building.

The new building on Pearl Street incorporated into its design many of the Moorish elements of the older building, although this style was already on the wane by the time of its construction. However, it would appear that the influence of the Moorish style Plum Street Temple in Cincinnati still had an impact on this largely German-American Reform congregation (see p. 104). The congregation continued to grow in the 1900s and an addition in a compatible Moorish design was added in 1924. Both the building and the addition are unaltered and have a high degree of integrity.

Following World War II, many members began moving to the suburbs and a new synagogue was needed. The congregation moved into its new facility in 1956 and this building became home to several other denominations. Scheduled for demolition in 1981, the building was saved by the Pearl Street Temple Emanuel Foundation formed by members of various civic groups. In 1986, the building was purchased by the City of Denver and leased to the Temple Center Foundation for use as a multi-activity center, thus assuring its continued presence near a cluster of historic places of worship built in the early years of the twentieth century.

Temple Emanuel
Synagogue,
Denver, Colorado

Hope Lutheran Church

310 South Third, Westcliffe

ARCHITECT / BUILDER:
Reverend John Reininga
CONSTRUCTION / DEDICATION DATE:
1917

THE HOPE LUTHERAN CHURCH is one of the oldest Lutheran congregations in Colorado and, from its inception in 1870, has played an important role in the history of Custer County. Its founders, German pioneers, settled in a remote area with the hopes of developing a self-sufficient agricultural colony. To that end they even brought with them a small flour mill. What they lacked, however, was a pastor. One finally arrived in 1872, enabling the congregation to build the first of its four churches. The community's remote location discouraged clergy and for long periods of time the church's pulpit stood empty, but still the congregation survived. As mining declined, agriculture became more important and the tiny Lutheran farming community of Westcliffe prospered, being named the county seat of Custer County in 1923.

With prosperity came pastors who chose to stay. One, Reverend J. Reininga, designed the present church and designed and carved its elaborate altar. The altar consists of Gothic spires and arches and a life-size figure of Christ. The most notable exterior feature of the building is its 96-foot high tower, visible for miles in every direction. The church continues its role in the community and survives as a monument to the perseverance of a small group of German settlers who followed their dreams westward.

Hope Lutheran
Church, Westcliffe,
Colorado

Swedish Evangelical Lutheran Church of Ryssby

North 63rd Street, vicinity of Boulder

ARCHITECT / BUILDER:
L. P. Kimmons, builder

CONSTRUCTION / DEDICATION DATE:
1881-1882

THE CHURCH SERVED as a religious and social center for a small Swedish settlement in rural Boulder County that flourished from about 1869, when Swedish settlers first arrived, until 1914 when the congregation merged with one in Longmont. Constructed of rough-cut sandstone quarried from a nearby homestead and set in random courses, the building is considered a vernacular adaptation of traditional Swedish vernacular architecture. It shares features in common with its model, the parish church in Old Ryssby, Sweden, including the floor plan, tower design, window placement, semi-circular communion railing, and vaulted ceiling painted sky-blue. The church in Old Ryssby, however, was much larger, more elegantly appointed, and had smooth white exterior walls.

The church was abandoned until 1924 when descendants of the Ryssby colonists began to hold biannual meetings in it. In 1969, the church was renovated and in 1970, a new tower was built to replace the one destroyed by lightning in 1914. The church remains as an important landmark for those of Swedish descent living in Colorado and its biannual services attract visitors from a wide area.

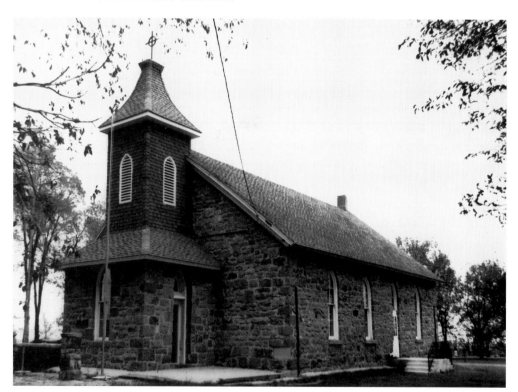

Swedish Evangelical
Lutheran Church
of Ryssby,
Ryssby, Colorado

Wyoming

WYOMING REFERS TO ITSELF as the "Cowboy" state, thus perpetuating its mythical image dating back to the development of the livestock industry in the latter part of the nineteenth century. The myth was embellished and received worldwide publicity because of Colonel William "Wild Bill" Cody and his Wild West Show. But there is far more to the state's history than what is portrayed in pulp fiction, films, and television. Before the arrival of the cavalry, cowboys, miners, and railroad crews, Wyoming was occupied by Indian tribes, including the Eastern Shoshones, a nomadic buffalo-hunting people. Evidence of their worship is the medicine wheel located in the Big Horn Mountains, where religious services continue to be held. All remained peaceable until the discovery of the South Pass through the Rocky Mountains in 1824 that opened the Oregon Trail to thousands of pioneers moving westward to Oregon. The increasing number of white people traversing traditional Indian land as well as settling on it led to a series of conflicts that were not resolved until 1868, when the Indians reluctantly agreed to settle on reservations. The nomadic Shoshones were sent to the Wind River Reservation in Fremont County where they were taught how to farm and were converted to Christianity. The log Holy Saint John Chapel was built for the Shoshone Episcopal Mission by the Reverend John Roberts in 1890, the smallest of three churches on the Mission site. The chapel continues to be used by the Shoshones for religious purposes and related congregational activities.

Roman Catholics established St. Stephen's Mission in 1884 for Arapahos forced to settle on the same reservation. **St. Stephen's Church**, constructed in 1928, is an unassuming frame structure, made unique by its decoration. Its exterior is covered with traditional Arapaho geometric red, black, and white designs that are also found on beaded or painted dance costumes and on traditional artifacts.

The Union Pacific Railroad reached its winter terminal of Cheyenne in the fall of 1867; soon after came an Episcopalian clergyman determined to introduce morality into what he perceived as a lawless society. The Episcopal Church was enjoying a revival at this time and saw the West as a region ripe for proselytizing. Its audience in Wyoming included wealthy and adventurous Englishmen who were establishing many of the area's large cattle ranches. An Episcopal parish was organized in Cheyenne in 1868 on land donated by the railroad. In August of that year, a small frame Gothic church was erected, the first in the territory of Wyoming. It was soon outgrown and by 1885, construction began on **St. Mark's Episcopal Church**. However, before it could be completed disaster struck; an unusually frigid winter killed thousands of cattle, causing the region to experience a major financial depression. But, with the help of a loan from the Episcopal American Church Building Fund, the church was completed.

With the westward movement of the railroad came a diverse group of settlers–ranchers and cowboys, railroad officials and rail laborers, merchants and entrepreneurs. Their actual numbers were small; thus one church often served various denominations. This was the case of **France Memorial United Presbyterian Church**, built in 1882 for a congregation organized in Rawlins in 1869. It continues to serve as the city's social, cultural, and religious center for people of all faiths.

The collapse of the cattle market coincided with the arrival of a large influx of farmers into northern Wyoming precipitating predictable battles among ranchers and farmers over land ownership. The infamous Johnston County War of 1892 has been immortalized in print and film, as has the cattlemen and sheepherders gun fights. The penny press glamorized the warfare, but the U.S. Army had to be called in to quell it. Enhancing the state's image, however, were its national parks, the first being Yellowstone established in 1872, followed by other national parks, forests, monuments, recreation areas, and historic sites. All these made tourism one of Wyoming's most important industries, contributing to its being granted statehood in 1890.

German immigrants in Laramie opened the city's rolling mills and a brewery. Numbering about 400 persons, they laid the cornerstone for a Lutheran church in 1890, the first German church in the state. Services in **St. Paulus Deutsche Evangelische Lutherische Kirche** (known now as St. Paul's United Church of Christ) were conducted in German until 1932.

Mormons settling in Lincoln County in southwestern Wyoming near the Utah border built the Auburn Rock Church in the late nineteenth century. One of the oldest buildings in the Star Valley, it was used for religious purposes for the Church of Jesus Christ of Latter-day Saints as well as a public meeting place for the community.

Douglas was known as Tent Town when it was founded in the 1880s as a market center for the surrounding region, a role it continues to play. It is also the site of one of Wyoming's oldest frame Gothic Revival churches, **Christ Episcopal Church** constructed in 1898, that illustrates the widespread popularity of this style even in relatively remote, sparsely populated areas of the nation.

St. Mark's Episcopal Church

1908 Central Avenue, Cheyenne

ARCHITECT / BUILDER:
Architect: Henry M. Congdon of New York City
CONSTRUCTION / DEDICATION DATE:
1886–1888

T HE CONGREGATION'S small frame Gothic Revival building dedicated in 1868 was Wyoming's first church building. The cattle industry prospered during the early 1880s and with it came a desire for culture, beauty, and buildings of permanence and dignity. The decision was made to replace the modest frame church with a larger, more elaborate one constructed of stone. Lots were purchased and a New York City architect was hired to design a building that would reflect the heritage of many of its members. Thus, according to tradition, St. Mark's is based on the style of Stoke Poges Church near London, built in 1080, made famous in the poem by Thomas Gray, "Elegy in a Country Church Yard."

The walls and roof of the church were completed when disaster struck in 1886 in the form of a bitterly cold winter that killed thousands of cattle on the open range. The depression that followed prevented the congregants from fulfilling their financial obligations to the church, thus requiring them to accept a loan from the American Church Building Fund in order to complete construction. Eleven of Wyoming's governors have been members of St. Mark's and President and Mrs. Franklin D. Roosevelt worshipped with the congregation during a visit to Wyoming. Although improvements and changes have been made to the building, care has been taken to retain the original design; the basic furnishings have been left as they were in 1888, including the original altar, wooden fixtures, and pews.

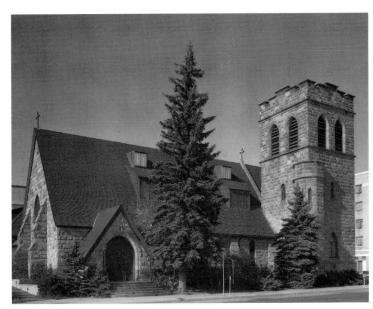

St. Mark's
Episcopal Church,
Cheyenne, Wyoming

France Memorial United Presbyterian Church

Third and Cedar Streets, Rawlins

ARCHITECT / BUILDER:
Not available

CONSTRUCTION / DEDICATION DATE:
1882

THE PRESBYTERIAN CHURCH OF RAWLINS was organized in 1869, one year after the town was established at a site where the Union Pacific railroad tracks paused before moving westward. A small frame church, built on land donated by the railroad, was dedicated in 1871. As it was the only church within 100 miles in every direction, it attracted traveling preachers and people representing various Protestant denominations. Ten years after its dedication, the congregation decided to construct a new stone church. As the congregation did not have sufficient funds to pay all the construction costs, a mortgage was negotiated with a member, James France. France ended up paying off the mortgage himself, and in gratitude for his donation, the congregation changed the name of the church to the "Mrs. Elizabeth France Presbyterian Church," now shortened to its present name.

The church, completed in 1882, is the only one in the city constructed of stone and is an early example of the Gothic Revival style in Wyoming. It is one of the oldest remaining structures in Rawlins and serves as a landmark in the city. Although additions have been made to the building, it continues to retain its architectural integrity.

France Memorial
United Presbyterian
Church,
Rawlins, Wyoming

St. Paul's United Church of Christ

ST. PAULUS DEUTSCHE EVANGELISCHE LUTHERISCHE KIRCHE

602 Garfield, Laramie

ARCHITECT / BUILDER:
Designed by George Berner
CONSTRUCTION / DEDICATION DATE:
1886

THE CONGREGATION WAS ORGANIZED in 1885 by German immigrants who wanted to secure the services of a minister to preach to them in their own language. After meeting in Laramie's Presbyterian Church for five years, the congregation decided to build their own building. Designed and constructed by a member of the congregation, George Berner, it is the first German church in Wyoming. Over the years, the congregation has undergone several changes of name and affiliation, adopting its present name in 1957.

The brick Gothic Revival building is the oldest remaining church structure in Laramie and one of the more elaborate Lutheran churches in the state dating from this period. Apart from an addition to the east end in 1922, the church looks much as it did when constructed. It remains an important visible reminder of the many people of German heritage who settled in Wyoming.

St. Paul's United
Church of Christ,
Laramie, Wyoming

Christ Episcopal Church

Corner of 4th and Center Streets, Douglas

ARCHITECT / BUILDER:
G. W.G. Van Winkle
CONSTRUCTION / DEDICATION DATE:
1898

SETTLERS MOVING WESTWARD with the frontier brought with them their memories of churches left behind. Many of Wyoming's early settlers came from northeastern states where the Episcopal faith was enjoying a revival. A part of that revival was a renewed interest in the Gothic style for church buildings. Elaborate Gothic Revival church plans had to be modified for export to frontier towns where money, technology, and material were often in short supply. Richard Upjohn's publication, *Rural Church Architecture,* was one source for ideas, and may have been the inspiration for this church which displays many of the features found in his book—steeply pitched roof, lancet windows, buttresses, and vertical planking on the exterior.

The church was the focal point of the town's cultural, social, and religious life and was used by other denominations before the construction of their own churches. Later churches were built of brick, leaving Christ Episcopal as not only the oldest church in Douglas, but the only one built of wood. Unfortunately, the building's historic character has been severely compromised by the addition of wide horizontal siding that has destroyed its graceful lines.

**Christ
Episcopal Church,
Douglas, Wyoming**

Montana

THE BIG SKY COUNTRY OF MONTANA was claimed by the French in 1682, who then ceded it to Spain before reclaiming it in 1800. Although some explorations were undertaken, neither France nor Spain established any permanent settlements. In 1804, the year after the United States acquired the land as part of the Louisiana Purchase, Lewis and Clark set out from St. Louis on their historic journey up the Missouri River in search of the Northwest Passage. Although they did not find a waterway linking the Mississippi River with the Pacific Ocean, they were able to map this hitherto unexplored area, opening it to fur traders and missionaries who followed in their footsteps.

Many of the fur traders were French Canadian Roman Catholics who brought with them experienced Iroquois trappers who taught the local Salish (Flathead) Indians their skills and introduced them to Christianity. The local tribes' relationship with the trappers was positive, resulting in their decision to embrace Christianity. Along with their friends the Nez Perce, the Salish sent representatives on a dangerous journey to St. Louis in search of a priest, a "Black Robe." Their request was granted by the Bishop of St. Louis and they were sent a Belgian-born Jesuit, Pierre Jean de Smet, one of the West's most remarkable and successful missionaries. In 1841, on the banks of the Bitter Root River, a favorite camping site of the Salish, he established the first Catholic mission in the Northwest Territory. A small log church constructed in 1846 was replaced by a more elaborate building, but trouble with the Indians forced the mission to close in 1850. It did not reopen until 1866 when the present **St. Mary's Mission** was constructed.

The Homestead Act passed in 1862 and the discovery of the first major gold strike in the region that same year quickly brought Montana to the attention of the rest of the nation. The Territory of Montana was carved out of Idaho Territory in 1864, mining camps and farming communities were established, and in 1889, Montana—with all its riches—entered the Union. The state's eastern prairie lands attracted farmers and ranchers, while the natural resources of the mountainous West, precious metals, and seemingly endless forests, brought in entrepreneurs, prospectors, and laborers.

With the discovery of gold at the Grasshopper diggings in 1862, the gold camp of Bannack was founded and thousands of hopeful miners stampeded to Montana's first boomtown. With them came missionaries intent on introducing an element of morality into the camps. By 1864 the Methodists had established a church in Bannack, but six years later the mine was played out and many of the miners moved on. Those that stayed helped erect the Methodist Church at Bannack in 1877, a small frame building typical of many of the churches built in Montana's mining towns.

Far more elaborate is the Episcopal church in Anaconda, the site of a huge smelter erected in 1883 by Montana's "Copper King," Marcus Daly. The town quickly grew after Daly established his smelter; congregations were formed and churches built, including a Methodist church that was also used by Episcopalians. The success of the smelter, and perhaps the fact that Mrs. Marcus Daly was an Episcopalian, led to the building of the stone Romanesque Revival **St. Mark's Episcopal Church** in 1890.

In 1864, four prospectors from Georgia whose luck was running out discovered gold in a gulch they ironically named "Last Chance Gulch." Better known today as Helena, the gold camp became the center for extensive gold and silver mining that produced fabulous wealth for many prospectors. The city's financial clout led to its being named the capital of Montana in 1889. One of the most successful mines was the Drum Lummon discovered by Thomas Cruse, an Irish Catholic immigrant. Thanks to Cruse and other prominent and wealthy Catholics, Helena became home to many grand buildings, including the **Cathedral of Saint Helena**, constructed between 1908 and 1924.

The state's oldest Jewish settlement dates from 1864, when Jewish merchants began arriving in booming Helena. The following year they organized the First Hebrew Benevolent Society, which became the nucleus for **Temple Emanu-El** founded in 1887. The congregation's Moorish-style synagogue, literally standing in the shadows of the Cathedral of Saint Helena, was completed in 1891. The congregation disbanded in the 1930s and the building is now owned by the Helena Diocese.

Organized efforts to encourage immigrants to settle in Montana began as early as 1869. The 1862 Homestead Act made land available on the prairies of north-central and eastern Montana and work was available in the state's mines, smelters, and railroads. Many of those who came were Germans and Scandinavians who would begin by working in the mines or smelters but later, at the encouragement of railroads that owned much of the land, became farmers or stockmen. Norwegian Lutherans formed agricultural communities and built churches that were cultural centers binding new communities in remote locations. One that has survived, **Bethany Lutheran Church** outside of Oilmont, is a modest building erected by Norwegian immigrants that has become a landmark on the prairie.

Surrounded by mountains, the Gallatin Valley became home to "Hollanders" arriving from older settlement areas in Michigan and Iowa. They established an ethnic enclave that still is identifiable. The completion of the railroad in the 1880s opened the area to settlement, at first attracting Germans seeking a good place to grow malting barley for beer. As the region is fertile but arid, an irrigation company was formed and soon the land was producing large amounts of barley. This attracted the "Hollanders," who were followed by Dutch immigrants recruited by the Board of Domestic Missions of the Presbyterian Church in America. Initially the Dutch worshipped in Presbyterian churches, but in 1903, they formed their own Christian Reformed Church. A small church built in 1904 on Church Hill (later spelled Churchill) near Manhattan was replaced in 1911 by the present Christian Reformed Church, a large frame structure seating about 600 people, considered the largest rural church west of the Mississippi, and the central focus of its ethnic community.

St. Mary's Mission

Stevensville, Ravalli County

ARCHITECT / BUILDER:
Father Anthony Ravalli
CONSTRUCTION / DEDICATION DATE:
1866; 1879

F ATHER ANTHONY RAVALLI, a Jesuit priest from Ferrara, Italy, arrived in the Bitter Root Valley in 1845 and built the first grist mill and saw mill in Montana. For a time St. Mary's Mission prospered, but trouble with the Indians led to its abandonment in 1850. In September 1866, Father Ravalli, accompanied by other clergy, returned to St. Mary's which they found in ruins, but within a month they built this church, dedicated on October 28, 1866.

Father Ravalli was a true Renaissance man. Not only was he able to construct grist and saw mills, he also designed and built the new altar for St. Mary's that stands under an alcove whose intricate scroll work he carved. He also carved the candlesticks that flank the altar and fashioned from plaster an almost life-size statue of St. Ignatius dressed in a deerskin cassock, which he painted Jesuit black. In 1879, he drew the plans and supervised the expansion of the church building, doubling its size. He was also a physician, serving both Indians and whites from a small pharmacy building beside the church. St. Mary's did not survive long after the death of this gifted man in 1884. On October 17, 1891, the Salish Indians were forced to leave Bitter Root Valley for a reservation to the north. A new parish was established in the nearby town of Hamilton, and in 1954, a new church was built south of St. Mary's Chapel to serve the town of Stevensville. The church remains, however, and is a major tourist attraction in this part of the Bitter Root Valley.

St. Mary's Roman
Catholic Mission,
Bitter Root Valley,
Stevensville, Montana

St. Mark's Episcopal Church

601 Main, Anaconda

ARCHITECT / BUILDER:
Not available

CONSTRUCTION / DEDICATION DATE:
1890-1891

AFTER FIRST MEETING in a Methodist church and then upstairs from a saloon, the Episcopalians in Anaconda decided it was time that they built a church of their own. Marcus Daly's smelter was booming, as was the town, and the future looked promising. In 1889, a lot was purchased and plans were made for the church's construction. This was not to be a modest frame church similar to those in most mining communities; rather, the congregants chose to build a handsome Romanesque Revival building using buff sandstone quarried near Garrison. The cost was $10,000, far more than the congregation could afford, even though Mrs. Marcus Daly was a member. In 1892, the church was closed for several months due to a smelter shutdown and the rector moved to Nebraska. A year later a new rector was called, the economy picked up, and in 1896, Mrs. Daly donated a large pipe organ.

The church remains in use although it has undergone some changes over the years, including a red brick, one-storied flat-roofed addition squaring off the space between the south transept and apse. All that remains of Marcus Daly's smelter is its 585-foot brick smokestack.

St. Mark's
Episcopal Church,
Anaconda, Montana

Cathedral of Saint Helena

530 North Ewing Street, Helena

ARCHITECT / BUILDER:
A. O. Von Herbulis

CONSTRUCTION / DEDICATION DATE:
1908-1924

HELENA WAS NOT ONLY MONTANA'S CAPITAL, but between the years 1880 and 1893, it was also the state's most wealthy city. The concentration of wealth made it possible to erect buildings on a grand scale, public edifices like the governor's private mansion completed in 1888 and the state capitol dedicated in 1902, and religious buildings, in particular the Cathedral of Saint Helena. The Helena Diocese at the time of the cathedral's construction numbered about 50,000. Thomas Cruse, a wealthy mine owner, donated over $100,000 to its construction. Sited on a knoll overlooking Last Chance Gulch,

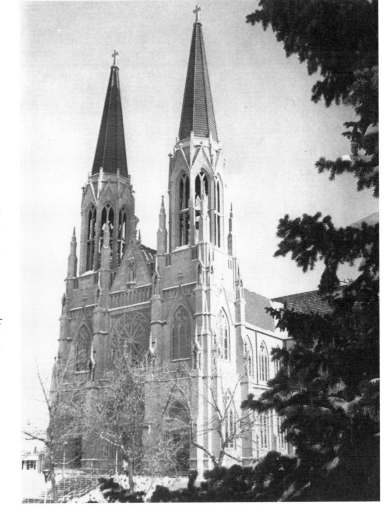

Helena's main street, the cathedral dominates the entire city. Its architect, A. O. Von Herbulis of Washington, D.C., was trained in Europe, which is evident in the building's design that reflects his familiarity with Gothic churches in Europe, including the Cathedral in Cologne, Germany, the Votive Church in Vienna, Austria, and Amiens Cathedral in France. The cathedral's twin spires rising to 230 feet are the tallest structures in Helena. While the cathedral's exterior remains essentially unchanged, the interior has undergone extensive renovations. However, the cathedral's most outstanding feature remains unchanged—its 59 stained glass windows made by the F. X. Zettler firm of Munich.

The cathedral has long been one of Helena's outstanding tourist attractions, receiving thousands of visitors each year.

Cathedral of St. Helena, Helena, Montana

Temple Emanu-El

515 North Ewing, Helena

ARCHITECT / BUILDER:
Heinlein and Mathias
CONSTRUCTION / DEDICATION DATE:
1891

L OCATED IN A RESIDENTIAL NEIGHBORHOOD a block away from the Cathedral of St. Helena stands the first synagogue constructed in the Pacific Northwest. The congregation, consisting of influential legislators, merchants, and community leaders, was founded in 1887, just as Helena entered its most prosperous period. The synagogue, built in 1891, echoes the community's prosperity. The Moorish style building, designed by the prominent local architectural firm of Heinlein and Mathias, was built of granite, sandstone, and red porphyry blocks, its twin towers capped with green onion domes. Helena's boom busted in the 1930s and the Jewish community began to dwindle. It soon became impossible for those who remained to maintain the synagogue and it was sold to the city for $1 and remodeled to be used as a state office building.

The building, lacking its distinctive onion domes, belongs now to the Helena Roman Catholic Diocese; it still retains much of its exterior integrity–a visual reminder of Helena's once prosperous and influential Jewish community.

Temple Emanu-el Synagogue (now offices of Catholic Diocese of Helena), Helena, Montana

Bethany Lutheran Church

One quarter mile south of Gus Blaze Road, Oilmont

ARCHITECT / BUILDER:
Not available

CONSTRUCTION / DEDICATION DATE:
1925

T
YPICAL OF THE MANY SMALL wood frame churches built by immigrant groups who came to settle in Montana's mining camps and farming communities, Bethany Lutheran Church, set in a vast landscape of windblown wheatlands, symbolizes the importance of the church as an ethnic group's cultural and religious center. Built by the area's original homesteaders, it reflects the boom and bust patterns of Montana's dryland farming era when immigrants were encouraged by railroads to settle on the semi-arid prairie.

Bethania Norsk Evg. Luthersk Menighed, as it was then known, was organized in 1912. The congregation met in homes and the local school before land was donated to build a church. However, an economic depression following crop failures and World War I delayed construction. Finally in 1923, the church's Ladies' Aid chapter approved plans to fund a permanent church building. The women purchased a building and moved it to the site. With the men contributing much of the labor and the women many of the furnishings, the church was completed and ready for services by 1926.

Bethany Lutheran remained active for about 25 years, until the 1950s when services were discontinued and the congregation merged with St. Luke's in nearby Shelby. The church is used for community gatherings and remains in good repair, thanks to the interest of local groups and individuals.

Bethany
Lutheran Church,
Oilmont, Montana

Idaho

I DAHO, KNOWN FOR ITS UNUSUAL SHAPE and famed potatoes, was originally part of the Oregon country claimed by the United States, Great Britain, Spain, and Russia. Spain and Russia eventually withdrew their claims, leaving the United States and Great Britain to compete for the area's rich resource of furs. When the fashion for furs began to wane, so too did Great Britain's interest, resulting in the British ceding jurisdiction of the entire region south of the 49th parallel to the United States. Idaho received its present boundaries following the formation of Montana Territory in 1864 and Wyoming Territory in 1868.

The Lapwai Mission, established in 1836 by itinerant Methodist missionaries, was the first in Nez Perce County. On their heels came the famed Jesuit missionary, Father Pierre Jean de Smet in 1840. Two years later Father Nicholas Point established the first Catholic mission among the Coeur d'Alene Indians near the Coeur d'Alene River. A temporary chapel of bark remained in use until Father Anthony Ravalli, a Jesuit priest born in Ferrara, Italy, was called upon to design the **Coeur d'Alene Mission of the Sacred Heart** in the 1850s. The mission remained in use until 1877; after years of neglect it has recently been restored to its original appearance.

Many people traveled through southeastern Idaho along the Oregon Trail, but few chose to settle there. However, as land became less available in Utah, Mormons began moving northward from the Great Basin area, establishing the territory's first permanent white settlement in 1860 in Franklin. Many of the Mormons who settled in Franklin and in Chesterfield, a second community established nearby, were polygamists; this prompted the territorial government to enact a law, upheld by the Supreme Court, depriving polygamists of the right to vote. The law remained in effect until the Mormon church formally rejected polygamy in 1893. The enactment of the law, however, did not deter the planners of Chesterfield. The town was laid out and the **Chesterfield Ward Meeting House of the Church of Jesus Christ of Latter-day Saints** was erected. The village was all but abandoned in 1941, but the meetinghouse is maintained as a museum by the local Daughters of Utah Pioneers.

The Mormons' dry farming techniques and irrigation transformed Idaho's arid but fertile soil into productive farmland. Ultimately agriculture became one of the state's major industries. However, another natural resource, minerals, was the magnet that was to finally attract thousands of settlers.

In a story often repeated throughout the West, the cry of gold in 1861 brought in prospectors, miners, and entrepreneurs who settled in boom towns like Hailey, located in the center of the rich Wood River mining district. The town was given a further economic boost several years later when a branch of the Oregon Short Line Railroad was extended into it. In 1885, Hailey's prosperous citizens erected one of the earliest brick churches in Idaho, the Gothic Revival style Emanuel Episcopal Church, distinguished by the Celtic cross topping its bell cope.

The arrival of railroads spurred further development of the territory's mineral deposits, leading to Idaho entering the Union in 1890. Boise, a military post and service center for nearby mining camps, was named its capital. New towns began developing as railroad termini and as sites for large smelting plans. One town that had both industries was Mackay, platted in 1901. Among the town's first buildings was **Mackay Methodist (Community) Church**, a modest frame structure erected in 1901, typical of many churches built in Idaho's mining towns.

Not all newcomers were interested in mining; some were homesteaders, including Finnish farmers who began settling in central Idaho's isolated mountain country in 1896. By 1915, 85 Finnish families were living in the area of Long Valley, including the family of Reverend John William Eloheimo, one of the founders of the Suomi (Finnish) Synod of the Lutheran Church in America. At first the Finns attended a Methodist church in a neighboring town, until the Finnish Ladies' Aid Society was able to raise enough funds to build **Long Valley Finnish Lutheran Church** in 1917. Although the building is no longer used as a church, the same Society continues to maintain it.

Perhaps one of Idaho's more unusual churches is Our Lady, Queen of Heaven, in Oreana in southwestern Idaho. It is an example of the creative adaptive reuse of a historic property, in this case a historic store transformed into a church. The town's founder, a miner who became a prosperous cattleman, constructed a series of stone buildings including a general store built of mortared lava rock. Through the years the property changed hands until 1961 when the current owner, Albert Black, donated it to the Catholic Church. A volunteer group remodeled the building, adding a belfry, buttresses, and a porch, thus transforming it into a church.

Idaho's first permanent Jewish settlers began arriving in 1865, some as merchants, others as potato farmers and ranchers. In 1895, the first Jewish congregation in Idaho was organized by Moses Alexander, who later became mayor of Boise and governor of the state. The congregation, which consisted mainly of people of German-Jewish ancestry, erected **Congregation Beth Israel** in 1896, the oldest synagogue in the state.

Coeur d'Alene Mission of the Sacred Heart

(CATALDO MISSION)

Caldwell

ARCHITECT / BUILDER:
Father Anthony Ravalli, architect, builder

CONSTRUCTION / DEDICATION DATE:
begun circa 1850

BUILT SOME TIME AFTER 1850 by Jesuit missionaries and Coeur d'Alene Indians, this log and adobe church is the oldest surviving mission church in the Pacific Northwest and is also the oldest extant structure in Idaho. Located in a remote setting on a hill overlooking the Coeur d'Alene River and valley, with a mountain backdrop, the church was designed by an Italian Jesuit priest, Father Anthony Ravalli. The building reflects Father Ravalli's familiarity with the classical Baroque architecture of his native country, and of his order's mother church, Il Gesu, in Rome.

This simplified version of a Baroque church was constructed using simple available tools including several broad-axes, an auger, some rope and pulleys, and a pen knife. An improvised whipsaw was used by the Indians to cut down the huge pine trees used in its construction. The priests executed all the interior decoration including the hand-carved altars, statues, ceiling details, and paintings.

The mission remained in use until 1877. It is believed that the Jesuits' influence discouraged many Coeur d'Alenes from joining Chief Joseph during the Nez Perce War of 1877.

A restoration project in the mid-1970s repaired or replaced all damaged material in the church, copying, where necessary, the original pieces.

Coeur d'Alene
Mission of the
Sacred Heart
(Cataldo Mission),
Caldwell, Idaho

The Chesterfield Ward Meeting House of the Church of Jesus Christ of Latter-day Saints

Chesterfield

ARCHITECT / BUILDER:
Not available

CONSTRUCTION / DEDICATION DATE:
1887-1892

THE RURAL VILLAGE OF CHESTERFIELD is located on the foothills of the Chesterfield mountain range. As was typical of the Mormon settlement pattern, a town grid street system was imposed on the hilly landscape. The most prominent buildings, the church and school, are located on the highest points in town where they have a magnificent vista of the valley. Platted in 1883, log, slab (squared logs), and frame buildings were constructed by the Mormon settlers. Several homes, two stores, the tithing office, and church were all built of locally fired orange brick. At its peak, over 400 people, dry farmers and their families, lived within a mile of the village. The town was also a frequent campsite and grazing area for travelers on the Oregon Trail which crossed the area.

The rectangular brick meetinghouse features a hipped porch and a half-round lunette window set into the front gable containing its dedication date. The town has been unoccupied for a number of years and many of its buildings are in various stages of disrepair. The church, however, has been maintained as a museum by the local Daughters of Utah Pioneers.

Chesterfield Ward
Meeting House
of the Church of
Jesus Christ of
Latter-day Saints,
Chesterfield, Idaho

Mackay Methodist Episcopal Church

(MACKAY COMMUNITY CHURCH)

Custer Street and Park Avenue, Mackay

ARCHITECT / BUILDER:
Not available

CONSTRUCTION / DEDICATION DATE:
1901

THE MACKAY METHODIST EPISCOPAL CHURCH is one of the earliest *new* buildings erected in Mackay during its boom year of 1901. Many of the town's first buildings were moved from Houston, another mining town four miles away. Along with the buildings came the town's Methodist minister, who elected to have a new church built in Mackay. Thanks to the efforts of the Ladies' Aid Society, the church's entire debt was paid off in three years.

Mackay was also home to a Roman Catholic church and an Episcopal church, neither of which was able to maintain a full-time pastor. As a result the Methodist Episcopal Church became locally known as the "community church," attended by people representing various Protestant denominations.

The exterior of the wood frame and clapboard church is apparently unaltered, with the exception of a small, compatible post-1945 addition at the rear. The interior has undergone more change, including a new chancel and furnishings. The building was a community center for the mining and agricultural region of the Upper Lost River Valley until 1980; currently it is privately owned.

Mackay
Methodist Episcopal
(Community) Church,
Mackay, Idaho

Long Valley Finnish Lutheran Church

Farm to Market Road, Lake Fork

ARCHITECT / BUILDER:
John Ruuska and John Heikkila, builders
CONSTRUCTION / DEDICATION DATE:
1917

THE PICTURESQUE Long Valley Finnish Lutheran Church is a well-preserved example in an unspoiled rural setting of the modest churches built by diverse ethnic groups who came to settle in the West. Idaho had two Finnish settlements: this one settled by religious Finns who were members of the Evangelical Lutheran Church and a second group, known as North Idaho Finns, composed of miners active in the Socialist movement. Rather than a church, they left behind the Enaville Workers' Hall.

The Finns in Long Valley were homesteaders who began to arrive in 1896. Money was scarce, but because of the efforts of the Ladies' Aid Society, funds were collected and the church was built on land donated by one of its members. The volunteer labor was supervised by two local Finnish carpenters, John Ruuska and John Heikkila. The building, although now used only on special occasions, still has its hundred-year-old pump organ, a podium and sacrament table made from Long Valley pine by a member of the congregation, and a Finnish Bible brought to Idaho by one of the immigrant families. The painting of Christ above the table was donated by the Ladies' Aid Society, who continue to maintain the building.

**Long Valley Finnish
Lutheran Church,
Lake Fork, Idaho**

Congregation Beth Israel Synagogue

1102 State Street, Boise

ARCHITECT / BUILDER:
Two St. Louis architects; names unavailable
CONSTRUCTION / DEDICATION DATE:
1895

IDAHO'S JEWISH POPULATION never numbered over 500, but in 1915 one of the founders of Beth Israel, Moses Alexander, began the first of two terms as governor of the state. Jews began to settle in Boise in 1865 when it was a service community for nearby mining districts as well as a military post established to protect Oregon Trail travelers. Most were of German-Jewish ancestry who gathered together to worship in private homes or in rented halls. A congregation was formed in 1895, and the following year this synagogue was constructed.

The synagogue is basilican in shape without transepts and stands on a foundation built of local sandstone, but the rest of the exterior is shingled. Vaguely Moorish, it reflects the congregants' awareness of the popularity of this style among Jews in the late nineteenth century. Its most outstanding feature, however, is a large rose window on its façade, more reminiscent of the Gothic style than Moorish.

The building underwent a complete restoration in the early 1980s and remains in use by its original congregation.

Congregation Beth Israel Synagogue, Boise, Idaho

Utah

U TAH'S AWESOME AND FORBIDDING landscape initially discouraged all but the most daring or desperate sojourners. Few if any of its early visitors envisioned it as a land of milk and honey, but for one group, anxious to find a secure place to practice its faith, Utah, with its rim of mountains surrounding a Great Basin, was Zion.

Two years before the end of the Mexican War and the transfer of the territory to the United States, an advance guard of Mormons reached a valley located between the Wasatch Mountains and the Great Salt Lake and saw promise where others saw only a barren, arid wasteland. The ordeals experienced by the Mormons are an important part of the history of America's westward expansion in the nineteenth century. It has been argued that the evolution of this church at any other time and in any other place is inconceivable. Brigham Young, who had assumed leadership of the Mormons following the murder of Joseph Smith, Jr., in Navoo, Illinois, in 1844, promised his followers deliverance–an exodus that turned into a chaotic flight from increasing persecution. On July 24, 1847, an ailing Brigham Young viewed the Great Salt Lake and proclaimed, "This is the place." On the site that became Salt Lake City, less than 2,000 Mormons set out to create the "State of Deseret" that was to stretch north and west into what is now Oregon and Idaho and southwest to the Pacific Ocean, establishing a Mormon corridor of settlements. Deseret never became a reality, but the United States government created the Territory of Utah in 1850, naming Brigham Young its governor. By that time over 11,000 people had settled in Utah; 95 percent were Mormons.

Ingenuity in developing irrigation methods, backbreaking work tilling the soil and building towns, "miracles" of gulls that ate crop-destroying crickets, and the 1849 California gold rush that transformed Salt Lake City into a major trading post, all contributed to the territory's growth and prosperity. "Gentiles" now began entering in increasing numbers attracted by work on the transcontinental railroad, completed in 1869, and in the mines. Their numbers were offset by the Mormons' assiduous missionary efforts, especially in Great Britain, Germany, and Scandinavia. Their missionary and economic successes made it inevitable that Mormon theocracy and American democracy would come in conflict resulting, at one point, in the United States government actually abolishing the corporation of the Mormon church. It wasn't until the Mormons agreed to prohibit polygamy that Utah was finally admitted into the Union in 1896.

It has been said that the Mormons might be in the West, but they are not entirely of it.

That is evident in the architectural styles imported from the East that were selected for many of their sacred buildings. Mormons have three sacred building types: temple, tabernacle, and meetinghouse. Most "Gentiles" are familiar with the famed temple in Salt Lake City, built between 1853 and 1893. Unlike earlier temples built in Navoo and Kirtland, this one was not to be used for any purpose other than as a sacred space open only to communicants to receive sacred instructions and prepare to meet God. Brigham Young selected the temple's architect, Truman Angell, and contributed ideas for its design. Young and Angell combined elements from Romanesque and Gothic architecture to create a soaring building that still gives the impression of being a fortress symbolizing the spiritual strength of the church and its role as a fortress against its enemies.

Tabernacles, intended to serve as congregational buildings of a stake, a term similar to diocese, were most often built in Eastern styles, such as the **St. George Tabernacle**, a lovely Colonial Georgian structure. A meetinghouse, a smaller and less elaborate building, serving its ward as a place of prayer, school, and community hall, would also reveal influences from popular architectural styles, particularly the Gothic Revival introduced into Utah by Protestant denominations. A surviving example is the Salt Lake Eighteenth Ward Meetinghouse built in 1881.

Although Utah is certainly more religiously homogeneous than any other state in the United States, it is unfair to describe it as a Mormon monotheocracy. Other faiths were able to establish a presence in the state, including the Methodists who founded a mission in Utah in 1869 and by 1872 had four churches, including the **First Methodist Episcopal Church**, built in 1906 for a congregation organized in Salt Lake City in 1870.

As happened elsewhere in unpopulated areas of the West, when there were too few people of one Protestant denomination to support a church, they would join together to build a "community church" such as the small Victorian Gothic Green River Church erected in 1907.

Mormons, following church counsel, avoided involvement in mining, opening the door for others to exploit the state's mineral riches. The "father of Utah mining" was General Patrick Connor, a Roman Catholic who urged his co-religionists to jump on the bandwagon. Bishop Lawrence Scanlan, arriving in the 1870s as a missionary to attend to the needs of the increasing numbers of Roman Catholics, was responsible for the erection of a number of Catholic churches, including the beautifully restored **Cathedral of the Madeleine** in Salt Lake City, built between 1889 and 1909.

Many of the "Gentile" immigrants, seen by the Mormons as "outsiders," found comfort and identity in their ethnic communities and neighborhoods. In 1900, there were three Greeks in Utah; ten years later their numbers had increased to over 4,000, mainly men recruited by Greek labor agents working for the railroads and mines. Holy Trinity Greek Orthodox Church, built in 1924, at one time dominated its Greek neighborhood in Salt Lake City. Other Greeks working in the coal mines of Carbon County built their own church, the **Hellenic Orthodox Church of the Assumption** in Price, dedicated in 1916.

Salt Lake City has a relatively large Japanese population, including a substantial number who were converts to Christianity. Their neighborhood is now gone, thanks to "urban renewal," but the Japanese Church of Christ, built in 1924, continues to serve descendants of its founders.

Although Utah was a "free" state, Mormons denied priesthood to blacks, thus excluding them from all temple rites. This has changed, but many of Salt Lake City's African-Americans continue to worship in the Trinity African Methodist Episcopal Church built in 1909 for a congregation organized in the 1880s.

German-speaking Jews, initially welcomed by the Mormons as "brothers," erected the first synagogue in Salt Lake City in 1883. Three other congregations were formed between 1891 and 1921. However, a decision by the Mormons not to trade at Jewish stores compelled many Jewish merchants to relocate elsewhere, including in Ogden, a "Gentile" city where they founded **Congregation B'rith Sholem** in 1921.

St. George Tabernacle

Five blocks west of the St. George Temple, St. George

ARCHITECT / BUILDER:
Miles Romney
CONSTRUCTION / DEDICATION DATE:
1863-1876

D ESIGNED BY THE ENGLISH ARCHITECT Miles Romney in a Colonial Georgian style, the St. George Tabernacle is considered the most beautiful of those built during the Brigham Young era. Constructed of local red sandstone blocks, the tabernacle's engaged two-stage central tower that dominates its façade reflects the architect's knowledge of the seventeenth- and eighteenth-century London churches designed by Christopher Wren and James Gibbs and their Colonial copies.

The St. George Tabernacle follows the general plan of other tabernacles inspired by the Old Provo Tabernacle, the first built outside of Salt Lake City. The raised-basement story of the St. George Tabernacle was originally used for religious instruction, cultural activities, and administrative meetings; it is now a Family History Center for the church. The main focus of the upper story is a two-tiered rostrum at the west, a centrally placed pulpit, and choir seats.

Tabernacles are congregational buildings that in their size and central position in the community serve to remind Mormons of their covenants and obligations. While the origin of the use of the term tabernacle for these structures remains uncertain, it does convey the prestige these buildings have as second in hierarchical importance to temples. The presence of both a temple and tabernacle in a community, as is the case in St. George, indicates that the city is an important center for the Church of Jesus Christ of Latter-day Saints.

St. George Tabernacle
of the Church of
Jesus Christ of
Latter-day Saints,
St. George, Utah

First United Methodist Church

203 South 200 East, Salt Lake City

ARCHITECT / BUILDER:
Frederic Albert Hale

CONSTRUCTION / DEDICATION DATE:
1905

FIRST METHODIST DATES its founding back to 1870 when Methodist missionaries began to actively try to convert Mormons in Utah back to "true Christianity." Initially services in Salt Lake City were held in an unfinished hayloft over a livery stable and then in a building located on Main Street. A church, constructed in 1871, served the congregation until the present building was dedicated in 1906. It is the oldest surviving Methodist church in the state as well as being the only Utah church designed by Frederic Albert Hale. Hale was a prominent Salt Lake City architect who designed many mansions and commercial structures for the city's non-Mormon population, who were in mining and business ventures.

What is notable about this church is Hale's use of a variation of the auditorium plan that had become popular in the late nineteenth century for nonliturgical denominations whose focus was on preaching. The brick church has an octagonal plan flanked on three sides by towers that provide entrances into the octagonal sanctuary and include stairways leading to the balcony level that curves along five sides of the octagon. The entire building remains essentially intact, although some changes were made to the altar and choir loft in 1960.

The building's significance lies both in its introduction into Salt Lake City of a new architectural style and its association with the history of Methodism in Utah.

**First United
Methodist Church,
Salt Lake City, Utah**

Cathedral of the Madeleine

331 East South Temple, Salt Lake City

ARCHITECT / BUILDER:
C.M. Neuhausen, Bernard O. Mecklenburg
CONSTRUCTION / DEDICATION DATE:
1900-1909

THE BEAUTIFULLY RESTORED gray sandstone Cathedral of the Madeleine was designed by C. M. Neuhausen, a Salt Lake City architect. The building's Romanesque Revival exterior reveals the influence of H. H. Richardson, while the interior is in the Gothic Revival style. Neuhausen died before the building was completed and Bernard O. Mecklenburg was hired to complete the towers and roof.

Mormons shunned mining, but others readily exploited the state's mineral wealth. Thousands of the mine owners and laborers who came to Utah were Roman Catholic. Salt Lake City had a Catholic church by 1871, but it wasn't until the arrival of Bishop Lawrence Scanlon that churches were built in most of the state's mining communities. It was under Scanlon's supervision that the Cathedral of the Madeleine was constructed. Much of the money used to build and furnish the cathedral came from Utah's Catholic mining tycoons, but additional funds came from an important historical source–the so-called "Pious Fund" established by early Jesuit missionaries for building churches in California. In 1902, two centuries after the fund's establishment, the money was made available to build a cathedral for the Salt Lake Diocese, illustrating the continuing impact of Catholic missionary efforts in the American West.

**Cathedral
of the Madeleine,
Salt Lake City, Utah**

Hellenic Orthodox Church of the Assumption

61 South Second East Street, Price

ARCHITECT / BUILDER:
Lars Gunderson, contractor

CONSTRUCTION / DEDICATION DATE:
dedicated in 1916

IN SPITE OF TWO REMODELINGS and one fire-induced renovation, the basic architectural integrity of the original yellow brick church remains intact. Initially in the traditional Greek cross plan, a new entrance consisting of two towers on the façade and an inside balcony were added. The fire resulted in new icons being commissioned and other restoration work.

The first Greeks to arrive in Carbon County, where Price is located, were brought in as strike breakers. By 1916 there were at least 3,000 Greek men working in the mines. An effort to construct a Greek church had begun four years earlier when a group met with Greeks from nearby Helper, where church services were held in a Greek coffee house. The two communities decided to build a church in Price. On the day of the church's consecration, special trains brought Greek miners from all the coal mines to Price for the celebration. They were met by an Italian band which escorted them to the church.

Initially most Greek miners came to the New World with the intention of earning as much money as possible and then returning to their homeland. The building of a church provided them with a sanctuary, a secure place, but it also came to symbolize their intention of making America their permanent home. Wives and girlfriends were sent for and, like so many pioneers who preceded them, the Greeks added their contributions to the nation's ethnic and religious diversity, this time in a state that is often perceived as religiously homogeneous.

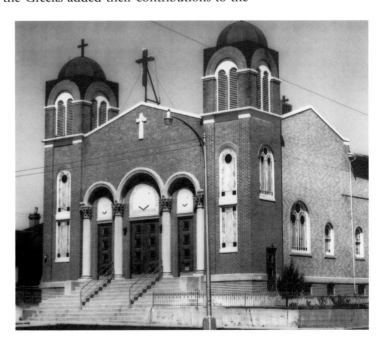

Hellenic
Orthodox Church
of the Assumption,
Price, Utah

Congregation B'rith Sholem Synagogue

2750 Grant, Ogden

ARCHITECT / BUILDER:
Not available

CONSTRUCTION / DEDICATION DATE:
1921

EVERAL JEWISH SETTLERS were in Utah as early as 1854, but it wasn't until the development of the mining industry in the mid-1860s that the community began to develop. Brigham Young offered them space in the Hall of the Seventies on Temple Square in Salt Lake City to hold religious services. This was a rather ironic, but undoubtedly deliberate, choice in that the Hall was modeled after the Sanhedrin, the supreme political, religious, and judicial body of Jews living in Palestine during the Roman period. Jewish merchants came into conflict with Mormons over the establishment of the Zions Cooperative Mercantile Institute, a church-operated general store designed to keep Mormon money in Mormon hands, prompting many of them to leave Utah or to relocate in non-Mormon "Gentile " mining communities, such as Ogden.

In 1890 a Jewish congregation, originally named Ohab Sholem, was organized in Ogden. Services were held in a clothing store and other rented quarters until a rabbi was hired in 1917. With his urging, land was purchased and in 1921 a small single-story brick synagogue, described as "mainly American [in style], but show[ing] a slight Grecian influence," was dedicated. It is the only synagogue in Utah built outside of Salt Lake City. Still in use for weekly Friday night services, the building remains virtually unaltered; a Jewish star and its name, "Congregation B'rith Sholem," carved into its tympanum proclaim its identity.

Congregation B'rith Shalem Synagogue, Ogden, Utah

Arizona

ARIZONA HAD A SETTLED POPULATION for centuries before the arrival of Spanish explorers and missionaries. The territory's culturally diverse American Indian population comprised Navajo in the Four Corners area, Papago in the south, Hopi in the northwest, and Apache. Most now live on large reservations, but evidence of their culturally advanced civilizations remains throughout the state. The Spanish began occupying Arizona in 1700, but the constant attacks by Apache Indians limited their number. As a result, following the end of the Mexican-American war in 1848, people of Spanish and Mexican descent living in Arizona numbered only 1,000.

Although the Spanish were few in number they left behind one of the most beautiful and historic churches in the nation, **San Xavier del Bac Mission** near Tucson, which was founded in 1700 by a Jesuit priest for the Papago Indians. The present church, built after the Jesuits were expelled by the Spanish crown and replaced by Franciscans, is possibly the mission's third building. Built of burned adobe brick by Papago laborers and Spanish-American craftsmen, San Xavier del Bac is considered the finest surviving example of Mission architecture, also referred to as Spanish Colonial architecture, in the United States.

The retention of adobe as a building material centuries after it was introduced is evident in Santa Cruz Roman Catholic Church, also located in Tucson. The Hispanic parish was formed by Spanish Carmelite priests expelled from Mexico during that nation's 1910 Revolution. The church was designed by Tucson's Bishop Henry Granjon in the Spanish Colonial Revival style with Moorish details, including a minaret-like bell tower. Completed in 1919, it is the largest known extant mud-adobe building in Arizona.

Anglo settlers began entering Arizona in the mid-nineteenth century, attracted by the discovery of valuable metals, particularly copper. As happened elsewhere in the nation, with them came their religion which had to find expression in what was for Easterners an alien environment. In the north, where timber was plentiful, churches were built of wood, but in areas where lumber was scarce, it was necessary for the builders to make adaptations. Thus one finds **St. Paul's Episcopal Church**, a Gothic Revival building in Tombstone, built of adobe. It is the state's first Episcopal church and in its style marks the beginning of Anglo influence in Arizona.

Mormons moving south from Utah began to settle in Arizona during its territorial period beginning in 1863. The establishment of Mormon chapels was closely associated with the creation of new towns where their missionary efforts were often successful. Such was the case in Prescott, where the Mormon Chapel, dedicated in 1918, is one of only two structures in the city to be built entirely of dressed blue granite masonry quarried at a nearby site.

The Navajo were never brought into the mission system or subjugated by the military during the period of Spanish occupation of Arizona. It wasn't until St. Michael's Mission was established in 1898 by the Franciscans that the Navajo agreed to accept a permanent Catholic mission. The mission consists of a school and a modest **Chapel** initially built to be a trading post.

Phoenix had a modest beginning in 1864 as the site of a hay camp supplying forage to nearby Camp McDowell. Its location on the site of a prehistoric Indian village inspired its early Anglo residents to name it after the bird that rises from the ashes of a lost civilization. The town became an important market and entertainment center for soldiers, prospectors, and cowboys, complete with the requisite saloons, gambling halls, and rowdiness. Phoenix's first real boom began in 1911 when the Roosevelt Dam on the Salt River began to provide water for power and irrigation. The development of the state's natural resources and its concomitant population increase resulted in Arizona being granted statehood in 1912, the last of the 48 contiguous states to enter the Union. Phoenix, as the capital, continued to expand, propelled in part by the coming of the railroad that provided it with a direct link to markets in the East.

Mirroring the growth of the city is the increase in its number of places of worship, jumping from seven churches in 1892 to 32 by the early 1920s, then 50 more in the next decade. Although places of worship were built in all the traditional and mainstream architectural styles current in the United States, the most prevalent styles, regardless of denomination, are those identified with the Southwest: Mission Revival, Spanish Colonial, and Spanish Eclectic. The present **Basilica of St. Mary's Cathedral**, built in 1903 for the oldest Catholic parish in the Salt River Valley, is a pastel-colored stucco over brick building whose exterior is in the Mission Revival style tempered with Romanesque features, while its interior is entirely in the Romanesque style, resulting in a sense of dislocation upon entering the sanctuary.

Methodist missionaries, not too surprisingly, arrived in Arizona with the earliest settlers, setting up missions in a territory that, to quote from the church history of Tanner Chapel, had been "little touched by the refining influences of civilization. . . . " Tanner A.M.E. Chapel, located in Phoenix, was organized by African-Americans who arrived in the city in the 1880s; it is named after Bishop B. T. Tanner, presiding bishop of the Colorado Conference. The chapel, organized in 1887, has had several homes. Its present brick Gothic and Romanesque Revival building constructed in 1929 is one of the largest A.M.E. churches in the Southwest.

The construction of the Atlantic and Pacific Railroad in the late nineteenth century led to the establishment of many permanent communities at strategic railway points. Flagstaff, one of those communities, was settled in 1882 by a mixed group of settlers, including Mexicans, Chinese, and African-Americans. A Presbyterian congregation organized in 1891 built a church the following year, but when the Presbyterians merged with the Methodists in 1915, the city's Protestant Mexican community acquired the building. Now named **La Iglesia Metodista Mexicana, El Divino Redentor**, it is the oldest church building in Flagstaff and the only extant one built of locally cut pine wood.

San Xavier del Bac Mission

9 miles south of Tucson on U.S. 89

ARCHITECT / BUILDER:
Not available

CONSTRUCTION / DEDICATION DATE:
completed in 1769

THE MISSION OF SAN XAVIER DEL BAC was founded by a Jesuit priest, Eusebio Francisco Kino, a beloved missionary to the Papago Indians. He laid the foundation for the mission's first church in 1700. In the years that followed it was replaced by several others until work began on the present building in 1783, the most magnificent building surviving from the period of Spanish domination of the Southwest. It was built during the residency of Father Bautista Velderrain, a Franciscan who took charge of the mission after the Jesuits were expelled from the Spanish Empire. Its architect remains unknown, but its Baroque style and decorative elements would suggest that he was familiar with Spanish church architecture, either in Spain or in Mexico. The Papago Indians were probably responsible for making and laying the abode bricks used in the construction, but it is thought that the more sophisticated vaults were built by imported laborers.

Soon after its completion the Spanish Empire and its mission system collapsed, followed by the Mexican revolution that began in 1810. The church, without a pastor, began to fall into ruin, but thanks to the efforts of the Papago people and the interest of others, it has survived and today remains a functioning parish church.

San Xavier del Bac
Mission Church,
Tucson, Arizona

St. Paul's Episcopal Church

Safford and 3rd Streets, Tombstone

ARCHITECT / BUILDER:
Endicott Peabody

CONSTRUCTION / DEDICATION DATE:
1882

TOMBSTONE IS PERHAPS best known, thanks to popular films, as the site of the shootout at the OK Corral. However, at the time this church was built, the city was far more than a hang-out for gun fighters and gamblers. An Episcopal congregation was already organized and meeting in the county courthouse when the decision was made in 1882 to erect a church that was completed under the leadership of Reverend Endicott Peabody of the famous Massachusetts Peabody family. Peabody returned to Massachusetts the year after the church was built and went on to found the famed and exclusive Groton School for Girls.

The building's Gothic Revival style was the style of choice for Episcopal churches, but this is perhaps one of the few in Arizona built of adobe. The adobe bell tower was eventually replaced with one built of brick.

As possibly the oldest Protestant church building in Arizona, it is surprising to find that practically every detail of the church is original and in good repair. Original stained glass windows, pews, organ, and even lamps originally from sailing ships and now electrified, all survive.

The church continues to serve an Episcopal congregation.

St. Paul's
Episcopal Church,
Tombstone,
Arizona

St. Michael's Mission

St. Michaels west of Window Rock, Apache County

ARCHITECT / BUILDER:
Not available

CONSTRUCTION / DEDICATION DATE:
Remodeled as a church in 1898

THE NAVAJO PEOPLE RESISTED missionary efforts until difficult circumstances during the Civil War caused them to seek help. At that time the United States government withdrew all its soldiers from the Southwest to serve in the war, forcing the Navajos to be rounded up and placed into captivity. Upon their release they sought to reclaim their land. Difficulties ensued, causing them to turn to the Franciscans for help. In response, the Franciscans established St. Michael's mission in 1898, the first permanent Catholic mission to the Navajo.

The modest building that served as the mission church was a remodeled trading post. The stone walls were plastered on the inside, chimneys were raised, and its single room partitioned to make six rooms. A large room at the west end was the chapel and one on the east a combined kitchen, dining, living room. In between were four small bedrooms. The partitions, however, could be removed if space was needed for a classroom. The missionaries had to construct their own benches, cupboards, and bookcases, and even inside doorways.

It is not the mission building that is of importance, but rather the contributions the Franciscans made in publishing numerous books on the Navajo language and the assistance they provided the tribe in its successful attempts to acquire more land.

The 640-acre site is owned by the Sisters of the Blessed Sacrament, who provide financial support to the mission.

St. Michael's
Mission Chapel,
Apache County,
Arizona

The Basilica of St. Mary's Roman Catholic Church

231 North 3rd Street, Phoenix

ARCHITECT / BUILDER:
R. A. Gray, George Gallagher
CONSTRUCTION / DEDICATION DATE:
dedicated in 1914

C ATHOLIC SERVICES WERE FIRST HELD in Phoenix in 1870. A decade later an adobe church seating 400 was constructed; it was completely refurbished in 1897. By the turn of the century the church was too small and in need of additional repairs. Its priest, Father Novatus Benzing, with assistance of Brother Leonard Darscheid of St. Louis, sketched an idea for a larger church in the Gothic Revival style that would seat 800. However, after the sketches were given to the architects, R. A. Gray and George Gallagher, it was transformed into a building featuring a Mission Revival exterior and a Romanesque interior. Built on the site of the old church that was torn down, its basement was dedicated in 1903, but the construction of the superstructure was delayed for ten years while funds for its completion were raised.

The building remains virtually unchanged, but the number of its parishioners has declined. It has been designated a basilica by the Vatican because of its historic importance to the people of Phoenix.

The Basilica of
St. Mary's Roman
Catholic Church,
Phoenix, Arizona

La Iglesia Metodista Mexicana, El Divino Redentor

(MEXICAN METHODIST CHURCH OF FLAGSTAFF)

319 South San Francisco Street, Flagstaff

ARCHITECT / BUILDER:
Not available

CONSTRUCTION / DEDICATION DATE:
1891

THE ONE-STORY WOODEN vernacular Gothic Revival church was constructed in 1891 for a Presbyterian congregation, who used it until 1915 when it merged with an Anglo Methodist congregation, forming the Federated Community Church. Soon after, a Mexican Methodist mission, formally established in 1917, began to use the building. In 1925, the church was purchased by a local Anglo attorney who donated it to the Methodist mission; they moved it seven and one-half blocks and rededicated it as Iglesia Metodista Mexicana, El Divino Redentor.

Although the church has undergone some modifications, it remains significant for several reasons, architectural and historical. It is the oldest church in Flagstaff and the only extant one built primarily of locally cut pine wood. Although wood was readily available and a common building material in early Flagstaff, all of the city's surviving pre-1940 religious structures are constructed of locally quarried stone.

Historically the church is important for the role it has played as a religious and social center for Flagstaff's Mexican-American Methodists. The church continues to serve in this capacity to a congregation that includes descendants of some of the original members.

La Iglesia
Metodista Mexicana,
El Divino Redentor,
Flagstaff, Arizona

Nevada

NEVADA'S CHARACTER IS DEFINED by its contrasts. Its arid and forbidding landscape initially discouraged early explorers and settlers, but that began to change in the mid-nineteenth century when the discovery of the vast mineral wealth hidden beneath its arid hills began attracting thousands of treasure hunters. One group, who had arrived earlier, with no interest in gold or silver, did find the area attractive: Mormons established Nevada's first permanent settlement, Mormon Station, in 1850. At the time the territory was part of the Mormon State of Deseret encompassing Utah and the entire Great Basin, including what is now Nevada. Five years later a second Mormon settlement was established at Las Vegas, an oasis first visited by Paiute Indians and then later by Spanish explorers. The Mormons used the fort and mission there for three years; only the fort survives as Nevada's oldest inhabited building, ironically in a city that flourishes from activities contrary to Mormon practices and beliefs. Perhaps this is best illustrated by one of Las Vegas's "historic" churches, The Little Church of the West, the city's first permanent wedding chapel. Built in 1942 as part of a large hotel complex, it is a miniaturized replica of a mining town church.

In the decade following the discovery of gold and silver, and the legendary Comstock Lode in particular, Nevada was transformed into a booming mining territory. The area's riches prompted Congress to create the Nevada Territory that initially included only part of the Great Basin. However, as additional mining sites were discovered, Congress kept expanding the territory at the expense of Utah, possibly as a way to displace Mormons who discouraged mining activities because of the people of questionable character it attracted. Finally, it was the territory's mineral wealth needed to help finance the Civil War, plus the need for two more Republican votes to pass the 13th Amendment abolishing slavery, that motivated Congress to quickly admit Nevada into the Union in 1864, naming Carson City its capital.

For the rest of the nineteenth century Nevada flourished and floundered, reflecting the perils of having an economy based on one industry–mining. Ghost towns abound, haunting memories of what was, but other towns have survived; some, like Carson City, Virginia City, and Las Vegas, are tourist destinations.

Carson City was founded in 1858 as a market and social center for nearby mining settlements. Its prosperity during the 1860s and 1870s is legendary, attracting eastern entrepreneurs who organized and built **St. Peter's Episcopal Church** in 1867, a frame Gothic Revival building that would be at home on the plains and prairies to the east. Also contributing to the town's prosperity was the government mint responsible for coining the abundant silver coming out of the Comstock Lode located 15 miles northeast, near Virginia City.

Samuel Clemens, better known as Mark Twain, and Bret Harte are only two of the notable people who took up residence in the boom town of Virginia City. Working as reporters on the *Territorial Enterprise,* Nevada's first newspaper, they let easterners know of the riches being uncovered in the West, particularly the Comstock Lode that gave the town its reputation for wealth and licentiousness. Virginia City's population reached its peak of 20,000 in the 1870s. A variety of people, including Irish, Cornish, Mexican, Italian, and Chinese miners and eastern entrepreneurs, all came here to seek their fortune. But despite its reputation as a rough and tumble wild west boomtown, home of the famous Bucket of Blood Saloon, the town was not bereft of religious institutions. The city experienced a devastating fire in 1875 that destroyed all churches save one, the Presbyterian Church, built in 1867 with funds raised by its congregation from mining stocks. The frame Gothic Revival church was abandoned for many years but has recently been restored and is open for services.

During Virginia City's boom years, **St. Mary's in the Mountains Roman Catholic Church** had between 3,000 and 5,000 members, reflecting the size of the town's Irish, Mexican, and Italian population. The present brick church, constructed in 1877, is the congregation's fourth building.

The Catholic Church has a long history in the Great Basin, predating the creation of the Nevada Territory. Initially dominated by Irish and Mexican immigrants, the arrival of Italians, Basques, and others changed its ethnic character. The fate of the Catholic Church mirrored the state's economy, boom and bust. A Catholic church built during one of the state's later "boom" eras initiated in 1931 by the State Legislature's legalization of gambling is **Immaculate Conception Church** in Sparks, a town that had its first boom in 1904 as a result of the arrival of the Southern Pacific Railroad.

Reno, Nevada's second largest city, began as a rail center for mining camps at Goldfield and Tonopah. Land, offered by the railroad at a public auction in 1868, immediately attracted settlers and the town became a bustling regional market and social center, a role it continues to play. At the same time Reno was founded, so too was its first Methodist congregation; two years later the congregation had its first church. The present Gothic Revival First United Methodist Church, constructed in 1925, is one of the first poured concrete buildings in Reno.

Four people organized Reno's **First Church of Christ, Scientist** in 1904, but following a dramatic increase in membership in the 1930s a new church was constructed, right in the midst of the Depression. The congregation, known for its support of minority groups, hired Paul R. Williams, an African-American architect, to design its new building, an excellent example of Colonial Revival architecture.

The instability of depending on only one industry to support the state's economy became painfully evident to its leaders when the Comstock lode collapsed, leading to a depression that lasted until the beginning of the twentieth century. Irrigation was one solution, providing arid areas with needed water that encouraged agriculture. The discovery of copper also helped. Unlike gold and silver that was extracted quickly from the earth, copper mining can take decades, providing communities with a long-term economic base. One of those communities is Ely, founded in 1868 as a silver-mining camp. It wasn't until the mines converted to copper mining that the town began to flourish, increasing its population from several hundred to 3,000. The stability of copper mining and the town's location near the Utah border attracted Mormon settlers, making it one of the rare areas in which Mormons and mining co-existed. Their commitment to the community is evident by the construction of **Ely Latter-day Saints Stake Tabernacle** dedicated in 1928.

Mining and agriculture continue to contribute to Nevada's economy, but their importance has been eclipsed by gambling, which was legalized in 1931. Nevada's contrasts are no more evident than in the glittering gambling centers like Reno and Las Vegas literally located next door to vast, uninhabited wilderness areas, peopled only by the ghosts of miners.

St. Peter's Episcopal Church

312 North Division Street, Carson City

ARCHITECT / BUILDER:
builder: Corbett Brothers

CONSTRUCTION / DEDICATION DATE:
1867, 1873

WOOD, THE PRIMARY BUILDING MATERIAL of St. Peter's Episcopal Church, coupled with its Gothic Revival style reveal the origins of its congregants. It also illustrates how quickly this style traveled westward in style books and the memories of settlers. Although the architect remains unknown, it is possible the congregants were familiar with Richard Upjohn's book on rural church architecture, or, like immigrants from abroad, depended on their memories of the churches they left behind.

An indication of how rapidly Carson City expanded can be seen by the need to enlarge the church six years after its completion. Of particular interest on the interior is its elaborate arcaded three-bay chancel screen supported by fluted Corinthian columns and the stained glass window in the gable above the gallery containing the figure of King David playing the harp.

The church is now used by the Episcopal Church for secular programs.

St. Peter's
Episcopal Church,
Carson City,
Nevada

St. Mary's in the Mountains Roman Catholic Church

Corner of Taylor and E Streets, Virginia City

ARCHITECT / BUILDER:
Not available

CONSTRUCTION / DEDICATION DATE:
1877

THIS LARGE BRICK GOTHIC REVIVAL CHURCH is the fourth structure erected by the parish. The former churches were all destroyed, the third may have been dynamited during the fire of 1875 that destroyed all the city's churches save one. When this building was constructed, it was lavishly decorated with balconies of rosewood and stained glass windows, including a rose window with trefoil tracery. It has since been stripped of much of its furnishings and decoration, not as a result of vandalism, but as a reflection of what happened when the Comstock Lode ran out and the city's population went from a high of 20,000 to the present 1,500.

Although bereft of its original decoration, St. Mary's remains open for services and is highlighted in the city's published walking tour.

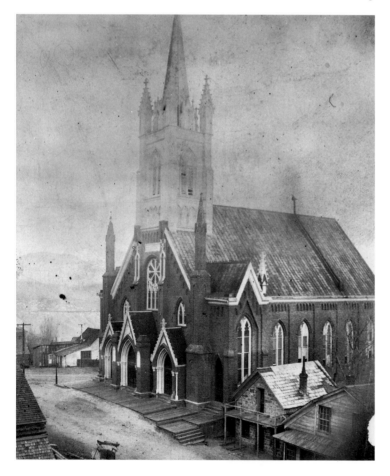

St. Mary's in the
Mountains Roman
Catholic Church,
Virginia City,
Nevada

Immaculate Conception Roman Catholic Church

590 Pyramid Way, Sparks

ARCHITECT:
Frederick Joseph DeLongchamps
CONSTRUCTION / DEDICATION DATE:
1932

THIS SMALL, ELEGANT, RED BRICK CHURCH is one of two buildings in Sparks that the prominent Nevada architect Frederick Joseph DeLongchamps designed in what is called the "Mediterranean Revival style," a style reminiscent of churches in Italy built during the eleventh and twelfth centuries. Here the effect is diminished somewhat by the addition of a vestibule and porch built to provide handicapped access that obscures the building's original façade. The church was built to replace an earlier one that was destroyed by fire in 1930.

Immaculate Conception is notable not only for its architecture but also for the fame of its architect, whose firm erected over 500 buildings in a variety of styles, and its distinction of being one of the first Catholic churches built in the state after Nevada was granted diocesan status by Pope Pius XI in 1931.

The church remains in use and other than the addition retains its architectural integrity.

Immaculate
Conception Roman
Catholic Church,
Sparks, Nevada

The First Church of Christ, Scientist

First Street 5 blocks east of Casino District, Reno

ARCHITECT / BUILDER:
Paul Revere Williams

CONSTRUCTION / DEDICATION DATE:
1938-1940

THE STUCCO AND WOOD CHURCH is an excellent example of the Classical Revival style adopted for many Christian Science churches. What distinguishes this structure is the reputation of its architect and the important role its members played in identifying social issues and promoting reform.

Paul Revere Williams (1894–1980), an African-American architect, was born in Los Angeles. He studied at the School of Art and the Beaux-Arts Institute of Design in Los Angeles and became a certified architect in 1915, one of the few blacks to achieve this distinction in the first decades of this century. Over the course of his career he designed over 500 buildings, including four in Reno. It is unclear why the members selected Williams, except it could be related to their support of minority groups coupled with Williams' fame as an architect. Although he enjoyed some recognition during his lifetime, his fame faded following his death and it is only recently that his work has begun to be recognized by historians and architects.

This building is no longer a church. Its owners are seeking an alternate use for it.

First Church of
Christ, Scientist,
Reno, Nevada

Ely Latter-day Saints Stake Tabernacle

900 Aultman Street, Ely

ARCHITECT / BUILDER:
Joseph Don Carlos Young, contractor
CONSTRUCTION / DEDICATION DATE:
1927-1928

MORMONS WERE IN NEVADA prior to the territorial period, although Ely's Mormon community didn't develop until the arrival of the railroad in 1906 and the opening of the copper mines. Ely, located in former Utah Territory, had its first organized branch of the Latter-day Saints (L.D.S.) in 1915; for two decades the Mormons met in temporary quarters until Ely was formally organized as a ward in 1926. Then efforts began to erect a stake tabernacle. The building, one of the few in the Colonial Revival style in the Great Basin, was opened in 1928; its contractor, Joseph Don Carlos Young, was the grandson of Brigham Young.

This tabernacle was replaced by a newer facility in 1957, and is now the Centennial Fine Arts Building, which is being restored as of this writing. The building retains its architectural integrity, remaining a symbol of its Mormon builders, who reestablished their roots in land that once was under the control of Utah.

Ely Latter-day Saints Stake Tabernacle (Centennial Fine Arts Center, White Pine Community Association), Ely, Nevada

10

Pacific Region

California
Oregon
Washington
Alaska
Hawaii

THIS REGION COMPRISES A TRIANGLE: California and Alaska anchor its corners, Hawaii is at the apex, and Washington and Oregon form part of its base; the rest is in British Columbia. This vast triangle encompasses many regions, but here they are compressed into one that receives its identity by a feature they share in common, the Pacific Ocean. A closer study, however, reveals two other characteristics shared by the five states–their relative isolation from the rest of the country and their great internal diversity as evidenced in geography and climate. Combined, these shared characteristics were to have an impact on their settlement patterns that, as will be seen, differ in important respects from those experienced in other regions of the country. Within the boundaries of this region is one of the nation's first frontiers and its last.

California is a case in point. As one of the first areas of the nation to be settled by Europeans, California initially developed at least three distinct cultural regions–Spanish and Mexican along much of the coastal area south of San Francisco; Russian north of that city; and beginning with the 1849 gold rush, a diverse migrant population rushing to the gold fields in the central area.

Washington and Oregon are often referred to as the Pacific Northwest, an area characterized in one geography book as being "strongly subject to maritime influence and rugged terrain."[1] The two states also share a similar settlement pattern in that they were generally ignored, except by fur trappers, until the mid-1840s when the promise of free land and the discovery of gold spurred thousands of pioneers to undertake the treacherous journey westward along the Oregon Trail. The completion of the Northern Pacific Railroad to Seattle in 1883, and the Great Northern ten years later, gave farmers and the lumber industry a much-needed link to eastern markets as well as providing a less hazardous journey westward for potential settlers.

Hawaii and Alaska, the nation's last frontier, for all their differences do share more than their proximity to the Pacific Ocean. As the last two states to join the Union, they are also the only ones that are not part of the contiguous United States. Contributing to their sense of isolation is the fact that except for a single highway that connects coastal southern Alaska with the United States, both states can only be reached by air or sea. They also share the distinction of having entered the Union mainly for their strategic military positions, as well as the usual economic and political ones. The Department of Defense remains Alaska's primary employer and Hawaii is the center of Pacific operations for all branches of the armed forces, who together employ 25 percent of the state's work force.

PRECEDING PAGE:

Holy Ghost Roman Catholic Church, Kula, Hawaii

California

FROM THE SEMI-NOMADIC TRIBES that once occupied the land and spoke at least ten different languages to the vast variety of ethnic and religious groups who began arriving in the eighteenth century, diversity has always characterized California. Explorers from Spain and Britain laid claim to this land in the sixteenth century, but it was essentially ignored for two centuries until Spain, hearing rumors of El Dorado, the mythical city of gold, and fearing Russian and British expansionism in the western hemisphere, began active colonization–its last effort at empire building.

Franciscan priests, accompanying Spanish expeditions, constructed a chain of 21 missions one day's march apart along the El Camino Real beginning in San Diego in 1769, and ending at San Francisco Solano in 1823. The missions were self-supporting entities that experienced some success with the Indians during their short existence. Secularized following the establishment of the Republic of Mexico in 1810, their land was to be given to Indians, but instead ended up in the hands of a few wealthy and powerful families who allowed the mission buildings to deteriorate. Early in this century the ruined buildings began to attract the attention of artists, tourists, and ultimately, preservationists, resulting in many being restored as popular tourist attractions, including **La Purísima Concepción**, founded in 1787.

Russian explorers sailing along the California coast were not seeking El Dorado, but rather sea otter and supplies for their Alaskan colonies. They built Fort Ross north of San Francisco in 1812 to protect their interests, but in 1841, when the fur trade collapsed, sold it to a Swiss immigrant, Captain John Sutter, who later achieved fame because of a discovery on his land. However, not all Russians left; some settled in a neighborhood of San Francisco known as Russian Hill, where they organized an Orthodox Parish in 1864 that was raised to the status of a cathedral in 1870. The parish's first church, destroyed in the 1906 earthquake, was replaced by Holy Trinity Cathedral, built in 1909. The cathedral's architect is unknown, but whoever drew its plans was obviously familiar with Chicago's Holy Trinity Cathedral designed in 1900 by Louis Sullivan (see p. 126).

California officially became part of the United States following the conclusion of the Mexican American War in 1848. It swiftly entered the Union two years later, because of an unexpected discovery that shaped its future. By the early 1840s, "foreigners" had begun to trickle into California. One, Captain John Sutter, not only purchased Fort Ross, but also received a 50,000-acre land grant along the Sacramento River from the Mexican government in 1839. He laid out the town of Sacramento, which later became the state's capital, and established a large agricultural empire. It was on Sutter's land, along the South Fork of the American River, that one of his workers, James Wilson Marshall, made a discovery in January 1848 that set the course for California's future. An attempt to keep his discovery secret failed, and soon the cry of gold circled the globe. People began flocking to California, each seeking a share of El Dorado. While religion may not have been their primary concern, it is surprising how quickly they sought out or established places of worship, as seen in the history of St. Francis of Assisi Church in San Francisco. From its founding in 1848, its priests have been offering sermons and hearing confession in the many languages of the miners–Spanish, French, Italian, German, and Chinese. The Gothic Revival church, dedicated in 1860, survived the 1906 earthquake, as did Old St. Mary's Cathedral, erected in 1854. Although it was gutted by fire and scheduled for demolition, an interfaith coalition was able to raise funds to pay for restoring St. Mary's. Damage caused by a second earthquake 90 years later has placed its future in doubt, but once again the greater community is coming to its rescue.

Places of worship built by newcomers often resemble those they left behind. The Anglos in Sonora who erected **St. James Episcopal Church** in 1859, the state's first Episcopal church, were obviously trying to replicate the buildings they left behind. So, too, were the Chinese miners who erected the **Won Lim Temple** in Weaversville in 1873. They made certain that its façade was painted to resemble the blue tiles and stone of traditional Chinese temples. The Jewish merchants in San Francisco who built Temple Emanu-El in 1864, destroyed in the 1906 earthquake, and its offspring, **Ohabai Shalome**, consecrated in 1895, consciously chose the Moorish style currently popular for synagogue architecture.

The gold rush lasted only a few years, boom towns blossomed and quickly faded, but San Francisco survived and prospered, becoming the largest and most cosmopolitan city on the West Coast until World War I. Its replacement was Los Angeles, *El Pueblo de Nuestra Señora de los Angeles*, the center of Catholic and Spanish California. What is less well known is that over 50 percent of the men who founded the colony of Los Angeles in 1781 were of African descent. Although essentially untouched by the gold rush, by the 1850s southern California was home to a mixed population of Hispanics and Anglos. Catholicism prevailed, as seen by the construction in 1876 of the **Cathedral of St. Vibiana**, in the center of the expanding village. Recently damaged by an earthquake, the fate of the oldest building in the designated historic core of Los Angeles remains uncertain.

Southern California wasn't really "discovered" until the transcontinental railroad to Los Angeles was completed in 1881. The railroad's promotion of cheap fares, the lure of sunshine, irrigation, and the promise of land, all were to contribute to transforming southern California into a mecca for those seeking to fulfill the American dream. In spite of the region's hedonistic reputation, it became one of the most "churched" areas of the nation, leading Christopher Rand to observe that "there are probably more religions in Los Angeles than in the whole previous history of mankind."[2] Catholicism now had competition. Exotic religious structures were erected, such as the First Hebrew Christian Church built in 1905 in Boyle Heights that has a large open scroll on its roof, and is described as a New Yorker's idea of architecture in Los Angeles. First Baptist Church in Ventura, north of Los Angeles, designed by Robert Stacy-Judd, is in a mixed Art Deco and Mayan style. Perhaps most interesting, however, is the impact that the restoration of the Spanish missions had on California architecture, resulting in the introduction of two new styles–the Mission Revival and the Spanish Colonial Revival. **St. Mary Magdalen Chapel** in Old Camarillo, dedicated in 1913, beautifully illustrates the span of California's religious architecture, stretching from the mission churches built in the eighteenth and early nineteenth centuries to mission style churches built in the twentieth century.

La Purísima Concepción

2295 Purisima Road, Purisima

ARCHITECT / BUILDER:
Soldiers and workmen from the presidio in Santa Barbara
CONSTRUCTION / DEDICATION DATE:
1815-1818

FOUNDED DECEMBER 8, 1787, by Fr. Fermin Lasuen, the mission's first buildings were hastily constructed in 1788 and replaced by more permanent adobe structures in 1802. Home to over 1,000 people, the mission flourished in the years following its rebuilding, only to be completely devastated by an earthquake and flood on December 21, 1812.

The padres, however, were not defeated. A safer site was selected four miles away and many of the new buildings were constructed with walls over four feet thick to resist future earthquakes. Unlike most missions that are built in the form of a quadrangle, La Purísima has a linear layout consisting of a cemetery and adjoining church, military quarters and workshops, and padres' quarters. But it was not natural causes that ultimately destroyed the missions—it was human events, particularly Mexico's declaration of independence in 1810, followed by Indian revolts and the secularization of the missions. In 1844, with few Indians remaining at the mission, it was sold to Don Juan Temple of Los Angeles. By the time the National Park Service took possession of the site in the 1930s, only fragments of its walls and a few pillars remained. After thoroughly researching the mission, plans were developed by the Park Service for its restoration. They were finally carried out in 1951, when the entire mission was rebuilt, the largest and most complete historic restoration in the West.

La Purísima
Concepción Mission,
Purisima, California

St. James Episcopal Church

Washington Street, Sonora

ARCHITECT / BUILDER:
Reverend John G. Gassman
CONSTRUCTION / DEDICATION DATE:
1859

SONORA, FOUNDED BY MEXICAN MINERS and named after their hometown, soon became one of the largest and wealthiest towns in the mother lode country. St. James was organized in 1857 by the town's "leading citizens," Anglo entrepreneurs, who originally met in a courthouse until a decision was made in the spring of 1859 to erect a church. The bishop in San Francisco sent Reverend John G. Gassman to take charge of its construction; he is listed as serving as the architect of the church. The building is a typical example of the popular Carpenter Gothic Revival style featuring vertical board-and-batten sheathing, here painted red, giving it its popular name, "the little red church."

St. James never had a large congregation, and over the years it saw its membership as well as the population of the town steadily decline as the gold played out. Sonora, and St. James, did survive and the town later became the seat of Tuolumne County and a market center. St. James, picturesquely situated at the head of Washington Street, is the oldest Episcopal church building in California.

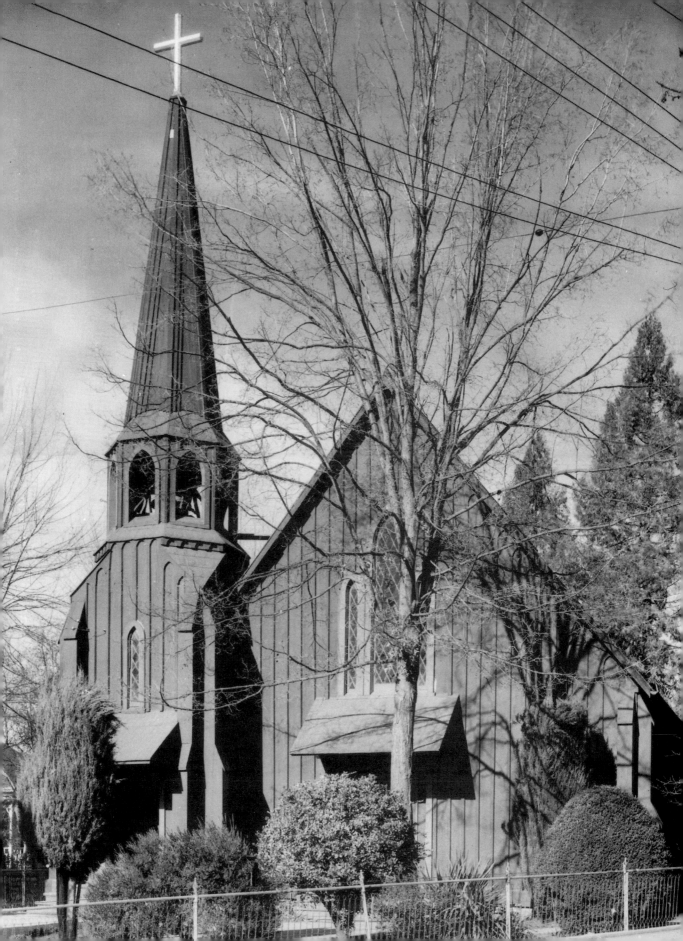

Won Lim Temple

(CHINESE JOSS HOUSE)

Oregon and Main Streets, Weaverville, Trinity County

ARCHITECT / BUILDER:
Not available
CONSTRUCTION / DEDICATION DATE:
1874

CHINESE IMMIGRANTS BEGAN TO ENTER the port city of San Francisco in 1850. Most were denied citizenship because of their color; thus they were unable to own land or file mining claims. Despite hostility and discrimination, Chinese immigrants did become miners, often reworking old claims or mining for others. Chinese miners arrived in Trinity County in 1850; by 1880, they numbered nearly 2,000 and had constructed three Taoist temples. The Won Lim Temple is the only one to survive. It is the second one built by its members; the first, built in 1852 or 1853, burned down in 1873 and was replaced the following year by the present building.

Located a distance from other Chinese communities, the Chinese in Weaverville chose to build a traditional temple reminiscent of those left behind in their homeland. Constructed of wood, the front of the building is painted to resemble the blue tiles and stone traditionally used for temples. Its roof ornaments, the most elaborate of any Chinese temple in California, include carvings of fish and dragons. Statues of the temple's two main gods, Bok Aie and Kuan Kung, are on the central section of the main altar. They, along with other statues of gods and goddesses housed in the temple and the door guardian, were made in Weaverville of local clay.

The temple, the oldest still in use in California, is now part of Joss House State Historic Park.

Won Lim Temple
(Chinese Joss House),
Weaverville,
California

Ohabai Shalome Synagogue

(BUSH STREET TEMPLE)

1881 Bush Street, San Francisco

ARCHITECT / BUILDER:
Moses J. Lyon
CONSTRUCTION / DEDICATION DATE:
1895

T HIS BUILDING EMBODIES an important part of San Francisco's history. By 1850, the city was home to two Jewish congregations; one founded by Poles and Englishmen, Shearith Israel, the other by Germans, Temple Emanu-El. Temple Emanu-El, erected in 1864, was one of the first synagogues in the nation to incorporate Moorish elements into its design. At the time of its construction, the congregation made a decision to affiliate with the liberal Reform movement, alienating members who preferred a more traditional ritual. The dissenters formed a new congregation, Ohabai Shalome, and in 1865 built a synagogue that remained in use until this building was consecrated in 1895.

The new synagogue is a romantic melange of historic styles—Venetian, Moorish, Romanesque, and Gothic. The architect's goal apparently was to design a building that was monumental and unique, but would not be mistaken for a church. Remarkably, all this was accomplished with milled and carved redwood, in places painted to resemble marble. The congregation used the building until 1934, when it was purchased by Japanese Zen followers and became the home of the Soto Mission. Occupied by a Christian group during World War II, it was returned to the Japanese, who continued to use it as a Zen Center until 1973, when it was purchased by the city's Redevelopment Agency. Aside from missing its towers, the synagogue is virtually intact. Funds are currently being raised to restore the building to its original appearance for use as a performing arts center.

Ohabai Shalome Synagogue (Bush Street Temple), San Francisco, California

Cathedral of St. Vibiana

Second and Main, Los Angeles

ARCHITECT / BUILDER:
Ezra Kyser
CONSTRUCTION / DEDICATION DATE:
1876

BUILT WHEN LOS ANGELES'S POPULATION was only 9,000, nearly half of whom were Roman Catholic, St. Vibiana, humbled but proud, is the oldest structure within the city's shabby historic district. Like its namesake, a young Italian woman martyred in the third century, this historic building appears to be on the verge of martyrdom, in the form of demolition by those who oppose its preservation.

Damaged by the 1994 earthquake, its west face obscured by a 1922 limestone addition, it is not easy for the viewer to appreciate St. Vibiana's simple but elegant beauty. The architect drew his inspiration from Barcelona's Church of San Miguel del Mar, a Spanish Baroque monument that was an appropriate model for a church built for a predominantly Hispanic parish. Changes made to the church do not detract from its historic integrity, but instead reflect its continuous use for over a century. Robert Venturi, a Pritzker-winning architect, in an eloquent letter sent to the Los Angeles city council, observed that landmarks like St. Vibiana's ". . . embody the beginnings, the oldest memories, the founding principles on which the city was formed."

Cathedral of
St. Vibiana,
Los Angeles,
California,
circa 1950

St. Mary Magdalen Chapel

Ventura Boulevard, Camarillo

ARCHITECT / BUILDER:
Albert C. Martin
CONSTRUCTION / DEDICATION DATE:
1914

P ERCHED ON A KNOLL OVERLOOKING Ventura Boulevard in Old Camarillo is a beautiful mission style church built by Juan Camarillo as a family chapel in memory of his parents. It is modeled after a church he had seen at his parents' birthplace in Mexico, as reinterpreted by Albert C. Martin, a Los Angeles architect who also designed the Ventura Courthouse.

No expense was spared on the chapel's construction. It has a family crypt under its southwest corner, a courtyard used as a gathering space with a fountain modeled after the one at the Santa Barbara Mission, and a wing on the east set aside as a family museum. The interior, decorated in oak and white marble, has 13 stained glass windows depicting the life of Christ. Created in Munich, Germany, prior to World War I, they remained in storage there until being shipped to Camarillo after the war.

The chapel was used by the Camarillo family for 25 years until it was given to the archdiocese of Los Angeles in 1940 for use as a parish church. When a larger church was built, the chapel was transformed into a parish center and school. It remains a prominent landmark in Camarillo, embodying the history of the community's founding family and illustrating the revival of interest in mission style architecture in the early twentieth century.

St. Mary Magdalen Chapel, Camarillo, California

Oregon

O REGON'S NAME IS FOREVER LINKED with the 2,000-mile trail wending westward from Independence, Missouri, to its fertile river valleys. Spurring the Great Migration of over 300,000 pioneers that began in 1843 and lasted three decades was the promise of free land and a fresh start. The territory, however, was not unknown to European and American explorers. A Spanish expedition sighted its southern coast in 1542 and the English explorer Sir Francis Drake sailed along its northwest coast in 1579. The English began establishing trading posts in the late eighteenth century, but the British fur monopoly was short-lived. American competition began soon after Meriwether Lewis and William Clark returned from their historic explorations and reported about the bountiful land they had seen. John Jacob Astor, the founder of the Pacific Fur Company, established a trading post named Astoria in his honor in 1811. It was located on the site of a campsite of Lewis and Clark that later became a destination for settlers and missionaries. The Gothic Revival Grace Episcopal Church, erected between 1885 and 1886, is the oldest church building in continuous use in Astoria and for years was the hub of a number of missions in the surrounding area.

Although Astor sold his company to the British during the War of 1812, this did not discourage other American fur traders and missionaries from entering the area. Soon they outnumbered the British and began demanding the right to establish a provisional government. Their rallying cry, "Fifty-four Forty or Fight" for the northern boundary of the United States was answered in 1846, when both sides compromised, accepting the 49th parallel as the border with Canada. Oregon had a territorial government in 1849, and a decade later entered the Union. Salem was named its capital.

Founding Salem in 1841 was the famed Methodist missionary Jason Lee who had established the first mission to the Indians in Oregon in 1834. Support for his efforts came from the New York–based Missionary Society of the Methodist Episcopal Church. After having only limited success proselytizing the scattered and decimated tribes left in the area, the Methodists began to turn their attention to encouraging immigration to Oregon and establishing a school in Salem that eventually became Willamette University. After organizing a congregation in 1841, a church was built in 1852 in the Classic Revival style familiar to its Yankee congregants. Replacing it is the **First Methodist Episcopal Church of Salem**, built between 1871 and 1878 in the popular Gothic Revival style. The church is an important landmark on the town square otherwise occupied by government buildings.

Right on the heels of the Methodist missionaries came the Roman Catholics who ministered to the needs of the early fur trappers and traders, primarily Roman Catholic French Canadians married to Indian women. When the fur trade went into a decline many of the

French Canadians and their families chose to remain in the territory, settling in an area known as "French Prairie," the first permanent farming community in Oregon. In 1836, they built a log church, hoping to attract a Catholic priest to serve their small community. A Jesuit missionary did arrive three years later, and in 1846 the parishioners built St. **Paul Roman Catholic Church**, the first brick church erected in Oregon and probably the oldest brick building standing in the state.

Many of the pioneers braving the Oregon Trail were Americans from eastern states, contributing to Oregon's predominantly Anglo population. This is evident in the names of many of its communities, including Portland, the state's largest city, named after Portland, Maine, the hometown of one of its two founders; this was an improvement over their initial choice, "Stumptown." The city's deep water harbor at the confluence of the Columbia and Willamette rivers made it a natural trading center, attracting many New Englanders who went on to become shipping magnates and bankers. One who arrived in 1851 donated land for the building of **Calvary Presbyterian Church**, whose cornerstone was laid in 1882. Designed by a prominent local architect, Warren H. Williams, it is one of the finest examples of wood frame Victorian Gothic architecture in the state.

Fourteen miles west of Portland stands a far more modest church that was also built by settlers arriving from the East. The congregation was established in 1844 by five pioneer families who had come to Oregon in the Great Migration of 1843 to homestead on free land. In 1853, with the help of new members, they built West Union Baptist Church, a simple frame building of hand-sawn lumber. It is the oldest Baptist church in Oregon and one of the state's earliest surviving examples of a rural pioneer church. Although no longer in use, it is being maintained by the Oregon Baptist Convention.

But not everyone settling in Oregon was American born. The **Greasewood Finnish Apostolic Lutheran Church**, a small Gothic Revival building, is in the center of the Greasewood Finnish American farming settlement area. Built between 1884 and 1887 by Finnish immigrants and Finnish Americans, this beautifully restored church continues to serve as a gathering place for descendants of the original settlers.

German-speaking homesteaders who began arriving in the latter part of the nineteenth century also built simple wood frame churches, many in the prevailing Gothic Revival style. One that continues to serve its community is Macksburg Lutheran Church, built between 1892 and 1894. The building's actual construction, however, was undertaken by Mennonite carpenters from the nearby community of Needy who volunteered their skills.

German Lutherans also began settling in Oregon's urban areas. They built a white clapboard Gothic Revival church in Portland in 1890 that after nearly 60 years was replaced by a new building, dedicated in 1950. **Zion Lutheran Church**, designed by Pietro Belluschi, is an outstanding example of his Northwest Regional style that uses simple vernacular forms and native materials.

Congregation Temple Beth Israel, organized in 1858, is the oldest Jewish congregation in the Pacific Northwest. The congregation's current building, completed in 1928, is a modern interpretation of the Byzantine style. At the time of its construction it was hailed in the local newspaper "as one of the most brilliant architectural accomplishments on the Pacific Coast and unique among synagogues of the country."

First Methodist Episcopal Church of Salem

(FIRST UNITED METHODIST)

600 State Street, Salem

ARCHITECT / BUILDER:
Cass Chapman, Chicago; W. F. Boothby, Salem
CONSTRUCTION / DEDICATION DATE:
1871-1878

BUILT ON THE SITE of the congregation's first church erected in 1852, the First Methodist Church of Salem is a large brick Gothic Revival building with a lofty wood belfry and spire, a dominant feature on Salem's town square otherwise occupied by county, state, and federal government buildings. The church was built between 1871 and 1878 from plans supplied by Chicago architect Cass Chapman and reduced in scale by one-eighth to lower the costs. Salem contractor and architect Wilbur F. Boothby was engaged in 1877 to prepare plans and supervise completion of the final stages of construction, including the belfry and spire. As the congregation grew, so did the church. Additions were made in 1935 and again in 1967, and while the chancel has been altered substantially, the auditorium remains spatially intact. Externally, the original appearance of the church has changed little since its completion in 1878.

First Methodist Church, with its historic relationship to the founding of Salem and of Methodism in Oregon, is the only church building in the city antedating 1880. This well-maintained structure is a relatively rare example of high style Gothic Revival church architecture in Oregon outside of Portland; its spire is one of the very few tall spires still standing in the state.

First United
Methodist
Church of Salem
(historic
illustration),
Salem, Oregon

St. Paul Roman Catholic Church

St. Paul, Marion County

ARCHITECT / BUILDER:
Elwood M. Burton, Portland: 1866 addition
CONSTRUCTION / DEDICATION DATE:
1846, 1866, 1898, 1995

S EVERELY DAMAGED IN AN EARTHQUAKE in 1993, St. Paul's, rebuilt in its original Gothic Revival style, was rededicated in 1995. It is the oldest brick church in the Northwest, and is the first structure visible upon entering St. Paul, a small farming community 25 miles southwest of Portland. Its bell tower crowned with spire and cross dominate the flat landscape and serve as the focal point of the town.

The community, founded by retired French Canadian fur trappers, built a log church in 1836 that served until the present building was begun in 1846. A four-sided brick sacristy was added to the northwest end in 1866, and in 1898 Portland architect Elwood M. Burton designed a brick vestibule and belfry to replace the original spire at the southeast end. Burton also oversaw the completion of the church's interior.

Following the earthquake, the entire structure was taken down brick by brick and restored, using the original bricks and concrete block reinforcements. The original clay bricks were manufactured on the site. Tradition holds that Indian women did most of the brick-making. The pit behind the church from which the clay had been excavated was still visible in the 1930s. The lumber came from a nearby sawmill launched in 1838, the first in Oregon that was independent of the Hudson's Bay Company.

Except for the two years St. Paul's was closed for rebuilding, no other congregation of any denomination in Oregon has been worshipping at the same site for a longer time.

**St. Paul Roman
Catholic Church,
St. Paul, Oregon**

Calvary Presbyterian Church

(THE OLD CHURCH)

1422 S.W. 11th Street, Portland

ARCHITECT / BUILDER:
Warren Heywood Williams
CONSTRUCTION / DEDICATION DATE:
1882-1883

D URING THE 1870s AND 1880s, as Portland prospered, a number of Gothic Revival churches of wood frame construction were built in the city. Calvary, also known as "The Old Church" and considered the most elaborate, is the sole survivor in this category, the oldest church standing on its original site in the city.

The congregation, consisting of many of Portland's most successful citizens, was formed in 1880, a time when the Presbyterian Church began to expand in the city. Among its members was William S. Ladd, a banker and entrepreneur who donated the land for the church. Warren Heywood Williams, the leading Portland architect of the day, contributed its design and supervised its construction. The cornerstone was laid in 1882 and the building was completed the following year.

Williams, born in New York City in 1844, immigrated to San Francisco with his father, an architect, in 1850. The great fire in Portland in 1872 drew Williams to the city, where he quickly established a reputation as a stylish designer. The most distinctive feature of Calvary, a board-and-batten building finished with Gothic details, is its louvered belfry tower and spire on the southwest corner that encloses the access into the church. A porte cochere is adjacent to the vestibule. The building remains in use and is considered one of the important examples of late nineteenth-century architecture in Oregon.

Calvary
Presbyterian Church
(The Old Church),
Portland, Oregon

Greasewood Finnish Apostolic Lutheran Church

Finn Road at Finland Cemetery Road, 5 miles west of Adams

ARCHITECT / BUILDER:
Not available

CONSTRUCTION / DEDICATION DATE:
1884-1887

FINNISH IMMIGRANTS, including many landless and impoverished peasants, came to America to take advantage of the land available for homesteading in the undeveloped American frontier. Some chose instead to labor in the copper mines in Michigan and the iron mines opening in Minnesota. Those who wanted to farm began arriving in Umatilla County, Oregon, in 1877 at the beginning of a land rush that developed the dry-land wheat industry for which the county is now famous. They wrote to their friends and families in Minnesota and Michigan, urging them to give up the difficult and dangerous labor in the mines and join them in Oregon. Many accepted, and by 1884 there were enough to construct this simple one-room, wood frame church with simple Gothic detailing. The building remains essentially unchanged except for the addition in 1910 of a cloakroom and entry vestibule on the east.

Commanding a 360-degree view of rolling wheat fields and the Blue Mountains, its siting makes it visible and accessible from all directions, and is indicative of the importance of the church in community life. Its simplicity reflects the beliefs of its founders, members of the Apostolic branch of the Lutheran Church known as Laestadians, after a Scandinavian Lutheran revivalist named Laestadius.

The church was closed in 1965, but was carefully restored in 1985-1986 by descendants of its builders and is in excellent condition.

**Greasewood
Finnish Apostolic
Lutheran Church,
Adams, Oregon**

Congregation Temple Beth Israel

1931 N.W. Flanders, Portland

ARCHITECT / BUILDER:
Morris H. Whitehouse, Bennes and Herzog, and Herman Brookman
CONSTRUCTION / DEDICATION DATE:
1926-1928

I N 1858, THE APPROXIMATELY 30 Jewish families living in Portland organized Congregation Beth Israel. They built their first synagogue, a frame Gothic building, in 1861. It was replaced in 1887 by a larger, more elaborate Moorish/Gothic structure that served the congregation until it was destroyed by fire in 1923. For five years the congregants worshipped in the Beth Israel school, constructed in 1923 next to the destroyed synagogue, until their new building was completed in 1928.

The Portland firms of Whitehouse and Associates, Bennes and Herzog, and Herman Brookman were associated in the design of the new building. Most of the principals were trained in the East. Morris Whitehouse was trained at the Massachusetts Institute of Technology and Herman Brookman was an apprentice to Harry T. Lindeberg, the designer of many estates for wealthy Long Islanders.

Designed in a modern version of the Byzantine style, the octagonal, domed synagogue is built of reinforced concrete with a facing of stone, brick, and terra-cotta. The interior has a spacious central octagonal auditorium and gallery covered by the dome; its focus is the *bimah* (platform) and the cast bronze doors of the Ark.

The synagogue is well preserved and distinguished by its scale and crafts details. It is one of Portland's outstanding architectural achievements.

Congregation
Temple Beth Israel
Synagogue,
Portland, Oregon

Washington

STATE BOUNDARIES ARE OFTEN ARBITRARY, having little relationship with those of nature. This is clearly demonstrated when one looks at a map of the State of Washington where the towering crests of the Cascade Mountains neatly divide the state into two regions, each with its own distinct topography, climate, and economy.

Washington's face toward the Pacific Ocean consists of forested and snow-capped mountains, fertile valleys, and a dramatic coastline dominated by Puget Sound and peppered with hundreds of islands. The region's mild coastal climate and abundant rainfall support rain forests thick with trees and vegetation. The Cascades form a natural barrier separating western Washington from the far different area immediately east of the mountains known as the Columbia Plateau, named for the Columbia River that creates a vast arc known as the Big Bend. This region, which consists of semi-arid rolling hills bisected by dry canyons, was transformed into productive farmland by the introduction of irrigation in the 1950s. The Oregon-Washington border area and much of eastern Washington are known as the Inland Empire, a rich irrigated farming area.

While cities in the East were rapidly expanding in the nineteenth century, this land remained pristine, visited only by intrepid explorers, fur traders, and the ubiquitous missionaries who followed in their footsteps. As early as the mid-sixteenth century Spanish and English explorers sailing along its coast claimed the land for their nations, but neither explored it further. It was the dream of the elusive Northwest Passage that propelled a second round of exploration, resulting in the discovery of the mouth of the Columbia River in 1778 by the American explorer Robert Gray, who claimed the land for the United States. Spain withdrew its claim, leaving the United States and Britain to battle for possession. Meanwhile, fur trappers and traders plied their trade with the Indians, missionaries sought to save their souls, and Lewis and Clark made it to the West Coast. Americans who followed in Lewis and Clark's footsteps established a provisional government in 1843 and, joining in with their countrymen in Oregon, began to agitate for the region to be annexed to the United States. In 1846, the United States-Canada border was set at the 49th parallel, and the Oregon Territory was created, a large expanse of land that was divided in 1853 to create the Washington Territory that included part of Idaho and Montana.

In 1857, the Roman Catholic Mission at Tulalip in the Puget Sound region was founded. A church erected ten years later was destroyed by fire in 1902 and the mission site was temporarily abandoned, until St. Anne's Roman Catholic Church was constructed in 1904 on a wooded hillside overlooking Tulalip Bay. The white frame Gothic Revival building is the last remaining symbol of Catholic missionary work among the Indians at this location. It continues to serve the Indian population of Tulalip Reservation which numbers about 500.

As white settlers began to arrive and push the poorly organized Indian people off their traditional lands, the missionaries' focus shifted to the needs of the newcomers. One of the first congregations organized in Washington, and the oldest Protestant church to survive in the state, is at Claquato in western Washington, a way-station for all overland travel from the Columbia River to the little port settlements of Olympia and Steilacoom. **Claquato Church**, built in 1858 for a Methodist congregation, has been restored as a memorial to the pioneers of Lewis County.

Port Gamble was one of the earliest and most important lumber-producing centers in the Puget Sound region. The area's great forests attracted New Englanders, including a group from Maine who established a lumber mill in Port Gamble that by the 1870s evolved into a multi-million-dollar industry. The homes and churches they built transformed this remote outpost into a New England town. A Congregational church built in 1870 was modeled after the First Congregational Church of East Machias, Maine, home of the town's founders. Now known as **St. Paul's Episcopal Church**, the building survives as a symbol of the importance people attach to recreating a known world in a wilderness environment.

Until the opening of the Oregon Trail in the 1840s, the only practical way to get to the Pacific Northwest was by sailing around Cape Horn. The trail, while equally treacherous, nevertheless became the passageway of choice for over 300,000 pioneers. Indian battles and the Civil War slowed down migration, but following the cessation of hostilities, the rush began. This was also a time of religious revival throughout the United States that even had an impact on Indian people in the Pacific Northwest. The Indian Shaker sect, peculiar to this region, is unrelated to the Protestant one of the same name founded in 1774 by Mother Ann Lee. The Indian sect was founded by John Slocum, a Squaxin Indian, following his seemingly miraculous resurrection in 1881. The **Indian Shaker Church** built in 1924 on the Tulalip Reservation is one of the last to be built on Puget Sound in conformance with sect tradition.

Settlement of Seattle began in 1851; four years later an Episcopal parish was established. Services were held in a small frame Methodist church until the congregation was able to erect its own building in 1876. Demolished in the catastrophic fire that destroyed much of Seattle in 1889, it was replaced by **Trinity Parish Episcopal Church**, designed in an English country parish Gothic Revival style by an English architect, John Graham, Sr., who had recently moved to Seattle.

Contributing to Seattle's renewal and growth following the devastating fire was the arrival of the transcontinental railroads in 1883 and 1893. The railroads, anxious to see the territory occupied, provided settlers with inexpensive transportation. The 1897 Klondike gold rush in the Yukon also helped, transforming the city into a supply depot for prospectors and miners. Prosperity and the increase in population contributed to Washington being admitted to the Union in 1899. Olympia, the site of the first United States Custom House in the Northwest, was named its capital.

Jobs in the expanding lumber industry attracted large numbers of Scandinavians, including Swedish Baptists who had migrated west from Minnesota and built Preston Baptist Church in King County in 1902. Norwegian Lutherans settling in the town of Utsalady on Camano Island found work in the sawmill and built Camano Lutheran Church in 1904.

Spokane, established in 1810 as a trading post for the Northwest Fur Company, began expanding in 1872 as its nearby falls began supplying power for grain and lumber mills. Like Seattle, much of Spokane was destroyed by a devastating fire in 1879. Following the fire, members of the **First (Westminster) Congregational Church** opted to replace their frame structure with a massive brick Richardsonian Romanesque structure that is Spokane's oldest standing church.

Claquato Church

3 miles west of Chehalis on Hwy. 6, Claquato

ARCHITECT / BUILDER:
Lewis H. Davis, builder
CONSTRUCTION/DEDICATION DATE:
1858

THE CHURCH AND VILLAGE are the result of the foresight and fortitude of one man, Lewis H. Davis. In 1853, he filed for a donation claim of 640 forested acres where he then built a sawmill. He donated the first lumber from the mill for the building of a community church that was also to serve as a school. Dedicated by the Methodists, the church was constructed entirely through volunteer effort. Davis's brother-in-law made the doors and casings; a village blacksmith forged the nails; and other settlers donated their labor. Pews, pulpit, and a pastor's chair were donated by pioneers in a nearby town. The bronze bell, purchased by public subscription, was cast in Boston and shipped around the Horn to Washington. All the original fixtures remain intact, save for

the pastor's chair. The simple frame Classical Revival church has a belfry consisting of a square capped with an octagon decorated with "spikes" symbolizing a crown of thorns.

Davis raised funds to improve roads, enabling the town to become an important way-station for all overland travel from the Columbia River to the ports of Olympia and Steilacoom. The railroad, however, chose to go through Chehalis, three miles to the east, causing Claquato to go into decline. The church closed, but was restored in 1953 by Chehalis Post Number 22, of the American Legion, with financial help from the county. It is the oldest extant Protestant church in Washington.

**Claquato Church,
Claquato,
Washington**

St. Paul's Episcopal Church

Northwest end of Kitsap Peninsula near entrance to Hood Canal, Puget Sound, Port Gamble

ARCHITECT / BUILDER:
Modeled after First Congregational Church, East Machias, Maine
CONSTRUCTION/DEDICATION DATE:
1870

PORT GAMBLE, ONE OF THE EARLIEST and most important lumber-producing centers of the Puget Sound region, is the finest surviving example of that region's many nineteenth-century lumber towns. It was founded by Captain William C. Talbot of East Mathias, Maine, who arrived in Puget Sound in 1853 aboard the schooner Julius Pringle, searching for a sawmill site. Leaving a crew to build a mill, he returned to San Francisco to pick up his partners, including Andrew J. Pope, who had joined the gold rush in 1849. By 1875, the company was the largest holder of timberlands in the Territory of Washington, producing 99 million feet of lumber annually.

The church is modeled after the First Congregational Church of East Machias, Maine, the home of the Pope and Talbot families. Even its divided and numbered pews are copied from the church in Maine. Now known as St. Paul's Episcopal Church, it is considered the most outstanding of Washington State's earliest churches. It is being maintained by the Pope and Talbot Company.

St. Paul's
Episcopal Church,
Port Gamble,
Washington

Indian Shaker Church

North Meridian Avenue, west of Marysville

ARCHITECT / BUILDER:
Church members

CONSTRUCTION/DEDICATION DATE:
1924

THE INDIAN SHAKER CHURCH on Tulalip Reservation is one of the last buildings to be constructed on Puget Sound in general conformity with sect doctrine. It is among the best preserved examples of Indian Shaker architecture, a tradition peculiar to the Pacific Northwest. The rectangular frame structure is unpainted in conformity with tradition, but its style, particularly its belfry, appears to be based on that of St. Anne's Roman Catholic Church on Tulalip Bay, except the belfry is on the west end, as opposed to the east.

The Shaker sect, a Messianic and healing sect, was founded in 1881 by John Slocum, a member of Squaxin band who lived on a homestead near Olympia. Believing he had been resurrected and instructed by God to lead sinners into a Christian way of life, he carried his mission to Indians throughout the region. Leadership later shifted to a figure known as Mud Bay Louis, who erected the sect's first church at Mud Bay. Despite legal sanctions and years of suppression and persecution by the state, the sect's followers finally were granted a charter in 1891 and became a regularly constituted church body free to practice their religion openly. The sect was introduced to the Indians of Tulalip Reservation around 1896. Opposition by the Roman Catholic Mission of St. Anne and the Indian Agency resulted in the sect's slow growth and the late date of this church built on the reservation. The church requires maintenance, but is still used on occasion for services.

Indian Shaker Church, Marysville, Washington

Trinity Parish Episcopal Church

609 Eighth Avenue, Seattle

ARCHITECT / BUILDER:
1891: Henry Starbuck; 1903: John Graham, Sr.
CONSTRUCTION / DEDICATION DATE:
1891; 1903

BUILT IN 1891 AND REBUILT AND ENLARGED following a fire in 1902, Trinity Parish Church is the mother church of Seattle's Episcopal parishes and missions. Tracing its history back to the first recorded Episcopal service held in Seattle in 1855, a parish was formally organized in 1865, and a church built in 1870. The church was used until 1889 when it was destroyed in the Seattle fire of that year. In 1891, a new church, designed by Henry Starbuck of Chicago, was built in the English Gothic Revival style, except its tower and spire were never completed. In 1902, a fire of undetermined origin badly damaged the church, destroying its interior. An architect, John Graham, Sr., was immediately hired to redesign a larger church. Graham, one of Seattle's most prolific and talented architects, was born in Liverpool, England, and came to Seattle at the turn of the century. In redesigning the church, he retained its Gothic Revival style and much of the exterior stone walls, but increased the dimensions of the transepts, squared off the sanctuary, and added the tower and spire omitted from the original. With new stained glass windows made in Germany and an altar made of Italian marble, the "new" church is one of the most beautiful in Seattle, having been designated a Seattle landmark in 1976.

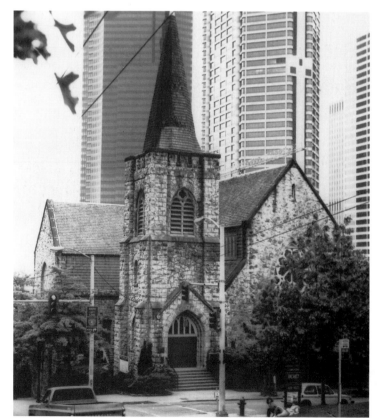

Trinity Parish Episcopal Church, Seattle, Washington

Westminster Congregational Church, First Congregational Church

401-411 South Washington, Spokane

ARCHITECT / BUILDER:
Worthy Niver and John K. Dow
CONSTRUCTION/DEDICATION DATE:
1890

T
HE FIRST CONGREGATIONALISTS arrived in the area of Spokane in 1838, establishing mission churches to the Indians. The area's first permanent congregation was founded in 1879 by Reverend Henry T. Cowley, a missionary from Seneca Falls, New York. A small frame church built in 1870 may have survived the fire that destroyed much of Spokane. In 1889, land was purchased for a new church and local architects, Niver and Dow, were hired to design it. Their plans reveal their familiarity with the latest in church design. The church's Richardsonian Romanesque styling would suggest they had access to the *Congregational Book of Plans for Churches and Parsonages* published in 1853 that advocates the use of the Romanesque style. They also may have seen plans or drawings of Richardson's trend-setting Trinity Church in Boston, begun in 1877 (see p. 20). The interior of the church originally had an Akron Plan that advocates placing the pulpit in the southwest corner with the pews arranged in a semicircle around the sanctuary (see p. 109). However, that was changed in 1909 when the pulpit was moved to the center of the south wall. The financial panic of 1893 forced the congregation to merge with Westminster Presbyterian, explaining the origin of its present name.

The building has undergone modifications and additions, but its historic importance to the city of Spokane has not diminished. It remains, as it is known, the "first church of Spokane."

First (Westminster)
Congregational Church,
Spokane, Washington

Alaska

A LASKA, TWO AND A HALF TIMES the size of Texas, was purchased from Russia in 1867 at the bargain basement price of $7.2 million, or less than two cents an acre. Not everyone cheered the purchase, and it soon became known as "Seward's Folly," immortalizing Secretary of State William H. Seward who negotiated the sale. It is unclear why the United States was determined to purchase what many considered a "barren, worthless Godforsaken region." Some historians argue that the United States was seeking to expand its control of the continent; others have suggested that a rumor that Brigham Young's Mormons were considering moving into the territory unnerved many members of Congress. Or, perhaps, Seward was simply prescient, recognizing the strategic importance of the region and its potential mineral riches. Whatever the motives, Alaska quickly proved to be neither worthless nor Godforsaken.

For thousands of years before the first Russian explorers arrived in 1741, Alaska was occupied by at least four native groups, each with a distinct culture and each living off the land's bounty. Russia was not interested in acquiring Alaska to expand its empire or to save the souls of its "heathen" people, but rather to acquire its bounty of otter and seal fur. The Russian-American Company was chartered in 1799 by the tzar for that sole purpose, and over the next 60 years Russian settlements were established along the territory's coasts.

Although unwelcomed by fur trappers and traders, missionaries, sponsored by the Russian Orthodox Church, began arriving in the 1790s settling first in the town of Kodiak on the Kodiak Archipelago, where they erected the first Russian Orthodox church in America in 1794. While that church no longer exists, **Saints Sergius and Herman of Valaam Russian Orthodox Chapel** on Spruce Island, built in 1895, honors Father Herman, the first American saint of the Russian Orthodox church.

There were never more than 800 Russians in Alaska, but the impact of Russian orthodoxy and its distinct form of religious architecture is still visible in the state's numerous Russian Orthodox churches, all dating to the period following the U.S. acquisition of the territory. All share similar plans—a longitudinal axis running from west to east beginning with a vestibule, and followed by a nave and iconostasis enclosing the altar that is set in the sanctuary. Variations were allowed in the shapes of the nave and sanctuary, as seen in the rare cruciform plan of Saint Michael the Archangel Cathedral in Sitka, built originally in 1848 and reconstructed in its original form in 1966 following a fire.

For years the U.S. government virtually ignored Alaska, but missionaries continued to see it as a territory ripe for evangelizing. One of the first Protestant missions was established in 1877 at a site where American troops were stationed; it was also the site of a Tlingit Indian village: Fort Wrangell on Wrangell Island. The Presbyterian missionaries were less interested in the souls of the soldiers than imposing American religion and values on the natives. They organized a missionary church in 1879 for the conversion of the Tlingit and a second Presbyterian church for the unruly American soldiers and miners. Reverend Harry P. Corser arrived in 1899 to minister to both churches, but found the Tlingit dissatisfied with the Presbyterian church's discriminatory policies. Deciding that the solution lay in integrating both congregations, Corser founded a new congregation, naming it People's Church, reflecting its openness to all people, and built a new building that later became **St. Philip's Episcopal Church**. Corser was ordained an Episcopal priest in 1907.

Gold finally put Alaska on the map; the first discovery was in Juneau in 1880, followed in 1896 by the major gold strike in the Klondike. Thousands of fortune seekers began to pour into Skagway, the closest port, and with them came even more missionaries to tame the wild miners as well as evangelize the native people. Episcopal missionaries were already active along the Yukon River prior to the discovery of gold, ministering to Indians, and encouraging them to build new settlements near the missions. Most mission buildings, including churches, were modest, but occasionally one finds exceptions, such as **Saint Peter's-by-the-Sea Episcopal Church**, built in 1899 in Sitka, which was the seat of Alaska's first Episcopal bishop, Peter Trimble Rowe. Bishop Rowe was responsible for raising funds to build the church and also did much of the stone work himself.

Gold was also discovered in the creeks and beaches near Nome in 1898. Anarchy reigned as over 25,000 people crowded into temporary housing that was gradually replaced by modest wood-framed structures. Few buildings survive from the gold-rush era, but one, **Saint Joseph's Roman Catholic Church**, built in 1901 and transformed into a warehouse in 1946, has been moved from its original site and is in the process of being preserved.

Alaska's population continued to increase with the passage of the 1903 homestead act opening government land to would-be farmers, followed by the establishment of the Territory of Alaska in 1912. The territory made its first bid for admittance into the Union in 1916, but it was denied due to the decline in gold deposits and a dramatic concomitant drop in its population. For example, Nome went from a population of over 12,000 in 1900 to 852 in 1920! The situation had an equally dramatic reversal with the onset of World War II and the Japanese occupation of the Aleutian Islands, which motivated the military to construct the 1,500-mile Alaskan Highway linking the territory with the Lower 48. The highway, the advent of commercial airlines, and jobs related to the military precipitated a second population boom, this time resulting in Alaska's admission into the Union as the 49th state in 1959, with Juneau named its capital. Half of the state's population resides in Anchorage, because of the military and the discovery of oil. Although Catholic and Protestant churches have been built there, the continuing vitality of the Russian Orthodox Church is visible right outside of Anchorage in Eklutna Village Historical Park, home to two Russian Orthodox churches. One, **Saint Nicholas Russian Orthodox Church**, was built in 1897 and restored in 1976-1977. The other, New Saint Nicholas Church, was built between 1954 and 1962 by Mike Alex, a Tanaina Indian chief, and his sons.

Saints Sergius and Herman of Valaam Russian Orthodox Chapel

Monk's Lagoon, Spruce Island

ARCHITECT / BUILDER:
Repaired by Father Gerasim

CONSTRUCTION / DEDICATION DATE:
1895-1896; repaired in 1930s

S
PRUCE ISLAND IS LOCATED ten miles north of the town of Kodiak; it can only be reached by sea or air. The small frame chapel, set in the woods about half a mile from the water, was built to commemorate the one hundredth anniversary of the introduction of Russian orthodoxy to America and was named after Father Herman, a member of the first Russian Orthodox Mission to Alaska, and its last survivor. Father Herman opened an orphanage for natives and Creoles (half Russian and half Native) on Spruce Island and began to permanently reside there sometime after 1808. Following his death in 1836, he, along with a disciple, were buried on the island. The chapel was erected between their two graves.

The chapel is now identified with Father Herman, who in 1970, thanks in great part to the efforts of Father Gerasim who repaired the chapel, became the first American saint of the Russian Orthodox Church. Father Herman's remains have since been moved to Kodiak; the chapel remains in use for special services several times a year.

Saints Sergius
and Herman of
Valaam Russian
Orthodox Chapel,
Spruce Island,
Alaska

St. Philip's Episcopal Church

446 Church Street, Wrangell

ARCHITECT / BUILDER:
Oscar Carlson, H. D. Campbell, builders
CONSTRUCTION / DEDICATION DATE:
1903

THE CHURCH, CONSTRUCTED ON DONATED LAND with donated labor and materials, stands on the crest of a hill east of downtown Wrangell. Initially built as the Peoples' Church, it was an attempt by Reverend Harry P. Corser to integrate two Presbyterian congregations–one that ministered to the Tlingit and the other organized for "Americans." Corser, increasingly dissatisfied with the Presbyterians' treatment of native people, ultimately was ordained an Episcopal priest and the Peoples' Church became St. Philip's Episcopal Church.

The church has a "T"-shaped floor plan with the cross of the "T" in the front and the nave extending from it; its gable roof is crowned with a bell tower. A double outside stairway was added in 1934. The building has undergone some modifications, both on the interior and exterior, including moving a stairway and the addition of three arched stained glass windows to the rear gable, including the central one dedicated to Reverend Corser.

Changes on the interior are mainly cosmetic; the marble altar of locally quarried stone, sanctuary furniture and rails built of local yellow cedar, and arched apse all remain unchanged.

St. Philip's
Episcopal Church,
Wrangell, Alaska

Saint Peter's-by-the-Sea Episcopal Church

611 Lincoln Street, Sitka

ARCHITECT / BUILDER:
H. L. Duhring, Jr.
CONSTRUCTION / DEDICATION DATE:
1899

ALTHOUGH SITKA IS THE CENTER of Russian orthodoxy in Alaska, and the site of Saint Michael the Archangel Russian Orthodox Cathedral, this did not discourage Protestant missionaries from trying to gain inroads among the natives. One of the missionaries, Sheldon Jackson, was successful in gaining government support for his efforts, including the college that bears his name, Sheldon Jackson College, founded as the Sitka Mission in 1878, the oldest educational institution in the state.

The Episcopalians' success is evident in the decision made by the newly named Episcopal bishop of Alaska, Peter Trimble Rowe, in 1899 to build a church and rectory in the heart of Russian Orthodox country. A portion of the building funds for St. Peter's-by-the-Sea was donated by an affluent couple from Utica, New York, who had visited Sitka in the summer of 1897. The rest was raised by a committee composed entirely of women. A Philadelphia architect, H. L. Duhring, Jr., was hired to draw plans based on Bishop Rowe's conception of what the church should look like; John W. Dudley, Recorder for the General Land Office in Sitka, supervised construction. The church, while small in size, is unique in appearance; it is one of the few stone buildings in Alaska. Displaying features that indicate the bishop's and architect's familiarity with the Richardsonian Romanesque style, such as the rose window set in a large pointed arch framed by the front gable, the building with its heavy timbering, random rubble stone, and wood shingling is typical of many small churches built in the United States at this time. The interior retains its original wooden pews; a reredos, added in 1932, was designed by Lester Troast, a Juneau architect.

St. Peter's-by-the-Sea Episcopal Church, Sitka, Alaska

Saint Joseph's Roman Catholic Church

Hammon Consolidated power plant complex, Nome

ARCHITECT / BUILDER:
J. B. Randall, Seattle architect
CONSTRUCTION / DEDICATION DATE:
1901

MOVED FROM ITS ORIGINAL SITE in 1946 and transformed into a warehouse, St. Joseph's Roman Catholic Church, after three years on Alaska's most endangered structures list, is in the process of being restored as a visitor center. Originally located at Steadman and King's Place, the building was erected in 1901 when the Alaska gold rush created the town of Nome. The rectangular wood-framed church, with a lower, gable-roofed sanctuary, had an 88-foot steeple that supported a large, electrically lit cross that served as an important navigational landmark on the Alaskan plateau. The steeple, along with the sanctuary, were removed and warehouse type doors installed when the building was transformed into a warehouse.

Although mining continues to be important to Nome's economy, the end of the gold rush witnessed a decline in the city's population. In 1993, the National Trust awarded Nome a Preservation Services Fund grant to help prepare a feasibility study that recommended future uses for the church. As a result of that study, funding was obtained for its restoration as a visitor center. The building has been moved again and placed on a permanent foundation. Its restoration includes the addition of a new steeple similar to its original one.

St. Joseph's Roman Catholic Church, Nome, Alaska (prior to conversion to a warehouse)

Saint Nicholas Russian Orthodox Church

Eklutna Village Historical Park, Greater Anchorage

ARCHITECT / BUILDER:
Not available

CONSTRUCTION / DEDICATION DATE:
1897; restored in 1976-1977

EKLUTNA, 25 MILES NORTHEAST OF ANCHORAGE, is the site of a village established by a group of Tanaina Indians who moved here from Knik in 1897. The small, hewn-log church with a gable roof, is one of only a few nineteenth-century Russian Orthodox churches remaining in Alaska. Two-thirds of its simple interior is devoted to the nave, which is separated from the sanctuary by a large floor-to-ceiling iconostasis decorated with beautiful moldings and supporting several oil on canvas icons.

Prior to the restoration of the old church in 1976–1977, Chief Mike Alex and his sons began construction in 1954 on a new Saint Nicholas Church to the south of the old one, completing it in 1962. The church resembles the 1897 structure in general form, but is a frame structure. Some of its icons came from the abandoned Aleutian village of Unga. An example of the willingness of the Russian Orthodox to incorporate native traditions can be seen in the nearby cemetery, where a synthesis of beliefs resulted in a unique burial custom–the use of brightly painted spirit houses. The Tanaina traditionally cremated their dead and placed the ashes in a spirit house; the Orthodox encouraged inhumation. The compromise is that the dead are now buried and the grave covered with a blanket. After 40 days a small gable-roofed spirit house, each unique in its decoration, is erected above the grave. Fences around the grave, crosses placed at the foot of the grave, and the graves facing east are all part of the Russian Orthodox tradition.

St. Nicholas Russian
Orthodox Church,
Eklutna Village,
Alaska

Hawaii

S UGAR, PINEAPPLE, AND SWAYING GRASS SKIRTS are what most Americans knew of the Hawaiian Islands before the horrifying events of December 7, 1941, awakened them to the Islands' strategic importance. In the course of World War II, over 400,000 American service personnel were stationed on the Islands, their presence accounting for the fourth time in the Islands' known history that outsiders changed the course of their culture and economy.

The first outsiders possibly came over 1,000 years ago from the Marquesas Islands 2,500 miles to the southwest. The Islands may have had a few inhabitants, but they were soon overwhelmed by the newcomers and by the Polynesians who followed them several hundred years later. Centuries of isolation allowed the Polynesians to develop a distinct social and religious system. Each island was ruled by a hereditary chief whose powerful priests controlled a polytheistic religion practiced at fixed places of worship and based on a series of elaborate taboos. Living in relative peace and in harmony with nature, the Islands' population grew to 300,000 by the late eighteenth century, the period that witnessed its second invasion by outsiders, led by Captain James Cook whose landing on the island of Kauai on January 20, 1778, forever changed the Islands' destiny.

Cook was initially welcomed by the Islanders as a "god," but a dispute over nails resulted in his death at their hands in 1779. This tragic event did little to diminish the excitement over the discovery of the Islands' strategic location as a mid-Pacific way-station for the growing American-Asian trade. The Islands were also in a state of change as they were in the process of being unified under the powerful rule of King Kamehameha I, who welcomed the commercial opportunities offered by whaling ships and other vessels. Many whalers were New Englanders who, after exhausting the Atlantic Ocean, were now turning their attention to the riches of the Pacific Ocean. At times they would hire Hawaiians familiar with the Pacific Ocean to be seamen on their ships. Some of the Hawaiians would return with the New Englanders to their Atlantic harbors. One was a Hawaiian sailor who was converted to Christianity at Yale College and managed to convince Congregational missionaries there that the Islanders were in need of salvation. The timing could not have been better. When the Reverend Hiram Bingham arrived from Boston in 1820, the islands were in turmoil following the death of King Kamehameha. His son, Liholiho, exposed to western culture, had abolished the taboo system, thereby lessening the power of the priests and subsequently the native religion. This prepared the way for the missionaries, who found the Islands a "fruitful field" where they could successfully sow the seeds of Christianity.[3]

The first missionaries landing at Kaulua on the island of Hawaii immediately set about constructing churches, simple utilitarian buildings similar to the meetinghouse at **Waioli** on the island of Kauai, initially built in 1832, and subsequently destroyed and rebuilt several times. Fire and hurricanes destroyed many of the early churches, but undaunted, the missionaries and their followers would immediately build new ones. Many were erected during the 1830s when Hawaii was experiencing its own great awakening. With the increase in converts, the missionaries were now able to build "real" churches, that is, ones similar to those they left behind. Thus, scattered throughout the Hawaiian Islands, in various stages of ruin and repair, are numerous vernacular interpretations of New England meetinghouses. Perhaps the largest and best known is **Kawaiahao Church (First Church)** on Oahu, completed in 1842, the congregation's fifth structure.

French Roman Catholics also sent missionaries to the Islands, but their first attempt to establish a mission in 1831 was successfully rebuffed by Protestants. They had better luck in 1839, when they forcibly convinced King Kamehameha III to declare religious tolerance in the Islands, preparing the way for later immigrants, primarily Catholic Europeans, who began arriving in the late nineteenth century. The Islands' first Catholic church, Our Lady of Peace Cathedral in Honolulu, was begun in 1840 and completed three years later. By the end of the nineteenth century, the number of Roman Catholics was equal to Protestants, thanks in part to the growth of Hawaii's sugar and pineapple industries that required imported labor. Among those recruited were indentured Portuguese immigrants from the island of Madeira who worked in the fields on the island of Maui. There they built their unique church, **Holy Ghost Catholic Church**, in 1894, the only octagonally shaped building in Hawaii to date from the nineteenth century.

Possibly the best known Roman Catholic priest in Hawaiian history is Father Joseph de Veuster, better known as Father Damien, who arrived on the island of Molokai in 1873 to minister to lepers. Called the "Martyr of Molokai," and nominated for sainthood, he rebuilt the settlement and erected numerous churches both in the settlement and in so-called "healthy" districts. One of the latter is St. Joseph Catholic Church, a tiny frame Gothic Revival structure constructed in 1876 in the community of Kamalo by native help working under the supervision of Father Damien; it was restored in 1971.

The arrival of westerners may have brought "religious salvation" to the Hawaiians, but it devastated their culture and population. By 1850, their numbers had dwindled to 75,000. This, coupled with competition from the Catholic Church, saw many of Hawaii's Protestant churches losing members and being abandoned. Ironically, the Congregational faith went into a decline at about the same time American control of the sugar and pineapple industry grew. Soon, powerful American planters were able to overthrow the monarchy and establish a revolutionary government that requested annexation by the United States, a request that was finally honored in 1898. Requests for statehood, however, were continually refused until 1959, after Alaska was admitted into the Union, and the strategic importance of Hawaii was recognized.

Several reasons have been advanced as to why Hawaii was continually refused entry into the Union, particularly in light of its control by Americans and its strategic location. The popular answer is its distance from the mainland; more likely it was due to its large Asian population, particularly Japanese Buddhists, whose arrival marks the Islands' third "invasion" by outsiders.

Buddhism was first introduced into Hawaii by Chinese plantation laborers who began to arrive in the mid-nineteenth century, but were quickly outnumbered by Japanese laborers who by 1900 comprised the largest ethnic group on the islands. A Japanese Buddhist Jodo mission was established in 1894 and five years later a Jodo Shin (True Jodo) mission began, with the latter sect becoming the more successful; others have since been introduced. Many of the first temples built by Japanese Buddhists, like the churches of the Congregationalists who preceded them, were simple interpretations of the buildings in their homeland often combined with elements borrowed from local architecture. An outstanding example is **Daifukuji Soto Zen Mission**, dedicated in 1919 in Honalo on the big island of Hawaii, the oldest Soto Zen temple in Hawaii.

A lesser number of Japanese immigrants chose to practice their native Shinto religion, but its national character made it less exportable than Buddhism. A Shinto shrine was built in 1898 in Hilo on the island of Hawaii. Another one, **Mau Jinsha Mission** on the island of Maui, was constructed in 1915 under the supervision of a master carpenter from Japan.

Hawaii's fourth invasion came as a result of Japan's military strike of December 7, 1941. The territory's Japanese citizens were rounded up and in their place came hundreds of thousands of American military personnel, to be followed after the war by an invasion of tourists.

Old Waioli Hui'ia Church

Off SR 56, Hanalei, Kauai

ARCHITECT / BUILDER:
1921 restoration supervised by Hart Wood, Architect
CONSTRUCTION / DEDICATION DATE:
1832; 1834; 1841; 1912

THIS IS THE THIRD CHURCH built on this site. The first was a huge thatch structure built in 1832 prior to the arrival of the Reverend William Alexander. Destroyed by fire two years later, it was immediately replaced by a similar structure that was destroyed in 1837. In 1841, Reverend Alexander dedicated a third building, the present Old Waioli Hui'ia Church. It is an imposing timber building with an open four-sided *lanai* (porch) surrounding it. Its tall hipped thatched roof is considered to be a derivation from nineteenth-century American buildings and a modified copy of a roof used in earlier Hawaiian structures. It is a prototype of the double pitched hipped roofs that are now identified as "modern" Hawaiian. The original roof was thatched, later replaced by shingles, then galvanized iron, back to shingles. Shortly before the church was dedicated a belfry was constructed behind the main structure. Measuring 24 feet in height, it houses a bell imported from Boston.

A new church was built in 1912 and this building was converted to a Sunday school and hall. It was restored in 1921 and again in the 1970s. Damaged by Hurricane Iniki, it is again undergoing restoration and is rescheduled to open in the fall of 1997.

**Old Waioli
Hui'ia Church,
Hanalei,
Kauai, Hawaii**

Kawaiahao Church

(FIRST CHURCH)

957 Punchbowl Street; 553 South King Street, Honolulu

ARCHITECT / BUILDER:
Reverend Hiram Bingham
CONSTRUCTION / DEDICATION DATE:
1838-1842

A LTHOUGH IT IS NOT THE OLDEST surviving religious structure in the Islands, because it is the church founded and designed by the Reverend Hiram Bingham, it is considered the most important and representative church of the Protestant missionary period. The present church, called the "Westminster Abbey of Hawaii," is the congregation's fifth home. Its first, a thatch-roofed, wooden structure, was erected in 1821. The congregation's earlier buildings were destroyed by fire, some by accident, one possibly by arson.

Bingham prepared the drawings for the present church replicating the Classical Revival style of New England meeting-houses favored by Congregationalists, which in turn look to James Gibbs's St. Martin-in-the-Fields, London, as a model (see p. 11).[5] Sources of material and funds for constructing the church were local and imported. The king contributed $3,000 and also donated stone, lime, and timber. Additional funds were raised in New Haven; Center Church (see p. 56) even donated some of its furnishings.

The building has been restored and altered several times since it was erected, including a complete reconstruction in 1925–1927 to replace wood damaged by termites.

Kawaiahao Church
(First Church),
Honolulu, Hawaii

Daifukuji Soto Zen Mission

Mamalahoa Highway, Honalo, Hawaii

ARCHITECT / BUILDER:
Not available

CONSTRUCTION / DEDICATION DATE:
Dedicated in 1921

THE CONGREGATION WAS ESTABLISHED in 1914, and under the direction of Reverend Kaiseki Kodama a temple was constructed. The present building, located about 200 yards north of the original temple, was built under the ministry of Reverend Meido Kakiura and was dedicated in 1921.

The mission is a one-story, frame building rendered in a typical Japanese Buddhist temple style for Hawaii. The use of the metal roof and single wall construction derive from Hawaii's plantation tradition, while the roof forms, the movement from the earth plane to the elevated temple, decorative portico, and use of the verandah all derive from Japan. The interior of the main hall has been remodeled, but in a fashion sensitive to the original structure. It contains an altar with a statue of Kannon by Sosaku Miki, a master sculptor in Japan.

The temple is considered an excellent example of a Buddhist temple constructed in Hawaii in the early twentieth century.

Daifukuji Soto
Zen Mission,
Honalo, Hawaii

Maui Jinsha Shinto Mission

472 Lipo Street, Wailuku, Maui

ARCHITECT / BUILDER:
Seichi Tomokiyo, Ichitaro Takata, master carpenters
CONSTRUCTION / DEDICATION DATE:
1915

B UILT DURING THE ERA of Emperor Taisho to commemorate the second year of his reign, this temple is on land in Kahului leased from the Hawaiian Commercial and Sugar Company for 99 years.

Two master carpenters from Japan were responsible for its construction. The small shrine section was built first, followed by the larger ceremonial hall. The major portions of both, in the traditional manner, were built without the use of nails or paint. Carvings and ornamental painted plaques are its only decoration.

Maui Jinsha was at its Kahului location until 1953 when, due to its alien property status, it was moved to its present Wailuku location on property owned in fee by the church. With great effort, the shrine was transported intact, and lifted into place by a crane. The main hall was taken apart and assembled piece by piece at its new location.

Mau Jinsha Shinto Temple, Wailuku, Maui, Hawaii

Holy Ghost Roman Catholic Church

Lower Kula Road, Kula, Maui

ARCHITECT / BUILDER:
Father James Beissel
CONSTRUCTION / DEDICATION DATE:
circa 1894-1897

THE OCTAGONAL HOLY GHOST CHURCH was built by indentured Catholic Portuguese immigrants who came to work on sugar plantations. Some, following the fulfillment of their contracts, chose to homestead in a green belt on the slope of the dormant Haleakala volcano. By 1882, the community had grown large enough to request a priest. Father James Beissel, a Prussian priest and confidant of Father Damien of Molokai, arrived and between 1894 and 1897, designed the Holy Ghost Church and supervised its construction.

The frame church, according to tradition, derives its unique form from the fact that it corresponds with the shape of a replica of the crown of Queen Elizabeth (Isabella) of Portugal who reigned in the thirteenth century, which the church houses. The crown plays an important role in the Portuguese community's Holy Ghost celebration which transpires at Pentecost, where it is afforded a place of honor at the feast.

Although the parish numbers less than 200 families, funds were raised to underwrite a complete restoration of the church, described by Reverend Beissel as "the jewel" of the many churches built on the Islands.

NOTES

1. Stephen S. Birdsall and John W. Florin, *Regional Landscapes of the United States and Canada,* 4th ed. (New York: John Wiley & Sons, Inc., 1992), 428.

2. Quoted in "Archdiocese of Los Angeles: From Its Establishment to the Present," Archdiocese of Los Angeles Archival Center, n.d.

3. Alan Gowans, *Fruitful Fields: American Missionary Churches in Hawaii* (Honolulu: Department of Land and Natural Resources, State Historic Preservation Division, 1993), 1ff.

FACING PAGE:
**Holy Ghost Roman
Catholic Church,
Kula, Maui, Hawaii**

Glossary

ARCHITECTURE

ADOBE Unburnt brick dried in the sun, commonly used for building in the southwestern U.S.

AEDICULE Usually a niche or opening framed by **columns, piers,** or **pilasters** supporting a **lintel, entablature,** or **pediment.**

ALTAR Where the communion table is placed in a church.

APSE A projecting part of a building, especially of a church; usually semicircular in plan.

ARCH Almost any curved structural member used to span an opening.

ARCADE A series of arches supported by **piers** or **columns.**

ASHLAR Cut stone masonry.

ATRIO Term used for a front courtyard surrounded by a low wall found in southwestern churches. Also called *atrium.*

AXIS An imaginary line passing through a building about which its principle parts are arranged.

BALDACCHINO A canopy on **columns** frequently built over an **altar.**

BAPTISMAL FONT A container to hold water used for the ritual of baptism; may vary in size according to the ritual.

BAPTISTERY A separate building or a part of a church used for baptismal purposes.

BASILICA A rectangular building designed along a longitudinal axis, leading from a **narthex** through the **nave,** that often has flanking aisles, culminating at an **apse** located at the opposite end. Within the Roman Catholic faith, it refers to the status of a church.

BAY A subdivision of the interior space of a building.

BELL TOWER The tower in which bells are hung, usually on the front **façade** corner. The upper story or room in which the bells are hung is called the belfry.

BIMAH Also spelled bema. Greek for platform. Usually refers to the platform in a synagogue where the lectern and/or table is located. In modern synagogues the **Torah Shrine** (Ark) stands against its rear wall.

BUTTRESS A vertical mass of masonry built against a wall to strengthen it.

CAPITAL The crowning member of a **column, pier,** or **shaft.** Comes in different styles.

CHANCEL That part of the east end of the church in which the main **altar** is placed; reserved for clergy and choir. This is sometimes called the "choir." Do not confuse with choir loft.

CHAPEL In a church, a separate space containing an **altar** dedicated to a saint. In a synagogue, this refers to a small prayer hall located near the main sanctuary.

CLAPBOARD A narrow board used to cover frame buildings.

CLASSICAL STYLE Inspired by architecture of ancient Greece and Rome, periodically revived as Classical Revival or Neoclassical.

CLERESTORY A clear story, i.e., a row of windows in the upper part of a wall.

CLOISTER A courtyard surrounded by covered walks, frequently found on the south side of churches or monasteries.

COLONNADE Passage lined with columns bearing a straight **entablature.**

COLUMN A kind of supporting **pillar** with a round **shaft,** base, and **capital.**

COMMUNION RAIL The railing that separates the **chancel** from the **nave.**

CONVENT A separate building used as living quarters for nuns.

CORBELLING Brick or masonry courses, each built out beyond the one below.

CORNICE The projecting crowning member of the **entablature.**

CRENELLATION Notched or indented tops of walls, usually in towers.

CROSSING The area where the **transept** intersects the **nave.**

CRUCIFIX A cross with the figure of Jesus crucified upon it.

CRUCIFORM Cross-shaped, as the plan of a church.

CRYPT A **vaulted** chamber, wholly or partly underground, usually under the **chancel.**

CUPOLA A small structure on top of a roof or a building, used as a lookout, to complete a design, or to hang bells in, etc.

DISTYLE-IN-ANTIS A **portico** with two columns between **pilasters.**

DOME A curved **vault**, often on a circular base.

ENGLISH BOND PATTERN Bricks are in alternate courses of headers (ends) and stretchers (sides).

ENTABLATURE Horizontal beams resting on **columns** or **pilasters.**

ETERNAL LIGHT *Ner Tamid* [Heb.]. The perpetual light hanging in front of the **Torah Shrine** in all synagogues.

FAÇADE The front or principle face of a building.

FLEMISH BOND PATTERN Bricks laid of alternating headers (ends) and stretchers (sides).

GALLERY A balcony; usually found in the rear of the **nave.**

GOTHIC STYLE A medieval style usually characterized by the use of pointed **arches** and ribbed **vaults**. Revived in the mid-19th century.

ICONOSTASIS A partition or screen on which **icons** are placed, separating the altar from the main part of the church.

LANCET WINDOW A window terminating in an acutely pointed **arch.**

LINTEL A horizontal beam spanning an opening, such as a window or a door.

LUNETTE A semicircular opening; often used to describe a window shape.

MENORAH A seven-branched candelabrum found in synagogues; it is associated with the Jewish temple in Jerusalem.

MIHRAB A prayer-niche in a **mosque**; faces Mecca.

MINARET A tall, slender tower connected with a **mosque**. Usually has a balcony from which the muezzin calls the people to prayer.

MINBAR The high **pulpit** in a **mosque.**

MOSQUE A Muslim place of worship.

NARTHEX The porch or entrance hall preceding the main hall of a place of worship.

NAVE The great central space in a place of worship, usually flanked by aisles.

NICHE A hollow or recess, generally in a wall, as for a statue.

OCULUS A circular window.

PEDIMENT The triangular gable end of a classical style building; also found over windows and door-ways.

PEW One of the long, fixed benches that usually constitute the seats of a church; may be a compartment separated by low partitions.

PIER Heavy, solid masonry support.

PILASTER A rectangular **column** projecting only slightly from a wall.

PILLAR Any vertical support including a **column, pilaster,** and **pier.**

POLYFOIL APSE An **apse** with several protruding rounded spaces or foils.

PORTE COCHERE A large gateway allowing vehicles to drive into the courtyard.

PORTICO A roofed space, open or partly enclosed, forming the entrance on the main **façade.** Often composed of **columns** supporting a **pediment.**

PULPIT A platform or raised structure in a place of worship from which the clergy conducts the service.

RECTORY A parsonage, a house for the clergy.

RIB A slender arched support in **Romanesque** and **Gothic vaults**.

RICHARDSONIAN ROMANESQUE A style of architecture based on the Medieval Romanesque style as interpreted by Henry Hobson Richardson (1838-1886), an influential American architect.

ROMANESQUE STYLE A Medieval style characterized by the use of a round **arch**, usually with heavy masonry construction. Revived in the mid-19th century.

ROOD SCREEN A screen separating the **nave** from the **chancel**, surmounted by a sculpture of Christ on the cross (**crucifix**).

ROSE WINDOW A great circular window filled with tracery, often found on the **façades** and at the ends of **transepts**.

SACRISTY A small chamber for vestments and ritual objects; see **Vestry**.

SANCTUARY A consecrated place; the most sacred part of any religious building, especially that part of a church in which the **altar** is placed.

SANCTUARY LIGHT A perpetual light found hanging in the **sanctuary** of some churches.

SHAFT the part of a **column** between the **capital** and base.

SIDE AISLE A corridor running parallel to the **nave** and separated from it by an **arcade** or **colonnade**.

SIDE ALTAR An additional **altar** in a church, located along the **side aisle**.

SOFFIT The underside of an **arch, lintel, cornice,** or stairway.

SPIRE A tall, sharply pointed summit, usually erected on a tower or roof. Can refer to the entire **steeple**.

STEEPLE A tall structure, usually topped with a **spire,** surmounting a tower or roof.

TORAH SCROLL The Five Books of Moses written in Hebrew on a scroll kept in the **Torah Shrine** in all synagogues.

TORAH SHRINE A cupboard or enclosed niche in which the **Torah Scrolls** are kept in a synagogue; usually located on the **bimah**.

TRACERY Branching ornamental stonework generally used in a window. It supports the glass and is characteristic of **Gothic** architecture.

TRANSEPT The part of a **cruciform** church crossing at right angles to the greatest length between the **nave** and the **chancel**.

UNDERCROFT The basement area under the **nave**.

VAULT A ceiling built on the principle of the **arch**.

VESTRY A room used to store vestments; in some churches it is used for other purposes, such as Sunday school or as a **chapel**. See **sacristy**.

SCULPTURE AND PAINTING

ALTARPIECE A painting placed above and behind an altar.

BULTOS Three-dimensional statues of saints carved of wood and painted in bright colors, found in southwestern churches.

DIPTYCH An **altarpiece** consisting of two panels or leaves hinged so that they can be folded together.

ENTHRONED MADONNA A pictorial or sculptural motif depicting Mary sitting on the throne of heaven holding infant Jesus.

FRESCO Painting on plaster walls. A **mural** painting.

ICON A representation in painting, enamel, etc., of some sacred personage, executed according to a convention or tradition. Usually found hanging on the **iconostasis** in an Orthodox church, or on the walls.

MEDIA The material from which an art object is made. For example, in painting it could be oil, acrylic, watercolor, **fresco**; in **sculpture** it could be stone, metal, wood, **plaster,** or **terra-cotta**. Needlework is another medium.

MOSAIC Patterns or pictures made by imbedding small pieces of stone or glass (**tesserae**) in cement on surfaces such as walls or floors.

MURAL A picture either painted on the wall (see **fresco**) or a large wall-sized painting.

PIETA A pictorial or sculptural motif of the Virgin Mary holding her crucified son.

RELIEF SCULPTURE Statue which is not freestanding but which is carved or cast so that it projects from the surface of which it is a part.

REREDOS A screen or partition wall, usually ornamental, behind an **altar**.

RETABLOS Images of saints painted on panels of wood; found in southwestern churches.

SANTOS Painted images of saints in southwestern churches.

SCULPTURE IN THE ROUND Freestanding figures carved or modeled in three dimensions.

STATIONS OF THE CROSS A sculptural or pictorial depiction of the fourteen stages of the passion of Christ.

TERRA-COTTA Hard baked clay used for **sculpture** or as building material, may be glazed or painted.

TESSERAE Small pieces of glass or stone used in making **mosaics**.

TRIPTYCH An **altarpiece** consisting of three panels.

Bibliography

ARCHITECTURE

Andrews, Wayne. *American Gothic: Its Origins, Its Trials, Its Triumphs.* New York: Vintage Books, 1975.

Bates, Grace. *Gallatin County Places and Things.* 2nd ed. Manhattan, Mt, 1994.

Bishir, Catherine W. *North Carolina Architecture.* Chapel Hill: University of North Carolina Press, 1990.

Blumenson, John J. G. *Identifying American Architecture: A Pictorial Guide to Styles and Terms: 1600-1945,* rev. ed. New York: W. W. Norton, 1981.

Broderick, Robert C. *Historic Churches of the United States.* New York: Winifred Funk, 1958.

Bruhn, Paul A., compiler. *Vermont's Historic Architecture: A Second Celebration.* Shelburne, Vt.: New England Press, 1985.

Burns, John A., et al., eds. *Recording Historic Structures: Historic American Buildings Survey / Historic American Engineering Record.* Washington, D.C.: AIA Press, 1989.

Bushman, Richard L. *The Refinement of America: Persons, Houses, Cities.* New York: Alfred A. Knopf, 1992.

"Cleveland Sacred Landmarks." *Gamut: A Journal of Ideas and Information.* Cleveland: Cleveland State University, 1990.

Coomber, James, and Sheldon Green. *Magnificent Churches on the Prairie.* Fargo, N.D.: Institute for Regional Studies, North Dakota State University, 1996.

Cornwall, Aaron Woolley. *A Pictorial History of the Anglican Churches in Colonial America 1607–1776.* Winston-Salem: Cornwall Photography, 1988.

DeLong, David G. *American Architecture: Innovation and Tradition.* New York: Rizzoli, 1986.

Dezurka, E. R. "Early Kansas Churches." *Kansas State College Bulletin* xxxiii, 5 (April 1, 1949): Bulletin 60.

Donnelly, Marion Carol. *The New England Meeting Houses of the Seventeenth Century.* Middletown, Ct.: Wesleyan University Press, 1968.

Eckert, Kathryn Bishop. *Buildings of Michigan.* NY, Oxford: Oxford University Press, 1993.

Ehrlich, George. *Kansas City, Mo: An Architectural History, 1826–1990,* rev. ed. Columbia, Mo.: University of Missouri Press, 1992.

Erpestad, David, and David Wood. *Building South Dakota: A Historical Survey of the State's Architecture to 1945.* Pierre, S.D.: South Dakota State Historical Society, 1997.

Fitch, James Marston. *Historic Preservation: Curatorial Management of the Built World.* New York: McGraw-Hill, 1982.

Five Views: An Ethnic Historic Site Survey of California. California Department of Parks and Recreation, Office of Historic Preservation, 1988.

Gamble, Robert. *Historic Architecture of Alabama: A Primer of Styles and Types: 1810-1930.* Tuscaloosa: University of Alabama Press, 1990.

Garner, John S. *The Midwest in American Architecture.* Urbana: University of Illinois Press, 1991.

Gebhard, David, and Gerald Monsheim. *Buildings of Iowa.* New York: Oxford University Press, 1993.

Gebhard, David, and Robert Winter. *Los Angeles: An Architectural Guide.* Salt Lake City: Gibbs-Smith, 1994.

Gowans, Alan. *Fruitful Fields: American Missionary Churches in Hawaii.* Honolulu: Department of Land and National Resources, State Historic Preservation Division, 1993.

——. *Styles and Types of North American Architecture: Social Function and Cultural Expression.* New York: Icon Editions, 1992.

Hall, Douglas Kent. *Frontier Spirit: Early Churches of the Southwest.* New York: Abbeville Press, 1990.

Hamilton, C. Mark. *Nineteenth Century Mormon Architecture and City Planning.* New York, Oxford: Oxford University Press, 1995.

Hayes, Bartlett H. *Tradition Becomes Innovation: Modern Religious Architecture in America.* New York: Pilgrim Press, 1983.

Henry, Jay C. *Architecture in Texas, 1895–1945.* Austin: University of Texas Press, 1993.

Historic America: Buildings, Structures, and Sites, recorded by HABS/HAER. Washington, D.C.: Library of Congress, 1983.

Hitchcock, Henry-Russell. *Rhode Island Architecture.* New York: DeCapo Press, 1965.

Hoagland, Alison K. *Buildings of Alaska.* New York: Oxford University Press, 1993.

Holisher, Desider. *The House of God.* New York: Crown Publishers, 1946.

Huber, Leonard. *Landmarks of New Orleans Architecture.* New Orleans: Louisiana Landmarks Society, 1984.

Kemp, Jim. *American Vernacular: Regional Influences in Architecture and Interior Design.* New York: Viking, 1987.

Kennedy, Roger. *American Churches.* New York: Steward, Tabori and Chang, 1982.

Krell, Dorothy, et al. *The California Missions: A Pictorial History.* Menlo Park, Calif.: Sunset Publishing, 1991.

Lane, George, and Algimantas Kezys. *Chicago Churches and Synagogues.* Chicago: Loyola University Press, 1981.

Lane, Mills. *Architecture of the Old South.* New York: Abbeville Press, 1993.

——. *Architecture of the Old South: Georgia.* Savannah, Ga.: Beehive Press, 1986.

——. *Architecture of the Old South: Kentucky and Tennessee.* Savannah, Ga.: Beehive Foundation, 1993.

——. *Architecture of the Old South: Louisiana.* New York: Abbeville Press, 1990.

——. *Architecture of the Old South: Maryland.* New York: Abbeville Press, 1991.

——. *Architecture of the Old South: Mississippi and Alabama.* New York: Abbeville Press, 1989.

——. *Architecture of the Old South: North Carolina.* Savannah: Beehive Press, 1985.

——. *Architecture of the Old South: South Carolina.* Savannah: Beehive Press, 1984.

——. *Architecture of the Old South: Virginia.* New York: Abbeville Press, 1989.

Loth, Calder, and Julius Trousdale Sadler, Jr. *The Only Proper Style: Gothic Architecture in America.* Boston: NY Graphic Society, 1975.

Luebke, Frederick C. *Nebraska: An Illustrated History.* Lincoln: University of Nebraska Press, 1995.

Mackintosh, Barry. *The Historic Sites Survey and National Historic Landmarks Program: A History.* National Park Service, 1985.

Maddex, Diane, general editor. *Landmark Yellow Pages.* Washington, D.C.: The Preservation Press, 1990.

Maine Catalog. Historic American Buildings Survey. National Park Service, Department of the Interior. Maine State Museum, 1974.

Mallary, Peter T. *New England Churches and Meeting Houses.* New York: Vendome Press, 1985.

Markovich, Nicholas, et al., ed. *Pueblo Style and Regional Architecture.* New York: Van Nostrand Reinhold, 1990.

Marlowe, George Francis. *Churches of Old New England.* New York: The Macmillan Co., 1947.

McCue, George, and F. Peters. *A Guide to the Architecture of St. Louis.* Columbia, Mo.: University of Missouri Press, 1989.

Momaday, N. Scott. *A Sense of Mission: Historic Churches of the Southwest.* San Francisco: Chronicle Books, 1994.

Morrone, Francis. *The Architectural Guidebook to New York City.* Salt Lake City: Gibbs-Smith, 1994.

Murtagh, William J. *Keeping Time: The History and Theory of Preservation in America.* Pittstown, N.J.: Main St. Press, 1987.

Mutrux, Robert. *Great New England Churches*. Chester, Conn.: The Globe Pequot Press, 1982.

Nicholson, William S. *Historical Homes and Churches of Virginia's Eastern Shore*. Accomac, Va.: Atlantic Publications, 1984.

Nicolletta, Julie. *The Architecture of the Shakers*. Woodstock, Vt.: The Countryman Press, 1995.

Noble, Allen G. *To Build in a New Land: Ethnic Landscapes in North America*. Baltimore: Johns Hopkins Press, 1992.

Pacyga, Dominic A., and Ellen S. Kerrett. *Chicago City of Neighborhoods*. Chicago: Loyola University Press, 1986.

Pearce, Sarah J. *A Guide to Colorado Architecture*. State Historical Society of Colorado, 1983.

Pearson, Esther. *Early Churches of Washington State*. Seattle: University of Washington Press, 1980.

Perrin, Richard W. E. *Wisconsin Architecture: HABS*. Department of the Interior, National Park Service, 1965.

Poppeliers, John C., et al. *What Style Is It? A Guide to American Architecture*, rev. ed. Washington, D.C.: Preservation Press, 1983.

Promised Land on the Solomon: Black Settlement at Nicodemus, Kansas. Department of the Interior, National Park Service, n.d.

Purdy, Martin. *Churches and Chapels*. Oxford: Butterworth Architecture, 1991.

Ranson, David F. "One Hundred Years of Jewish Congregations in Connecticut: An Architectural Survey." *Connecticut Jewish History*, 2 (1): Fall, 1991.

Rifkind, Carole. *A Field Guide to American Architecture*. New York: Bonanza Books, 1980.

Robinson, Willard B. *Reflections of Faith: Houses of Worship in the Lone Star State*. Waco, Tx.: Baylor University Press, 1994.

Rosenthall, William A. *The American Synagogue in the Nineteenth Century*. Cincinnati: HUC-JIR, 1982.

Scott, Pamela, and Antoinette J. Lee. *Buildings of the District of Columbia*. New York: Oxford University Press, 1993.

Shane, Wesley I. *The Iowa Catalog: HABS*. Iowa City: University of Iowa Press, 1979.

Shelgren, Olaf William, Jr., Cary Lattin, and Robert W. Frasch. *Cobblestone Landmarks of New York State*. Syracuse: Syracuse University Press, 1978.

Sheppard, Carl. *The Archbishop's Cathedral*. Santa Fe, N.M.: Cimarron Press, 1995.

Slade, Thomas M., ed. *HABS Indiana*. Historic Landmarks Foundation of Indiana. Bloomington: Indiana University Press, 1983.

Smith, G. E. Kidder. *The Beacon Guide to New England Houses of Worship*. Boston: Beacon Press, 1989.

Smith, Mary Lorraine, ed. *Historic Churches of the South*. Atlanta: Tupper and Love, Inc., 1952.

Speck, Lawrence W. *Landmarks of Texas Architecture*. Austin: University of Texas Press, 1986.

Spector, Tom. *The Guide to the Architecture of Georgia*. Columbia: University of South Carolina Press, 1993.

Staehr, C. Eric. *Bonanza Victorian: Architecture and Society in Colorado Mining Towns*. Albuquerque: University of New Mexico Press, 1975.

Starr, Eileen F. *Architecture in the Cowboy State: 1849-1940*. Glendo, Wyo.: High Plains Press, 1992.

Stern, Robert A. M. *Pride of Place: Building the American Dream*. Boston: Houghton-Mifflin, 1986.

Stipe, Robert E., and Antoinette J. Lee. *The American Mosaic: Preserving a Nation's Heritage*. Washington, D.C.: US/ICOMOS, 1987.

Stiritz, Mary M. *St. Louis: Historic Churches and Synagogues*. St. Louis, Mo.: Landmark Association of St. Louis, Inc., 1995.

Tinterow, Gary. *Two Centuries of American Synagogue Architecture*. Waltham, Mass.: The Rose Art Museum, Brandeis University, 1976.

Upton, Dell, ed. *America's Architectural Roots*. Washington, D.C.: The Preservation Press, 1986.

Weber, David J. *The Spanish Frontier in North America*. New Haven: Yale University Press, 1993.

Wedda, John. *New England Worships*. New York: Random House, 1965.

Weissbach, Lee Shai. *The Synagogues of Kentucky: Architecture and History*. Lexington: University Press of Kentucky, 1995.

Whiffen, Marcus. *American Architecture Since 1780: A Guide to the Styles*, rev. ed. Cambridge, Mass.: MIT Press, 1992.

Whiffen, Marcus, and Frederick Koeper. *American Architecture, 1607–1976*. Cambridge: MIT Press, 1983.

Willard, Ruth. *Sacred Places of San Francisco*. San Francisco: Presidio Press, 1985.

Wischnitzer, Rachel. *Synagogue Architecture in the United States: History and Interpretation*. Philadelphia: Jewish Publication Society, 1955.

Wrenn, Tony P., and Elizabeth Mulloy. *America's Forgotten Architecture*. New York: Pantheon, 1976.

RELIGION, GEOGRAPHY, AND HISTORY

Albanese, Catherine L. *America, Religions and Religion*, 2nd ed. Belmont, Calif.: Wadsworth Publishing, 1981.

Allen, James Paul, and Eugene James Turner. *We the People: An Atlas of America's Ethnic Diversity*. New York: Macmillan, 1988.

Arnold, Morris A. *Colonial Arkansas, 1686–1804: A Social and Cultural History*. Fayetteville: University of Arkansas Press, 1991.

Birdsall, Stephen A., and John W. Florin. *Regional Landscapes of the United States and Canada*. New York: John Wiley & Sons, 1992.

Borchert, John R. *America's Northern Heartland: An Economic and Historic Geography of the Upper Midwest*. Minneapolis: University of Minnesota Press, 1987.

Bradley, Martin B., et al. *Churches and Church Membership in the United States, 1990*. Atlanta: Glenmary Research Center, 1992.

Bradshaw, Michael. *Regions and Regionalism in the United States*. Jackson: University of Mississippi Press, 1988.

Buenker, John D., and Lorman A. Ratner, eds. *Multiculturalism in the United States: A Comparative Guide to Acculturation and Ethnicity*. New York: Greenwood Press, 1992.

Dinnerstein, Leonard, and David M. Reimers. *Ethnic Americans: A History of Immigration*, 3rd ed. New York: Harper and Row, 1988.

Dyrud, Keith P., Michael Novak, and Rudolph J. Vecoli. *The Other Catholics*. New York: Arno Press, 1975.

Engbrecht, Dennis D. *The Americanization of a Rural Immigrant Church: The General Conference Mennonites in Central Kansas, 1874–1939*. New York: Garland Press, 1994.

Gaustad, Edwin Scott. *Historic Atlas of Religion in America*, rev. ed. New York: Harper and Row, 1976.

——. *A Religious History of America*, rev. ed. San Francisco: Harper, 1990.

Golab, Caroline. *Immigrant Destinations*. Philadelphia: Temple University Press, 1977.

Holmquist, June Drenning, ed. *They Chose Minnesota: A Survey of the State's Ethnic Groups*. St. Paul, MN: Minnesota Historical Press, 1981.

Jamison, Wallace N. *Religion in New Jersey: A Brief History*. Princeton: D. Van Nostrand Co., Inc. 1964

Kasmin, Barry P., and Seymour P. Lachman. *One Nation Under God*. New York: Harmony Books, 1993.

Lieberson, Stanley. *From Many Strands: Ethnic and Racial Groups in Contemporary America*. New York: Russell Sage Foundation, 1988.

Lincoln, C. Eric, and Lawrence H. Mamiya. *The Black Church in the African American Experience*. Durham, N.C.: Duke University Press, 1990.

Madison, James H., ed. *Heartland*. Bloomington: Indiana University Press, 1988.

Marty, Martin. *The New Shape of American Religion*. New York: Harper & Row, 1959.

——. *A Nation of Behavers*. Chicago: University of Chicago Press, 1976.

——. *Modern American Religion: The Irony of It All.* Chicago: University of Chicago Press, 1986.

——. *Modern American Religion: The Noise of Conflict: 1919–1941.* Chicago: University of Chicago Press, 1991.

——. *Pilgrims in Their Own Land: 500 Years of Religion in America.* Boston: Little, Brown and Co., 1984.

Murrin, Mary R., ed. *Religion in New Jersey: Life Before the Civil War.* Trenton: New Jersey Historical Commission, 1985.

Neusner, Jacob, ed. *World Religions in America: An Introduction.* Louisville: Westminster/John Knox Press, 1994.

Samuelson, Myron. *The Story of the Jewish Community of Burlington, Vermont.* Burlington, Vt.: Myron Samuelson, 1976.

Sherman, William C., and Playford V. Thorson, eds. *Plains Folk: North Dakota's Ethnic History.* North Dakota Centennial Heritage Series: North Dakota Institute for Regional Studies, North Dakota State University, 1988.

Shortridge, James R. *Peopling the Plains: Who Settled Where in Frontier Kansas.* Lawrence: University Press of Kansas, 1995.

——. *The Middle West: Its Meaning in American Culture.* Lawrence: University Press of Kansas, 1989.

Ward, David. *Cities and Immigrants: A Geography of Change in Nineteenth Century America.* New York: Oxford University Press, 1971.

Wertheimer, Jack, ed. *The American Synagogue: A Sanctuary Transformed.* Cambridge: Cambridge University Press, 1988.

Williams, Peter W. *Popular Religion in America: Symbolic Change and the Modernization Process in Historical Perspective.* Englewood Cliffs, N.J.: Prentice Hall, 1980.

Wind, James. *Places of Worship: Exploring Their History.* The Nearby History Series, Vol. 4. American Association of State and Local History.

Zelinsky, Wilbur. *The Cultural Geography of the United States.* Englewood Cliffs, N.J.: Prentice Hall, 1973.

Illustration Credits

COVER

Susan Hebard for the State Historical Society of North Dakota, National Register of Historic Places.

PREFACE

Page ix, Joni Gilkerson, Nebraska State Historical Society.

INTRODUCTION

Page 1, The Peterborough Historical Society; **p. 3,** Jim Gautier.

CHAPTER 1 America's Religious Heritage

Page 8, Historic American Buildings Survey, Library of Congress; **p. 11,** Engraving by T. Malton, courtesy Witt Library, Courtald Institute of Art, University of London; **p. 12,** Archives / Research Library, Virginia Department of Historic Resources; **p. 15,** courtesy The Historic New Orleans Collection, Museum / Research Center; **p. 16,** Historic American Buildings Survey, Library of Congress.

CHAPTER 2 New England

Page 20, Massachusetts Historical Commission; **p. 22,** Mark C. Bisgrove, Historic American Buildings Survey, Library of Congress; **p. 23,** Maine Historic Preservation Commission; **p. 25,** Maine Historic Preservation Commission; **p. 26,** Maine Historic Preservation Commission; **p. 27,** Maine Historic Preservation Commission; **p. 29,** Maine Historic Preservation Commission; **p. 32,** Charles Bonenti, Vermont Division of Historic Sites; **p. 33,** Louise Roomet, Vermont Division for Historic Preservation; **p. 34,** Vermont Division for Historic Preservation; **p. 35,** National Register of Historic Places; **p. 36,** John R. Axtell, Vermont Division for Historic Preservation; **p. 37,** John R. Axtell, Vermont Division for Historic Preservation; **p. 40,** Willis T. Rich, courtesy of the New Hampshire Division of Historical Resources; **p. 41,** Gretchen Langheld, courtesy of the New Hampshire Division of Historical Resources; **p. 42,** Lisa Mausolf, courtesy of the New Hampshire Division of Historical Resources; **p. 43,** Perron Studio, courtesy of the New Hampshire Division of Historical Resources; **p. 44,** Sarah R. McDonald, courtesy of the New Hampshire Division of Historical Resources; **p. 46,** Clark Linehan, National Register of Historic Places; **p. 47,** author; **p. 48,** Ray Sawyer; **p. 49,** JoAnne Devereaux ; **p. 50,** Chris Rediehs, Historic Boston Incorporated; **p. 51,** (left) author; (right) National Register of Historic Places; **p. 52,** National Register of Historic Places; **p. 55,** Stanley P. Mixon, Historic American Buildings Survey, Library of Congress; **p. 56,** John Warner Barber, published by Hitchcock & Stafford, New Haven; **p. 57,** Connecticut Historical Commission; **p. 58,** Connecticut Historical Commission; **p. 59,** Connecticut Historical Commission; **p. 62,** Arthur W. LeBoeuf, Historic American Buildings Survey, Library of Congress; **p. 63,** Jack E. Boucher, Historic American Buildings Survey, Library of Congress; **p. 64,** Jack E. Boucher, Historic American Buildings Survey, Library of Congress; **p. 65,** National Register of Historic Places; **p. 66,** Warren Jagger, Rhode Island Historical Preservation and Heritage Commission; **p. 67,** Warren Jagger, Rhode Island Historical Preservation and Heritage Commission.

CHAPTER 3 Middle Atlantic Region

Page 70, Michael Horowitz, courtesy of the Eldridge Street Project, Inc.; **p. 74,** Gerald Paul Vanderhart; **p. 75,** Arnold Moses, Historic American Buildings Survey, Library of Congress; **p. 76,** National Register of Historic Places; **p. 77,** Michael Horowitz, courtesy of the Eldridge Street Project, Inc.; **p. 78,** Samuel Gruber; **p. 79,** G.T. Hess, Adventist Historic Ministry; **p. 82,** National Register of Historic Places; **p. 83,** R. Merritt Lacey, Historic American Buildings Survey, Library of Congress; **p. 84,** National Register of Historic Places; **p. 85,** courtesy Historic Preservation Commission, Paterson, New Jersey; **p. 86,** M. R. Kralik, National Register of Historic Places; **p. 87,** Michael Brooks, Historic American Buildings Survey, Library of Congress; **p. 90,** National Register of Historic Places; **p. 91,** author; **p. 92,** , National Register of Historic Places; **p. 93,** Jack Boucher, Historic American Buildings Survey, Library of Congress; **p. 94,** National Register of Historic Places; **p. 95,** National Register of Historic Places.

CHAPTER 4 East North Central Region

Page 98, Carl F. Waite, Historic American Buildings Survey, Library of Congress; **p. 102,** National Register of Historic Places; **p. 103,** National Register of Historic Places; **p. 105,** Jack E. Boucher, Historic American Buildings Survey, Library of Congress; **p. 106,** courtesy Library/Archives, Reorganized Church of Jesus Christ of Latter-day Saints, Independence, Missouri; **p. 107,** courtesy Library/Archives, Reorganized Church of Jesus Christ of Latter-day Saints, Independence, Missouri; **p. 108,** National Register of Historic Places; **p. 109,** Evan Golder; **p. 111,** Eric Gilbertson, National Register of Historic Places; **p. 112,** Eric Gilbertson, National Register of Historic Places; **p. 113,** National Register of Historic Places; **p. 114,** National Register of Historic Places; **p. 115,** M. Tekulve, National Register of Historic Places; **p. 116,** Emil J. Pierdos, National Register of Historic Places; **p. 117,** National Register of Historic Places; **p. 119,** Mackinac Island State Park Commission, National Register of Historic Places; **p. 120,** courtesy St. Paul's Cathedral; **p. 121,** Public Information Department, City of Detroit, National Register of Historic Places; **p. 122,** Michigan History Division; **p. 123,** Dr. Donald J. Bruggink, National Register of Historic Places; **p. 125,** Charles D. Keifer, Inspired Partnership; **p. 127,** National Register of Historic Places; **p. 128,** Illinois Historic Preservation Agency; **p. 129,** Ray Pearson, Historic American Buildings Survey, Library of Congress; **p. 130,** Harold Allen, Historic American Buildings Survey, Library of Congress; **p. 131,** Harold Allen, Historic American Buildings Survey, Library of Congress; **p. 132,** Judith Bromley; **p. 135,** John Demby, National Register of Historic Places; **p. 136,** National Register of Historic Places; **p. 137,** Wisconsin Landmark Commission; **p. 138,** Mark Wade, Milwaukee County Historical Society; **p. 139,** Nancy Belle Douglas, National Register of Historic Places.

CHAPTER 5 West North Central Region

Page 142, Joni Gilkerson, Nebraska State Historical Society; **p. 143,** Historic American Buildings Survey, Library of Congress; **p. 144,** State Historical Society of Iowa; **p.148,** Doug Ohman; **p. 149,** Doug Ohman; **p. 150,** Doug Ohman; **p. 151,** Doug Ohman; **p. 152,** author; **p. 153,** Doug Ohman; **p. 156,** State Historical Society of Iowa; **p. 157,** National Register of Historic Places; **p. 158,** State Historical Society of Iowa; **p. 159,** John F. Gaston, National Register of Historic Places; **p. 160,** courtesy Mother Mosque of America; **p. 163,** Deon K. Wolfenbarger, National Register of Historic Places; **p. 164,** Emil Boehl, Missouri Historical Society; **p. 165,** Gerald Lee Gilleard, National Register of Historic Places; **p. 166,** Tom Chesser, National Register of Historic Places; **p. 167,** James M. Denny, National Register of Historic Places; **p. 169,** Martha Hagedorn-Krase, National Register of Historic Places; **p. 170,** David von Riesen, Historic American Buildings Survey, Library of Congress; **p. 171,** David von Riesen, Historic American Buildings Survey, Library of Congress; **p. 172,** National Register of Historic Places; **p. 173,** Ralph A. Coffeen, National Register of Historic Places; **p. 174,** Martha Hagedorn-Krase; **p. 175,** National Register of Historic Places; **p. 177,** Janet Jeffries Spencer, National Register of Historic Places; **p. 178,** Joni Gilkerson, National Register of Historic Places; **p. 179,** Janet Jeffries Spencer, National Register of Historic Places; **p. 181,** Joni Gilkerson, National Register of Historic Places; **p. 182,** R. Bruhn, National Register of Historic Places; **p. 184,** Janet Jeffries Spencer, National Register of Historic Places; **p. 188,** National Register of Historic Places; **p. 189,** Wolff Janson, National Register of Historic Places; **p. 190,** Orlando Goering, National Register of Historic Places; **p. 191,** South Dakota State Historical Society, National Register of Historic Places; **p. 192,** author; **p. 195,** National Register of Historic Places; **p. 197,** Susan Hebard, National Register of Historic Places; **p. 198,** National Register of Historic Places; **p. 199,** National Register of Historic Places; **p. 200,** National Register of Historic Places; **p. 201,** National Register of Historic Places.

CHAPTER 6   South Atlantic Region

Page 204, National Register of Historic Places; **p. 206,** State Historic Preservation Office, South Carolina Department of Archives and History; **p. 208,** Edward M. Rosenfeld, Historic American Buildings Survey, Library of Congress; **p. 209,** Sue Fox, National Register of Historic Places; **p. 210,** Edward F. Heite, National Register of Historic Places; **p. 211,** David Ames, Historic American Buildings Survey, Library of Congress; **p. 212,** National Register of Historic Places; **p. 215,** author; **p. 216,** Historic American Buildings Survey, Library of Congress; **p. 217,** Dwight McNeill; **p. 218,** Jan Cigliano; **p. 219,** author; **p. 221,** Anthony Hathaway, Historic American Buildings Survey, Library of Congress; **p. 223,** Aaron Levin, Jewish Historical Society of Maryland, Inc.; **p. 224,** Elizabeth Booth, National Register of Historic Places; **p. 225,** Dan O'Toole, c/o Blakeslee-Lane, Inc., National Register of Historic Places; **p. 226,** National Register of Historic Places; **p. 227,** Aaron Levin, Jewish Historical Society of Maryland, Inc.; **p. 228,** Aaron Levin, Jewish Historical Society of Maryland, Inc.; **p. 229,** Aaron Levin, Jewish Historical Society of Maryland, Inc.; **p. 230,** Michael Dersin; **p. 233,** Historic American Buildings Survey, Library of Congress; **p. 234,** Sarah Driggs, National Register of Historic Places; **p. 235,** Michael Rierson, National Register of Historic Places; **p. 236,** The Valentine Museum, Richmond, Virginia; **p. 237,** Virginia Historic Landmarks Commission; **p. 240,** Richard Cheek, Historic American Buildings Survey, Library of Congress; **p. 241,** Jack E. Boucher, Historic American Buildings Survey, Library of Congress; **p. 242,** Richard Cheek, Historic American Buildings Survey, Library of Congress; **p. 243,** James E. Harding, National Register of Historic Places; **p. 244,** Elizabeth Nolin, National Register of Historic Places; **p. 247,** Tony Vaughn, North Carolina Department of Archives and History; **p. 248,** Michael Southern; **p. 249,** M.B. Gatza, Mecklenburg Historic Landmarks; **p. 250,** Frances Benjamin Johnston, Historic American Buildings Survey, Library of Congress; **p. 251,** Adolph Gluck; **p. 253,** C.O. Greene, Historic American Buildings Survey, Library of Congress; **p. 254,** Charles N. Bayless, Historic American Buildings Survey, Library of Congress; **p. 255,** William S. Chiat; **p. 256,** Elias B. Bull, National Register of Historic Places; **p. 257,** C.O. Greene, Historic American Buildings Survey, Library of Congress; **p. 258,** John E. Wells, State Historic Preservation Office, South Carolina Department of Archives and History; **p. 261,** Historic American Buildings Survey, Library of Congress; **p. 262,** Martha Zeigler; **p. 263,** James R. Lockhart, National Register of Historic Places; **p. 264,** National Register of Historic Places; **p. 265,** National Register of Historic Places; **p. 268,** Katherine Monahan, Ph.D.; **p. 269,** National Register of Historic Places; **p. 270,** National Register of Historic Places; **p. 271,** National Register of Historic Places.

CHAPTER 7   East South Central Region

Page 274, Ed Babst, National Register of Historic Places; **p. 278,** E.W. Russell, Historic American Buildings Survey, Library of Congress; **p. 279,** Charles A. Heppernan, Choctaw County Historical Society; **p. 280,** Mobile Press Register, National Register of Historic Places; **p. 281,** J. E. Scott, Jr., Fouts Commercial Photography; **p. 282,** Historic American Buildings Survey, Library of Congress; **p. 285,** Richard J. Cawthon, Mississippi Department of Archives and History; **p. 286,** Mary W. Miller, Historic Natchez Foundation, National Register of Historic Places; **p. 287,** National Register of Historic Places; **p. 288,** *Mississippi Today*; **p. 289,** Sam Gruber; **p. 292,** Tennessee Historical Commission; **p. 293,** Historic American Buildings Survey, Library of Congress; **p. 294,** Birdsong Photography, courtesy Sacred Heart Church; **p. 295,** National Register of Historic Places; **p. 296,** Robert E. Dalton, National Register of Historic Places; **p. 297,** Kentucky Heritage Council; **p. 299,** John Walden, National Register of Historic Places; **p. 300,** National Register of Historic Places; **p. 301,** Stephen Foster Drama Association, National Register of Historic Places; **p. 303,** National Register of Historic Places.

CHAPTER 8   West South Central Region

Page 306, Bob McCormack, National Register of Historic Places; **p. 310,** courtesy The Historic New Orleans Collection; **p. 311,** National Register of Historic Places; **p. 312,** National Register of Historic Places; **p. 313,** National Register of Historic Places; **p. 314,** National Register of Historic Places; **p. 317,** Sarah Brown, National Register of Historic Places; **p. 318,** J. Wiedower, Arkansas Historic Preservation Program, National Register of Historic Places;

p. 319, Claudia Morrow, Arkansas Historic Preservation Program, National Register of Historic Places; **p. 320,** P. Zollner, Arkansas Historic Preservation Program, National Register of Historic Places; **p. 321,** Dianna Kirk, Arkansas Historic Preservation Program, National Register of Historic Places; **p. 324,** Eva Osborne, Oklahoma State Historic Preservation Office; **p. 325,** National Register of Historic Places; **p. 326,** Annetta L. Cheek, National Register of Historic Places; **p. 327,** Don Simmons, National Register of Historic Places; **p. 328,** courtesy of the Art Institute of Chicago; **p. 331,** National Register of Historic Places; **p. 332,** Roy Pledger, Historic American Buildings Survey, Library of Congress; **p. 333,** Texas Historical Commission, National Register of Historic Places; **p. 334,** Calvin Littlejohn, National Register of Historic Places; **p. 335,** Samuel Gruber.

CHAPTER 9   Mountain Region

Page 338, Wyoming Division of Cultural Resources; **p. 343,** Jim Gautier; **p. 344,** Jim Gautier; **p. 345,** Jim Gautier; **p. 346,** Jim Gautier; **p. 347,** Jim Gautier; **p. 350,** National Register of Historic Places; **p. 351,** National Register of Historic Places; **p. 352,** David Anderson, National Register of Historic Places; **p. 353,** National Register of Historic Places; **p. 354,** National Register of Historic Places; **p. 357,** Jack E. Boucher, Historic American Buildings Survey, Library of Congress; **p. 358,** Rick Allesandro, National Register of Historic Places; **p. 359,** National Register of Historic Places; **p. 360,** National Register of Historic Places; **p. 363,** Montana Historical Society; **p. 364,** John N. DeHaas, Jr., National Register of Historic Places; **p. 365,** Diocese of Helena Archives; **p. 366,** Diocese of Helena Archives; **p. 367,** National Register of Historic Places; **p. 370,** Historic American Buildings Survey, Library of Congress;; **p. 371,** National Register of Historic Places; **p. 372,** Fred Walters, National Register of Historic Places; **p. 373,** Patricia Wright, National Register of Historic Places; **p. 374,** Idaho State Historical Society, National Register of Historic Places; **p. 378,** National Register of Historic Places; **p. 379,** Jana Money, Utah State Historical Society Photograph Archives; **p. 380,** Utah State Historical Society Photograph Archives; **p. 381,** National Register of Historic Places; **p. 382,** National Register of Historic Places; **p. 385,** Melissa Stapley, Territorial Newspapers; **p. 386,** Frederick D. Nichols, Historic American Buildings Survey, Library of Congress; **p. 387,** Arizona State Parks Board, National Register of Historic Places; **p. 388,** author; **p. 389,** Bill Perreault, National Register of Historic Places; **p. 393,** National Register of Historic Places; **p. 394,** Nevada Historical Society, National Register of Historic Places; **p. 395,** National Register of Historic Places; **p. 396,** Hale Day Gallagher Co.; **p. 397,** Martin / Healey Studios.

CHAPTER 10   Pacific Region

Page 400, Rick Reagan, National Register of Historic Places; **p. 405,** William S. Chiat; **p. 407,** Roger Sturtevant, Historic American Buildings Survey, Library of Congress; **p. 408,** Roger Sturtevant, Historic American Buildings Survey, Library of Congress; **p. 409,** Courtesy of Felix M. Warburg, A.I.A.; **p. 410,** Jack E. Boucher, Historic American Buildings Survey, Library of Congress; **p. 411,** author; **p. 415,** Vern Serex, National Register of Historic Places; **p. 416,** Edward H. Fitzgibbon, National Register of Historic Places; **p. 417,** National Register of Historic Places; **p. 418,** Steve Randolph, Umatilla County, National Register of Historic Places; **p. 419,** Reed Elwyn and Jon Horn, Lewis and Clark College, National Register of Historic Places; **p. 423,** National Register of Historic Places; **p. 424,** courtesy St. Charles Episcopal Parish; **p. 425,** Elizabeth Walton Potter, National Register of Historic Places; **p. 426,** L. Garfield, National Register of Historic Places; **p. 427,** Jacob Thomas, National Register of Historic Places; **p. 430,** Kreta / Merculief, St. Herman's Seminary Collection (Kodiak), National Register of Historic Places; **p. 431,** K. Cohen, Wrangell Historical Society, National Register of Historic Places; **p. 432,** Alfred Mongin, Alaska Division of Parks (Anchorage), National Register of Historic Places; **p. 433,** Historic American Buildings Survey, Library of Congress; **p. 434,** National Register of Historic Places; **p. 438,** National Register of Historic Places; **p. 439,** Historic American Buildings Survey, Library of Congress; **p. 440,** courtesy Don Hibbard, State of Hawaii, Department of Land and Natural Resources, State Historic Preservation Division; **p. 441,** John Wright, State of Hawaii, Department of Land and Natural Resources, State Historic Preservation Division; **p. 443,** Rick Reagan, National Register of Historic Places.

Index